Industry, Services, and Agriculture

THE UNITED STATES AND EUROPE IN THE 1990s

CAPITAL MARKETS AND TRADE
Claude E. Barfield and Mark Perlman, editors

INDUSTRY, SERVICES, AND AGRICULTURE
Claude E. Barfield and Mark Perlman, editors

POLITICAL POWER AND SOCIAL CHANGE
Norman J. Ornstein and Mark Perlman, editors

RESHAPING WESTERN SECURITY
Richard N. Perle, editor

Industry, Services, and Agriculture

The United States Faces a United Europe

Edited by
Claude E. Barfield and Mark Perlman

The AEI Press

Publisher for the American Enterprise Institute
WASHINGTON, D.C.

1992

Distributed by arrangement with

University Press of America
4720 Boston Way
Lanham, Md. 20706

3 Henrietta Street
London WC2E 8LU England

Library of Congress Cataloging-in-Publication Data

Industry, services, and agriculture : the United States faces a united
 Europe / edited by Claude E. Barfield and Mark Perlman.
    p.   cm. — (AEI studies ; 524)
    Includes bibliographical references.
    ISBN 0-8447-3755-0 (c).
    1. European Economic Community countries—Industries.
2. Agriculture—Economic aspects—European Economic Community
countries. 3. Competition—European Economic Community countries.
4. Competition—United States. 5. Europe 1992. I. Barfield,
Claude E. II. Perlman, Mark. III. Series.
HC241.2.I48 1991
338.094—dc20   91-33598
                                                    CIP

ISBN 0-8447-3755-0

1 3 5 7 9 10 8 6 4 2

AEI Studies 524

The AEI Press
Publisher for the American Enterprise Institute
1150 17th Street, N.W., Washington, D.C. 20036

Printed in the United States of America

Contents

LIST OF FIGURES

Acknowledgment

The American Enterprise Institute would like to thank the following foundations and corporations for their support of the AEI project, The United States and Europe in the 1990s: the Pew Charitable Trusts, the General Electric Company, the German Marshall Fund of the United States, IBM, the American Express Company, the Samsung Group, Robert Bosch Gmbh, and the Swedish Employers' Confederation.

Contributors

CLAUDE E. BARFIELD is coordinator of Trade Policy Studies at the American Enterprise Institute.

MARK PERLMAN is University Professor of Economics at the University of Pittsburgh.

JONATHAN D. ARONSON is professor of international relations at the University of Southern California.

DOMINIQUE BOCQUET is professor at the Institut d'Etudes Politiques de Paris.

JOHN BUTCHER is a member of Parliament and of the U.K. Conservative party.

ROBERT L. CARTER is Norwich Union Professor of Insurance Studies at the University of Nottingham.

GORDON CLONEY is president of the International Insurance Council.

GEZA FEKETEKUTY is counselor at the Office of the U.S. Trade Representative.

GEOFFREY FITCHEW is director general of financial institutions at the Commission of the European Communities.

CLAUDE G. B. FONTHEIM is the principal of Fontheim & O'Rourke and executive director of Alliance General & Co.

WERNER HEIN is a partner at Wilkinson, Barker, Knauer & Quinn.

MICHAEL HODIN is vice-president for public relations at Pfizer International, Inc.

PAUL M. HORVITZ is Elkins Professor of Banking and Finance at the University of Houston.

RALPH ICHTER is chairman of Euroconsultants, Inc.

CLAIBORNE H. JOHNSON, JR., is corporate vice-president of the Communications Services Division of the Technical Services Group, EDS.

NANCY JOHNSON is manager of international trade, E. I. du Pont de Nemours and Company.

OAKLEY JOHNSON is vice-president of corporate affairs at AIG.

TIMOTHY JOSLING is professor at the Food Research Institute at Stanford University.

DANIEL M. KASPER is director of transportation practice for Harbridge House.

G. MUSTAFA MOHATAREN is director, trade policy and competitive analysis, General Motors Corporation.

HEINRICH VON MOLTKE is deputy director general of internal market and industrial affairs for the Commission of the European Communities.

PETER OBERENDER is professor of economics at the University of Beyrouth.

FABRIZIO ONIDA is director of CESPRI at the Luigi Bocconi Commercial University.

MICHEL PETIT is director of agriculture and rural development for the World Bank.

R. RICHARDSON PETTIT is Duncan Professor of Finance, University of Houston.

ROBERT G. ROGERS is manager of government relations for Siemens Corporation in the United States.

PAUL C. ROSENTHAL is a partner of Collier, Shannon & Scott.

W. R. ROWLAND is director and group general manager, Royal Insurance Holdings.

JOHN SAULT is agriculture counselor at the Embassy of Australia in Washington, D.C.

FRED M. SCHERER is Ford Motor Company Professor of Business and Government at the John F. Kennedy School of Government at Harvard University.

HARMON SCHWEITZER is director of international marketing and business development for Network Systems International of AT&T.

WARNER R. SINBACK is manager of telecommunications services for GE information Services.

MICHAEL SKARZINSKI is U.S. assistant secretary of commerce for trade development.

FREDERICK SORENSON is director of air services for the Commission of the European Communities.

STEWART H. STEFFEY, JR., is senior vice-president of CIGNA Worldwide, Inc.

CHRISTIAN STOFFAÉS is deputy director of Electricité de France.

DANIEL SUMNER is U.S. deputy assistant secretary of agriculture for economics.

STEFAN TANGERMANN is professor of agricultural economics at the University of Gottingen.

JAMES R. TARRANT is special negotiator for transportation affairs in the Bureau of Economic and Business Affairs at the Department of State.

SIDNEY TOPOL is chairman of Scientific Atlanta, Inc.

FRANK D. WEISS is head of the Research Group, Foreign Economy and Structural Change, Kiel Institute for World Economics.

MASARU YOSHITOMI is director of the Economic Research Institute, Economic Planning Agency of Japan.

Introduction

Claude E. Barfield and Mark Perlman

In 1985 the twelve members of the European Community began designing and implementing an ambitious plan for regional integration unequaled in recent history. If all goes according to this single-market plan, European market barriers will fall, a unified market of more than 320 million consumers will emerge, goods and capital will flow with greater ease across national borders, businesses will benefit from new market opportunities, and dramatic economic gains will be achieved through efficiency improvements and specialization in production.

But will all go according to plan? And what does the plan mean for non-EC firms and countries? Troubling issues of reciprocity, for example, remain to be defined in practice, and a number of restrictive trade practices and protective enclaves remain outside the integration process.

European and American authors in the following chapters temper enthusiasm with skepticism as they take a closer look at these issues in the context of a number of key economic areas. The three broad economic sectors first merit a brief overview, to give some perspective to the individual studies that follow.

Two points distinguish the manufacturing sector. First, although manufacturing (excluding construction and energy) represents less than 30 percent of Community gross domestic product, it accounts for almost 70 percent of total trade in goods and services. Second, significant differences exist among the twelve members—a factor that may prove critical in determining the pace, if not the nature, of the European integration process. For example, four countries (Germany, France, the United Kingdom, and Italy) dominate the others, accounting for almost 80 percent of industrial production in the Community.

The unique role of agriculture is also difficult to overlook. By almost any measure of its economic importance, it has had a disproportionate effect on both internal and external EC relations. For example, agriculture accounts for 3.5 percent of Community GDP, but it dominates the EC budget, accounting for two-thirds of total Community expenditures. Furthermore, a common market in Europe until relatively recently was defined by agriculture. Intra-EC trade

1

has doubled over the past twenty years, and in 1987 nearly 60 percent of total agricultural imports came from other member countries. Policy discussions have been anything but harmonious, however, especially with non-EC countries. In recent years, U.S.-EC trade disputes have become particularly caustic, as U.S. agricultural exports to the European Community have declined and American producers have faced increasing competition from European rivals in third-country markets. The most notable dispute derailed the Uruguay Round of international trade negotiations in December 1990 and may do so again unless compromises are reached on reforming the current system of European farm subsidies—a system that represents roughly 50 percent of the annual $250 billion global bill for farm subsidies.

By contrast, services represent a new area for international negotiations, an area whose economic importance is large and getting larger for both domestic economies and international trade. Services account for the largest share of employment and national production in most advanced economies, representing more than 60 percent of GDP in the United States and in Europe. The GATT in a recent report also found that during the 1980s the value of trade in commercial services such as financial and management services grew at an average rate two and one-half times the rate of goods. This finding is particularly impressive given the limited accounting methods and the serious undercounting in service trade statistics.

Although service activities are growing more rapidly than is the production of goods, it is important to note that the two are becoming increasingly intertwined. The GATT estimates, for example, that roughly one-fourth of service outputs are now used as inputs into goods production, underlining further the importance of improving the productivity performance of services and opening this sector to greater competition. This will not be easy. Governments have in the past regulated services with an intensity and form rarely found in goods industries, through such measures as administrative actions or regulations that favored domestic suppliers over foreign rivals and kept markets severely fragmented. As a result, measures to open markets in this area in Europe, while promising dramatic economic gains, will be as difficult to design as to implement.

Against this background, this volume examines four manufacturing industries: automobiles, steel, pharmaceuticals, and telecommunications equipment. Next the book turns to the service sector to consider telecommunications services, air services, financial services, and insurance, followed by two essays on agriculture that conclude the volume. Individually and collectively, the essays illustrate how the planned and contemplated changes in Europe are already reshaping corporate strategies and the competitive climate in the various sectors. Together they also chart a course for U.S. policy makers, offering detailed and informed analysis on both current and emerging areas of friction. The authors also make recommendations for advancing American interests in Europe, as well as for advancing the interests of other non-European nations in the 1990s.

As director of a European research institute, Fabrizio Onida opens the volume with a useful overview of the political-economic forces at work in Europe and the likely impact on industrial structure, economic growth, and international trade relations. He takes the position that European moves toward unity will be a positive force that will accelerate continental integration and "contribute to worldwide integration rather than to divisive bloc-to-bloc strategies."

Building on the work of Victoria Curzon of the University of Geneva, Onida describes current moves toward European integration as a Ferrari model sparked and powered by the principle of mutual recognition. Simply stated, this means that EC members agree to accept each other's differences in regulatory regimes and not to restrict trade practices in domestic markets if they are compatible with the legal institutions of their respective member countries of origin. By requiring more than national treatment, Onida argues that the full application of this principle will lead to liberalization and deep integration, as member states are forced to change in order to compete for the investment and skills of footloose multinational firms. It is this competition between member states and market-driven reform that sets the current programs for economic cooperation apart from the original EC gradualist, "steamroller" model or the minimalist, "miniweight" approach of the EFTA countries.

Taking a Schumpeterian view of dynamic economic competition between firms, Onida further argues that the European gains from integration will flow largely from dramatic and accelerated changes in the European industrial structure. In particular, average firm size is expected to increase as formerly protected, small, and inefficient firms are forced through competition to exit, while innovative firms expand and enter new markets. Key to this process is the role of external investment flows and of interfirm collaborative alliances. He is particularly optimistic about the prospects for the European technology programs (such as Esprit and Race) to reduce fragmentation and to increase the competitive position of the European electronics industry.

He is equally optimistic about the prospects for market access for firms from non-EC member countries, arguing that Fortress Europe is not only undesirable but also implausible. As evidence, he cites the rising importance of multinationals, technological interdependence, and general economic interdependence with the rest of the world. From this, Onida concludes that the forces at work both in Europe and in the broader global arena not only boost the cause of greater integration, but dramatically complicate the economics and politics of trade policy; they will therefore limit residual protective tendencies.

Frank Weiss takes a closer look at this conclusion in his study of the European steel and automobile industries. His theme is posed as a question in the title of his chapter: "Will the Automobile Industry Go the Way of the Steel Industry?" Weiss notes at the outset that both industries seem good candidates for eliciting government protection. Both are characterized by high firm concentration, high regional concentration, and highly unionized and large work forces. Both also are directly affected by a gradual relocation of production, from established centers to new areas and countries.

How, then, does one explain the quite different patterns of government intervention and protection that characterize the postwar history of the two sectors? Weiss argues that the steel sector from the beginning became the object of common community policy, while automobiles remained the province of individual national policies. He traces the evolution of EC steel policy from 1960 to 1990, documenting the rise of a system that combined subsidization of losses with output quotas put in place to keep subsidization costs under control. During the 1980s, the external effects of the system in effect constituted equivalent tariff rates varying between 17 and 25 percent, which resulted in large welfare losses for the European Community.

In the automobile sector, a different tale unfolded during the same period. Decisions regarding the automobile industry remained in the hands of national leaders, resulting in a crazy-quilt, porous pattern of protection and in no EC-wide move toward closing markets. Weiss credits Count Otto Lambsdorff, the German Free Democratic party leader, with masterminding a key maneuver that changed the course of EC automobile trade policy in the late 1970s. While serving as Germany's economic minister, he stole a march on EC bureaucrats by secretly negotiating an agreement on voluntary export restraints for his country alone, thus heading off what would have been a precedent-setting move for a community-wide VER for automobiles. Subsequently, individual EC nations concluded separate deals, and the resulting system fell far short of the more tightly controlled protection for the steel industry.

In closing, Weiss expresses fears that 1992 will produce a protectionist regression in the automobile sector because of new commission authority to establish community-wide rules. He is cautiously optimistic, however, and believes that new forces for trade liberalization within the commission will combine with outside pressures from the United States and others to open national markets over time for both automobiles and steel.

Transition concerns are also the subject of Peter Oberender's chapter on the Community's pharmaceutical industry, clearly the largest in the world. Currently, the industry almost everywhere (but particularly in industrialized countries) is significantly affected by national licensing policies regarding customer safety, involving quality control in the production as well as distribution of the products. The Europeans now face the need to redesign myriad production and distribution regulations as the market widens; furthermore, the sheer immensity of the administrative regulatory task all but boggles the mind. Yet, whatever the effect, the European Court of Justice has turned a skeptical eye on national regulations purportedly designed to protect customers, but in actuality serving to strangle trade between member countries.

Market barriers masquerading as nondiscriminatory regulations are also of considerable interest in the telecommunications equipment sector. Claude Fontheim, in his analysis of the European deregulation process in this sector, highlights procurement policies as a source of continuing friction in U.S.-EC trade relations.

Fontheim first examines the requirements of the commission's 1987 Green Paper on telecommunications, then turns to the specific proposals on the European Community deregulation agenda that will expose American equipment firms to both new opportunities and risks in the 1990s. He offers in particular an unusually lucid description of the proposed changes, and he highlights three areas—the 50 percent local content rule, the lack of transparency in the type approval process and standard process, and the narrow definitions of what constitutes a European firm—as the particular problem areas for U.S. corporations. He concludes that the liberalization process has clearly started but that protective enclaves in areas such as infrastructure equipment remain outside this process, and political obstacles still need to be overcome at the member-state level.

In terms of a U.S. policy response, Fontheim analyzes the difficulties with three possibilities that have been considered. These include, first, designation of the European Community as a "priority country" under the Telecommunications Title in the 1988 Trade Act in an effort to stimulate negotiations; second, attempts to reserve a position at the EC 1992 bargaining table; and third, renegotiation of the GATT agreement on government procurement.

5

On a more general note, the bargaining table will also need to include another dimension—namely, the tightly regulated and increasingly important service sector. Telecommunications, as Jonathan Aronson has demonstrated in previous works, will be particularly important in this respect, because of the links to information services as well as the interdependent relationship between liberalization of trade in equipment and in services. In his essay in this volume Aronson explores whether the emergence of an integrated European market will restrict or will promote trade opportunities in telecommunications and information services, and how non-European, in particular American, corporations will be treated as the European Community moves to pry open traditional national monopolies. He is both pessimistic and optimistic about the likely results.

He traces the evolution of European telecommunications policy over the past two decades in the context of the continuing debate over liberalization and the migration of authority from individual member states to Brussels. This examination provides a rare chronicle of the diminishing status and shrinking mandate of the national Postal, Telegraph, and Telephone monopolies, in the continuing debate over liberalization and the migration of authority from individual member states to Brussels. He concludes on a somewhat positive note: although not all roads will lead to Brussels in telecommunications, as national authorities will retain some control, still, consumers and non-European corporations will enjoy the opportunities of a more competitive environment in the 1990s. Particular attention is given to the emerging markets for value-added services and advanced radio communications, as the areas of greatest opportunity for U.S. telecommunications service providers.

Writing before the scheduled close of the Uruguay Round, Aronson is also somewhat optimistic about the potential for international negotiations with nonmember countries. Although the extension of GATT to telecommunications services is fraught with difficulties, he suggests that important steps toward international agreements are likely, especially in establishing principles of transparency and market access in the enhanced telecommunications sphere.

Air services constitute another area ripe for multilateral negotiations, but Daniel Kasper argues that at this time the forum should be smaller than the GATT, as in U.S.-EC negotiations. In looking ahead to commercial air wars in the 1990s, Kasper examines the economic and political forces that are reshaping airline services and the emerging new world aviation order.

For starters, the market will be a global one. Kasper points out that American "deregulation and the economic logic of hubbing made international expansion by U.S. carriers virtually inevitable." Increased competition forced airlines to rationalize routes and exploit economies of scale and scope. The hub and spoke system that emerged also made it easier for U.S. carriers to expand internationally, by adding service to international markets as another spoke to be served by their domestic hubs, putting their smaller and less efficient foreign rivals at a further disadvantage. The lure of international markets for U.S. carriers is further enhanced by the traffic and profit rates, which are expected to surpass those of domestic markets. For European carriers, the attraction is the large American domestic market as well as the operating base necessary to compete for transatlantic traffic.

The path forward to a global market, however, will continue to be a rocky one. It will require fundamental changes not only in national regulatory systems, but also in the form of international negotiations. Kasper rejects the current Byzantine system of agreements between individual EC member states and the United States as an untenable approach for the future. What is needed, he argues, is direct negotiations between the European Community and the United States that can grant American access to the internal, integrated EC market.

Kasper finds in the European Second Package of Liberalization measures the beginnings of a common Community air transport policy, but the outline is less than encouraging. The intent is to push for a barrier-free European market by 1993, but outsiders—like the United States—will be blocked at least temporarily from participating. A principal problem, Kasper argues, is the order of negotiations. The first round is expected to include only EC members, then to expand to include other European nations to form a Europe-wide market, and finally to include negotiations with North America and Asia.

How should the United States respond, Kasper asks, to this European strategy for liberalization? We lose by waiting, he answers. By waiting for the Europeans first to establish a common market and then to negotiate, access problems of American carriers are not only prolonged, they are probably made more difficult. After battles are fought over internal market reforms and delicate compromises are designed, even willing European negotiators will find it difficult to garner support for substantive market access negotiations with the United States. The threat, in Kasper's words, is "another odious CAP—this time a 'Common Aviation Policy.' "

Furthermore, as in the United States in the 1980s, deregulation in the Community in the 1990s will be marked by consolidation. The Europeans start the process with fewer airlines, however, and the specters of tight European cartels and oligopolies subsequently loom large on the horizon. What is the solution? Foreign investment and international competition now—not only in evolving European industry, but also in U.S. industry, Kasper concludes.

Trade in insurance services, by contrast, is already partly integrated, although points of friction remain. Robert Carter's chapter on trade issues between the United States and the European Community in the area of insurance not only presents an evenhanded review of the potential trade conflicts between the two partners, but also more broadly provides the reader with a succinct but thorough primer on the structure and workings of the insurance industry in advanced industrial economies.

The opening section of the chapter describes the activities of insurance companies, including their arrangements for risk spreading and transfer through coinsurance and reinsurance. A discussion of the role of insurance companies in savings and investment markets is also included in this section. Carter then turns to the economics of the production of insurance services, and he delineates the role of capital, human, and information resources in this production. He stresses in particular the increasing importance of information technology in the internationalization of insurance services.

The next section of the chapter describes in some detail the composition, structure, and size of both the U.S. and the EC insurance markets. Carter points out that although individual EC country markets are quite small, the European Community as a single market will represent some 22 percent of life insurance premiums (the United States, 30 percent; Japan, 33 percent) and 26 percent of nonlife insurance premiums (the United States, 46 percent; Japan, 12 percent).

Having set the stage with this background information, Carter then turns to an analysis of the insurance trade between the European Community and the United States and of the degree to which the two economies are already integrated. This analysis is followed by a detailed examination of the directives that the European Community is producing as it moves toward a common European market for insurance and an analysis of the potential impact of these new regulations on U.S. and other non-EC insurance companies.

Carter concludes the chapter with a description of the remaining barriers to insurance trade on both sides of the Atlantic, and with recommendations for reducing those barriers, particularly under the auspices of current GATT negotiations.

Financial services other than insurance also figure prominently on the European internal market agenda. Barriers that restrict the movement of capital and the provision of financial services across borders, for example, are scheduled to be eliminated. Together the changes are expected to account for one-third of the total increase in the EC's GDP from the completion of the internal market. And they will dramatically reshape the regulatory structure in Europe. At the center of everyone's attention are the EC proposals to offer common banking, insurance, and securities licenses that would enable European financial institutions to offer an unprecedented array of services throughout Europe.

How these changes will affect the ability of U.S. firms to compete in Europe and in the U.S. financial market is the subject of the chapter by Paul Horvitz and Richardson Pettit. Their approach differs from the well-worn path of trying to predict how the European Community will treat non-EC firms and the issue of reciprocity. They leave speculation on this matter to others and focus instead on what the impact will be on American business interests under several scenarios and on what American policy makers should do in return.

On the European side, Horvitz and Pettit consider the issue of national treatment versus strict reciprocity within the context of the Second Banking Directive and the investment and insurance directives. If the European Community adopts reciprocal national treatment as its standard, for example, Horvitz and Pettit are optimistic about the prospects for American firms. They argue in particular that although American firms will be restricted at home by existing U.S. law from offering the same variety of services offered in Europe, universal banks in Europe will not have a significant cost advantage. In addition, consumer demand and capital positions are not expected to impair the ability of American banks and other financial institutions to compete and benefit from the expanding, integrated European marketplace. The authors also predict that the U.S. financial structure will not be significantly affected by the EC initiative.

The authors do not, however, consider this outcome to be a positive one in terms of American economic welfare. Instead, they turn their spotlight on U.S. policy makers and argue that greater liberalization is needed. Rejecting conventional wisdom, they further argue that strict reciprocity on the part of the European Community can benefit the United States *if* policy makers respond by accommodating the European Community and making similar moves toward eliminating banking restrictions at home. In this sense the authors have managed to translate the popularly perceived threat of EC strict reciprocity into their best-case scenario, in which liberalization in Europe leads to liberalization at home. Whether pressure and counter-pressure will work remains to be seen. Tension either way promises to characterize the transition.

Conflict is nothing new for those familiar with the economics and politics of agricultural trade. Timothy Josling's chapter, written from the standpoint of one living in the United States, reviews the history of the current agricultural policy tensions between the United States and various European countries. Earlier (and until very recently) major importers of American agricultural products, these countries are now emerging as major international export competitors. His analysis offering generalization about various policies as they pertain to countries and to products is anchored in specific production facts.

Josling's views are put forth within a framework of three observations: his estimate of the annual, worldwide, increased demand for agricultural products, approximating 2.5 percent; his perception of conflicts between domestic political-agricultural policy and the demands of the European Community rules; and his realization that several commodity markets (for example, wheat) seem to be currently satiated.

His essay takes up governmental domestic programs that were seemingly intended to stabilize or to make safer for consumption various types of agricultural output, but which in practice, he sees, lead to international trade restrictions.

Finally, Stefan Tangermann closes the volume with a discussion of the problems being experienced by Europeans, who are pressing to develop an integrated European common (market) agricultural policy at the same time as they are being criticized by Americans, who are aggressively pressing for more open world agricultural trade. Domestically, the efforts of the several European countries have been all but dominated by the political strength of each country's sometimes small but always powerful agricultural sectors. Actually, the intra-Common Market trade opportunities have since the late 1960s been, on the one hand, at least nominally free of restrictions. On the other hand, the existence of an asymmetrical Green Money system of agricultural exchange rates, along with Monetary Compensation Amounts, has served to complicate these transactions.

Tangermann believes that in the future, such integration of national policies as occurs will come not through harmonization of each country's standards with those of the other countries, but through the effects that a common agricultural policy will introduce— particularly as it is affected by the outcome of the Uruguay Round GATT talks. Change toward more open agricultural markets will occur, he believes, but only gradually and with pressure and counterpressure.

This volume is one of four published from the AEI project, The United States and Europe in the 1990s. Under the auspices of this major research effort, AEI commissioned a series of twenty-eight papers analyzing the problems and prospects for U.S.-European relations in the areas of trade, finance, agriculture, defense, social policy, political institutions, and world diplomacy.

In March 1990, AEI convened a four-day conference in Washington, D.C., to present the analysis and conclusions of the commissioned papers. Panels of experts provided supporting or dissenting conclusions, and these written statements are also included in this volume. The other volumes in this series are

Reshaping Western Security: The United States Faces a United Europe. Richard Perle, ed.

Capital Markets and Trade: The United States Faces a United Europe. Claude E. Barfield and Mark Perlman, eds.

Political Power and Social Change: The United States Faces a United Europe. Norman J. Ornstein and Mark Perlman, eds.

PART ONE
Overview

1

Structural Change and International Integration of the European Single Market

Fabrizio Onida

Since the early 1980s the climate of opinion in Europe and the United States concerning their economic integration and the performance of their respective markets has swung between two extremes. In Europe the mood has changed from Europessimism to Europhoria, in anticipation of a single internal market. The pendulum has moved in the opposite direction in the United States. The enthusiasm surrounding the economic recovery pushed forward by Reaganomics has given way to concern for the loss of technological and financial leadership to Japan and Europe. Little can be said about the technical competition, structural changes, and international integration that the single market may bring without some understanding of the circumstances behind these swings.

The first factor to consider is the unexpected strength of the recovery of domestic demand, output, and employment in the United States in 1981–1986, after the second oil shock. In sharp contrast, the European recovery was rather sluggish, in part because the German government had been reluctant to give the "German locomotive" a second trial after its disappointing experience with the active monetary and fiscal policies implemented in 1978–1979 under pressure from the Bonn (1978) G-7 Summit. From the U.S. perspective, Europe appeared to be neither a free market nor a system undergoing an investment-led mobilization of its economic potential, as was the case in Japan.

As for the U.S. situation, several American and European economists attributed the improvement to a sudden increase in the marginal efficiency of investment in the United States, which had begun to attract massive capital inflows from firms in Europe and Japan in search of profitable investment opportunities. The unusual strength of the dollar, following its prolonged weakness in 1978–1979, before Ronald Reagan took office, was by and large, taken to be a symptom

15

of good health and a rapidly improving supply side, rather than a disruptive trend.

Second, the managers of large multinational enterprises were struck by the record-high profits that U.S. and Canadian companies and foreign subsidiaries were making in comparison with European companies and the European subsidiaries of U.S. enterprises. This led some observers to conclude, "Europe is no longer the automatic choice it once was as a base for multinational investment: the fragmented nature of its markets makes trade especially difficult, particularly the lack of harmonization across national boundaries and the protectionist attitude of different Member States towards its own industries" (*Financial Times* 1984).

Indeed, in the first half of the 1980s direct U.S. investment in Europe came to a standstill and then dropped from roughly $80 billion to $70 billion. By the end of 1987, however, American investments in Europe had zoomed to $120 billion (see tables 1-1 and 1-2).[1]

Third, American business, not to mention European business itself, saw the national fragmentation and the protectionist attitude of the members of the European Community (EC) as a serious obstacle to coherent European industrial policy. The turmoil of the 1970s seemed to have greatly undermined the chances for European economic, financial, and monetary integration:

> There was a long period of relative silence from Brussels, the dreadful 1970's with all its problems, and there were times when there was no objective for the European Community. There is no more fascinating document of those times than Roy Jenkins' 1977–81 diary which shows clearly that during his entire presidency no one quite knew where the Community was or should be going. It was in the 1980's only, and even then towards the mid-1980's, that a new objective was identified (Dahrendorf 1989).

At the time that the historical decision was made to introduce a European monetary system (EMS) as a framework for macroeconomic integration, its full implications were not yet understood. Until 1983, the countries of the European Community (EC) frequently revised their exchange rates. Countries such as France and Italy were occasionally forced to reintroduce foreign exchange controls and various types of financial regulations to prevent their EMS exchange policy from putting undue stress on their official reserves. All this greatly dampened enthusiasm for the new design of European integration.

Fourth, international businesses became particularly concerned about early indications of an EC attempt to impose various regulations on the European labor market. One proposal (the Vredeling directive) even recommended that the employees of transnational companies become more involved in managerial affairs.

When the dollar declined and the U.S. "twin deficits" showed no sign of budging, attitudes toward the U.S. performance in relation to that of Europe changed. And when the single market project emerged in 1985–1986, Europessimism began to wane.

The EC Council passed the Single European Act in June 1985. It was subsequently ratified by the governments concerned and implemented through a stream of EC Commission directives designed to have the European internal market in operation by the end of 1992. The act was seen as a harbinger of a new European economic renaissance that would put to rest the gloomy predictions of all those who felt the focus of economic growth in the world had definitely shifted to the Pacific basin.

A large majority of European observers, including myself, think that the Single European Act will trigger far more than a psychological reversal. According to a business opinion survey conducted by the Commission of the European Communities (1988b, chap. 8), most companies and countries—except for Greece and to some extent France—expect 1992 to be a source of business opportunities rather than risks (table 1-3). Although on average the optimism seemed higher at the company level than at the country level, the opposite appeared to be the case among the countries of the deutsche mark bloc (the Federal Republic of Germany and Benelux), precisely those countries in which one might have expected to find some fear that European integration would bring macroeconomic instability and inflation.

The Single Market as a Model of Mutual Recognition and Jurisdictional Integration

By and large, I share Victoria Curzon Price's (1989) vision of the single European market as an ambitious third model of European integration, which she calls the "Ferrari model." It differs from two previous models: the "lightweight mini" applied to the countries of the European Free Trade Association (EFTA) and the "steamroller" model devised for the pre-1985 EC countries. The EFTA model is characterized by trade liberalization (but does not bind member countries to a common external tariff) and almost zero commitment to the coordination of economic policies. The original steamroller model of EC-6 reflected a gradualist approach, as explained below.

The 1992 project incorporates the basic federalist principles of both EFTA and the European Community: namely, subsidiarity and

17

TABLE 1-1

OUTWARD STOCKS OF DIRECT FOREIGN INVESTMENT, BY MAJOR HOME COUNTRY AND REGION, 1960–1985
(billions of U.S. dollars)

Countries and Regions	1960 Value	Total (%)	GDP (%)	1975 Value	Total (%)	GDP (%)	1980 Value	Total (%)	GDP (%)	1985 Value	Total (%)	GDP (%)
Developed market economies	67.0	99.0	6.7	275.4	97.7	6.7	535.7	97.2	6.7	693.3	97.2	8.0
United States	31.9	47.1	6.2	124.2	44.0	8.1	220.3	40.0	8.2	250.7	35.1	6.4
United Kingdom	12.4	18.3	17.4	37.0	13.1	15.8	81.4	14.8	15.2	104.7	14.7	23.3
Japan	0.5	0.7	1.1	15.9	5.7	3.2	36.5	6.6	3.4	83.6	11.7	6.3
West Germany	0.8	1.2	1.1	18.4	6.5	4.4	43.1	7.8	5.3	60.0	8.4	9.6
Switzerland	2.3	3.4	26.9	22.4	8.0	41.3	38.5	7.0	37.9	45.3	6.4	48.9
Netherlands	7.0	10.3	60.6	19.9	7.1	22.9	41.9	7.6	24.7	43.8	6.1	35.1

Canada	2.5	3.7	6.3	10.4	3.7	6.3	21.6	3.9	8.2	36.5	5.1	10.5
France	4.1	6.1	7.0	10.6	3.8	3.1	20.8	3.8	3.2	21.6	3.0	4.2
Italy	1.1	1.6	2.9	3.3	1.2	1.7	7.0	1.3	1.8	12.4	1.7	3.4
Sweden	0.4	0.6	2.9	4.7	1.7	6.4	7.2	1.3	5.8	9.0	1.3	9.0
Other[a]	4.0	5.9	3.1	8.5	3.0	1.7	17.4	3.2	1.9	25.6	3.6	3.3
Developing countries	0.7	1.0	—	6.6	2.3	—	15.3	2.8	—	19.2	2.7	—
Centrally planned economies of Europe	—	—	—	—	—	—	—	—	—	1.0[b]	0.1	—
Total	67.7	100.0	—	282.0	100.0	—	551.0	100.0	—	713.5	100.0	—

— = not available.

a. Australia, Austria, Belgium, Denmark, Finland, Greece, Ireland, New Zealand, Norway, Portugal, South Africa, and Spain.

b. 1983, rough estimate.

SOURCE: United Nations Center on Transnational Corporations (1988).

TABLE 1-2
INWARD STOCKS OF DIRECT FOREIGN INVESTMENT, BY MAJOR HOST REGION, 1975–1985
(billions of U.S. dollars)

Countries, Regions, and Areas	1975			1983			1985		
	Value	Total (%)	GDP (%)	Value	Total (%)	GDP (%)	Value	Total (%)	GDP (%)
Developed market economics	185.3	75.1	4.5	401.0	75.6	5.1	478.2	75.0	5.5
Western Europe	100.6	40.8	5.8	159.6	30.1	5.6	184.3	28.9	6.6
United States	27.7	11.2	1.8	137.1	25.9	4.2	184.6	29.0	4.7
Other[a]	57.0	23.1	7.0	104.3	19.7	6.0	109.2	17.1	5.7
Japan	1.5	0.6	0.3	5.0	0.9	0.4	6.1	1.0	0.5
Developing countries and territories	61.5	24.9	6.4	138.4	24.4	7.4	159.0	25.0	8.5
Africa[b]	16.5	6.7	15.7	19.6	3.7	9.4	22.3	3.5	10.8

Asia[c]	13.0	5.3	3.2	40.1	5.8	4.9	49.6	7.8	5.7
Latin America and the Caribbean[d]	29.7	12.0	8.9	73.2	13.8	11.9	80.5	12.6	13.6
Other[e]	2.3	0.9	2.1	5.4	1.0	2.4	6.6	1.0	3.4
Total[f]	246.8	100.0	4.9	539.4	100.0	5.5	637.2	100.0	6.1

a. Australia, Canada, Japan, New Zealand, and South Africa.
b. Botswana, Cameroon, Central African Republic, Congo, Côte d'Ivoire, Egypt, Gabon, Ghana, Kenya, Liberia, Libyan Arab Jamahinya, Malawi, Mauritius, Morocco, Nigeria, Senegal, Seychelles, Sierra Leone, Togo, United Republic of Tanzania, Zaire, Zambia, and Zimbabwe.
c. Bangladesh, China, Hong Kong, India, Indonesia, Malaysia, Pakistan, Philippines, Republic of Korea, Singapore, Sri Lanka, Taiwan Province, and Thailand.
d. Argentina, Barbados, Brazil, Chile, Colombia, Dominican Republic, Ecuador, Guyana, Jamaica, Mexico, Panama, Paraguay, Peru, Trinidad and Tobago, Uruguay, and Venezuela.
e. Fiji, Papua, New Guinea, Saudi Arabia, Turkey, and Yugoslavia.
f. Excluding the centrally planned economies of Europe, for which no precise data are available.
SOURCE: United Nations Center on Transnational Corporations (1988).

TABLE 1-3
POLL OF EUROPEAN FIRMS ON OPPORTUNITIES AND RISKS IN THE COMPLETION OF THE INTERNAL MARKET
(percent)

Industry as a Whole	Bel-gium	Den-mark	West Ger-many	Greece	Spain	France	Ire-land	Italy	Luxem-bourg	Nether-lands	Por-tugal	United Kingdom	EUR-12
					For your company								
Opportunities much greater	35	12	15	15	26	9	33	26	20	26	35	21	19
Opportunities somewhat greater	38	42	37	40	33	36	33	38	40	25	25	45	37
About the same/ don't know	25	42	41	19	30	49	28	30	40	44	30	29	37
Risks somewhat greater	2	3	6	21	6	5	3	5	0	2	11	4	5
Risks much greater	0	1	1	5	5	1	3	1		3	7	1	2

						For the economy of your country							
Net effect (a)	+71	+50	+45	+29	+48	+39	+60	+58	+60	+46	+42	+61	+49
Net effect (b)	+53	+31	+30	+20	+35	+24	+45	+42	+40	+35	+35	+41	+33
Opportunities much greater	35	15	17	14	25	7	23	21	40	30	31	18	18
Opportunities somewhat greater	45	44	33	19	24	29	43	28	20	32	23	38	31
About the same/ don't know	18	33	43	19	37	40	17	36	40	31	22	33	38
Risks somewhat greater	2	7	6	29	6	20	14	10	0	5	16	10	10
Risks much greater	0	1	1	19	8	4	3	5	0	2	8	1	3
Net effect (a)	+78	+51	+43	−15	+35	+12	+49	+34	+60	+55	+30	+45	+36
Net effect (b)	+57	+33	+30	−10	+26	+8	+35	+25	+50	+42	+27	+31	+26

NOTE: Net effect (a) = Percentage difference between firms saying opportunities were greater (+) and firms saying risks were greater (−). Net effect (b) = Weighted difference (%) between firms saying opportunities were much greater (+1) or somewhat greater (+0.5) and firms saying risks were much greater (−1) or somewhat greater (−0.5).
SOURCE: Commission of the European Communities (1988a).

a tolerance of national differences within a federal regime. But it goes beyond the gradualist, or functionalist, approach of EC founders Jean Monnet and Robert Schumann, which progressively slowed down the momentum of European integration during the 1970s and early 1980s. The crucial new step in the 1992 project has been its endorsement of the revolutionary principle of mutual recognition and equivalence as a basis for integration. Mutual recognition means that no member country can bar from its own territory the free trade of goods and services that are compatible with the legal institutions of the member countries in which they originate, except in the few circumstances referred to in Article 36 of the Treaty of Rome (which pertain to public morality, security, and public health).

According to the functionalist approach, a fully integrated Europe can only come about in small steps, through a gradual harmonization of national rules. Technicians and negotiators play a dominant role in this scheme, trying to establish a federal regime that respects the differences of the member countries and observes the subsidiarity principle, "Never allow a higher-level institutional body to undertake a task that a lower-level body could accomplish as well" (Curzon 1989: 24; Padoa Schioppa 1987). The hope is that "one day the nation state [will] be caught, like Gulliver, by hundreds of sovereignty-stripping agreements" (Curzon 1989: 27). Despite the emphasis on the subsidiarity principle, this harmonization process runs the risk of tolerating regional price differences and distortions over the long term, as well as market fragmentation.

The principle of mutual recognition, which originated in the Court of Justice ruling on Cassis de Dijon in 1978, is bound to accelerate competition among firms, consumer tastes, and institutions.[2] It will probably allow EC countries to pursue even more ambitious forms of economic integration than the North American Free Trade Area does under its present arrangements (Pelkmans 1988). Thus the single market may indeed become "one of the best, most market-oriented blueprints for economic cooperation that has ever been devised" (Curzon 1988: 41).

The principle of mutual recognition provides the impetus for the progressive elimination of physical, technical, fiscal, and financial barriers. It is expected to trigger a chain of macroeconomic and microeconomic effects that will move the EC countries toward their 1992 target of static efficiency, "X efficiency," and dynamic efficiency and ultimately lead to increased output (see figures 1-1 and 1-2). In particular, this principle will make it possible to bypass the many lines of resistance and captive market fragmentation that give rise to inefficiency when price differences persist within the integrated area.

FIGURE 1–1
INTEGRATION AND THE EFFECTS OF SIZE OF MARKETS

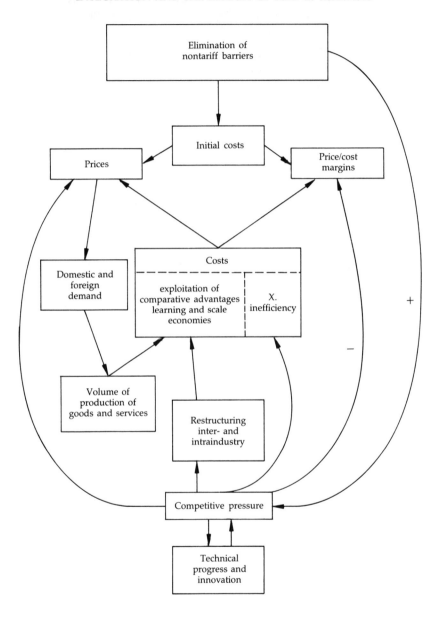

Note: The + sign indicates an increase; the − sign indicates a reduction.
SOURCE: Commission of the European Communities (1988a).

FIGURE 1–2
PRINCIPAL MACROECONOMIC MECHANISMS ACTIVATED IN THE COURSE OF COMPLETION OF THE INTERNAL MARKET

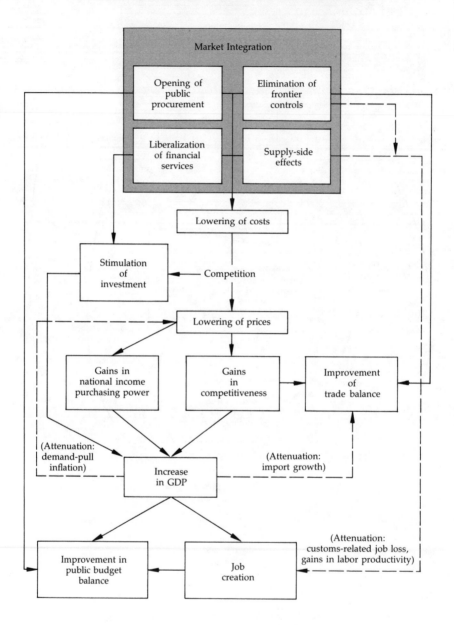

SOURCE: Commission of the European Communities (1988a).

Some numerical model simulations suggest that the community welfare gains from reducing these price differences and related captive markets may even surpass the gains that technical economies of scale achieve through the increased specialization of producers within an integrated market (Smith and Venables 1988). Although prices declined in the 1980s, after their strong rise in the second half of the 1970s, substantial differences, on the order of 10 percent and more, still show up in most services, durable consumer goods, and food products subject to excise taxes.

The breakdown of captive market rules and of the various invisible barriers to trade closely resembles the cartel-breaking impact of the jurisdictional integration that accompanied the sustained growth Europe experienced after the Industrial Revolution (Olson 1982: chap. 5). The distributive coalitions or rent-seeking organizations that emerge with different intensity under all political regimes (and become an unpleasant party for the Smithian invisible hand) are bound to resist all-encompassing free-trade schemes. But a central government can ensure free trade in much the same way that the U.S. Constitution does—by prohibiting member states from imposing barriers to the interstate movement of goods and people.

The problem is that stable societies whose political borders do not change tend to foster more collusions, cartels, and distributive coalitions (that is, organizations for collective action). These organizations can reduce a society's capacity to adapt to changing environmental conditions (which are shaped by technology, tastes, and value judgments) and thereby slow down its rate of growth (Olson 1982: chap. 3).[3] Although one should be careful about drawing generalizations from history, Mancur Olson's observation that broadening political boundaries and free trade has often provided a powerful boost to prosperity, whereas maintaining market fragmentation and rigidities has often led to a decline, offers a useful guideline for Europe in the 1990s (Dahrendorf 1989: 1).

Of course, it is not certain that all the member countries will meet the tight schedule for implementing the EC directives. The most recent biannual report of the Commission of the European Communities on the progress of the single market (1989a) notes that, of the 279 measures recommended in its White Paper (1986), the European Council had approved 127 by late spring 1989, under heavy pressure from the commission, but there were long delays in enacting the corresponding national legislation. Of the 68 measures whose deadline for approval has already passed, only 2 have been incorporated into the national legislation of all twelve EC countries. Those with the best record of approval are the United Kingdom, France, Germany,

Benelux, and Denmark, each with 45–55 directives in effect. Italy and Spain have been the worst performers, with 29 and 30 directives, respectively, surpassing only Portugal (21 directives). The delay in Spain and Portugal is more justifiable than in Italy, given that newcomers must struggle to adopt about 1,000 old directives they inherited upon entering the Community less than three years ago (see Buchan 1989; *Economist* 1989). Political pressure has been mounting throughout the member countries, and as recently as mid-1990 few in Brussels, at any rate, appeared concerned about any delay in the transition to January 1, 1993.

Changing Industrial Structure in an Open Economy

A closer analysis of the probable impact of the 1992 market suggests that the expected gains from technical economies of scale, increased efficiency, and dynamic (learning) economies will be rooted in deep and accelerated changes in the European industrial structure. These changes will be reflected in average firm size, concentration indexes, rates of entry and exit turnover, and the reshuffling of property and management. Three changes in particular can be expected to occur.

First, the single market is likely to wipe out small, inefficient firms that depend entirely on national or local captive markets, often linked to the government's procurement of goods and services in areas such as energy supply, telecommunications, and public transportation.[4] Because these firms do not employ many people, the social cost of their exit will be relatively low. With the disappearance of these firms under competitive pressure, inefficient price differences within the European Community are likely to dwindle.

Second, many small, large, and medium-size firms that are unable to withstand the competition from intra-EC imports and from more efficient domestic rivals will undergo property and management restructuring as a result of takeovers or mergers that will try to overcome structural weaknesses and reestablish true market potential. Most of these inefficient firms possess a valuable stock (in sunk costs) of equipment, manpower, skills, and distributive networks that more efficient competitors are willing to reshape and incorporate in a broader technological and managerial framework rather than scrap. Many of the firms that survive beyond 1992 are likely to be well endowed with market factors (including trademarks, dealers, distributive and after-sale assistance network), but may need to improve their technology and management. This will be one of the main factors leading to a new wave of direct investment and interfirm cooperative agreements among both European and non-European

28

firms, as explained in the next section.

Third, the internal market is likely to provide more incentives for efficient newcomers, who will be lured into it by greater profit opportunities. This change will partly offset the increase in the supply concentration ratio that the first two changes are likely to cause.

Note, too, that the transition to 1993 will not just be a matter of integrating continental *markets*. Continental industrial and service *structures* must also be integrated. Most firms, especially smaller ones, are probably not yet completely aware of this perspective (and perhaps are still too optimistic about their future).

The Role of Direct Investment

As already mentioned, the industrial restructuring of 1992 will create new opportunities for cross-country investment within and outside the European Community. Some direct investment within the European Community may be replaced by larger trade flows, as invisible trade barriers (especially those tied to local public procurement) and transport costs are lowered. At the same time, there are good reasons to believe that direct intra-EC investment will actually increase: (a) a more integrated but nonhomogeneous market offers greater incentive to oligopolistic and monopolistic competitive firms to reinforce and stabilize their marketing network; (b) greater market integration implies that the cost of coordinating cross-country management operations within multiplant companies will be lower, information will flow faster, cultural and linguistic barriers will not be as high, and it will be easier to comply with different national regulations and infrastructures; and (c) the recent entry of new peripheral countries into the European Community is providing multiplant firms opportunities for exploiting locational advantages (Buckley and Artisien 1988).

However skeptical one may be about institutional and psychological obstacles to greater intra-EC mergers and acquisitions (see table 1-4), there is enough evidence to indicate that the pressure of soaring competition has already helped increase the volume and share of intra-European equity and nonequity operations.[5] A few examples illustrate this recent trend: Daimler-MBB (defense); CGE-Alcatel, GEC-Plessey-Siemens, Bosch-Jeumont Schneider and Plessey (telecommunications); Fiat Marelli-Matra and CIR-Valéo (car components); Fiat IVECO-Ford U.K. (trucks); VW-SEAT (cars); Olivetti-Triumph Adler (office equipment); SGS-Thomson (semiconductors); Electrolux-Thorn EMI and Electrolux-Zanussi (domestic appliances);

29

TABLE 1-4

NUMBER OF MERGERS AND ACQUISITIONS IN THE EUROPEAN COMMUNITY, 1985–1988

Industries	Mergers and Acquisitions Involving First 1,000 European Firms			Mergers and Acquisitions Involving European Firms with Sales over ECU 1 Billion		
	1985–1986	1986–1987	1987–1988	1985–1986	1986–1987	1987–1988
Food	34	52	51	17	35	40
Chemical	57	71	85	33	51	57
Electric and electronics	13	41	36	9	12	23
Mechanical	29	31	38	17	20	26
Computers	1	2	3	0	1	3
Metal manufacturing	17	19	40	4	11	32
Vehicles	10	21	15	3	11	14
Wood, paper, and furniture	27	25	34	5	8	18
Mining	10	9	12	7	4	9
Textiles, clothing, and footwear	9	6	14	2	2	4
Building	14	9	33	8	11	29
Other	6	7	22	3	5	13
Total	227	303	383	108	171	268

SOURCE: Commission of the European Communities (1989a).

Asea-Brown Boveri (electrical engineering); and Moét Hennessy-Guinness (wine and beer).

Lower barriers to trade and factor movements within the Community are also likely to attract direct investments from firms in other regions fearing increased invisible discrimination against outsiders. The idea that Europe will become a fortress is difficult to accept, however, as explained below. More important, non-EC producers will have an incentive to expand and consolidate their multiplant operations, or at least their network of commercial subsidiaries, within a growing and less fragmented EC market. After all, a more unified market benefits all producers in that market, regardless of their nationality.

A significant role is already being played by some non-EC producers, notably the EFTA countries Sweden, Norway, and Switzerland, whose high degree of internationalization has been associated with the EC market for a long time. In 1986, for example, EC-9 shares of the manufactured exports of Switzerland, Austria, Sweden, and Norway amounted to more than 40 percent, which was greater than the EC market shares of member countries such as the United Kingdom and Denmark (table 1-5). The EC market also absorbed about 50 percent of the total foreign production of Swedish multinationals and—as might be expected—a larger share of total sales by Swedish multinationals (38 percent) than their domestic market sales (24 percent) (Swedenborg 1988).

American and Japanese investors are also active in Europe. Indeed, European subsidiaries of U.S. multinational firms have long been entrenched in the European market. The lowering of trade barriers inside the European Community will no doubt induce U.S. parent companies to consolidate their existing European network by selling off or rationalizing subsidiaries originally set up mainly to act as insiders within national captive markets (particularly in telecommunications, pharmaceuticals, and electrical engineering). ITT, for example, recently sold its European telecommunications business to Alcatel, and Honeywell completed a similar divesture in computers, which it sold to Bull. Conversely, U.S. parent companies may be encouraged to relocate their European production (or, indeed, their world production) to specific EC areas offering lower production costs or to engage in selective acquisitions (as in the recent Ford-Jaguar, GM-Saab, and Pepsico-BSN cases), being more able than before to exploit the opportunities of a less fragmented continental market.

Although Japanese parent companies are latecomers in the European market, they are already pushing hard to increase their equity and nonequity direct involvement in the enlarged European market. The single market provides them an even greater incentive to increase

TABLE 1-5

Trade Matrix for Western European Exports of Manufactures, 1986
(percentage of total exports)

Importing Nation	Exporting Nation												
	Nor-way	Fin-land	Swe-den	Den-mark	United King-dom	West Germany	France	Italy	Nether-land	Bel-gium/ Luxem-bourg	Switzer-land	Aus-tria	Port-ugal
Norway	0.0	5.1	11.4	11.3	1.5	1.5	0.8	0.7	1.5	1.0	0.9	1.2	2.5
Finland	2.8	0.0	6.4	2.9	1.0	1.2	0.7	0.7	0.9	0.6	0.8	1.0	2.2
Sweden	13.6	15.3	0.0	13.5	2.8	3.1	1.7	1.3	2.3	1.6	1.9	2.2	5.3
Denmark	6.6	3.6	7.4	0.0	1.7	2.3	1.1	1.0	2.0	1.4	1.4	1.4	2.9
United Kingdom	11.5	10.2	10.7	10.0	0.0	9.1	9.4	7.5	11.9	9.7	8.2	5.0	15.1

West Germany	13.0	8.8	10.9	13.8	12.0	0.0	17.2	18.9	22.9	21.1	21.8	35.2	18.1
France	3.6	4.2	5.2	4.9	8.0	12.4	0.0	16.6	10.9	18.9	9.3	4.7	17.1
Italy	2.6	1.7	3.3	2.2	4.7	7.6	10.3	0.0	5.4	6.1	7.3	7.0	3.3
Netherlands	5.8	3.3	4.6	4.1	5.9	8.6	4.6	3.1	0.0	14.3	2.9	2.8	6.6
Belgium-Luxembourg	1.8	1.5	4.2	2.0	5.8	7.1	8.9	3.4	15.4	0.0	2.2	2.9	3.3
Switzerland	1.5	1.3	2.1	2.1	2.7	6.1	4.4	4.7	2.3	2.2	0.0	8.4	3.1
Austria	0.7	1.0	1.1	1.1	0.7	5.6	1.0	2.5	1.4	1.1	3.9	0.0	1.4
Portugal	0.4	0.2	0.5	0.5	0.7	0.6	0.9	0.9	0.6	0.4	0.7	0.4	0.0
EFTA 8	37.1	35.7	34.6	42.4	11.1	29.5	20.0	19.3	22.9	18.0	17.8	19.6	32.5
EC 6	26.8	19.5	28.2	27.0	36.4	35.5	41.0	42.0	54.6	60.4	43.5	52.6	48.4
EC 9	45.3	33.5	46.8	37.5	38.8	47.5	52.4	51.4	69.1	71.9	53.8	59.4	66.4
EFTA 5	18.6	22.7	21.1	31.0	8.7	17.5	8.6	9.9	8.4	6.5	7.5	12.8	14.5

SOURCE: Wijkman (1989).

local production than it does U.S. companies well beyond "screw-driver operations," which may be easier to organize but are much more fragile from a political point of view. The preferred locations of Japanese parent companies (the United Kingdom, Netherlands, Belgium, Germany, and more recently Spain and France) are those from which they can serve the enlarged European market through a mix of locally produced goods and exports from Japan (Fukuda 1988).[6]

Interfirm Cooperation as a Tool for Dynamic Competition

The single market also provides an excellent opportunity for interfirm cooperation, a vital instrument for Schumpeterian dynamic competition. This concept is well-known in the corporate and political culture of Japan and has gained a following throughout Europe since the early 1980s, but has only recently been discovered by U.S. businesses and policy makers (Dertouzos et al. 1989). Ever since Schumpeter (1942: chap. 8) argued that large scale is a necessary condition for technical progress and "creative destruction" and that "perfect competition is not only impossible but inferior and has no title to being set up as a model of ideal efficiency," economists have been ambivalent about competitive rivalry and market concentration (Stigler 1982; Di Lorenzo and High 1988). Although rivalry and competition lead to greater efficiency, because of the need to survive in the market, excessive fragmentation of supply may cause resources to be misallocated and wasted in the race to obtain a patent or to support research and development (R & D) and in response to the free-rider phenomenon. Static and dynamic efficiency do not necessarily coincide, nor do they always function in the interest of consumer sovereignty. Innovation depends on "complementary assets" (Porter 1986; Teece 1986, 1989; Williamson 1981)—ranging from R & D to production, marketing, distribution, and after-sale assistance. Consequently, co-ordination and cooperation among business units, especially between users and producers (Von Hippel 1976; Kline and Rosenberg 1986; Lundvall 1988), become crucial activities for the single innovating firm trying to adapt to the ever-changing environment and to share the risks and costs of new investments.[7]

In the United States, interfirm cooperation is forbidden by anti-trust legislation, except in the area of R & D (since 1984). The extent to which these rules have actually been implemented and thus have hampered corporate cooperative agreements downstream is still open to discussion. Japan's experience has been almost the reverse, although it is far from the extreme cartelization and tightly knit oligopoly that some accounts depict. At present, the new wave of equity and nonequity interfirm agreements in Europe, not only in the field of precompetitive innovation, is providing a laboratory for dynamic competition and for the gradual development of new kinds of national antitrust legislation and practical regimes. A pragmatic approach to antitrust rules is already being tested on intra-German and on intra-European mergers by Daimler-MBB and GEC-Siemens-Plessey, respectively. American and Japanese companies are also fully engaged in these activities.

The danger that these mergers and cooperative agreements may become transformed into cartels must not be overlooked, however (Porter 1990). The line between rationalizing industrial structure and reproducing captive markets at a continental level may be a thin one. European governments are probably not yet fully aware that a Fortress Europe could well rise up in the distant future, under the anticompetitive hand of cartels fostered by various political and special-interest groups. For the time being, competitive forces appear to be at work as the countries of Europe prepare for the imminent collapse of their purely national captive markets. The cooperation that this competitive spirit has spawned in the field of technology (in programs such as Espirit, Race, Brite, and Eureka) may yield significant results—not so much because of the public financial support coming this way, but because of the opportunity Europe now has to strengthen its position in the international technology race.

Community transfers to industrial research and development within these programs currently amount to slightly more than 1 percent of the total being spent on R & D efforts by the twelve EC members and absorb roughly 2 percent of the total EC budget (which is still dominated by agricultural subsidies). Thus the risk of cartelized R & D is almost nonexistent, at least so far. Despite the limited amount of seed money, what can be done with it already sounds impressive if one takes into account Europe's largely unexploited potential in generating and diffusing new technologies (Sharp and Shearman 1987; Doz 1989). Just think of the possibilities that are opening up.

Scientific Cooperation. Scientists and researchers in the academic and nonacademic institutions of Europe, not to mention skilled technicians and managers in firms, have considerably less mobility than their counterparts in the United States. Their movement is hampered by institutional constraints and other barriers such as housing and language problems. Recent European programs in support of research and teaching exchanges (COMETT, SPES), for example, are forging closer ties among scientists and researchers and making it possible to tap the intellectual talents of those working in geographically peripheral areas. With greater scientific cooperation, scientists may have more influence on public policies in their fields of interest (*Nature* 1989).

Technological Independence. A great deal of empirical evidence now indicates that Europe is lagging behind in several highly pervasive new technologies: microelectronic and optoelectronic components, computers and data processing, consumer electronics, some advanced materials (mainly technical ceramics, functional ceramics for electronics, high-performance components), and some areas of biotechnology (genetic engineering, advanced fermentation, and separation technologies especially applicable to the food industry, among others) (Patel and Pavitt 1988; Pavitt and Patel 1988; Commission of European Communities 1989b). Considerable effort will have to be put into generic technologies, mainly microelectronic components and advanced materials (that is, the technologies needed to improve the performance of a wide array of final products) to avoid excessive dependence on foreign supplies (Barfield and Schambra 1986; Ergas 1987; Aigrain et al. 1989; Dertouzos et al. 1989; Scott 1989). Technological independence can be achieved through R & D cooperation between Europe's industrial and research organizations. Such cooperation is clearly lacking, outside of the relatively efficient German-Nordic interaction (Stankiewicz 1986; Onida and Malerba 1989).

Competitiveness. To be sure, Europe is not behind in all technological fields: think of nuclear energy, computer-integrated manufacturing, telecommunications equipment and services, artificial intelligence software and systems engineering, biotechnologies for pharmaceutical uses, and aerospace. But it does trail the United States and Japan in terms of several indicators of technological input and output: the number of researchers relative to the total labor force (table 1-6), R & D over sales and industrial value added (table 1-7), the absolute value of R & D expenditure by major firms in high-technology fields, R & D over GDP (figure 1-3), and per capita patents (table 1-8).[8]

Exports. On the whole, Europe's share of exports in high- and medium-technology industries, net of intra-EC trade, is quite respectable, although its performance in relation to Japanese exports is still weak where high-tech, electronic products are concerned (table 1-9). The reason is not difficult to find if one takes into account the imports that have penetrated the European market and upset the trade balance in these fields since the mid-1970s, the same period in which Japan took the maximum advantage of the even greater deterioration in the U.S. trade balance (figure 1-4).

TABLE 1-6

WORKERS IN R & D FOR EVERY 10,000 IN THE TOTAL LABOR FORCE,
1984–1986

Country	Number
United States[a]	69.0
Japan[b]	63.2
West Germany[c]	49.1
France[c]	41.2
United Kingdom[c]	32.8

a. In 1986.
b. In 1985.
c. In 1984.
SOURCE: *Nature* (1989).

TABLE 1-7

ANNUAL GROWTH OF INDUSTRIAL R & D COMPARED WITH OTHER
FACTORS, 1967–1983
(percent)

Country	R & D	Output	Profits	Profits/ Output	R & D Output	R & D Profits
Japan	10.7	5.4	1.5	−3.9	5.3	9.2
United States	4.1	2.4	−4.1	−6.5	1.7	8.2
France	5.8	3.1	—	—	2.7	—
West Germany	5.6	2.2	−0.6	−2.8	3.4	6.2
Italy	5.1	2.7	—	—	2.4	—
Netherlands	2.0	2.7	—	—	−0.7	—
Sweden	6.6	1.3	3.0	1.7	5.3	3.6
United Kingdom	1.1	1.7	−0.5	−2.2	−0.6	1.6
1967–1975	−0.5	2.2	−2.0	−4.2	−2.7	(1.5)
1975–1983	2.7	1.2	1.1	−0.1	1.5	(1.6)

— = not available.
SOURCE: Pavitt and Patel (1988).

European Standards. In view of the extensive fragmentation of national technical standards and national champions in high-tech fields, an all-out effort should be made to establish European standards, systems, and system networks. A move is already being made in this direction by European programs such as Race (in telecommunications) and, to a lesser extent, Espirit (in information technologies)

37

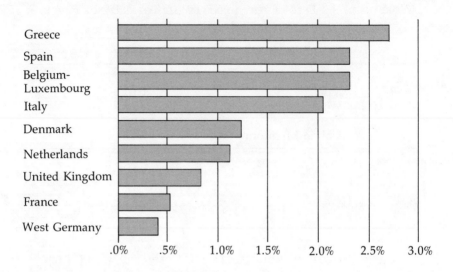

FIGURE 1–3
RATIO OF R & D SPENDING TO GDP IN THE EC, 1988

SOURCE: Commission of the European Communities (1989).

and Brite (in various fields of mechanical and electrical engineering). The continental standardization of technical specifications and safety requirements for products will not automatically detract from dynamic competition by, say, reducing the incentive to innovate or allowing particular standards to take precedence over others. If anything, the current and planned European programs for R & D expenditure (tables 1-10, 1-11) should concentrate more resources on joint research centers and on more flexible task forces, with a view to carrying out highly complex projects that cross national boundaries in areas such as health, telecommunications, energy, natural resources, and advanced transportation systems.

Why Not a Fortress Europe?

Although some national governments may still try to keep their captive markets going for a while, the single market is soon likely to put an end to such divisive strategies. Ample reason for not believing Europe will become a fortress can be found in its *patterns of external trade and investment*.

Historically, Western European trade has consistently followed a path of increasing interdependence with the rest of the world. The

38

TABLE 1-8

Trends in per Capita Patenting in the United States by Major OECD Countries, 1963–1968 and 1980–1985

(per million population)

Country	1963–1968	1980–1985
Japan	10.40	78.98
United States	236.13	157.88[a]
France	26.64	38.79
Italy	8.15	14.03
Netherlands	36.61	46.89
Sweden	65.30	89.12
Switzerland	140.74	182.34
United Kingdom	44.38	40.51
West Germany	55.32	97.01
Western Europe[b]	36.71	51.15

a. The differences in magnitude of per capita patenting between the United States and the other countries are an exaggeration of the differences in innovative activity as the propensity of U.S. firms to patent in their home country is higher than that of firms from other countries.
b. Western Europe is defined as the seven European countries listed above, plus Belgium, Denmark, and Ireland.
SOURCE: Pavitt and Patel (1988).

TABLE 1-9

Export Market Shares for Civil Markets Excluding Intra-EC Exchanges, 1986

Percentage of World Market	European Community	United States	Japan
High technology[a]	18.8	15.7	22.4
Medium technology[b]	28.0	12.1	15.8

a. R & D spending to production value ratio of more than 4 percent. This group includes the following industries: pharmaceuticals, office and data processing machines, professional and domestic electrical equipment, aeronautics, precision instruments, and equipment.
b. R & D spending to production value ratio of 1 to 4 percent.
SOURCE: Commission of the European Communities (1989a).

FIGURE 1–4
MERCHANDISE BALANCES IN HIGH-TECH PRODUCTS
IN RELATION TO WORLD TRADE IN HIGH-TECH PRODUCTS, 1970–1987

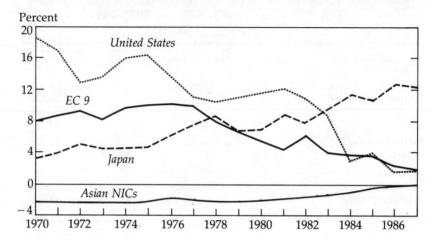

SOURCE: Centro Europa Ricerche (1989).

lowering of intra-EC barriers has not prevented dynamic net external
trade, even though the share of intra-EC trade over total EC trade has
risen about 56–57 percent since the 1986 oil countershock drastically
cut the OPEC share of world imports. Depending on the relative
cycle in European versus American domestic demand, the share of
external EC imports of manufactures over EC apparent consumption
of manufactures continued to rise during the first half of the 1980s,
although proportionately less than in the United States as a result of
the competitive loss that the strong dollar brought to American
producers in their own domestic market (table 1-12). This situation is
akin to the steady import penetration of Japanese manufacturing
domestic demand. The ratio of imports to GDP for the European
Community (excluding intracommunity trade) and the United States
is today close to 9 percent, against 6 percent for Japan. The ratios of
exports to GDP is about 10–11 percent for both the Community and
Japan, but less for the United States (table 1-13).

Technological innovation has long been pushing toward a global
market. Europe plays the global game. European multinational companies, at least in high-tech fields, reject technological autarky and
technological dominance as opposite, unfeasible alternatives. Self-
centered European growth appears implausible in an increasingly
global market calling for economies of scale in an interdependent

TABLE 1-10
EC Program for R & D, 1987–1991
(millions of ECUs)

Area of Concentration	Amount
Quality of life	375
Health	80
Radioprotection	34
Environment	261
Information and communication society	2,275
Information technology (Esprit)	1,600
Telecommunications (Race)	550
New services (DRIVE, DELTA, AIM)	125
Modernization of industrial sectors	845
Manufacturing industries (Brite)	400
Advanced materials (EURAM)	220
Basic materials	45
Standards and measurements (BCR)	180
Enhancement of biological resources	280
Biotechnology (BAP–BRIDGE)	120
Food technology (ECLAIR)	105
Agriculture	56
Energy	1,173
Fission	440
Thermonuclear fusion (JET)	611
Nonnuclear energy	122
Science and technology for development	80
Enhancement of ocean resources	80
Ocean sciences and technology	50
Fishing	30
European cooperation	288
Stimulation of human resources (science)	180
Use of major facilities	30
Forecasting and assessment (FAST–SPEAR)	23
Exploitation of research results	55
Total	5,396

Source: Commission of the European Communities (1989b).

TABLE 1-11

The European Community's Framework Program for Research
and Technological Development, 1990–1994

(millions of ECUs)

Area of Concentration	Amount
Diffusive technologies	
Information and communication technologies	4,108
Industrial and materials-related technologies	1,777
Management of natural resources	
Environment	928
Life-related science and technologies	1,295
Energy	1,866
Management of intellectual resources	
Human capital and mobility	852
Total	10,826

Note: Figures include a carryover of unspent resources from the previous framework program, for 1987–1991.
Source: Commission of the European Communities (1989a).

world. The EC countries feel that modern technological trends have already engendered the 1993 market (De Benedetti 1988). They feel the U.S. market, unlike the rather closed Japanese market, is already a domestic market, in which they make sales and purchases and participate in production, design, and R & D.

As already observed, national governments may continue to cling to some of their protectionist rules and captive markets. Even so, the principle of mutual recognition will create strong political pressure for broadening the scope of liberalization and open competition.

The U.S. and EFTA multinationals that have long been acquainted with the fragmented European market may well find themselves among the beneficiaries of the single market, owing to their know-how in handling logistical problems and distribution and in managing complex organizations. A knowledge of local market differences and opportunities is deeply embedded in their management and strategic planning and often puts them ahead of their direct European competitors, who are more used to devising strategies that will help them keep an upper hand in their national domestic markets than to competing in the continental arena. Think of the many European subsidiaries of U.S. multinationals in chemicals, pharmaceuticals, telecommunications, computers, and passenger cars.[9]

As the theory of effective protection suggests, the notion of Fortress Europe may not reflect the desires of all producers. Some may want protection for their final products and yet strongly oppose trade barriers on their imported intermediate inputs, which would put them at a disadvantage by leaving their foreign competitors to have access to low-cost intermediate inputs. Local producers of intermediate inputs, however, may press for more protection of infant industries in their own sectors. The result could be an unstable combination of conflicting interests, as emerged in the recent embarrassing negotiations between the European Community and Japan concerning electronic chips.[10]

Nonetheless, technological interdependence along the value chain in most modern manufacturing makes the concept of Fortress Europe increasingly implausible since it collapses the interests of various domestic producers into a single group. Moreover, technological change and technological dynamic competition make it increasingly difficult for national interest groups to become winners in a global market.

Even modern theories of strategic protectionism in imperfectly competitive and oligopolistic markets can hardly lead to safe predictions. As others have pointed out, "Free trade is not passé, but it is an idea that has irretrievably lost its innocence. Its status has shifted from optimum to reasonable rule of thumb" (Krugman 1987b: 132), and "the information requirements for suitable intervention, regardless of relation, are complex and outcomes are unusually sensitive to governments making the correct guesses and choices" (Bhagwati 1989: 40). "Managed trade is simply a bad idea. It replaces competition among firms with competition among bureaucrats" (Lawrence 1989).

Ruling out Fortress Europe does not at all imply giving up defensive action (as in the case of Japanese passenger cars)[11] or offensive action aimed at reciprocity (as in the Multi Fiber Agreement negotiations or in the efforts to maintain a trade balance in the field of motor vehicles). For its part, Japan must make certain that, when and if Europe's walls go up, its global companies qualify as insiders (*Economist* 1989: 31). Meanwhile, U.S. negotiators are particularly concerned with technical standards (the Deutsche Institut für Normung-DIN has 20,000 standards and its representatives preside over about 40 percent of the EC committees in charge of proposing Europewide technical standards) and reciprocity. Questions of origin and local content are mainly of concern to Japan (Montagnon 1988).

I should hasten to add, however, that national interests will undoubtedly persist and that different "national innovation sys-

TABLE 1-12
IMPORTS AS PERCENTAGE OF APPARENT CONSUMPTION, 1981–1982 AND 1985–1986

	European Community[a]		United States-Canada[a]		Japan		Total	
	1981–1982	1985–1986	1981–1982	1985–1986	1981–1982	1985–1986	1981–1982	1985–1986
Total manufactures								
Total	11.32	12.54	7.13	10.33	4.96	4.60	4.52	5.18
From developing countries	2.63	2.84	2.53	3.42	1.62	1.43	2.39	2.83
Textiles								
Total	11.85	13.35	5.30	7.80	4.71	5.37	5.51	6.70
From developing countries	4.49	4.98	2.21	3.23	2.18	2.13	3.04	3.60

Clothing								
Total	24.55	29.20	20.74	33.05	14.98	15.33	19.18	26.14
From developing countries	15.26	17.88	15.98	24.56	8.70	8.86	14.87	20.27
Chemicals								
Total	9.35	10.27	4.36	5.88	6.70	6.54	3.38	3.80
From developing countries	1.40	1.63	0.79	1.12	0.93	1.06	1.05	1.29
Transport equipment								
Total	9.69	11.79	10.24	13.05	2.46	2.39	1.80	2.29
From developing countries	0.80	0.88	0.36	0.80	0.17	0.09	0.46	0.69
Machinery and other manufactured goods								
Total	21.32	24.11	12.73	19.51	5.36	4.59	5.65	6.99
From developing countries	2.68	3.29	4.21	6.21	0.87	0.88	3.08	4.15

a. Imports in these cases exclude intra-area trade.
SOURCE: UNCTAD, Handbook of International Trade and Development Statistics (1988).

TABLE 1-13

RATIO OF MERCHANDISE EXPORTS AND IMPORTS TO GDP, 1980–1986

(percent)

Year	EC12[a]	United States	Japan
Exports			
1980	9.8	7.9	12.2
1981	10.3	7.5	12.8
1982	10.0	7.1	11.7
1983	10.1	6.4	12.5
1984	10.7	6.6	13.7
1985	10.8	5.8	13.6
1986	10.2	5.7	12.9
Imports			
1980	12.5	9.3	13.2
1981	11.3	9.0	12.0
1982	11.0	8.9	11.7
1983	10.8	9.4	11.5
1984	11.0	11.0	11.9
1985	11.1	10.8	11.2
1986	11.7	11.5	12.2

NOTE: Based on U.S. dollars at current prices.
a. EC data refer to extra-Community trade.
SOURCE: Commission of the European Communities (1988a).

tems," along with various combinations of "mission-oriented" and "diffusion-oriented" technology policies (Ergas 1987), are likely to prevent a cohesive EC-wide industrial policy from being implemented, at least in the foreseeable future. French policy makers, for instance, are likely to make some alliance with U.K. policy makers against Germany's numerous regulations and high technical standards. At the same time, the German and British governments strongly oppose the blatant protectionist attitude of the French government with respect to European "national champions." French and Italian fears of competition from Japan in the car market are countered by German and British distrust of administrative import barriers. Margaret Thatcher's (1988) comments at Bruges in this regard, as well as the views of several British officials (for example, Healey 1988; Lawson 1989) hardly square with the preference function supported by the French government.

Underlying these differences are four critical concerns, dubbed the "inconsistent quartet" (Padoa Schioppa 1987): free trade in goods and services, free capital mobility, monetary and exchange rate stability, and national monetary independence. The Delors Report (1989) and all recent official statements by European policy makers clearly suggest that EC members are prepared to abandon the fourth one (national monetary independence) in favor of a centrally coordinated European monetary system (EMS), rather than put the first three at risk. This does not rule out temporary recourse to specific technical regulations on short-term capital movements (such as leads and lags in short-term export and import credit) in order to cope with sudden speculations on intra-EC exchange rates, as long as some degree of fluctuation around officials parities is maintained before reaching Delors's stage three. But this has little to do with maintaining a basically open trade regime, internally or externally.

Internal Trade and Intra-EC Distribution of the 1992 Gains

The enlarged EC-12 is more likely than the original EC-6 to generate industrial specialization among the member countries (Krugman 1987a), given the entry of peripheral countries characterized by rather different rates of development. Such specialization within the single market will facilitate intraindustry trade among member countries (that is, trade in various product groups within traditionally classified sectors will increase relative to trade among sectors). Furthermore, it will still allow substantial redistribution among trading partners, as is the case with classical and neoclassical interindustry trade among countries endowed with different factors. The distribution of gains from trade is a crucial point to consider in assessing the costs and benefits of protection or trade liberalization.

On a static level, such distribution is determined by the particular terms of trade (ratio of average export price to average import price) that prevail at the start of the liberalization process. More significant on a dynamic level are trends in the terms of trade over time. A country specializing in goods characterized by greater seller market power and faster growth of demand is more likely to increase the valorization of its own human and technical resources, in comparison with a country specializing in serving slow-growing or quasi-perfect competitive markets. We can expect this to happen for a number of reasons.

More Leeway for Intraindustry Specialization. The impressive growth of intraindustry trade within the original EC-6 did not seem to hinge on whether member countries were endowed with similar factors. Just think of the massive labor migrations from Italy to France, Belgium, and Germany during the late 1950s and 1960s. If anything, member countries differed considerably in their natural resources.

Putting aside controversial definitions and measurements of factor endowments, one can expect intraindustrial trade in the European Community to stem from (a) the convergence of demand patterns and (b) greater interdependence through intra-EC direct investments. In both cases, I am assuming faster diffusion of information within the Community and greater mobility of capital and labor (economic integration beyond a customs union).

In a fully integrated continental market, most efficient enterprises of the member countries will become increasingly aware of the benefits to be derived from relocating their activities in order to better serve the integrated market. In so doing, they will try to take advantage of (a) the differences in factor costs and availability, (b) the different rates of growth and characteristics of local demand, (c) external economies and diseconomies, and (d) the location incentives provided by various national and local authorities.

Even in the absence of international capital mobility, recent models of trade based on imperfect markets and economies of scale (Helpman and Krugman 1985) suggest that, within an integrated area consisting of various regions endowed with different factors, intraindustry specialization may well develop together with traditional interindustry specialization, depending on the factor intensities of the industries. This result flows from the unpredictable pattern of trade arising from single firms specializing in single products within each sector and exploiting the opportunities of decreasing unit costs (static economies of scale).

If full capital mobility is introduced, there is an even greater probability of intraindustry specialization within regions of the integrated market. In fact, under the assumption of perfect capital mobility, the relative scarcity or abundance of capital of various regions cannot be precisely identified.

Regional differences in the cost of labor and other factors may well persist even in a fully integrated market, as is suggested by the recent history of the U.S. and Canadian markets. Note, too, that the availability of specific human, physical, and technological resources is not evenly distributed over the integrated continental market.

Intra- and interindustry specializations are difficult to predict for yet another reason. External economies and diseconomies of specific productive agglomerations, including crucial links between industry and knowledge-generating institutions, may well dominate processes of regional specialization for specific factor-intensive goods and services.

Different rates of growth and characteristics of domestic demand in different regions of the integrated market, including the adaptation customs of specific users, are also likely to encourage some relocation of activities closer to faster-growing regions, regardless of their specific endowments. Crude neoclassical models tend to disregard this factor, since they capture only pure price-cost competition. Within a modern framework of imperfect markets with imperfect information and significant external economies and diseconomies, however, nonprice factors of competition also play a crucial role, particularly distributive network efficiency, before-sale and after-sale assistance facilities, and closer geographical links between the users and producers of intermediate and capital goods (Marvel and Ray 1987; Jacquemin and Sapir 1988).

User-producer links are of utmost importance in the early phases of a product cycle. As long as the production function of the new product becomes standardized, firms may find it beneficial to relocate entire or partial phases of production purely as a cost-saving strategy.

All the foregoing considerations reinforce the first point, namely that the single market is likely to accelerate the trend toward intraindustry specialization in member countries. But imperfect markets, product differentiation, economies of scale, and external economies also hinge on the existence of asymmetrical gain from trade within the single market.

Redistribution of Gains from Trade among Member Countries. The benefits of the internal market arising from economies of scale and dynamic X efficiency will not necessarily accrue in the same degree in all regions of the European Community. A given region or country may find itself at the bottom end of the net benefits as a result of the following characteristics of specialization:

• Lower income elasticity of world demand, which implies more stringent constraints on the growth of countries' own domestic demand for imports, at least as long as full monetary unification does not completely remove the obstacles to large (and perhaps growing) intraarea trade imbalances.

• Higher degree of standardization and homogeneity, which provides less scope for monopoly rents (at least temporary rents, compatible with imperfectly free entry) and for related improvements in the terms of trade with other regions.

• Lower-quality segment of demand within a vertically differentiated range of products. Indeed, the producers of lower-quality goods face the unpleasant prospect of progressive losses in market shares, as the increasing per capita incomes within the single market induce consumers to abandon low-quality goods in favor of higher-quality goods (Shaked and Sutton 1984).

• Lower dynamic economies of scale (learning by doing, learning by using, learning by research). Hence, there will be less opportunity for increasing cost competitiveness over time and for the downstream diffusion of technological advantages.

Thus the internal market may bring about more acute regional imbalances, as suggested by early analyses of the dynamic effects of customs unions (Giersch 1949–1950). Predictions cannot be based on these grounds alone, of course. History has shown that the cumulative effects of specialization tend to be combined with continuous flows of technology and of managerial resources between more and less advanced areas (see the north-south models of Krugman 1979). The entry of newcomers, including producers in imitating countries (second comers, followers), characterize varying degrees of "market contestability" even when assuming a permanent oligopolistic structure of major suppliers (Baumol and Willig 1986).

However measured, regional inequalities in Europe (which can be divided into fifty-nine large regions), and individual member countries, are today larger than the regional inequalities in the United States (at least in forty-eight of its states) (Begg 1989; Boltho 1989). The synthetic index of standard of living for Europe's richest regions (Darmstadt and Oberbayern in Germany) is five times higher than that of its two poorest regions (Basilicata and Calabria in Italy). Although differences in the regional standard of living in Europe declined rapidly during the 1950s and 1960s, the rate has slowed down from the 1970s onward.

In the United States, regional inequalities have been constantly offset by the mobility of capital and domestic labor (particularly in the South and West and by the remarkable flexibility in wages. In addition, the U.S. fiscal system is designed to promote some income redistribution among states (unlike the regressive EC fiscal mechanism of agricultural duties and subsidies).

Although mechanisms need to be found to address Europe's regional imbalances (Commission of the European Communities 1977; Padoa Schioppa 1987; Begg 1989; Scott 1989), their targets and instruments have to be scrutinized carefully in order to avoid wasteful intervention and even the self-defeating effects of financial subsidies. A greater and more widespread supply of business services (real and financial), information technologies, and telecommunications and transport facilities are of much higher priority than the traditional transfer of income. Some regional imbalances may be efficiently tackled by less traditional infrastructural programs, with investment focused on new industries (for example, tourism and intensive high-tech research activities).

To correct structural imbalances among regions and promote the diffusion of technological and production opportunities, the integrated market must maintain a high degree of wage and labor flexibility:

> Wage differentiation between the centre and the periphery is thus essential for adequate growth. But it is also a necessary condition for an optimum allocation of resources in the spatial dimension. With inadequate wage differentiation, not enough jobs will move from the centre and look for jobs there waiting in desperate conditions at the outskirts of large cities or even in slum districts. Special upheavals and xenophobia, already now observable, may then become detrimental to European integration. This danger should warn us against the corporatist tendencies towards excessive labour market harmonisation. (Giersch 1989: 11)

> The road to fortress Europe is paved by the technocratic quest for ex ante harmonization within the Community. (Giersch 1989: 19)

EC members have had some difficulty formulating a European social statute. Even the Delors Report (1989: par. 29) sends mixed signals in the regard. On one hand, it emphasizes that intra-EC wage differences are necessary to offset productivity differences and external diseconomies; on the other hand, it explicitly calls for compensatory policies (to be implemented through investment programs, the infrastructure, and environmental actions) to avoid cumulative disequilibria between central regions and to take advantage of static and dynamic economies of scale, lower transport costs, and peripheral underdeveloped regions.

Summary

How long the Europhoria of the late 1980s and new-found hope for sustained growth will last is uncertain. The transition to the single market will not be without its hardships. Even so, businesses that have been surveyed appear to believe the benefits will outweigh the costs for individual countries and firms. This is especially the view of firms belonging to the strong-currency bloc (Germany and Benelux)—precisely those that one might expect to balk at monetary and exchange rate integration for fear of importing inflation and monetary instability from weak-currency countries.

To borrow Victoria Curzon's suggestive imagery, I see the single

51

market project entering a third and new phase of accelerated European integration (the Ferrari model), which differs from the traditional gradualist (steamroller) approach of EC-9 and the deep-rooted minimalist (miniweight) approach of the EFTA countries. This move toward a truly continental European economy is based on the principle of mutual recognition. The Community-wide acceptance of this principle, although it comes long after the famous 1978 decision on Cassis de Dijon, gives decisive support and credibility to the ambitious design and creates pressure for greater static and dynamic efficiency at the level of firms, markets, and institutions. Technical and institutional barriers to the project will undoubtedly be scrutinized, and there will be less scope for rent-seeking coalitions. Nonetheless, many fears concerning corporatism, managed trade, and technocratic regulations are far from removed.

The structural impact of the real and financial integration under the Ferrari model will consist of a dwindling of smaller inefficient firms, a massive reshuffling of the property and management of ailing firms (those unable to face the stronger competition but still endowed with human and physical assets that retain considerable value), and new entries of innovative firms. Intra-European mergers and acquisitions have already been taking place at a rapid rate in recent years. This does not mean that Scandinavian, Swiss, American, and Japanese firms have become passive spectators. Indeed, non-EC multinationals, which long ago learned how to deal with fragmented but integrating markets, may well be among the principal gainers from the single market.

Above all, the 1992 single market will provide an impetus to the continental integration of industrial and tertiary structures, not just markets. Firms, especially small and medium-size firms, are not yet completely aware of the potential of the single market in this regard. The real impact of full integration—that is, the gradual fall of invisible national barriers and of national and local captive markets—will become clearer as the process evolves. In the meantime, EC members are likely to become somewhat more realistic about the net benefits of 1992 from the perspective of their own firms.

The single market provides excellent opportunities for interfirm cooperative agreements (including agreements with non-EC firms). Such agreements, well-known in Japan's corporate and political culture, are becoming increasingly popular throughout Europe, albeit with some unusual country-specific features, and are drawing attention away from American businesses and policy makers. Cooperative agreements are crucial instruments of Schumpeterian dynamic competition, although there is always a danger that they may degenerate into collusive cartels.

Interfirm cooperation within European technology programs (such as Esprit and Eureka) may help European companies come up from behind in the electronic and intensive technology races. The problem is that cultural and institutional barriers continue to keep European scientists, researchers, and skilled technicians far less mobile than their counterparts in the United States. European technology programs, however, are greatly helping to improve this situation. Nor is European industry lagging in every aspect of the international technological competition, although the balance of trade in the high-tech industries has gradually shifted away from Europe since the mid-1970s. The fragmentation of national technical standards and captive markets for public procurement in high-tech fields are still a serious obstacle to the achievement of static and dynamic economies of scale.

Technological innovation is leading countries everywhere toward a global market and interdependence, so the European single market is bound to play the global game. Under those circumstances Europe is not likely to become a fortress or a battlefield under external dominance. At the same time, Europe's divergent national interests and various national innovation systems make it rather unlikely that a cohesive and EC-wide industrial policy will emerge.

Instead, the single market is offering more scope for intra-EC specialization that is closer to modern intraindustry patterns than to classical interindustry schemes. The most efficient firms recognize the opportunities awaiting them if they relocate their activities in order to better serve an integrating market by taking advantage of differences in costs, local tastes, the growth in local demand, specific external economies (especially those linked to user-producer relations), and specific locational incentives offered by local governments.

Admittedly, the internal market may reinforce regional inequalities, since they are not offset by labor mobility to the same degree that they are in the United States. Remembering their past disillusion, governments will undoubtedly put EC regional policies under close scrutiny. They should also put more emphasis on clearly focused development projects, infrastructures, and real services (rather than on income subsidies). Substantial interregional flexibility must be preserved where labor costs and regulations are concerned to avoid drawing business firms and skilled people to weaker regions endowed with less physical and human capital, poorer infrastructures, and higher transport costs in comparison with the richest markets.

The less fragmented and more self-conscious European economy that seems to be evolving in the 1990s will create opportunities for greater Schumpeterian competition, both within and outside its political borders. These events may well lead to some sort of future

European political unity, if one can look beyond the present turmoil and radical changes in Eastern Europe.

References

Agnelli, U. 1988. "Fortress Europe: A View from a European Automobile Manufacturer." Paper presented at the Prince Bertil Symposium, Corporate and Industry Strategies for Europe, Stockholm, November 9–11.

Aigrain P., G. Allen, E. Azantes e Oliveira, U. Colombo, and U. Markl. 1989. *Report of the Framework Programme Review Board*. Brussels, June.

Aoki, M. 1989. "Global Competition, Firm Organization and Total Factor Productivity." Paper presented at the OECD International Seminar on Science, Technology, and Economic Growth. Paris, June 5–8.

Barfield, C. E., and J. H. Makin, eds. 1987. *Trade Policy and U.S. Competitiveness*. Washington, D.C.: American Enterprise Institute.

Barfield, C. E., and W. A. Schambra, eds. 1986. *The Politics of Industrial Policy*. Washington, D.C.: American Enterprise Institute.

Baumol, W. J., and R. D. Willig. 1986. "Contestability: Developments since the Book." *Oxford Economic Papers* (November).

Begg, I. 1989. "European Integration and Regional Policy." *Oxford Review of Economic Policy* (Summer).

Bhagwati, J. 1989. "Is Free Trade Passé after All?" *Weltwirtschaftliches Archiv* 1.

Boltho, A. 1989. "European and U.S. Regional Differentials: A Note." *Oxford Review of Economic Policy* (Summer).

Buchan, D. 1989. "The Good, the Bad, the Indifferent." *Financial Times*, September 25.

Buckley, P. J., and P. Artisien. 1988. "Policy Issues of Intra-EC Direct Investment: British, French and German Multinationals in Greece, Portugal and Spain, with Special Reference to Employment Effects." In *Multinationals and the European Community*, edited by J. H. Dunning and P. Robson. Oxford: Blackwell.

Centro Europa. 1989. Report 3. Rome.

Centro Studi sui Processi di Internazionalizzazione. 1988. *International Agreements of Italian Firms: An Analysis with Specific Reference to the Role on Intra-EC Cooperation*. Report for the Business Cooperation Centre of the S.M.E. Task Force. Brussels: Commission of the European Communities.

Commission of the European Communities. 1977. *Report of the Study Group on the Role of Public Finance in European Integration* (McDougall Report). Brussels.

———. 1986. "Single European Act." *Bulletin of the E.C.*, Supplement 2.

————. 1988a. "1992: The New European Economy. *European Economy* (March).

————. 1988b. *Research on the "Cost of Non-Europe," Basic Findings.* Brussels.

————. 1989a. *Fourth Report of the Commission to Council and European Parliament on the Implementation of the White Paper on the Completion of the Internal Market.* Brussels, June 20.

————. 1989b. "Panorama of EC Industries." Brussels.

Curzon Price, V. 1988. "1992: Europe's Last Chance? From Common Market to Single Market." 19th Wincott Memorial Lecture. Occasional Paper 81. London: Institute of Economic Affairs.

————. 1989. "Three Models of European Integration. In *Whose Europe? Competing Visions for 1992.* London: Institute for Economic Affairs.

Dahrendorf, R. 1989. "The Future of Europe." *Whose Europe? Competing Visions for 1992.* London: Institute for Economic Affairs.

Dasgupta, P., and P. Stoneman, eds. 1987. *Economic Policy and Technological Performance.* Cambridge: Cambridge University Press.

De Benedetti, C. 1988. "Strategies for a Single European Market." *Financial Times,* European Business Forum, Rome, December 1–2.

De Jong, H. W. 1988. "Market Structures in the E.E.C." *The Structure of the European Industry,* 2d rev. ed., edited by H. W. De Jong. Dordrecht: Kluwer Academic.

Delors, J. 1989. Report to the Committee for the Study of Economic and Monetary Union on the Economic and Monetary Union in the EC. Brussels, April.

Dertouzos, M. L., R. K. Lester, and R. M. Solow. 1989. *Made in America. Regaining the Productive Edge.* Cambridge, Mass.: MIT Press.

Di Lorenzo, T. J., and J. C. High. 1988. "Antitrust and Competition, Historically Considered." *Economic Inquiry* (July).

Doz, Y. 1989. "Innovation, Technology and Competences: Mobilizing Capital in Companies." Paper presented at the OECD International Seminar on Science, Technology and Economic Growth, Paris, June 5–8.

Dunning, J. H., and P. Robson. 1988. "Multinational Corporate Integration and Regional Economic Integration." *Journal of Common Market Studies* (December).

Economist. 1988. "Europe's Internal Market—EEC 1992." July 8.

————. 1989. "Europe's Internal Market—EEC 1992." July 8.

Ergas, H. 1984. "Why Do Some Countries Innovate More than Others?" Center for Economic Policy Studies Paper 5. Brussels.

————. 1987. "The Importance of Technology Policy. In *Economic Policy and Technological Performance,* edited by P. Dasgupta and P.

Stoneman. Cambridge: Cambridge University Press.

European Community. 1988. *17th Report on Competition Policy*. Brussels.

Ferguson, C. H. 1989. "Macroeconomic Variables, Sectoral Evidence, and New Models of Industrial Performance." Paper presented at OECD International Seminar on Science, Technology and Economic Growth, Paris, June 5–8.

Financial Times (London). 1984. "Multinationals and European Integration: A Lack of European Harmony." April 5–6.

Fukuda, H. 1988. "Japanese Business and Investment in the European Community." *Financial Times*, European Business Forum, Rome, December 1–2.

Geroski, I. A. 1988. "Competition and Innovation." In *Research on the "Cost of Non-Europe," Basic Findings*, vol. 2, Commission of the European Communities. Brussels.

Giersch, H. 1949–1950. "Economic Union between Nations and the Location of Industries." *Review of Economic Studies*.

———. 1989. *Europe's Prospects for the 1990's*. Economic Papers of the Commission of the European Communities 76 (May).

Healey, D. 1988. "Will the Europe of 1992 Be Outward or Inward Looking?" *Financial Times*, European Business Forum, Rome, December 1–2.

Helpman, E., and P. R. Krugman, 1985. *Market Structure and Foreign Trade: Increasing Returns, Imperfect Competition, and the International Economy*. Cambridge, Mass.: MIT Press.

Islam, S. 1987. "What's Causing America's Capital Imports?" *Challenge* (September-October).

Jacquemin, A. 1987. *Collusive Behaviour: R&D and European Policy*. EEC Economic Papers 61 (November).

Jacquemin, A., and A. Sapir. 1988. "International Trade and Integration of the European Community." *European Economic Review* (September), special issue.

Jones, D. 1988. "Corporate Strategies for a Truly European Car Industry." Paper presented at the Prince Symposium on Corporate and Industry Strategies for Europe, Stockholm, November 9–11.

Kline, S. J., and N. Rosenberg. 1986. "An Overview of Innovation." In *The Positive Sum Strategy*, edited by N. Rosenberg and R. Landau. Washington, D.C.: National Academy Press.

Krugman, P. R. 1979. "A Model of Innovation, Technology Transfer and the World Distribution Income." *Journal of Political Economy* (April).

———. 1987a. "Economic Integration in Europe: Some Conceptual Issues." In *Efficiency, Stability and Equity. A Strategy for the Evolution of the Economic System in the European Community*, edited by T. Padoa Schioppa. Brussels.

————. 1987b. "Is Free Trade Passé?" *Journal Economic Perspectives*.

Lawrence, R. 1989. "Why Managed Trade Is a Bad Idea." *Financial Times*, June 7.

Lawson, N. 1989. "Quale tipo di spazio finanziario europeo?" Lecture at the Royal Institute for International Affairs, Milan, January 25.

Linder, S. B. 1961. *An Essay on Trade and Transformation*. New York: Wiley.

Lipsey, R. E., and I. B. Kravis. 1987a. *Saving and Economic Growth: Is the U.S. Really Falling Behind?* American Council of Life Insurance and Conference Board, Report 901. New York.

————. 1987b. "Competitiveness and Comparative Advantage of the U.S. Multinational Enterprises." *Banca Nazionale del Lavoro Quarterly Review* (June).

Lundvall, P. A. 1988. Innovation as an Interactive Process: From User-Producer Interaction to the National System of Innovation. In *Technical Change and Economic Theory*, edited by C. Dosi et al. London.

Marvel, H. P., and E. J. Ray. 1987. "Intra Industry Trade: Sources and Effects on Protection." *Journal of Political Economy* (December).

Montagnon, P. 1988. "Trading Places for the Future." *Financial Times*, September 30.

Nature. 1989. "Science in Europe." April.

Nomisma. 1989. *Fusioni Acquisizioni Concorrenza*. Bologna.

Olson, Mancur. 1982. *The Rise and Decline of Nations: Economic Growth, Stagflation and Social Rigidities*. New Haven, Conn.: Yale University Press.

————. 1986. "Supply-Side Economics, Industrial Policy, and Rational Ignorance." In *The Politics of Industrial Policy*, edited by C. E. Barfield and W. A. Schambra. Washington, D.C.: American Enterprise Institute.

Onida, F., and F. Malebra. 1989. "R&D Cooperation between Industry, Universities and Research Organizations in Europe." *Technovation* 9 (2–3).

Onida, F., and G. Viesti. 1988. *The Italian Multinationals*. London: Croom Helm.

Padoa Schioppa, T. 1987. *Efficiency, Stability and Equity: A Strategy for the Evolution of the Economic System in the European Community*. Bruxelles.

Patel, P., and K. Pavitt. 1988. "Measuring Europe's Technological Performance: Results and Prospects." Center for Economic Policy Studies Paper 36. Bruxelles.

Pavitt, K. 1980. *Technical Innovation and U.K. Economic Performance*. London: Macmillan.

Pavitt, K., and P. Patel. 1988. "The International Distribution and

Determinants of Technological Activities." *Oxford Review of Economic Policy* (Winter).

Pelkmans, J., in cooperation with M. Vanheukelen. 1988. "The Internal Markets of North America: Fragmentation and Integration in the U.S. and Canada." In *Research on the "Cost of Non-Europe," Basic Findings*, vol. 16, Commission of the European Communities. Brussels.

Porter, M. E. 1986. "Changing Patterns of International Competition." *California Management Review* (Winter).

———. 1990. *The Competitive Advantage of Nations*. Cambridge, Mass.: Harvard University Press.

Schumpeter, J. 1942. *Capitalism, Socialism and Democracy*. New York: Harper & Row.

Scott, A. 1989. *Completing the Internal Market: Some Implications for the Scottish Economy*. Royal Bank of Scotland Review (June), special 1992 edition.

Shaked, A., and J. Sutton. 1984. "Natural Oligopolies and International Trade." In *Monopolistic Competition and International Trade*, edited by H. Kierzkowski. Oxford: Oxford University Press.

Sharp, M., and C. Shearman. 1987. *European Technological Collaboration*. Chatham House Papers 36. London: Routledge & Kegan.

Smith, A., and A. J. Venables. 1988. "Completing the Internal Market in the European Community: Some Industry Simulations." *European Economic Review* (September), special issue.

Stankiewicz, R. 1986. *Academics and Entrepreneurs: Developing University-Industry Relations*. London: F. Pinter.

Stigler, G. J. 1982. "The Economists and the Problem of Monopoly." *American Economic Review* (May).

Swedenborg, B. 1988. "The EC and the Locational Choice of Swedish Multinational Companies." The Prince Bertil Symposium, Corporate and Industry Strategies for Europe, Stockholm, November 9–11.

Teece, D. J. 1986. "Profiting from Technological Innovation." *Research Policy* (December).

———. 1989. "Technological Change and the Nature of the Firm." In *Technical Change and Economic Theory*, edited by G. Dosi et al. London: Pinter.

Thatcher, M. 1988. Speech at opening ceremony of the 39th academic year of the College of Europe, Bruges. Extracts in *Financial Times*, September 21, 1988.

United Nations Centre on Transnational Corporations. 1988. *Transnational Corporations in World Development: Trends and Prospects*. New York.

Von Hippel, E. 1976. "The Dominant Role of Users in the Scientific

Instruments Innovation Process." *Research Policy* 5.

Wijkmen, P. M. 1989. "Patterns of Trade in the European Economic Space." *International Spectator* (January–March).

Williamson, O. E. 1981. "The Modern Corporation: Origins, Evolution, Attributes." *Journal of Economic Literature* (December).

2
Commentaries on Structural Change

A Commentary by John Butcher

We have a dilemma in the United Kingdom. We do not know whether to call the EEC by its old title, the Common Market, which refers to the six original countries, or by the new title, European Community.

Those who still wish to call Europe a common market are probably those who subscribe to Prime Minister Thatcher's view as put forward in her famous speech in Bruges in 1989. It is fundamentally misinterpreted by a large number of people. Those who see Europe as a growing and integrated community, who would call it the European Community, would probably subscribe to the view of Jacques Delors, who sees Europe not only trading within an intra–free-trade area, but taking on wider social responsibilities. Others espouse the views in Mrs. Thatcher's Bruges speech. They endorse a Europe that trades freely and has the minimum of intra-European barriers, but does not get bogged down in the minutiae of managing both intra-European and extra-European trade.

My second observation concerns the question of Germany's unification. When I was a young student, I spent a lot of time with friends from West Germany who were involved in exchange programs. I remember a German student of economics who talked about Middle Germany, by which he meant East Germany, and Middle Deutschland, by which he meant Germany to the east of East Germany—that is, parts of Poland.

In what we call East Germany, I see talented people of famous provinces like Brandenburg and Saxony and parts of what used to be known as Prussia. A look at East Germany's political tradition indicates that the SPD is in the ascendancy. This is completely uncharted territory in which I have no observations to make, but only questions to ask.

The economic condition of East Germany today, however, seems to parallel the economic condition of the United Kingdom between 1945 and 1947. Capital equipment was run down, people were tired, underinvestment had been a problem for a long time. But basic structures were intact.

Is East Germany going to take a postwar, British-Socialist attitude toward its problems, an Attlee–style approach with public utilities still publicly owned and 40–60 percent of GDP generated by publicly owned organizations?

They built the famous German miracle from a basic premise, real money. Once the people of West Germany had a real currency that could be exchanged for real goods that had real value, then the union could begin. In the aftermath of elections on March 18 we may see an SPD–style majority in some provinces. But will the SPD look to the failed public utilitarianism of Britain's immediate postwar period, or will it look to Fonme Chandl, and Leduny Erhard? I hope it is to Erhard for the sake of the people of the united Germany.

I now look at the question of Central Europe and Eastern Europe. In the first sentence of a widely syndicated newspaper article in September 1990, I wrote that I feared President Gorbachev was finished. To say that this brave and likable man is destined to fail because he started something that we in the West desperately want to see succeed gives no one, particularly in the West, any joy. But no amount of cheering from the touchdown line will help him resolve his dilemma; he is still proclaiming a top-down approach, a command economy. He wants his *glasnost* and *perestroika*. While in Bonn, at the time of Gorbymania, I fell in with part of the Russian entourage. I heard then that now famous Russian joke about the true meaning of *glasnost* and *perestroika*. The old Russian dog who had been in exile asked the young Russian dog who had stayed in Moscow, "What do *glasnost* and *perestroika* mean?" The young dog answered, "The chain that tethers us is shorter and the food bowl is farther away, but we are now allowed to bark." Gorbachev's problem is that his government sees discussion as a luxury for officials, while the Muscovite housewife is queuing longer for scarcer goods. And it will not be the KGB or the Soviet army that works for Mr. Gorbachev; it will be the Muscovite housewife. He may have redefined his job, he may be distancing himself from the party in due course, but the command economy will let him down.

We must decide what pressures and which trends will have an impact on us. The development of industrial and commercial trade policy within Western Europe points to the East. Some clear practical-ities must be looked at and some real work done while these bigger issues are being resolved.

Fabrizio Onida wrote about what this means for Japanese and European multinational companies. If we look, for example, at the value of acquisition deals made inside Europe by nation, we find the following. The United States, in the first nine months of 1989, deployed ECU 10 billion, which was 30 percent of the total cash spent on acquiring companies within the EC. France deployed the second largest sum at ECU 7,872 million, which was 23.5 percent of the total cash spent. Third was the United Kingdom at ECU 4,887 million, which was 14.6 percent of the total cash spent. Germany deployed half Britain's rate and was followed by Italy, Sweden, Belgium, and the others. So the United States is doing what it always was good at; it is building up its subsidiaries in Europe and acquiring synergic European companies. This will ensure continued existence of an international market inside Western Europe.

On open market measures, I turn to my excolleague Nicholas Ridley, who has spoken on state aid. In measuring whether Europe is constructing a level playing field, I draw your attention to figures that Ridley cites. In 1986 Italian state aid was eight times as high, French aid two times as high, and German aid 2.5 times as high as that of the United Kingdom. Ridley does not foresee the playing field being leveled off by 1992, and the commission is aware of this. We support the commission in its efforts to forbid new state aid schemes, but it must also tackle existing subsidies. Nonsense is made of the single market and fair competition by governments that prop up inefficient industries and subsidize business costs. So tackling this inequity must be a priority and a practical task of Europe today.

The United Kingdom has a reputation for talking tough on Europe about open market measures and a reputation for being practical to the point of irritation. Of the seventy-seven single market directives enunciated by the commission so far, seventy-four have been implemented already by the United Kingdom, and two will be implemented shortly. That means that the United Kingdom has been the main driver for free intra-European trade after Denmark.

The new figures for European research and development under the framework program between 1987 and 1991 show projected spending of ECU 5.617 billion on R & D programs. Within the field of information technology, ECU 2 billion out of a ECU 5.6 billion R & D program will go to information technology and telecommunications R & D.

The next biggest spender by category is energy. A total of ECU 1.5 billion is allotted for fission, fusion, and nonnuclear energy, and the rest is distributed over biological resources, quality of life questions, seabed and marine resources, and collaborative efforts on big science.

This spending indicates Europe's feelings of vulnerability; so it must make its presence felt in information technology, in telecommunications, and in energy questions. It is an opportunity, particularly in the area of defense and information technology, for further collaboration.

A Commentary by Heinrich von Moltke

Current moves toward European integration can be compared with a Ferrari, as to speed and precision. The internal market is misunderstood when someone says, the wages cannot be harmonized between Britain and Rumania and therefore the Common Market is coming to a halt. The problem is that no one has ever had the idea to harmonize all these things. The beauty of the internal market is that it leaves so many things to competition; it focuses only on the essentials, where harmonization is still essential. The rest is left to the workings of what Mr. Giersch has called the competition between locations.

This brings me to the next question. Is it going to be done on time? And what is going to come after 1992? People have said that 1992 is a moot issue: it is already being achieved. To a great extent that is true, because two-thirds of the decisions have been taken and a good deal of the transposition has been done. Of 1,007 measures to be transposed into national law by January 1, 1990, some 660 have been transposed—two-thirds. The rest may not come on time.

We will not achieve everything; but if we bring down the border controls by January 1, 1993, the most important step will have been taken, because the competitive pressure between locations will start working. The question will then be, Will the inevitable pressure toward harmonization be checked or not?

That question is important because it determines what the community wants and can want to be. Giving in to this pressure would probably create some trouble. If we want to be too perfect, how can we contemplate ever bringing the Eastern European countries into our orbit? It would not be feasible. Even inside the community, we cannot hope to be too perfect; we have still large inequalities between Portugal and Denmark. This model should be followed, but a certain number of additional measures may be called for.

A further question concerns the day-to-day administration. Will that remain as it is? Few people know how this internal market is going to be implemented. One of those few, the French ambassador, wrote an elucidating article about the internal market. He defined the territory of the internal market as twelve territories united only by a presumption of unity. That is correct, because the presumption of unity is the masterpiece of it. Mutual recognition rests on the basis of laws that are not the same but are presumed to be equivalent.

Therefore the whole administration will be left in the hands of national administrations with differing laws and differing practices. They will be asked to presume that what a neighbor does is equivalent and must be recognized, not stopped at the border.

This brings us to the question of monetary and economic union. I think it is going to come, but it would be foolish to give a timetable. Is it necessary to bring into the lawbook those articles that will be necessary to implement such a scheme when it is mature? Do the events that have occurred in Eastern Europe make this inevitable?

Some people think that we can no longer hope to plan the kind of Europe that embraces many issues outside the pure trade ones. I disagree. All of the East European countries will want to have some form of attachment to the Community. Some say it openly and some say it covertly, but all think the same thing.

To what unit do they want to be attached? Will it be something strong, or something that will slowly disintegrate from the sheer numbers being added to it? As on a bicycle, if you don't move forward, it will fall.

Can one stop the bicycle because others want to join? In the famous Peking Circus some twelve people can mount one bicycle, but only real artists can do that. In the case of Europe, the bicycle would fall.

Therefore we cannot have a bicycle; we need more wheels on our vehicle. It needs to move forward, or it will lose every attraction to the East European countries, as well as the capacity to help them effectively. And a lot of money and expertise will be needed to help these countries.

A wish has been expressed that the United States should work together with Japan to have some say in this Europe. The United States and Japan have already moved in this way. It is exactly what we would like to see happening. A parochial Europe is not what we want. It needs to keep in touch with the global economy, and only by investment can that be done—by joint ventures, by mergers in every kind of acquisition.

A lot of expertise can move from the Western world to the East European countries—expertise that will have to be developed quickly in order to keep people there.

Will it affect our north-south problem to drag investment into East European countries rather than Portugal and Spain? Our programs for investment in these southern countries are going to continue. Anything else will have to be in addition to what has been earmarked for the southern European countries. But of course, private companies cannot be ordered to invest in Portugal.

The East European countries will not necessarily have a very sophisticated demand. They want decent goods, but they don't need marvels of high technology. They need medium technology of the kind we are quite good at—our strong point in the race about technology.

The medium technology of countries like Portugal and Spain will require a much larger market now. Perhaps it would be a good idea to use our investment in these countries to supply more medium-technology goods.

For the high technology, linkups will have to happen and already have happened: the latest statistics are quite elaborate. The Europeans also are linking up. The figures for intra-European linkups have quadrupled over the past five years and doubled over the past two. They are now more or less at par with linkups on a purely national level, which shows that integration is working. Through these linkups we will create the Common Market or internal market. Whatever the name is, it will deserve the name of common.

A Commentary by Michael Skarzinski

My comments will focus on how the U.S. administration approaches the subject of the single market of Europe in the context of technology and innovation. Here are some assumptions.

• All markets are global, and a nation's industry and its individual companies must formulate and implement global strategies.

• Technology is mobile, and it cannot be contained.

• Governments, corporations, and individuals tend to arrange themselves to succeed and prosper in the long term.

• In the aggregate, market growth is generally based on success, merit, and other comparative advantages. Individual transactions and individual projects are not always based on comparative advantages, but countries always pursue their self-interest with varying degrees of nationalism.

There are indeed links among European industrial policy, trade, defense, and even aid like overseas development assistance. Both companies and governments note those connections, where they occur, and base their policy strategies on them.

Claude Fontheim posed the interesting question, What is a U.S. corporation? How does the concept apply to membership in, for example, Sematech or in other U.S. consortiums—the Microelectronics and Computer Corporation in Austin, Texas, which has its first

Canadian member, whose other members are U.S.? European technology consortiums embody various forms of industrial organization, forms of industrial arrangement.

What should be the U.S. response to the EC 1992 as an evolving process? Generally speaking, the Bush administration believes that EC 1992 is a very positive development, one that will contribute to the growth of the world economy and to the growth of technology.

There are some pitfalls that we can sink into, however, and we need to be alert to them. These are the issues that the United States discusses with the commission: various aspects of technology policy as well as reciprocity, national treatment, quantitative restrictions, rules of origin, local content, product standards, and the tie-in to multilateral trade negotiations. It is important to note that over a trillion dollars in trade is not covered by the GATT. Some of these issues, at least, fit into this discussion of high-technology policy: issues like intellectual property protection and government procurement in certain excluded sectors, notably telecommunications, for example.

What, then, should U.S. companies do? Apparently, they are doing much in the way of investment, but in general U.S. companies want to work with European and Japanese firms.

Claude Barfield mentioned Sematech earlier. At this moment Sematech and Jesse are trying to find ways to work together. Sematech does not cover every aspect of the semiconductor industry, only the manufacturing processes. The tools used to make semiconductors need to be added to the process, but gaps remain in the areas of materials, gases, and chemistry. Because of the very capital-intensive nature of technology, European, U.S., and Japanese companies need to work together because no one can do it all.

The single market offers both attractive opportunities and problems for U.S. companies. An individual company's position within the European market really determines whether that company views its experience there as positive or negative. A company that is organized to do business today in Europe or one that has invested recently is perhaps better poised to take advantage of opportunities than others that will follow.

A Commentary by Dominique Bocquet

Onida has convincingly denied the existence of Fortress Europe, but he could have bolstered his argument further. There are other rules that will benefit non-EC companies in the single market besides mutual recognition. One of them is what might be called the transparence principle of the single market.

To take an example, the legislation being adopted on public procurements in Europe will require public authorities to publish a notice, in the Community's official journal, of every significant purchase or order they intend to make. Obviously this will enable companies outside the Community to make tenders. Even if these procedures were to foster a kind of European preference, it would be limited by the GATT code and the transparence principle.

Also note that Heinrich von Moltke and his colleagues overseeing the internal market and industrial affairs of the European Community have been fighting against subsidies to industry, and they have forced national governments to cut their budgets. Indeed, most of the subsidies concentrated on specific sectors have been sharply reduced in Europe.

In addition to these self-imposed constraints, the European Community provides non-EC firms having subsidiaries in Europe with an important guarantee. Under the fifty-eight articles of the Rome treaty, these subsidiaries are considered EC companies, regardless of the owner. Thus IBM-Deutschland or Ford-Belgium are treated like European firms when it comes to providing access to markets.

But this action will have many other consequences, especially for European R & D programs. Many American firms are wondering whether they will be allowed to participate in these programs. If the firms are deemed European their subsidiaries will be fully entitled to apply for these programs, if they qualify for them—that is, if they present a proposal for a project together with a company within the Community.

There are two categories of European R & D programs. The first is made up of the programs managed by the European Commission, such as Race (in advanced telecommunications) and Esprit (in electronics). These programs have precise criteria that companies must meet to receive grants. Several American firms have already been selected to take part in these programs. The second category consists of intergovernmental programs, primarily Eureka. This program works in a different way. There is no limiting criterion but also no automatic settlement. Grants may even be provided by individual member states.

One of the most important Eureka projects is Jessy, in which three large European companies (Phillips, Thomson, and Siemens) have joined to conduct joint research on chips. One of these companies—Siemens—has just signed an agreement with IBM. I don't know whether IBM will receive a grant, but at least the partnership is an open one.

And so Europe will not, I hope, be a fortress. As Onida pointed out, however, the single market is also aimed at strengthening European cohesion, in part in response to the threat from Japan. But there are still many obstacles to cohesion, particularly to mergers within Europe, although I don't think the differences in the tax laws and social laws are among them. The multinationals are able to cope with those differences.

More serious are the merger regulations themselves. Until now, mergers have been implemented on a national rather than continental basis. A few years ago, for example, the French group, Thomson, was stopped from taking over the German firm, Gründig, despite the fact that the combined market shares of the companies throughout Europe were moderate. But the German cartel prevented the merger. Admittedly, there should no longer be any problems of this kind, for the power to control mergers has, since October 1990, been transferred to the European Commission.

Perhaps a more serious obstacle to mergers is that EC members have different conceptions of the relationship between finance and industry. In the Anglo-Saxon model, the stock market plays a large role in assessing the performance of companies and, if need be, in changing their management, by way of takeover bids. In contrast, the systems in Germany and Japan protect companies from takeover bids and place control of the companies entirely in the hands of either banks or management itself.

The point is that the border between these two systems runs right through the middle of the European Community. The question is, which of the two systems will prevail in Europe? I think this is a central concern for international firms.

In *Generation Europe*, Philippe Delleur and I suggest that, by and large, the Anglo-Saxon pattern will prevail. Takeover bids will probably be legalized everywhere in the Community, and this will mean a great deal of change in Germany, Italy, and the Netherlands. At the same time, countries will not want to make takeover bids too easy, for fear of weakening industry. Therefore several will no doubt try to protect some of their companies from takeover bids, but not all of them. This could mean more shareholdings by the banks. In any case, takeovers of firms in another country will remain a rare occurrence, if only for psychological reasons.

Since mergers are likely to be hampered, it is essential for the European companies to find other ways of getting together, especially when economies of scale are necessary. Therefore, fifty-fifty alliances cannot be ruled out, even though many of them have failed in the past for the lack of unified management, among other problems. But lessons have been learned from these failures. The recent Volvo-Renault agreement is a case in point.

First, the move has been gradual—proceeding through swaps of shares rather than an immediate merger, which was the strategy commonly used in the past. Second, the existing teams complement one another to some extent. Volvo is strong in the heavy truck business and in up-market automobiles, whereas Renault produces a wider range of car models. This will certainly make coordination easier.

Cooperation is also essential in R & D—but extremely difficult to achieve in a competitive environment, as the Americans have discovered. Their common research centers ran into many problems when they were created in 1984. To make a cooperative program work is like dealing with a theory of games problem: to improve cooperation between firms, you have to make it clear that the game will increase the joint payoff, and one of the ways of underlining that payoff is to reward cooperation with financial incentives. This is why grants are provided by the European R & D programs.

Beyond the mechanisms required to induce cooperation, of course, is the question of whether the interests of the European countries can converge. In my opinion, these differences in their interests (and in their approaches to free trade) are beginning to fade. Remember, too, that in many fields technologies will have to be developed on a worldwide basis. Therefore European firms will need external alliances. This is yet another argument against Fortress Europe.

To some extent, cooperation has been held up by the rather slow pace of the European decision-making process. It seems Europeans cannot reach an agreement without many drawn-out discussions. As a result, tension rises, which is not so surprising. Put any twelve persons in a meeting room, and if the meeting is long, what happens? Those who are inside start feeling anxious because they realize how hard it is for them to agree. Meanwhile, those outside the room are also feeling anxious because they think something like a plot is brewing inside the room! The construction of EC-92 has not been much different.

PART TWO
Industry

3
Will the Automobile Industry Go the Way of the Steel Industry?

Frank D. Weiss

As EC-92 approaches, trade between Europe and the United States in steel and automobiles merits close attention. Since the early 1970s, these industries have been the object of trade policies widely described as the new protectionism, which takes in all nontariff types of protection. As yet, few can agree on the impact or the cost of the measures undertaken in any industry under this label. The quantitative effects will no doubt become clearer once trade policy in Europe is centralized under the Commission of the European Communities and the EC Council in Brussels. This transfer of power is sure to have an impact on the substance of trade policy, but it is likely to be quite different for the automobile industry, which has not been subjected to central control in the post–World War II era, and the steel industry, which has.

Trade Relations and the New Protectionism

The economic basis of protectionist policy in both the U.S. and EC steel and automobile industries has been much the same: production has been relocated from established centers to other centers that are newcomers on the world markets. This phenomenon can be seen in the changing share of output in steel and automobiles among the supplying countries of the world since 1960 (table 3-1). Clearly, the United States was affected before Europe was, and steel came under relocation pressure before automobiles did. Table 3-1 understates the competitive pressure for relocation because the figures are distorted by the trade policy measures already carried out.

The cause of the relocation itself is also the same in both industries, although its progress may have been hastened by the particular circumstances in individual countries. These industries rank near the top in their use of skilled labor relative to other factors of production and thus are predisposed for rich country locations (see Wolter 1974;

73

TABLE 3-1
SHARE OF WORLD OUTPUT OF STEEL AND AUTOMOBILES, SELECTED REGIONS, 1960–1988
(percent)

Year	Steel				Automobiles			
	European Community[a]	Japan	United States	West Germany	European Community[a]	Japan	United States	West Germany
1960	28.2	6.4	26.4	9.8	35.5	—	47.7	12.5
1970	23.1	15.6	20.4	7.5	35.2	18.2	28.5	13.2
1975	19.4	15.8	16.7	6.2	31.1	21.0	27.3	9.7
1980	17.8	15.5	14.5	6.1	30.2	28.4	20.6	10.4
1981	17.8	14.3	15.7	5.9	28.9	29.8	21.1	10.4
1982	17.2	15.4	10.6	5.5	30.8	29.3	19.1	11.1
1983	16.5	14.7	11.6	5.4	29.9	27.6	22.9	10.3
1984	16.9	14.9	11.8	5.5	27.1	26.9	25.7	9.5
1985	18.8	14.6	11.1	5.6	26.8	27.1	25.7	9.8
1986	17.6	13.8	10.4	5.2	28.0	26.8	24.7	10.0
1987	17.1	13.4	11.0	4.9	29.3	26.4	23.5	10.0
1988	17.7	13.6	11.6	5.3	29.6	26.2	23.0	9.5

— = not available.

a. 1960, 1970: West Germany, Italy, France, United Kingdom. Since 1975, also including Belgium, the Netherlands, and Spain.
SOURCE: Calculated from Wirtschaftsvereinigung Eisen- und Stahlindustrie, *Statistisches Jahrbuch der Eisen- und Stahlindustrie*, various issues.

Dicke 1978). But as the poorer countries in the world catch up with the richer ones in terms of these factors, their share of world output changes. In addition, both industries are subject to significant economies of scale. Once a firm in a new location becomes competitive, older firms in older locations will feel considerable pressure.

When the underlying production technology became tradable internationally, national idiosyncracies increased the pressure for relocation, particularly in the United States (see Crandall 1987). Since both industries are heavily unionized, the wages they offer are significantly higher than they would be under competitive conditions in the labor market. This wage level was validated by an oligopoly in U.S. steel and automobile markets, which shared the scarcity rent it had created with the trade unions. As soon as sufficient outsider competition materialized, rents fell, and the wage level hurt international competitiveness. If this explanation holds, it constitutes additional pressure for relocation as formerly poor countries catch up and as technology becomes more freely tradable.

These adjustment pressures are widely recognized, but they alone do not explain why policy makers yielded to them in such degree, at least in the case of steel. Experience in other industries has varied widely. An interesting example of protection can be found in the footwear industry in a host of rich countries, where it flowered briefly in the early 1970s and then wilted away (Hamilton 1988). In contrast, steel protection in Europe seems to be far from sporadic, and automobile protection seems to be on the verge of unfurling. The effectiveness of the instruments used to carry out the new protectionism has varied greatly, depending on the time, place, and product. Even something as entrenched as protection to clothing and textiles under the auspices of the Multifiber Agreement (MFA) varies within the period of each contract renewal according to world demand, since the restrictions are quantitative. In the early 1980s it was close to zero in Europe (Hamilton 1986, 1988).

The effects of the new protectionism are often downplayed (see, for example, Yoffie 1983; Baldwin 1986), but the reason is easy to see. The instruments of the new protectionism are often bilateral. Hence, they can often be evaded legally through trade in substitutes produced in third countries. In the case of a bilateral voluntary export restraints (VER), one of the countries might set up a tariff factory in a third country. The automobile VER between Japan and the United States is a case in point (Feenstra 1987). The increased imports of European cars that were closer to Japanese cars than were American home-produced cars kept the cost of protection down. The situation in European automobiles is not too different. Four EC countries—

Spain, Italy, France, and the United Kingdom—have imposed VERs on imports from Japan. The quantitative restrictions are quire tight, except in the United Kingdom. But the European Community cannot forbid trade in domestically produced substitutes.

The effects of this mechanism for keeping the cost of protection down are discernible in the data on new car registrations in various EC countries when measured against Japan's and Germany's share of world production of automobiles. Their share changed very little after 1980 (although Japan's continued growing through 1980; table 3-1). VERs against Japanese automobiles came into effect in France and the United Kingdom in the late 1970s, but the restrictions in Spain and Italy were imposed even earlier. The VERs are reflected in the stable, limited market shares of Japan in the restricting countries (table 3-2). In all four EC countries, the expanding market share of Germany (table 3-3) in the 1980s (compared with the 1970s) is immediately apparent. At the same time, the open German market yielded increasing shares to Japan and fewer shares to domestic producers. Of course, the VERs are being accompanied by a great deal of trade diversion. Protection there is, but it is porous protection.

The situation in the steel industry could not be more different. Since 1980 the Community has negotiated a set of EC-wide VERs with the principal steel-supplying countries and has imposed anti-dumping duties against the uncooperative countries or extracted a price undertaking (a promise of a maximum price). In addition, the EC Commission has, until recently, allowed member countries to subsidize their steel industry in a particularly pernicious way—by covering the losses of steel enterprises and imposing limits on their output. Although the output quotas have been lifted, some subsidization is still tolerated. More important, the VERs have in effect isolated the Community's steel price from the world steel price. At times, this has reached tariff equivalents of 17–25 percent (Weiss et al. 1988: 15). Similarly, the trigger price mechanism isolated the U.S. price of steel from world markets far more effectively than the automobile VER with Japan was able to accomplish.

This difference in the degree of protection in the steel and automobile industries in Europe and the United States is usually explained on the basis of the costs and benefits for the interest groups involved (see Baldwin 1986; Weiss et al. 1988). But on these grounds *both* the industries are good candidates for protection. Both are characterized by a high concentration of firms, which obviates the free-rider problem in financing the lobbying for protection; a highly unionized labor force, which eliminates the same problem on the labor side; a large labor force, which means a large number of potential voters; and high regional concentration, which tends to lend the support of intermediate layers of government to the lobbying at the national level. Nonetheless, protection levels differ in the industries in Europe and the United States.

There is a further paradox. Countries with an established system of representation for their large interest groups are unlikely to have much protection anywhere (Olson 1982). The reason is simple: encompassing groups, if they claimed protection for themselves or for some of their members, would be internalizing the costs of protection and therefore would desist from such activity. Yet, the large EC country with the most effective set of encompassing representative institutions in place on both the labor and capital sides is West Germany, where the structure of protection in the two industries is most skewed. Free trade is permitted in automobiles, whereas significant border protection and domestic subsidization exist for steel.

If one relates protection to the political economy rather than to the spot markets that interest groups and governments recontract continuously, it becomes easier to understand the differences across industries. Note that some industries are not even included in the normal periodic bargaining on trade liberalization. They are subject to their own institutions, which have their own rules, often arrived at through international agreements.[1] Steel is one such industry. In Europe, the steel trade was removed from the domain of normal trade policy making quite soon after World War II, through the creation of the European Coal and Steel Community (ECSC). The ECSC was founded for reasons beyond the narrow economic sphere that had to do with the state of international relations in Europe immediately after World War II. Suffice it to say that these motives were stronger than any economic calculation, and, once in place, the new institution played by its own rules.

Policy in Europe's Steel Industry

Steel policy in the European Community soon came to be common policy, although this was not the case in the coal industry, which was also under the auspices of the ECSC.

Evolution of Policy. The first steps toward a common policy may be seen as responses to short-term problems of the business cycle, and they were harmless enough (for full details, see Dicke et al. 1987; Herdmann and Weiss 1985). In 1963 tariff and nontariff protection against imports from third countries was raised in response to a temporary decline in sales. These measures were renewed from year

TABLE 3-2
New Registrations of Japanese Cars in the European Community, 1970–1988
(percent of total new registrations)

Year	West Germany	Belgium	Netherlands	France	Italy[a]	Great Britain	Spain
1970	0.1	5.0	3.2	0.2	0.0	—	—
1971	0.1	7.2	6.8	0.2	0.1	—	—
1972	0.4	10.0	9.5	0.4	0.1	—	—
1973	1.1	12.1	11.4	0.7	0.1	5.6	—
1974	1.3	13.0	11.6	0.8	0.0	6.7	—
1975	1.7	16.6	15.5	1.6	0.1	9.0	—
1976	1.9	18.0	16.8	2.7	0.1	9.4	—
1977	2.4	19.3	19.8	2.6	0.1	10.6	—
1978	3.7	17.8	18.8	1.8	0.1	11.0	—
1979	5.6	17.9	19.1	2.2	—	10.8	—

Year						
1980	10.4	24.5	26.4	2.9	0.1	11.8	—
1981	10.0	24.8	24.4	2.5	0.1	11.0	—
1982	0.8	21.1	22.4	2.9	0.1	11.0	—
1983	10.6	22.5	23.5	2.7	0.1	10.7	1.0
1984	12.0	19.9	22.0	3.0	0.2	11.1	0.7
1985	13.3	19.7	22.3	3.0	0.2	10.8	0.7
1986	15.0	20.7	24.4	2.9	4.7	11.1	0.6
1987	15.1	20.5	25.9	2.9	0.8	9.7	0.7
1988	15.2	20.8	27.7	2.9	1.2	9.3	0.9

— = not available.

NOTE: 1970, 1971 data refer to sales of new cars.

a. 1983–1986 sales.

SOURCE: Calculated from Verband der Automobilindustrie, *Das Auto international in Zahlen*, various issues, and from Verband der Automobilindustrie, *Tatsachen und Zahlen*, various issues.

TABLE 3-3

New Registrations of German Cars in the European Community, 1970–1988
(percentage of total new registrations)

Year	West Germany	Belgium	Netherlands	France	Italy[a]	Great Britain	Spain
1970	77.5	36.5	39.7	10.9	16.1	—	—
1971	74.8	37.4	37.9	11.5	14.5	—	—
1972	73.8	36.3	34.3	11.2	12.5	—	—
1973	74.1	35.2	34.7	11.4	11.6	5.7	—
1974	73.3	31.7	31.6	9.4	10.0	4.6	—
1975	75.1	30.5	32.2	10.4	12.1	6.0	—
1976	78.3	31.4	34.5	12.1	14.9	8.1	—
1977	78.9	33.5	35.6	11.9	14.7	15.2	—
1978	78.1	35.1	37.3	11.1	13.3	14.0	—
1979	76.8	35.5	38.5	11.3	—	13.5	—

1980	73.7	34.2	36.5	12.1	16.0	22.7	—
1981	74.7	35.3	39.1	16.3	18.5	24.1	—
1982	75.9	38.5	41.0	17.6	18.8	27.6	—
1983	75.6	38.3	40.5	19.3	16.4	25.7	7.0
1984	73.3	40.4	41.6	20.6	16.2	23.4	5.5[b]
1985	72.8	40.8	43.2	21.7	18.0	23.8	35.5
1986	70.3	40.4	40.8	20.5	17.1	20.7	38.0
1987	70.8	41.4	40.6	20.0	17.7	17.1	38.3
1988	70.9	42.0	38.8	20.9	18.2	20.4	39.0

— = not available.

NOTE: 1970, 1971 data refer to sales of new cars.

a. 1983–1986 sales.

b. Including cars produced in Spain; 1983 and 1984 imported cars only.

SOURCE: Calculated from Verband der Automobilindustrie, *Das Auto international in Zahlen*, various issues, and from Verband der Automobilindustrie, *Tatsachen und Zahlen*, various issues.

to year, and in 1967 a voluntary export restraint was negotiated with Japan. Throughout this period, the EC Commission promoted the steel industry with financial assistance designed to increase capacity.

National subsidization policies were also beginning to proliferate. By 1980, a crisis was looming on the horizon and the detailed regulation of the steel market began in earnest. As in coal, the commission's role was not so much to distribute money to steel industries in the member countries, but to regulate how the subsidies were to be granted. Production quotas were introduced, and after the early 1980s import quotas—negotiated and imposed—were tightened.

This does not mean that all was harmony among Europe's steel producers. Germany's steel industry is, to an extent at least, a victim of these measures. It is probably the lowest-cost producer in the European Community, as its industry representatives claim, and therefore it benefits from foreign trade protection. But it is prevented from increasing exports to the other EC countries. Indeed, the German government opposed the introduction of production quotas, and publicly demanded an end to them and the subsidies. Furthermore, only one German steel company (Arbed) has received direct financial assistance to cover losses.

If these measures were so detrimental to the German steel industry, why did steel firms acquiesce in them? When the EC Commission announced in 1990 that it was imposing binding production quotas under Article 58 of the ECSC treaty, its purpose was in part to limit subsidies and in part to respond to the breakdown in the voluntary cartel of the steel companies (for details, see Grunert 1987: 237, 276ff.). But the quotas required the unanimous agreement of the European Council. The German government, with the support of the steel companies, alone resisted them and refused to give in unless it received a subsidy code, which was duly granted. Note, however, that the breakdown of the voluntary quota system had been precipitated by a German firm, Klöckner, which felt cheated by its low quota. This went hand in hand with a desire by German firms for enforced quotas after the cartel had broken: "An ironic and grotesque situation was thus created: the West German government, in isolation from other Community members, was leading a campaign against the implementation of Article 58, whilst at the same time German steel companies . . . were demanding—and had provoked—the management of the steel economy by the commission" (Grunert 1987: 277). Yet, this action paid off for the steel companies. To gain the German government's support, the commission granted the German companies far larger quotas than they otherwise would have obtained.

Once individual countries in the European Community started subsidizing individual steel companies by covering their losses, the rules had to be expanded to include the imposition of output quotas, lest the subsidization become completely uncontrollable.[2] And once the production quotas were introduced, they had to be imposed on German companies as well, as these would otherwise move down the average cost curve and eliminate the other EC producers from competition. The negotiations were concerned with the distribution of quotas, rather than the efficiency of the overall allocation. Because intercommunity trade had to remain free, production quotas seemed to be the answer. Since 1986, these have been lifted as capacity has been cut, but a market-sharing agreement with the United States, as well as a host of VERs with Japan and the NICs, is still in place.

The Effects and Costs of Steel Policy. The steel industry in this case can be characterized as a contestable market. This means that because there are no barriers to entry, pure profits cannot emerge, with the result that price equals average cost. If the fixed costs were low enough, contestability would converge to perfect competition; if fixed costs were high enough, one firm would supply the world market. This monopolist could earn no rent because the threat of entry forces it to charge no more than the average cost for its product.

This description of the steel industry may seem farfetched; hit-and-run competition, a requirement of contestability, seems difficult to swallow. But it should be remembered that technology in most steel-making operations has become fairly widespread. In addition, the success of minimills suggests that optimal plant size has tended to fall. Thus, if a firm incurs sunk costs upon entering steel making, the costs are likely to be fairly low. Tests of the structure of the steel industry were undertaken with a simulation model constructed on the basis of cost functions for different steel-processing techniques in various countries throughout the world (Lont and Mathiesen 1983; Mathiesen and Wergeland 1986). The results suggest that the international steel industry is actually perfectly competitive:

> The model was . . . used to simulate production and trade patterns under alternative assumptions regarding market structure—perfect competition, a general Nash-Cournot equilibrium and a Nash-Cournot equilibrium for some producers with the rest as a competitive fringe. The predicted patterns were confronted with actual world production and trade. The conclusion was that, despite apparently high concentration in the industry, the assumption of perfect competition gave the best fit (Haaland and Norman 1987).

83

For the present analysis, only the weaker form of competition, contestability, is required.

The subsidization and production quota system that has become prevalent in Europe has another peculiar feature that must be recognized. The subsidy does not apply to product output or factor input, but to losses. The subsidies are paid by national governments; the EC Commission only legalizes their payment. This makes the subsidy open-ended, so firms will have an incentive to produce as much as possible. To limit the extent of subsidization, the authorities had to introduce a system of production quotas. The quotas are not allocated to firms on the basis of efficiency considerations, but rather as the outcome of a bargaining process in which firms often use historic output to support their case.

This institutional feature of the steel protection system has important consequences for the social cost of intervention, as illustrated in figure 3-1. Average cost curves are shown for two firms: the efficient firm, AC_1, which incurs minimum average cost at the world market price P_w, and the inefficient firm, AC_2, which incurs minimum average cost even above the domestic price $P_w(1 + t)$. For simplicity, each is assigned an identical production quota, q^*. Firm 2 requires the subsidy $q^* [AC_2^* - P_w (1 + t)]$ to maintain operations. Firm 1 is earning a private profit of $q^* [P_w (1 + t) - AC_1^*]$. The social cost of such an institution is very large by the standards of an equivalent per unit output production subsidy of the most efficient firm: all of firm 2's output could be purchased at the world market price P_w; the extra social cost of production is $q^* (AC_2^* - P_w)$, which can be decomposed into the absolute subsidy amount plus the firm's output times the difference between domestic and world prices. In addition, this institution is forcing firm 1 to impose a loss on society, namely, the extra cost incurred by operating above the minimum average cost $[q^* (AC_1^* - P_w)]$, plus the extra output and cost reduction forgone (surface abc). Lost consumer surplus attributable to the nontariff barriers (NTBs) in steel should be added as a small footnote to this social loss.

The German steel industry is generally thought to be efficient at domestic prices, and perhaps at world prices (World Bank 1987), but one German company is not. It is the only one to have received the type of cost transfers analyzed here. It produced 10.3 million tons of rolled steel during the period 1981–1985. The firm received DM 3.4 billion in subsidies, or about DM 330 per ton (Herdmann and Weiss 1985). Had the company ceased production and had its quotas been transferred to other German firms, so that they could expand output and move down the average cost curve, it would have saved a total of

FIGURE 3–1
SOCIAL COST UNDER A PRODUCTION QUOTA AND SUBSIDY SCHEME

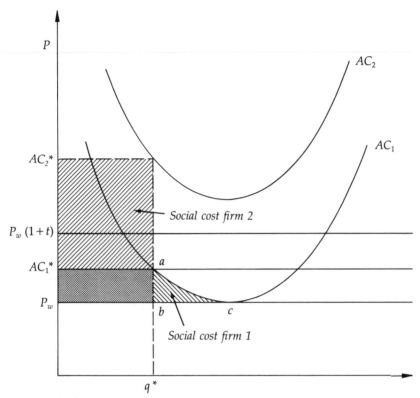

SOURCE: Author.

DM 5.7 billion. This would have been sufficient to bribe the company's workers not to work to the tune of DM 250,000 each, instead of the DM 45,000 that the laid-off workers actually received. The situation in the other European countries is more pronounced still. The six firms that received most of the subsidies produced 55 million tons of steel in 1981 and received DM 46 billion in the five-year period up to 1985. Had they ceased production, other companies could have produced the steel at a total cost of DM 50 billion less. This adds up to a social loss of DM 105 billion for the five-year period and ignores consumer surplus, which is dwarfed by these figures in any case.

Does it then pay (socially) for the government of the low-cost producer to subsidize its steel industry? The idea behind strategic trade policy is simple: an output subsidy enables a domestic firm to capture a larger share of the world market and hence profits (see, in particular Brander and Spencer 1983). Alternatively, the output subsidy enables the recipient firm to move down its average cost curve and reduce social cost at home. The proliferation of steel subsidies in Europe in the late 1970s can indeed be viewed as a subsidy competition among European states acting as agents of the steel producers. In consequence, third-country producers, primarily in the United States, were threatened with the loss of market, that is, with being pushed up the average cost curve. Two characteristics of the steel industry, even if there were no free entry, obviate the results, although not the logic of strategic trade policy. First, some of the firms were high-cost producers at any level of output. Supporting such firms by public policy implies not that a rent is preserved for the home country, but that real extra production costs are imposed at home. Second, even if there hadn't been any high-cost producers, overcapacity in the steel industry would have meant that everyone's unit costs were too high.

In a contestable market without quotas, it does not matter who produces. The only rationale for a subsidy is a political one—keep your own producers afloat until the other, higher-cost producers have cut capacity or gone out of business; or at least use the threat potential to keep domestic prices below what they otherwise might be. It always pays the low-cost producer's government to fight for a higher quota, and, if minimum average cost is truly at or below world market prices, to press for liberalization. This has in fact been the strategy of the German government, in accordance with the producer's interest organization. The quota system was dismantled after July 1988, but the issue of subsidies has by no means been cleared up (*Economist* 1988: 58). If this episode is repeated either in steel or in other industries, high costs will be incurred through "inefficient entry," namely, insufficient exit (see Horstmann and Markusen 1986). This example also illustrates that strategic trade policy results are extremely sensitive to entry and exit conditions, which firms must therefore take into account in choosing their strategies. It is not enough to observe a concentrated industry and infer therefrom that government intervention would lead to gains from trade.

Policy in the Automobile Industry

Because France, Spain, Italy, and the United Kingdom have VERs with Japan (the German one was either redundant, inoperative, or nonexistent), the automobile market is often said to be highly fragmented and highly protected.[3] This is somewhat of an exaggeration, although automobile models are admittedly not perfect substitutes for each other and some protection is afforded by the VERs. By the late 1970s almost all European car producers were clamoring for relief from Japanese imports. The EC Commission was ready to take on the role of negotiating a Community VER with Japan in order to expand its field of activities. But the commission wanted complete negotiating authority for every VER. The West German government was opposed to the transfer of power to the commission. At the same time, the economics minister, Otto Count Lambsdorff, was under pressure from some German automobile producers. In what must go into the annals of international trade diplomacy as a masterful application of the principles of political economy, he flew to Japan after secret negotiations had taken place—illegally kept secret from the EC Commission—and arranged a redundant VER with that country (Langdon 1981: 95; see also Bronckers 1983 and De Melo and Messerlin 1988). He thereby killed three birds with one stone: he prevented the commission from trespassing on his territory (Community-wide quotas were apparently no longer needed); he got the domestic industry off his back by making it look like something had been done; and he preserved free trade in Germany and more or less free trade in the Community.

There is some evidence that Lambsdorff knew what he was doing and that he was against import controls for Germany. The outcome could have been predicted to some extent from the domestic political economy and international circumstances. Lambsdorff's position and party (the FDP), combined with the industrial characteristics of the automobile industry, made the industry politically uninteresting to him. In addition, no important election was coming up. Perhaps most important, he could prevent the emergence of an institution with the right to make policy. This was, after all, the same minister who had been responsible for the German position on the steel industry in 1981–1982. Note, too, that the sometimes mentioned trade diversion (from the United States) failed to trigger increased protection in Germany. At the time, the United States had a functioning VER with Japan.

Lessons for Automobiles Taught by Steel Policy

Not everything about the commission's steel policy should be viewed negatively. What by the late 1970s was turning into a subsidization war among European countries and between European countries and the United States was defused politically. Quite apart from securing the market-sharing agreement with the United States, the commis-

TABLE 3-4

CAPACITY OF THE STEEL INDUSTRY IN EUROPE, 1970–1987

(thousands of tons)

Year	West Germany	France	United Kingdom	Italy	Belgium
1970	53,100	25,130	—	21,240	14,830
1975	62,859	33,632	27,080	32,780	19,024
1980	66,900	32,500	28,000	39,400	19,700
1985	48,899	28,464	23,721	36,200	14,614
1986	47,184	28,191	22,591	35,388	13,556
1987	47,121	27,073	22,870	36,547	13,561

— = not available.
SOURCE: Wirtschaftsvereinigung Eisen- und Stahlindustrie, *Statistisches Jahrbuch der Eisen- und Stahlindustrie* (1989).

sion realized that the proximate cause of the problem was one of excess capacity. The root cause was, of course, a shift in comparative advantage, but in an industry with high fixed coats this manifests itself as excess capacity (see Oberender and Rüter 1988). The commission merely legalized national subsidies but predicated them on capacity reduction. In this, it achieved a modicum of success (table 3-4). Together with buoyant demand, profitability has been temporarily restored. Subsidies of the pernicious kind have stopped, except in Italy, and output quotas have been done away with. What remains is a set of border measures against steel-producing countries. Because capacity cuts have gone no further, no further pressure for liberalization is likely to come from within Europe. It would have to come from third countries, either bilaterally or within a multilateral liberalization framework.

The automobile situation, however, is disquieting. The subsidization of automobiles is also becoming an issue in the European Community. So far, only one firm has been implicated—Renault. Bear in mind that the widely spread regional or R & D aids to industry are not the issue, because these extend across industries. Rather, it is the same practice of covering losses, which, as in the steel industry, forces all other producers to move up the average cost curve by maintaining uneconomic capacity.

More worrying is the expected reinstitutionalization of automobile policy. Apparently a German economics minister no longer has the freedom of movement he had when the domestic lobby was divided over the role of Japanese imports and he can no longer be a maverick. Moreover, his powers will become even more limited when discretionary potential is centered in Brussels. The EC Commission has presented its proposals for regulating the automobile market once it obtains the authority to do so in 1993.

The proposals have evolved over time, with Germany and the United Kingdom pushing for a liberal stance and Italy and France pushing for more restrictions. The commission foresees (as of November 1990) limiting the market share of Japanese producers, including transplants, to 20 percent of the EC automobile market. This limitation would expire five years after coming into effect in 1993. In keeping with the spirit of the 1992 program, rules concerning local content would be dropped. Over time, the commission's proposals have become increasingly liberal, both with respect to the market share allowed Japanese producers and with respect to the length of time that must elapse before complete liberalization is allowed. The latest version of the commission's proposal does not even foresee a Community-wide quota. Each restricting country is to liberalize within five years (*Frankfurter Allgemeine Zeitung*, December 11, 1990). Clearly, such a policy would constitute an unequivocal move toward liberalization; no new protective institution would be created, and the trade diversion mechanism described at the outset of this discussion would remain in operation.

If the only pressure for liberalization emanated from two of the big four in the European Community, the commission might not be moving quite so far in this direction. (The United Kingdom and Germany have taken this stance, by the way, because a great many Japanese transplants are produced in the United Kingdom on one hand, and the phenomenon of trade diversion is well understood in the German auto industry, on the other.) The other pressure for liberalization emanates from the United States and the ongoing Uruguay Round trade negotiations. There is so much pressure on the European Community for agriculture that it is loath to have to defend another sector internationally, and a restrictive market-sharing agreement would certainly be strongly opposed by the United States, which has now become home to substantial Japanese transplant operations.

Now that the EC Commission is leaning toward a more liberal market-sharing deal, the protectionist danger is no longer the quantitative costs of any particular restriction, but rather the setting of a new precedent. Once institutionalized, these rules would in effect take another industry off the international trade liberalization agenda. It would be like a Multifiber Agreement for automobiles, being at times more restrictive and at others less so, but not likely to be abolished.

Something else that hinders complete liberalization in automobiles and steel is the weakness of the opponent. Quite apart from a bilateral squabble in steel, both the United States and the European Community harbor interest groups that have the same opponent, namely producers in Japan. That country has relatively little power in commercial diplomacy because it has little threat potential: its imports of politically sensitive manufactures are too small to make a protectionist threat cut much ice in the other large trading nations, and it saves the little clout it has for its protectionist sinner—agriculture.

For all the adjustment problems and acrimony that international trade in steel and automobiles has spawned in the past twenty years, things are likely to be much quieter if the Uruguay Round is a success. Too many issues of overriding importance to the economy (and lately to foreign policy) are at stake for too many countries to let new restrictive rules become established for the two industries. Nor should it be forgotten that much adjustment has already been accomplished, albeit slowly. Nevertheless, were it not for the Uruguay Round, skepticism about liberal trade outcomes would be warranted. If the round fails, it will be warranted.

References

Baldwin, Robert E. 1986. "The New Protectionism: A Response to Shifts in National Economic Power." NBER Working Paper 1823. Cambridge.

Brander, James, and Barbara J. Spencer. 1983. "International R & D Rivalry and Industrial Strategy." *Review of Economic Studies* 50: 707–22.

Bronckers, Marco. 1983. "A Legal Analysis of Protectionist Measures Affecting Japanese Imports into the European Community." In *Protectionism and the European Community*, edited by J. H. J. Bourgeois et al. Antwerp.

Crandall, Robert W. 1987. *The Effects of U.S. Trade Protection for Autos and Steel*. Brookings Papers on Economic Activity 1. Washington, D.C.

De Melo, Jaime A., and Petrick A. Messerlin. 1988. "Price, Quality and Welfare Effects of European VER's on Japanese Autos." *European Economic Review*, 1527–46.

Dicke, Hugo. 1978. *Strukturwandel im wes deutschen Strassenfahrzeugbau*. Kieler Studien 152. Tübingen.

Dicke, Hugo, et al. 1987. *Die EG-Politik auf dem Prüfstand*. Kieler Studien 209. Tübingen.

Economist. 1988. "Unshackled," July 2, p. 58.

Feenstra, Robert C. 1987. "Automobiles Prices and Protection: The U.S.-Japan Trade Restraint." In *The New Protectionist Threat to World*

Welfare, edited by Dominick Salvatore. Amsterdam.

Frankfurter Allgemeine Zeitung. 1990. "Bei japanischen Autos bleibt Brüssel hart," December 11.

Grunert, Thomas. 1987. "Decision-Making Processes in the Steel Crisis Policy of the EEC: Neo-corporatist or Integrationist Tendencies?" In *The Politics of Steel: Western Europe and the Steel Industry in the Crisis Years (1979–1984)*, edited by Ives Mény and Vincent Wright.

Haaland, Jan I., and Victor N. Norman. 1987. "Introduction: Modelling Trade and Trade Policy." *Scandinavian Journal of Economics* 893: 217–26.

Hamilton, Carl B. 1986. "An Assessment of Voluntary Restraints on Hong Kong Exports to Europe and the U.S.A." *Economica* 53.

———. 1988. "The Transient Nature of the 'New' Protectionism: The Case of International Trade in Footwear." Paper presented at the International Seminar in International Trade, Oxford.

Herdmann, Ute, and Frank D. Weiss. 1985. "Wirkungen von Subventionen und Quoten—Das Beispiel der EG-Stahlindustrie." *Die Weltwirtschaft* 1.

Horstmann, Ignatus, and James R. Markusen. 1986. "Up the Average Cost Curve; Inefficient Entry and the New Protectionism." *Journal of International Economics* 20: 225–47.

Langdon, Frank. 1981. "Japan versus the European Community: The Automobile Crisis." *Journal of European Integration* 5 (1).

Lont, Anke, and Lars Mathiesen. 1983. *Modelling Market Equilibrium: An Application to the World Steel Market*. Bergen: Center for Applied Research.

Mathiesen, Lars, and Tor Wergeland. 1986. *Analyse ar verdens stalmarked*. Bergen: Center for Applied Research.

Oberender, Peter, and Georg Rüter. 1988. "The Steel Industry: A Crisis of Adaptation." In *The Structure of European Industry*, edited by H. W. de Jong. Dordrecht.

Olson, Mancur. 1982. *The Rise and Decline of Nations*. New Haven, Conn.

Swann, Dennis. 1984. *The Economics of the Common Market*. Harmondsworth.

Tarr, David G. 1988. "The Steel Crisis in the United States and the European Community: Causes and Adjustments." In *Issues in U.S.–EC Trade Relations*, edited by Robert E. Baldwin, Carl B. Hamilton, and André Sapir. Chicago.

Ven, Hans van der, and Thomas Grunert. 1987. "The Politics of Transatlantic Steel Trade." In *The Politics of Steel: Western Europe and the Steel Industry in the Crisis Years (1974–1984)*, edited by Ives Mény and Vincent Wright. Berlin.

Weiss, Frank D. et al. 1988. *Trade Policy in West Germany*. Kieler Studien 217. Tübingen.

Winham, Gilbert R. 1986. *International Trade and the Tokyo Round Negotiation*. Princeton.

Wolter, Frank. 1974. *Strukturelle Anpassungsprobleme der westdeutschen Stahlindustrie*. Kieler Studien 127. Tübingen.

Woolcock, Stephan. 1981. "Iron and Steel." In *International Politics of Surplus Capacity*, edited by Susan Strange and Roger Tooze. London.

World Bank. 1987. *World Development Report 1987*. New York: Oxford University Press.

Yoffie, David B. 1983. *Power and Protectionism*. New York.

———. 1984. "The Structure of Modern Protectionism: Past Patterns and Future Prospects." Harvard Business School Working Paper. Cambridge, Mass.

4
Commentaries on Automobiles and Steel

A Commentary by G. Mustafa Mohataren

I certainly share the view that the European Community's original plan to include all Japanese vehicles, whether imported or produced in Europe, in a sales restraint within the European Community would have been an unprecedented expansion of the scope of protection. No other developed country has done that.

Nevertheless, I do not believe that means the auto industry is headed along the same troubled path as taken by the steel industry. Indeed, I believe that the EC auto market following 1992 will be much more competitive than it is today.

Let me cite just three of the reasons why I think the EC market is going to be much more competitive. First, even as the European Community talks about putting a quota on the Japanese share they talk also about an increase in the quota, for which they have suggested a target ranging from 16 percent to 20 percent by the end of the decade. That may not seem like much, but in a 15 million car market it is a very large number of sales of Japanese vehicles. It is sufficient to allow not only the total output of plants the Japanese are building and of what they currently import to Europe, but also some room for imports to the United States.

Second, even without any relaxation of external restraints, the European Community plans to monitor state aid to the domestic EC auto industry, and this will lead to substantially increased competition among EC-based producers. The availability of such aid to Renault or the Rover group is probably the biggest remaining internal barrier to trade within the European Community. The knowledge that a company with which you are competing has access to state aid makes you much less aggressive than your competition, because you know you will not be allowed to win. If that state aid is monitored, companies will start to compete much more vigorously.

Furthermore, the companies eligible for state aid know they do not have to compete; they do not have to restructure and rationalize, and therefore they continue to operate at a much higher level than they otherwise would. More vigorous policing of such aid therefore should lead to rationalization of the EC auto industry, which in turn should eliminate the reason for providing the protection currently being demanded—that is, it should help the industry avoid the adjustment.

But the most important reason why the market will be competitive is that the underlying economics of the auto industry are very different from the underlying economics of the steel industry. In the case of steel, comparative advantage has shifted from Europe and the United States to Japan and the emerging countries of Latin America and Asia. That is not the case with autos.

A remarkable set of studies shows that auto production remains economically viable in Europe as well as in the United States. The study done by the MIT Motor Vehicles Program, perhaps the most quoted study on this subject, concludes that the competitive advantage in the auto industry is firm-specific, not country-specific. In other words, the Japanese firms have now demonstrated that they can produce at virtually the same cost in the United States and Europe as in Japan.

Unfortunately, the study also shows that on average the European auto industry is much less efficient than the U.S. and certainly the Japanese industries. This finding explains in part why there is pressure to include production in Europe within general sales restraint. But the fact that competitive advantage is firm-specific rather than country-specific also means that most forms of protection will not work. As long as some firms can produce at a much lower cost than others, a way will be found to sell a product.

Consider this case, for example: if the European Community imposes a sales restraint on the Japanese and the Japanese agree to it—sales restraints are always profitable for the country or group of companies that they are imposed upon—such a scheme would slow sales of Japanese name plates in Europe. But it won't affect the so-called joint venture relationship, such as Honda and the Rover group, to name one. Rover will find it profitable to expand its output of cars designed and produced according to Honda's methods, at much lower cost than that paid by other European producers. A removal of internal barriers by the European Community would make joint-venture arrangements much more attractive for other European firms as well. To the extent that one or another European company decides not to cooperate with the Japanese—as the French and the Italians have decided, historically—others can benefit tremendously by forming joint ventures with the Japanese. All our studies suggest that costs can easily be cut by about 20 percent in Europe, by using

Japanese production methods. A restraint on Japanese imports or Japanese production that artificially raises prices in Europe would make it very profitable for other companies to step in. That has happened in the United States to some extent, and I think it will happen in Europe also.

An added bonus is the role of countries such as the United Kingdom, which sees the Japanese investment in the U.K. auto industry as the most cost-effective way to rejuvenate more or less nonexistent domestic industry. Surely the United Kingdom will not tolerate efforts to restrict output from those plants. The United States has already declared its intention of challenging the European Community and the GATT if it decides to restrict exports from the United States.

The bottom line is that the European Community appears to be on the verge of substantially expanding the scope of protection. But it is premature to conclude that such a move would necessarily put the auto industry on the path toward increasing protection. As long as the average European auto plant requires twice as much labor as that required by the most efficient auto plant, there will be a profitable opportunity. I believe the worldwide auto industry is sufficiently competitive not to let that opportunity pass.

A Commentary by Paul C. Rosenthal

Because so much of U.S. steel policy is a reaction to EC policy and because the influence of Japan differs in steel and autos, it is important to look at U.S., EC, and Japanese relations in these industries in the 1980s before speculating about the 1990s.

Steel. In the late 1970s and early 1980s, Japan's steel industry was viewed as a threat to both the U.S. and EC industries. Japan arguably was the world's lowest-cost producer. The United States introduced a trigger price mechanism to deal with Japanese imports. The European Community, Frank Weiss explained, expanded its subsidies to the steel industry, restricted imports, and imposed production quotas. In addition, it approved minimum price levels. The concern of U.S. producers was not just subsidized imports from the European Community but the diversion of third-country exports from the closed EC market to the United States. Although they may have felt less competitive than the Japanese, they knew they could stay in the game

95

with Europe as long as the EC producers were unsubsidized. Although the United States took many actions concerning steel in the first half of the 1980s, one is particularly noteworthy. After many unfair trade cases and ultimately an escape clause were filed, the United States signed voluntary restraint agreements with the European Community and with Japan and other countries. Thus U.S. policy on steel in the remainder of the 1980s was a reaction not only to low Japanese costs but also to EC policy.

Interestingly, U.S. producers increased their productivity during these years and became the lowest-cost producers overall in the U.S. market—again, assuming no subsidies. A new threat to the Japanese and EC market share in the United States then arose—from newly industrialized countries such as South Korea. Indeed, the voluntary restraint agreements (VRAs) of 1989 were concerned with other countries as much as with Japan and the European Community.

No longer low-cost producers, the Japanese have had to struggle to stay in the U.S. market. The newly industrialized countries, many of which are heavily subsidized, are now a major threat to Japan's market share in the United States.

The Bush administration has pledged to end the steel VRAs in 1992. As part of this effort, it obtained an agreement—Steel Consensus Agreement—from the signatory countries to eliminate most steel subsidies. Whether these countries will adhere to the agreement remains to be seen. The European Community has signed the agreement, but will it stop subsidizing? Also, the relationship of the Steel Consensus Agreement to the negotiations being conducted in the Uruguay Round of the GATT talks also remains to be seen.

Automobiles. Another important point to note about the steel and auto industries is the marked difference in their investment strategies. In the steel industry, on one hand, Japanese companies have entered joint ventures in the United States, but U.S. companies do not have subsidiaries in Europe. In the automobile industry, on the other hand, Japan has plants in United States, and U.S. companies have plants in Europe. The U.S. VRAs that have been in place since 1981 have given the auto industry breathing room for further investment, which has clearly helped the big three auto companies improve their productivity. Even so, Japan remains a threat to automakers in the United States, not to mention the European Community.

A central question for U.S. and EC automobile policy will be how to treat Japanese subsidiaries, the so-called transplants, that have been particularly active in the United States. Japan has fewer transplants in EC countries in part because of their domestic content rules, or the threat of such rules.

U.S. and EC auto producers continue to see Japan as their opponent, as Weiss points out, but that is not necessarily true of the U.S. administration. In recent weeks, U.S. Trade Representative Carla Hills stated that she would use all tools in the U.S. arsenal to fight EC restrictions on imports from Japanese transplant operations in the United States. But the U.S. auto companies with EC production facilities may favor EC restrictions on such products, as well as on those produced in Japan.

Even U.S. auto companies without EC subsidiaries might favor such restrictions since cars produced by the Japanese transplants (at least to date) have far less U.S. content than those produced by the big three. According to a General Accounting Office (GAO) report issued in the summer of 1990, the big three had 88 percent domestic components in 1988, whereas the Japanese affiliate automakers in the United States had only about 38 percent. The GAO also found that Japanese auto transplants were responsible for 25,000 net job losses in the United States in 1988.

If the GAO report is accurate, why would U.S. trade policy fight EC restrictions on transplant exports to the EC countries? A better approach would be to have some minimal U.S. content—perhaps 50 percent content requirement, as is the case in the free-trade agreement between the United States and Canada—before a Japanese transplant-produced car could be considered American for EC trade policy purposes.

Other Observations. The 1990s could see several changes for steel, both in the United States and the EC countries. With depressed economies, less demand, and fewer sales to auto companies, the unfair trade conditions could make it necessary to continue the VRAs in the United States and the subsidies to EC steel. It is also possible—but not likely—that the Uruguay Round of negotiations might lead to a special agreement for the elimination of steel subsidies, one that would expand upon the Steel Consensus already in place. The downsizing and restructuring of the EC automobile companies that are likely to occur in the 1990s will no doubt produce some clamoring for government subsidies, as occurred in steel. Another important policy question is whether those subsidies for restructuring and downsizing should be permitted.

A Commentary by Heinrich von Moltke

The main argument in Frank Weiss's chapter is that the transfer of power from member states to the EC Commission can be expected to have an impact on the substance of trade policy. This argument is illustrated by a comparison between the steel industry and the automobile industry, the argument being that the steel industry has always been subjected to central control in the post–World War II era as the automobile industry has not. I disagree with this argument.

Contrary to what many people believe, no common trade policy exists in the field of steel. Legally, the coal and steel treaty is a free trade area, not a common market. This fact is made clear by Article 71, which states expressly that the responsibility of member states is not affected by the coal and steel treaty. Nevertheless, member states introduced identical tariffs on January 1, 1964. Why? They did so in order to simulate the effects of an inclusion of the steel industry into the common external tariff, which was created on the basis of the EC treaty.

Moreover, on January 1, 1964, the level of customs tariffs, which in many countries was approximately 5 percent, was increased to 9 percent—at that time, the rate foreseen by the Italian tariff. But this increase was not the result of the transfer of the decision-making power to the Community level. The decision making was not transferred. It was a common decision, reached by consensus. The main reason for it was that there was no legal equivalent in the coal and steel treaty to Article 113 of the EC treaty, which allows for majority decisions to be taken in the field of trade policy. So every decision that was taken over and beyond the rather meager powers conferred by the coal and steel treaty had to be taken unanimously.

But it cannot be denied that the prevailing bad times for the steel markets may have played a certain role. The main reason for the increase of customs tariffs in certain member countries was the impossibility of reaching an agreement on any other basis. What we witnessed in those days was another application of the rule that the convoy cannot be faster than the slowest sailing ship.

During the 1960s and well into the 1970s, this was the only element of a protectionist trade policy, if one can call it that. The fact that six member countries introduced quantitative restrictions with respect to East European countries can hardly be seen as another case in point. This was done not only with respect to steel products; on the contrary, wide product ranges were covered by such quantitative restrictions, believed necessary in order to compensate for the total lack of market prices in all state economies. No other quantitative restrictions were in place during that period, while in the United States the first voluntary restraint agreements (VRAs) were being negotiated under the leadership of Mr. Solomon, among others, with the European Community. It was the higher authority at that time.

This policy was followed by one relying on the trigger price mechanism, and subsequently on the well-known VRAs, so that the price level in the United States remained mostly above the price level prevailing in the Community—sometimes by as much as 15 to 20 percent.

It cannot be denied that the Community turned protectionist after 1974–1975; from one year to the next, demand fell by 20 percent, or 30 million tons. With prices going down by 150 to 200 marks a ton, many companies became unprofitable. Frank Weiss describes what happened then. The Community tried to cope with this problem through a voluntary system of market management. But ultimately, in 1977–1978, it had to make use of the highly interventionist instruments foreseen by the coal and steel treaty in the event of a manifest crisis. Most of what Frank Weiss says about this policy can be subscribed to, even though the decision on production quotas could be taken by majority voting and in fact was taken on that basis. The commission tried to buy off these member countries, which did not to the same extent follow other member countries in their subsidization. But the reason for this attempt was not to keep subsidies under control. The control on subsidies was achieved only by the code on subsidies.

What led to the production quotas was the danger that the markets of member countries with fewer subsidies would be swamped by cheap and subsidized products from other member countries, and that the reaction to such a threat would be the recourse to border closure measures under Article 37 of the Coal and Steel Community. In this sense, the highly questionable policy pursued by the Community during that period was mainly an attempt to maintain the unit of the common coal and steel market.

Unquestionably, Frank Weiss is correct in his description of the highly damaging effect of the subsidization policy followed by most European countries during that period. Economically, this policy was certainly an error. What is questionable is whether any alternative to this policy existed in the political reality of those days. The countries that paid the highest subsidies had nationalized their steel industries and were therefore taking political responsibility for their well-being, exposing them to social and political pressures. It would be incorrect to assume that the Community merely legalized those subsidies when the subsidy code was introduced in 1981. The commission was given authority to grant exceptions to its subsidy rules, and it has used these powers to make any exception conditional on corresponding capacity reductions. Through this policy the committee was able to reduce the overcapacity of our steel industry by almost 35 million tons.

This is the only argument that can be advanced to justify our subsidy policy, but it is an important one. Furthermore, the Community was not the only region in the world protecting its steel industry. Japan at that time was an impenetrable market, as it still is to some extent. The United States, through its trade policy measures, contributed to higher consumer prices, and calculations have shown that the amount the American consumer had to pay was more or less equivalent to the amount the European taxpayer paid in the form of subsidies. Neither production quotas nor subsidies exist any longer. The last exception to the prohibition of subsidies was granted to an Italian firm, and only under the condition of large capacity reductions.

The introduction by the Community of VRAs with its main steel supplies is nothing to be proud of, considering their effect on trade. Until 1974, the import penetration was approximately 7 percent in the European Community. By 1976 or 1977, it had reached approximately 10 percent. The VRAs negotiated in 1978 maintained that import penetration at the level of 10 percent—there has been no cutback. In the meantime, the VRAs have been drastically liberalized. Most of our suppliers will no longer be under any quantitative restrictions. For those countries (mainly East European) that continue to remain under such restrictions, the quantities will be increased by 15 percent, and several product categories will no longer be covered by such agreements. The Community policy aim is to lift these restrictions completely, very soon. Soon, therefore, the policy that the commission negotiated on behalf of its member states will no longer be called protection.

The Automobile Industry. Contrary to what one might assume, the automobile industry is already subject to the Community's decision-making power under Article 113 of the EC treaty. There is thus no need for transfer of power. It must be said, however, that our foreign trade policy in this field is still incomplete because import quotas are in place for Japanese cars in three member countries—quotas about which GATT has been notified, and which are legal under GATT.

These import restrictions were taken in the late 1960s in the case of Spain and Portugal, and in 1962 in the case of Italy. In the late 1970s and early 1980s, two other member states, France and the

United Kingdom, introduced import restrictions in the form of gray zone agreements with Japan, under the pressure of the recessions that threatened the existence of their car industries. The Community's trade policy today is split between those countries that apply the community trade policy—that is, a policy without any trade restrictions—and the five member states that continue to practice national quantitative restrictions with respect to Japanese car imports.

The reason why the community is now compelled to act against these national policies is the decision to complete the internal market by 1992. Import restrictions are having their effect not only with respect to direct imports from Japan; they also effectively fragment the internal market because of the continued existence of internal border controls that in the case of legal quantitative restrictions are authorized by the commission under Article 115 of the treaty. Article 115 allows the commission to protect national continuing trade policy measures against parallel imports, if it can be shown that economic necessity would justify such a move.

The question has been raised, What is now happening with Article 115? The commission is now gradually reducing the protection in the three above-mentioned national markets by gradually increasing the authorized parallel imports from other member countries. Therefore the market share of Japanese cars, including cross-country cars, is now close to 3 percent in Italy—no longer 0.7 percent as is often stated. The intention is to completely terminate any authorization under Article 115 by the end of 1992 and to negotiate a similar result for France and the United Kingdom. Why have we to negotiate a similar result? Simply because Article 115 is possible only with respect to two legal quotas, while the United Kingdom and France have gray zone agreements. So we cannot hinder them from applying these agreements other than by negotiating them away. We might attack them under the law, but it is not politically wise to do that.

These negotiations are not easy, since member states still practicing import restrictions have a blocking minority in the Council of Ministers for the harmonization measures needed to complete internal markets. We still have three directives to complete in order to get the European car as a technical model, thus introducing the European approval system, an essential element of the internal market. We need the necessary number of votes, and those with restrictions can block them.

These countries argue that their industries need a transitional period beyond 1992, during which they can take measures in order to reestablish their competitiveness. The commission, the Japanese government, and perhaps even the American automobile industry have recognized the need for such a transitional period. It has been said in the United States that the European industry is not fully competitive now. But the commission has always made it clear that this period cannot be open-ended and that after the preestablished date for its expiration, trade with the Community, including the five countries still protected, must be totally free. The commission has also made clear that during the transitional period Japanese imports to the nonprotected markets—which constitute the majority within the Community—should not be restricted at all. It has made clear that Japanese brands of cars manufactured outside Japan will not come under any kind of transitional arrangements.

The commission has thus put the automobile industry on the liberalization agenda. Even the transitional period would be a period of liberalization, since the Japanese market share of imported cars within the Community would continue to grow. This is a clear proof that the completion of the Community's trade policy in the automobile sector has a liberalizing effect.

In conclusion, I object to the proposal that the commission become a promoter of a regulated automobile market, which would be another international precedent for market sharing. Neither should it contemplate any sector agreement in GATT. The intra-Community competition has reduced the cost of the protected measures for the consumers to the extent that there is not much pressure from the consumers' side; but the pressure for liberalization comes from the commission and from the logic of the internal market, to which all member countries have subscribed. This is a strong political argument, and I predict that it will prevail, with or without pressure from third countries.

In fact, third countries are not in a strong position, as they have followed policies similar to the one now on its way out in the five member countries discussed. The Japanese market was effectively closed until only a few years ago, and its wish to protect its infant automobile industry was the cause of the introduction of some quotas in the early 1960s. In the case of the United States it is less clear. There were VRAs, and they continue to be practiced, although they are no longer required by agreement. The Community is not the only source of precedents, and the policy of the United States is not just a reaction to the Common Market.

The Subsidy Issue. In the early 1980s, many companies had to be bailed out. In America, it was Chrysler; in our Community, it was many others. Now we have a stiffening attitude at the commission.

In 1989 we introduced a new subsidy regime aimed at effectively limiting all types of aid, including regional aid.

In conclusion, the policy followed by the commission is similar to the one followed in the steel sector, but it will lead much more rapidly to completely freed markets. There is no danger from the transfer of power. When the five still lagging countries come to be included into our common trade policy, the ultimate result will be full liberalization.

A Commentary by Masaru Yoshitomi

My own comments for this study discuss the antidumping regulations on various high-tech products as well as automobiles. I agree with Mr. Weiss's analysis of the commission's proposal to put the brunt of the restraints on imported cars, in addition to Japanese cars produced in Europe. Even though Mr. von Moltke defended the commission's proposal by saying that the market share of Japanese cars would be increased from 11 percent to 16–20 percent, we do not know the basis on which such a calculation is made. The basic assumption is that no European car should be crowded out by any increase in Japanese cars produced by Japanese companies, regardless of the location. If that is the case, then competition would be limited, and the spirit of the recommendations would violate the policy of competition.

I also mentioned in my chapter many European attitudes that justify protection against Japanese products on the presumption that the Japanese market is effectively closed. Indeed, professional economists have struggled over how to measure the closedness or openness of markets, including autos and others. Nevertheless, other countries sometimes use the closedness of Japanese markets as an excuse to advocate the further closing of their own countries' markets. But after all, free trade, regardless of the closedness or openness of other countries' markets is valuable for its own sake, and we should not forget that.

5
Europe's Drug Market and Pharmaceutical Industry in the 1990s

Peter Oberender

The chemical industry now plays a vital economic role in countries throughout the world—not only as an employer, supplier, exporter, and importer, but also as the driving force behind innovative research and development. This industry will no doubt be greatly affected by economic integration in the European Community (EC), but it is far too complex an entity to treat in a brief discussion. Therefore I concentrate on one of its larger branches—pharmaceutical products, which provide a number of clues to the overall industry's prospects and to the kinds of opportunities and risks that lie in the path of development toward a common market in Europe. Germany's pharmaceutical industry is singled out for close attention because it accounts for 15.87 percent of the country's chemical products (figure 5-1) and also has a prominent position in the European Community. The discussion revolves around the following sets of questions:

• What institutional framework, particularly state regulations, surrounds the pharmaceutical market in Germany and in the other EEC countries? What is the composition and concentration of its supplies? What and how extensive are the barriers to entry? How is the market structured, how does it behave, and what results has it produced?

• What problems and gains will the Common Market bring? What changes can be expected? Will a harmonization take place, and, if so, how far-reaching will it be? Will the Community become a fortress?

• What can entrepreneurs and politicians from non-EC states (especially the United States) hope to gain from the integration? What strategies will countries need to use to remain in the market?

Germany's Pharmaceutical Industry

The pharmaceutical industry in Germany is best understood by examining the structure of its market and the parameters that make it competitive.

FIGURE 5-1

PRODUCTION OF CHEMICAL PRODUCTS IN WEST GERMANY, 1988

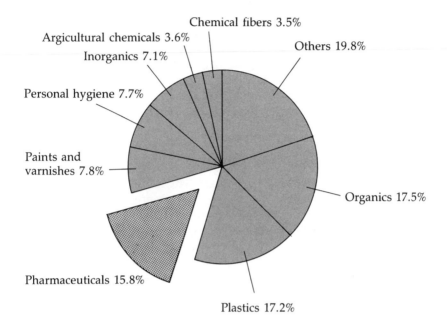

Chemical fibers 3.5%

Argicultural chemicals 3.6%

Inorganics 7.1%

Others 19.8%

Personal hygiene 7.7%

Paints and varnishes 7.8%

Organics 17.5%

Pharmaceuticals 15.8%

Plastics 17.2%

SOURCE: VCI, Jahresbericht 1988/89, Frankfurt/Main 1989, p.14.

Supply. The supply of pharmaceuticals in Germany is carefully regulated under legislation passed in 1961 and 1976 that covers the safety, efficacy, quality, and promotion of drugs. The more stringent requirements of the 1976 drug law, in particular, have increased the expenses of pharmaceutical companies and made it more difficult for potential newcomers to enter the market. To ensure certain standards of quality, 80 percent of all drugs may only be sold at pharmacies. From an economic point of view, this regulation gives rise to an artificial monopoly. To maintain their professional image, many companies also make the pharmacies the sole agents for the rest of their pharmaceutical sales mix. In doing so they not only strengthen the pharmacies' monopoly but they also discriminate against other channels of distribution. The retail price of drugs that are available only at a pharmacy (including the wholesale and retail trade margins) is fixed by legislators. In consequence, pharmacists cannot pursue their own competitive pricing policies.

In the past, druggists were not allowed to substitute a cheap drug with identical therapeutic qualities for a more expensive one prescribed by a doctor. This prohibition was partly lifted by the 1989 public health care reform act. Within the framework of fixed prices, product substitution is permitted. The anticompetitive effects of these various state interventions are compounded by the fact that only druggists may own and run a pharmacy.

A few additional rules set by druggists' associations further restrict competition among public pharmacies. For example, they have to limit their sales mix to goods "usually sold at pharmacies," and, in contrast to hospital pharmacies (which only supply hospital needs), they are not allowed to buy drugs in economy-size packages at low prices and sell them individually.

Production of drugs and foreign trade. The long-term development of drug consumption and increasing prosperity are closely connected. As the standard of living rises, so does the demand for medical care and the material and financial prerequisites for covering health care expenses. In 1988 the turnover in pharmaceuticals amounted to DM 23.823 billion, compared with only DM 2.350 in 1960. This enormous growth is the result of a rising per capita income combined with a disproportionate rise in the demand for health care, as mentioned above; immense progress in the development of more effective drugs; and the fact that the Statutory Health Insurance Organization (Gesetzliche Krankenversicherung, GKV) agreed to bear fully their members' expenditures on drugs until 1977. In that year the government set a ceiling on national drug spending. Table 5-1 presents selected figures on sales, employees, and foreign trade in the industry.

Concentration. At present, Germany has about 1,000 pharmaceutical companies, including the 475 members of the Bundesverband der Pharmazeutischen Industrie (BPI), which account for nearly 95 percent of aggregate sales. On the public pharmacy market, the shares of the leading companies have been on the decline for more than twenty years (tables 5-2 and 5-3). Sales of the top ten companies were fairly constant between 1973 and 1981 but have fluctuated considerably since then (figure 5-2). These changes reflect the dynamism of the market structure and the increasing intensity of competition (Vernon 1970–1971: 246 ff.).

The BPI interprets the shifts in the ranking of the top ten as a sign of fierce competition on the pharmaceuticals market (BPI 1989: 64). Note, however, that the absolute shares of the companies differ only slightly (in other words, small changes in absolute sales can have a significant effect on the top ten positions), and that the

TABLE 5-1

SALES, EMPLOYEES, AND FOREIGN TRADE IN WEST GERMANY'S
PHARMACEUTICAL INDUSTRY, SELECTED YEARS, 1960–1988

Factor	1960	1981	1988	1988 Increase (based on 1960)
Sales in billions of deutsche marks	2.350	16.770	23.823	10.1 times
Employees in thousands	n.a.	35.6	104.2	—
Exports in billions of deutsche marks	0.596	6.548	9.373	15.7 times
Export quota (percent)	25.4	39.0	39.3	
Imports in billions of deutsche marks	0.190	3.765	4.937	26.0 times
Import quota (percent)	8.1	22.5	20.7	

— = not available.
SOURCES: Statistisches (1962: 223–315), BPI (1989: 14), and VCI (1989: 71–85).

reasons for such alterations have not yet been found. Are they the
result of competitive activities, market changes, or changes in a single
company? National and international cooperation no doubt play a
role.

Thus concentration in the pharmaceutical industry (in the market
of public pharmacies) is relatively low in comparison with other
branches of industry and has gone down considerably during the
past two decades. The market situation is different for hospital
pharmacies. Although only the figures for 1974 are available, they

TABLE 5-2

SHARES OF LEADING COMPANIES IN WEST GERMANY'S PHARMACY
MARKET, 1966–1988

(percent)

Year	Top 5	Top 10	Top 20	Top 50	Top 100
1966	20.9	34.5	49.9	69.7	82.1
1970	19.8	33.1	48.3	71.1	85.5
1974	18.9	31.2	45.7	69.7	85.9
1978	17.5	27.5	41.4	65.1	83.6
1982	14.8	24.1	37.1	60.5	79.4
1986	12.3	20.2	32.7	56.8	77.7
1988	11.4	20.0	33.1	56.7	77.2

SOURCES: BPI (1988: 119; 1989).

TABLE 5-3

Shares of Leading Groups of Companies in West Germany's
Pharmacy Market, 1974–1988

(percent)

Rank	1974	1978	1982	1986	1988
Top 5	27.2	26.3	24.8	21.7	20.0
Top 10	44.4	41.2	38.6	33.5	32.2

Sources: BPI (1988: 119; 1989).

provide a reasonable indication of the situation. In that year the top twenty companies accounted for 65.8 percent of the market (compared with 45.7 percent on the public pharmacies' market); 13 percent of it was covered by Bayer, 5.3 percent by Hoechst. No company share on the public pharmacies' market exceeded 4 percent.

Most of the pharmaceutical companies (particularly the large ones) offer a great variety of drugs for sale, but 50 percent or more of their turnover takes place in only three or four therapeutic categories. In 1976 and 1977 Hoffmann La Roche did half of its German business in psychiatric drugs and antibiotics. Hoechst's sales mixture that year comprised approximately 180 finished drugs, but 30 percent of the preparations sold were Euglucon 5 and Insulin Hoechst. This information indicates the extent to which pharmaceutical companies depend on only a few products for their success. It is assumed that this dependence increases as the size of the company decreases.

Research and nonresearch companies. Some of the pharmaceutical industries invest in research and development (R & D) to increase their pharmacological knowledge. They develop and test chemical compounds with improved or new therapeutic qualities, and, if the tests prove successful they put the finished product on the market.

These drugs consist of hardware (the drug itself) and software (information about the ingredients, safety, efficacy, and the like). Imitators like Ratiopharm, Sanorania, or Siegfried copy only the hardware (after patent rights have expired), but do not concern themselves with the software. So, from the economist's point of view, identical drugs can be considered heterogenous goods. The problem is that the hardware and software are not traded separately in the market. To exclude imitators from participating freely in the software, an extra market for more detailed information about drugs and their peculiarities would have to be created.

To finance their R & D activities, innovative companies have to pass their costs on to the consumers, by way of higher prices. This

FIGURE 5–2

SALES RANKING OF THE LEADING PHARMACEUTICAL COMPANIES IN WEST GERMANY, 1970–1988

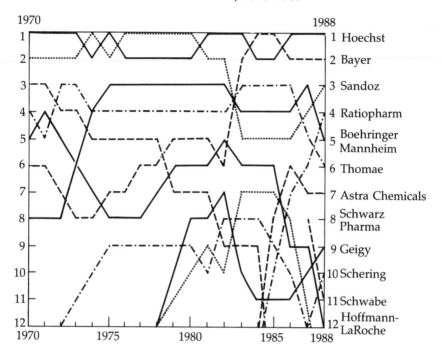

NOTE: Sales in public pharmacies at manufacturer's selling price.
SOURCE: BPI(1989: 65).

can be a problem when doctors are statutorily obliged to prescribe cheap generic drugs because the more expensive products of innovators will be discriminated against. At the same time, R & D activities can be used to justify exorbitant prices, for example, when market demand does not depend on the price, as in the case of persons insured against the costs of illness. Whether or not the market will accept innovations and reimburse R & D investments is always a journey into the unknown.

Barriers to market entry. The extent to which competition is present in the market depends on the barriers to entry. Three kinds of barriers have been identified: economies of scale, absolute cost advantages, and product differentiation. Regulations imposed by the government or professional associations can be added to this list. In the pharmaceutical industry, patent rights, the diversification of products

109

(protection of trademarks), and governmental restrictions on the admittance of new drugs all keep potential newcomers from entering the market.

The European Community agreed on a patent law in 1978, by which they extended the protection by patent from eighteen to twenty years. With the help of patent rights, innovative companies can isolate their market segment from potential competitors for a certain period of time. Two possibilities remain for those who wish to enter a market segment without infringing on a patent currently in force. One either applies for a license or tries to circumvent the patent by developing substances with identical therapeutic qualities. In the pharmaceutical industry today, however, licenses are hardly ever granted by innovators except on the basis of cross-licensing agreements. Small and medium-size companies usually do not own any patents or the right for an exchange. It takes a great deal of experience in the therapeutic category concerned, combined with sufficient financial backing, to circumvent a patent.

Since the protection of patents has a considerable effect on drug market competition, an important question to consider is whether protection should be abolished or weakened by coercive licenses. Even if a patent was not taken out for a new invention, the chance of being one jump ahead of one's competitors might induce companies to continue investing in R & D.

The protection of trademarks also plays an important role on the drug market. Many large established companies use goods carrying their trademark to influence young doctors' prescribing habits during their hospital training. The brand loyalty created this way is preserved and consolidated later by the companies' pharmaceutical advisers. Moreover, since little economic incentive is present in the German health service system at times, doctors often persist in prescribing their preferred brands, even if they are aware of cheaper alternatives. They rely on the reputation and experience of the manufacturers of proprietary goods to vouch for the quality, safety, and efficacy of the product. Thus brand drugs appear to have a competitive advantage over potential alternatives as a result of trademark protection, even when patents have expired.

In 1978 the standards of examination for new, innovative drugs were raised but market entrance was made easier for imitators, who were now allowed to apply for standard admission. That is to say, the new regulations discriminated against innovative companies and favored imitative ones. Although the barriers to entry connected with production engineering are low, governmental requirements for admission and production—as well as patent law, the protection of

FIGURE 5–3
System of Drug Distribution in West Germany

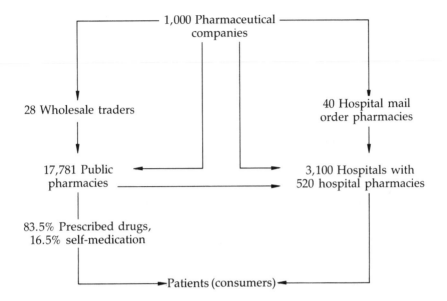

SOURCE: Author.

trademarks, and product differentiation—limit the number of potential newcomers, especially small and medium-size companies.

The structure of distribution. The channels of distribution are another distinctive feature of the German drug market (figure 5-3). The wholesale trade is characterized by competitive research. The number of independent enterprises dropped from ninety in 1960 to forty in 1981 and only twenty-eight today. Also note that doctors have a central position in the public pharmacies' market inasmuch as 83.5 percent of the drug sales stem from their prescriptions.

Demand. Drug demand depends to a large extent on the individual patient's health insurance program. In the case of freely obtainable over-the-counter (OTC) drugs (mainly drugs for minor ailments), the consumer not only decides on his or her demand (self-medication), but also has to foot the total bill (there is no reimbursement, except when an OTC drug is prescribed by a doctor). In this market segment, which accounts for 16.5 percent of the public pharmacies' sales, prices can play their normal economic role.

More than four-fifths of the drugs consumed in Germany are prescribed by doctors, with the health insurance companies covering

FIGURE 5–4
The Public Health System in West Germany

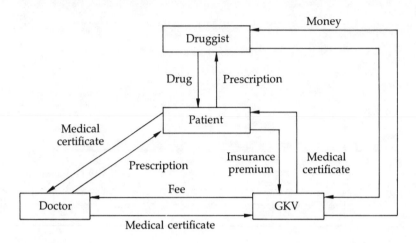

Source: Author.

the costs (complete or partial recovery). Blue- and white-collar workers whose earnings do not exceed DM 54,000 a year are subject by law to insure themselves against the costs of illness. At present, 99.6 percent of the German population have health insurance; 90 percent are insured by the GKV under a compulsory program, 8 percent by a private organization (Private Krankenversicherung, PKV), and 2 percent by their employer (the police and the military).

The GKV has two notable characteristics: (1) according to the principle of solidarity, each insured person enjoys the same benefits, regardless of earnings and insurance premiums, and (2) the insurance company directly pays the pharmacy, doctor, and hospital bills. The patient normally has nothing to pay. This procedure has changed somewhat, however, as a result of the 1989 Public Health Care Reform Act (Gesundheitsreformgesetz, GRG). Some fields of medical care have gone over to a system of reimbursement.

Under the social and public health policy, the GKV covers all costs in the case of illness (figure 5-4). As a result, demand in the health sector is totally price inelastic. Parts of the population try to get as many of the "free" insurance benefits as possible. Economically, they strive to realize the volume of saturation (and sometimes exceed it), where the marginal utility is 0. Their behavior is marked by a free-rider mentality and the moral hazard phenomenon.

If we assume there is no reimbursement and the demand curve for a certain drug is N_1 (figure 5-5), this curve is limited by the

FIGURE 5–5

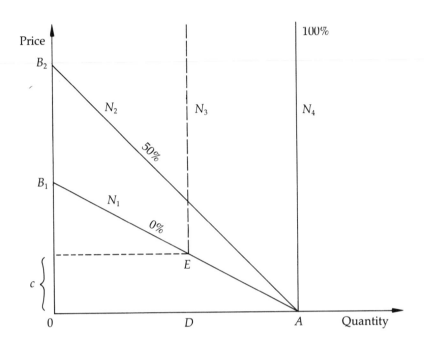

SOURCE: Author.

prohibitive price B, a price just so high that no one is willing to pay it, and the volume of saturation A, the amount of the drug people will consume if it is free. Now suppose a 50 percent reimbursement is introduced and causes the demand curve to turn clockwise around A until the price B_2 is twice as high as B (N_2). The higher the percentage of reimbursement, the more the demand curve turns around, until it becomes completely price inelastic and parallel to the price axis (of the coordinate system) in the case of a 100 percent restitution (N_3). If the patient has to pay a certain share of the drug price himself, C (at the moment DM 3), on drugs not affected by the new (fixed-price) regulation, the demand curve will be AEN.

Persons who are not compulsorily insured can voluntarily register with a private health insurance company (Private Krankenversicherung, PKV; see figure 5-6). They can select their own range of benefits at companies of their choice. Their drug expenses, for example, can be part or completely excluded from reimbursement (the

FIGURE 5–6
THE PRIVATE SYSTEM OF PROCURING PHARMACEUTICALS IN WEST GERMANY

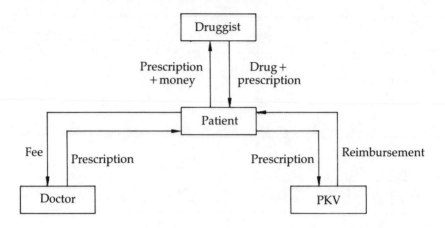

SOURCE: Author.

demand curve in figure 5-5 turns counterclockwise to the left). The premiums of the insured persons do not primarily depend on their incomes, but on the likelihood of becoming ill and on the extent to which the insurance should cover the health expenses (on the principle of equivalence, fees and possible benefits have to correspond.

In the case of the PKV, the insured person has to settle his bill first and gets his money refunded by the insurance company later (reimbursement system).

The market on the demand side works as follows. About 80 percent of the drug sales by public pharmacies consist of prescribed drugs. In this market segment, prices do not play a significant role and, because of the institutional features mentioned above, are scarcely noticed by the doctors. On the OTC market, however, the price-market mechanism works in the normal way. A commercial price is effective and the price elasticity of demand is considerably higher than in the case of drugs reimbursed by an insurance company.

The main reason for the significant difference between the strong (figure 5-7) burst of growth in the GKV drug expenditures and the slow-growing OTC trade is that the GKV table of benefits has constantly been extended. In consequence, GKV coverage has been substituted for self-medication in several therapeutic categories. In the future, if governmental regulation of drugs liable to reimbursement continues to increase, the tide may turn in favor of the OTC trade.

114

FIGURE 5–7

TRENDS IN THE GKV DRUG EXPENDITURE, THE OTC TRADE, AND THE
GROSS NATIONAL PRODUCT IN WEST GERMANY, 1970–1988

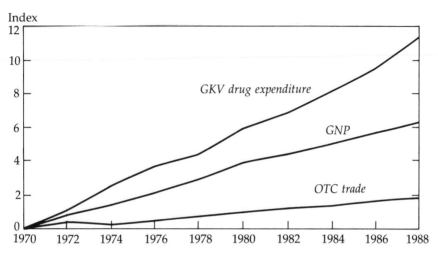

SOURCES: Cranz et al. (1982) and BPI (1987–1988).

The Parameters of Competition in Pharmaceuticals

The parameters of competition in the pharmaceutical industry are
price, product advertising and information, and research and development.

Price. Pharmaceutical companies seek extensive trade with hospitals
because they know the attending doctor will tell the family doctor
about the drugs prescribed when the patient is discharged, and the
future prescribing habits of young doctors and medical students can
be influenced during their hospital training. In addition, hospital
druggists have a better view of the market than doctors in private
surgeries and are not as easily swayed by the advertising of the
pharmaceutical industry. To them, price is the deciding factor in
buying drugs. As a result, prices play an important role in this
segment of the drug market. Pricing competition is fierce, and absolute prices as well as the rate of price increases stay well below the
level of the public pharmacies' market.

There the situation is different. Doctors and patients have no
reason to behave in a price-conscious way when drugs are covered by
health insurance. So demand is quite independent of price and price

115

changes (it is inelastic). The pharmaceutical companies do not pursue active pricing strategies because they cannot gain competitive advantage by doing so. Indeed, they are not particularly concerned with pricing competition since wholesale and retail margins are fixed by law.

Another factor to consider in connection with price is the problem of parallel imports, which arises when the prices of identical products differ from one country to another. Arbitrage dealings are usually thought to encourage competition. In this case, however, the arbitrage is not caused by the market process, but by governmental constructivist intervention and the still unrealized integration of the European economic and social systems. Parallel imports subject the German drug market to foreign intervention. This is not the way to heighten price competition.

Price competition is also limited by the circulation of drug lists. The primary purpose of these lists is to improve market transparency for the demand side (doctors and patients), but also to make it easier for the pharmaceutical companies to draw comparisons between their own and their competitors' goods (price, compound, size of package, etc.). If suppliers cannot gain a competitive advantage through active pricing policies, they will turn to other means.

Product. To gain an additional share of the market and to leave their competitors behind, the pharmaceutical companies began concentrating on the product. For a period of time, they went through intensive product competition as a great number of new drugs were introduced or old ones improved. The BPI now puts out a "red list" of some 8,550 drugs (produced by its members) that are based on 2,900 substances. The total number of drugs on the German market is about 15,000.

The Institute for Medical Statistics (London) has found that most doctors work with a maximum of 300–500 drugs. On a daily basis, they may prescribe 120–150 drugs. For public pharmacies the situation is similar: in 1988 62.5 percent of their drug sales fell to the share of only 500 drugs, 87.9 percent to 2,000.

As product competition increases, R & D expenditure also rises in an effort to develop the up-to-date technical knowledge that is needed to maintain product variety and innovation and to extend the life span of products affected by competition or to replace them. The number of new drugs has declined since the 1960s (figure 5-8). The principal reasons are that the ever-faster reactions of the competing producers have reduced the economic advantages of diversification and product differentiation has become more and more expensive

FIGURE 5–8
INNOVATIVE MEDICINES AND R & D APPROVAL RATES IN WEST GERMANY, 1967–1987

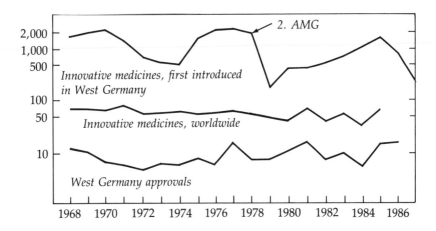

SOURCE: BPI (1988: 26, 27).

because of technological obstacles. The temporary increase between 1974 and 1976 and the subsequent drop were connected with the 2. AMG. Many companies rushed to apply for the approval of new drugs before the tighter qualifications came into force on January 1, 1978. The marked decline also reflected a falloff in the use of products as a competitive parameter.

In 1983 the BPI, the Kassenärztliche Bundesvereinigung, and the Arbeitsgemeinschaft der Berufsvertretungen Deutscher Apotheker (ABDA) recommended that pharmaceutical companies restrict themselves to the use of three standardized package sizes. By doing so, they not only reduced the alternatives on the demand side, but also limited the possibilities of product differentiation on the supply side. From the point of view of competition, such recommendations have the same effect as cartel agreements on standard specifications and types.

Advertising and Information. When product differentiation lost its effectiveness, the pharmaceutical companies began to rely on advertising and information (A & I) to promote their products.

By 1986, the share of A & I in the pharmaceutical industry's total expenditure had risen to 18.3 percent (DM 3.4 billion) (table 5-4). With the help of a narrow market and the activities of market research

117

TABLE 5-4

EXPENDITURES ON PHARMACEUTICAL ADVERTISING AND INFORMATION
IN WEST GERMANY, 1976–1986

(millions of deutsche marks)

Year	1976	1978	1980	1982	1985	1986
Scientific information	1,233	1,538	1,771	2,013	2,307	2,400
Advertising	476	575	590	686	815	953
Total	1,709	2,113	2,361	2,699	3,122	3,353

SOURCE: BPI (1983: 131).

agencies, pharmaceutical companies learned to assess their competitors' reactions to their A & I activities.

It became necessary, however, to bring the advertising budgets down to a justifiable, reasonable level. A one-sided reduction of a single company would have led to a slump in its demand. As a result, no firm wanted to be the first to cut its A & I expenditure. To resolve this problem, the BPI placed some voluntary restrictions on the delivery of free drug samples, the size of advertisements in professional journals, business gift giving, the size of pharmaceutical exhibition stands, and the spending on continuing education for doctors. A & I therefore lost much of its competitive significance, and fringe parameters such as pharmaceutical advisers became important. In 1987, 11,500 such advisers were at work trying to promote their companies' products.

Better market transparency for the doctors and a more critical attitude toward information and advertising are likely to make the work of these advisers harder in the future. In the long run, only superior products will prevail in the market.

Research and Development. Research and development also plays a substantial role in the pharmaceutical industry. It includes basic research, applied research, and development.

Only 15 of the approximately 1,000 drug producers in Germany carry on basic research, but there are 123 pharmaceutical research companies and their subsidiaries (which account for 80 percent of the sales to public pharmacies. These companies spent approximately DM 4.0 billion and DM 4.5 billion on R & D in Germany in 1988 and 1989, respectively. Their expenditure on R & D as a percentage of sales is shown in table 5-5. The figures for foreign companies are comparatively low because they have to contribute to the R & D expenses of the parent company.

TABLE 5-5

R & D Expenditures as a Percentage of the Pharmaceutical
Sales in West Germany, 1977–1987

Turnover (millions of deutsche marks)	German Companies			Foreign Companies in West Germany		
	1977	1980	1987	1977	1980	1987
0–7.5	3.6	1.7	2.5	2.2	2.0	2.2
7.5–15	5.4	3.0	4.0	3.7	1.0	2.2
15–45	5.0	5.4	4.5	3.1	2.0	4.7
45–150	10.5	10.0	10.2	3.9	3.5	4.6
More than 150	17.1	16.4	21.0	10.0	2.8	6.7

SOURCES: BPI (1979: 16; 1982: 15; 1989: 20).

Although R & D expenditure has increased steadily (in Germany, for example, it has risen from DM 0.6 billion in 1970 to DM 1.9 billion in 1981, DM 3.7 billion in 1987, DM 4.0 billion in 1988, and DM 4.5 billion in 1989), the number of active substances discovered from year to year has been falling. That is to say, the R & D productivity as a reflection of output and costs (input) has declined. This trend has been precipitated by tightened statutory controls on the admission, production, and control of drugs; decreasing marginal returns of R & D activities in the face of a fast-evolving traditional technology; and rising factor prices.

At the same time, there are some indications that large pharmaceutical companies in particular have succeeded in identifying the close links between their own R & D activities and their competitors' reactions. For some time the pharmaceutical industry has been moving toward R & D cooperation in the form of a division of labor and cross-license agreements or joint ventures in order to share the costs and risks of R & D activities and to avoid duplicating work unnecessarily.

The Regulation of Pharmaceutical Products in the European Community

The corporate bodies of the European Community have tried for years to integrate the European pharmaceutical markets, beginning with guidelines on the reduction of trade barriers (by way of national rules of admission) introduced on January 26, 1965. These guidelines have constituted the basis for all EC rules on pharmaceutical products. Subsequent directives have been concerned with the drawing up of petitions for admission, production and quality control, labeling, and product information.

EC Regulations. The admission of pharmaceutical products in the European Community consists of a somewhat complicated procedure. First, a pharmaceutical product must gain before it can be put on the market in a member state. The applicant can apply for national admission in one or more states at the same time. As soon as a pharmaceutical product has obtained national admission in any member state (it need not be the home country), the same documentation can be used to gain admission to at least two other EC member states. Possible objections of single member states are aired in the Committee for Proprietary Medicinal Products (CPMP), the representative of the national admission authorities. There is also a high-tech procedure; it is obligatory for pharmaceutical engineering products to go through a slightly different procedure in that they must first be scrutinized before they can be granted admission (May 1989: 129).

General directives for the further integration of the pharmaceutical market were issued in 1985. These consist of about 300 measures, 13 of which relate to the supply of pharmaceutical products. By 1988, about 45 percent of all the planned measures had been adopted. A further 45 percent are being discussed, and the remaining 10 percent—which include measures for nonprescription drugs—are under preparation (Cranz 1989:29ff.). The Commission of the European Communities plans to present further proposals concerning EC admission procedures, prices, the dissemination of information and publicity in professional and nonprofessional circles, the delivery and prescription of pharmaceutical products, and rules for pharmaceutical groups that have been excluded from regulation up to now (May 1989: 12ff.).

After customs regulations and quota limitations were reduced under the Treaty of Rome, several EC member states tried to hinder drug imports through nontariff trade barriers. The European Supreme Court interpreted these as a violation of Article 30 of the treaty, however, and heard complaints. It thus played an important role in the realization of free trade in pharmaceutical goods (for details, see Donnell 1981: 826ff.). The court has also ruled that the trademark protection for a pharmaceutical product is used up after its first introduction to the market of an EC member state. Consequently, the national property rights of owners who are affiliated with foreign producers or derive their industrial property rights from them cannot prevent the importation of their products.

National Regulations. National regulations within the European

Community have increased considerably since the early 1970s primarily because of a growing concern with safety and with the rising costs of health care. Safety, in particular, has affected product control, downstream market control, and product liability. Individual member states have interpreted safety in different ways, but, in general, they have given high priority to protecting the intended patient. Opinions differ widely on efficacy, however. In contrast to Germany, Denmark and France (like the United States) have a highly restrictive admission policy where efficacy is concerned.

Other national features that inhibit free pharmaceutical trade are the diverse regulations concerning price, costs, profits, recoverability, and publicity. The 1970s witnessed a gradual increase in state intervention within the framework of the cost-cutting policy in individual member states. Prices and quantities were the main targets. As the EC corporate bodies worked to integrate the regulations on the introduction of pharmaceuticals, member states began to close up their home markets. The pharmaceutical industry found itself caught between the two.

Price regulations and systems of refund. The most extensive restrictions on the prices of pharmaceuticals originate with the state and therefore have the greatest bearing on the free trade of goods within the European Community that is planned for 1993. Although the restrictions differ from one state to another (table 5-6), they should all be eliminated if a common market is to come into existence.

Every country of the European Community has some type of policy to control pharmaceutical expenditure. The methods used vary widely, as do the average price levels. Almost all the systems, however, incorporate an element of patient copayment and exempt over-the-counter products from regulation.

At one extreme, Germany leaves pharmaceutical firms free to set prices as they wish. Total expenditure is limited by strong pressure on companies to limit price increases and on doctors to economize, and by a negative list that excludes certain categories of comfort drugs from the reimbursement system. The situation in the Netherlands is similar. Prices are high in both countries.

In the United Kingdom, the profitability of pharmaceutical companies is controlled. A target is set for the sector as a whole; the level for each firm depends on its research effort and on its contribution to the British economy. Subject to these constraints, companies are allowed to set the prices at which their products are introduced. Irish prices are tied to those in the United Kingdom and in both cases are in the middle range.

France allows firms to set their own prices in principle, but in

TABLE 5-6:

	Belgium	Denmark	France
Pricing	On a cost basis	Price control according to cost structure and profit	Price rigging with the Health Department for refundable products; free price formation for nonrefundable drugs
Price rise	Admission required	Permission required	Permission required; price rise according to costs for research and development, exports, and domestic employment
Discimination of foreign products		None	Domestic drugs are favored in a price comparison; imported drugs are to be admitted as imitators
Positive/negative list; other regulations	Positive list with admission criteria: therapeutic and social interest, duration of treatment, substitution possibility and price comparison with similar drugs	Positive list with admission criteria: efficacy, safety, and cost-benefit analysis	Positive list with admission criteria: price, therapeutic benefit, domestic demand, and domestic research and development
Refund principle	Reimbursement of costs principle		

practice admission to the national reimbursement system is strictly controlled. Products are dealt with on an individual basis. The price agreed between the manufacturer and the reimbursement authority depends on those of competitive products and on the company's local activities in France. Belgium has a similar system. Prices are low in both countries, especially in France.

Denmark, Greece, Italy, Portugal, and Spain control the prices of individual drugs by the use of cost-plus methods. They also maintain

REGULATIONS FOR PRICING AND REFUNDS FOR DRUGS IN THE EC STATES

West Germany	Great Britain	Greece
No price control	Prices for prescription drugs are controlled by the NHS because the profit is fixed	On a cost basis
No control	No control	Admission required
None	PPRS favors domestic drugs	Favored refund of domestic drugs; pharmaceutical exchange rate was frozen on lowest level
Negative list according to economic efficiency; fixed amount regulation	Positive list for national health system prescriptions according to the following criteria: therapeutic benefit and medical necessity	Positive list
Benefits-in-kind principle	Benefits-in-kind principle	Benefits-in-kind principle *(table continues)*

positive lists. Prices are high in Denmark, below average in Italy, and very low in the other three countries.

In every EC country except Germany, the price at which a product is introduced cannot subsequently be changed without official permission. Such permission is often delayed, refused, or made contingent on the company expanding its local activities (Economists Advisory Group 1988: 9). Companies have tried to evade these hindrances by introducing new products. France, for example, intro-

TABLE 5-6 (continued)

	Ireland	Italy	Luxembourg
Pricing	No price control for innovations	For refundable drugs guidelines on a cost basis	On a cost basis, not higher than the country of origin
Price rise	Permission required	Admission required	No control
Discimination of foreign producers	None	Price advantages for domestic drugs	
Positive/negative list: other regulations	Positive list with admission criteria: efficacy, safety, and cost-benefit analysis	No positive lists with different obligations for additional contributions according to the following criteria: therapeutic efficacy and cost-benefit analysis	Positive list according to the following criteria: therapeutic benefit and cost-benefit analysis
Refund principle		Benefits-in-kind principle	Reimbursement of costs principle

duced 330 new substances from 1961 to 1985. In comparison, Germany introduced 268 new substances and the United States only 130 in the same period.

In addition to imposing price restrictions, almost all EC member states restrict the range of products with the help of positive and negative drug lists. Some countries also use those lists to limit drug imports. This action constitutes a violation of the provision in the Treaty of Rome prohibiting discrimination.

Ireland is the only EC country that does not have a refund list. The refund is not bound to a single medication. The only social criterion behind the Irish health care system is the claim. In the other EC countries, with the exception of Germany and the Netherlands, refundable medicines are recorded in positive lists. In Portugal, Denmark, the United Kingdom, and Italy, the state stipulates which preparations are to be on the list. Spain, Greece, and Belgium leave it up to the health insurance fund whether to record a drug on the positive list. In France, the decision is made by the health insurance funds, but it must be approved by the department responsible. In the

TABLE 5-6 (continued)

Netherlands	Portugal	Spain
No price control	After negotiation, on the basis of local prices, lowest European price; therapeutic benefit and cost-benefit analysis	For prescription drugs on a cost basis
No control	Admission required	Admission required
Frequent application of EWG in order to ward off the importing of foreign products.		
Negative/positive list fixed according to therapeutic benefit; cost- benefit analysis	Positive list admission criteria: therapeutic benefit, international comparison, cost-benefit analysis	Positive list with admission criteria: efficacy, safety, and cost-benefit analysis

Benefits- principle

SOURCE: Author.

Netherlands, the health insurance funds are advised by a panel of experts. In this case, the refund list is not mandatory but is only recommended to doctors. There is, however, an obligatory negative list. Only in Germany is it possible to obtain a 100 percent refund. It is restricted by a negative list for *Bagatellartzneimittel* (medication for minor illnesses). There is an additional list of comparative prices that does not, however, exclude single drugs from prescription.

Another hindrance to a common market lies in the pharmacy law, which varies greatly from one EC country to another. Furthermore, only three countries besides Germany—namely, Ireland, the Netherlands, and the United Kingdom—allow drugs to be sold in pharmacies or similar stores. These various regulations and trade barriers in the EC member states affect not only their respective home markets but also foreign markets, owing to the growing market interdependence.

The effect of margins and value added on price. Drug distribution is heavily influenced by state regulations throughout the EC countries, nearly all of which stipulate that certain drugs can only be made

TABLE 5-7

VALUE-ADDED TAX AND WHOLESALE AND PHARMACY MARGINS ON
DRUGS IN THE EUROPEAN ECONOMIC COMMUNITY, 1989

Country	Value Added	Wholesale Margin[a]	Pharmacy Margin[b]
Belgium	6/19	13.1	31
Denmark	22/22	3.7–16.8	24–45
France	5.5/18.6	9.7	30.44
Greece	6/(8)	22	24.5
Ireland	0.23	15	37.5
Italy	9/18	10.7	25
Netherlands	6/19	16.7	fixed amount, Hfl 10.35
Portugal	—	10	20
Spain	6/6	12	29.9
United Kingdom	0/15	10.5	33.3
West Germany	14/14	10.7–17.4	23.1–40.5

— = not available.
a. Wholesale margin as a percentage of the wholesale price (not including value added tax).
b. Pharmacy margin as a percentage of the ultimate consumer price (not including the value-added tax).
SOURCE: *Health Economics* (June 1989).

available at pharmacies. Wholesale and pharmacy margins, as well as value added, are also stipulated (table 5-7). As a result, a medication that may have a standardized purchase price in all the countries will vary in its pharmacy sales price (figure 5-9). These differences are reenforced under different inflation rates and, consequently, under different exchange rates within a system of flexible exchange rates. Differences in price often create an incentive for the entrepreneur to introduce pharmaceuticals from a low-price country into a high-price country.

Price and profit regulation. Price intervention can lead to particularly grave problems in the drug sector. In general, state intervention means that maximum prices are set on the basis of the costs of production rather than scarcity and competition in the market. The problem is that the costs of a product cannot be objectively determined, especially in multiproduct firms and especially when, as in the case of drugs, overhead costs are high (Riebel 1959: 237). This makes it difficult to calculate the contribution margin for research and development. Cost is particularly difficult to calculate when a

FIGURE 5–9
Ultimate Consumer Prices
(standardized purchase price of DM 10.-)

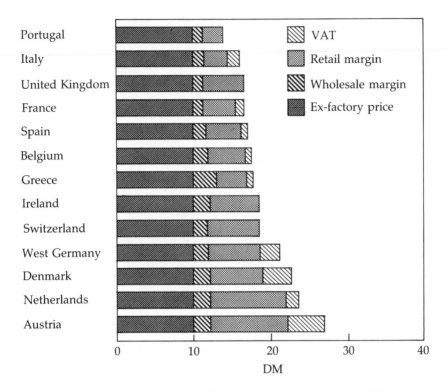

SOURCES: Prognos AG-Basel, 1976; Health Econ AG-Basel, June 1989.

product is introduced. Because there are usually scale effects, unit costs depend on the quantities produced and therefore on the volume of sales, which in turn is determined by a host of parameters and cannot be predicted in general.

Even if price regulation is not extreme enough to cause producer losses, it can reduce profits and thus the capability and willingness to pursue research and development. On the one hand, research and development will, in the long run, be directed toward the areas with a large sales potential because costs can be distributed over a greater number of units, and prices can be kept down, to appease the authorities. On the other hand, interest in rare diseases is likely to decline because of a small sales potential. Decreasing profits and profit expectations affect not only the direction of the research and development activities, but also their structure.

Under such circumstances, innovative research is likely to give way to more imitative investigations, and enterprises will turn increasingly toward markets with higher profit margins. If price increases can only be effected with the help of a new product, as in France, the entrepreneurs will rely on the product parameter. By varying and manipulating the product, its producers will try to circumvent the price structures and will legally be justified in doing so.

When prices are regulated, enterprises are less concerned with the conditions of competition and more with the expectations of the price-setting authority. Consequently enterprises are more ready to cooperate, and concerted action becomes easier for state institutions. The danger of increasingly coordinated conduct among the pharmaceutical companies is that state rules can lead to uniform cost estimation and then to cartels.

If research and development costs that arise abroad cannot be covered by drug imports because of a price regulation, the purchasers of drugs on the nonregulated markets will help finance pharmacological progress for these regulated markets by way of higher prices. Such a beggar-thy-neighbor policy constitutes an efficient strategy for the redistribution of income across countries. Furthermore, if foreign enterprises are discriminated against because their research and development costs are only partly accepted as costs by the authorities, they may decide to change their location from the exporting country to the respective importing country, depending, of course, on the opportunity costs.

Further problems arise from regulations that focus on profitability. Profit cannot be calculated unless the costs underlying the revenue are known. As already noted, it is extremely difficult to calculate costs objectively. In addition, such regulations encourage entrepreneurs to expand their costs—for example, by giving executives high salaries, fees, or other privileges—for fear that their profits will be considered too high by the supervisory office. Since profitability is the ratio of profit to contributed capital, there is a further incentive to work capital intensively to lower the profitability at a given profit. Such conduct can lead to a waste of capital.

Refundability. At the moment, the refundability of pharmaceutical products constitutes an entrance barrier in the various health care systems of the EC nations. The refusal of refund by a health insurance organization has the same effect as an import embargo, especially when a domestic drug of the same value is refundable. Such a strategy is employed rather often in some EC countries, such as England and France, in order to protect the domestic pharmaceutical industry, because in most cases it is impossible to prevent drugs from being introduced to the market. By these means, a second admission, in the form of refundability, takes place. In a relatively free market such as Germany's, these nontariff trade barriers can, through their cumulative effects, also distort competition in the form of drug imports (toward parallel imports or reimports).

Parallel imports. Parallel imports and reimports of drugs are another serious problem that can arise in the context of price regulation. In general, arbitrage dealing cannot be criticized as long as it is based on market forces. When price interventions abroad are the cause for such dealing, it is no longer arbitrage dealing in the usual sense, but discriminatory dealing, which amounts to importing foreign state interventions. On a short-term basis, it can help stimulate price competition. On a long-term basis, it constitutes a serious threat to the pharmaceutical industry since the financing of innovative research and development can no longer be guaranteed when prices and profits begin to sink. The decision of the European Supreme Court (ESC) to permit parallel imports can only be justified economically if the same guidelines are valid for all EC member states. As long as this is not the case, the jurisdiction of the European Community remains questionable. It could only be politically justified on the assumption that it would put pressure on the national governments to integrate their guidelines. In fact, such integration merits close attention and should not be delayed or else irreversible damage may be done, for example, to the German pharmaceutical industry, which is known for its innovativeness.

Intermediate result: diagnosis. The pharmaceutical industry has been under increasing political pressure in recent years. The scope for entrepreneurial action has narrowed under the growing body of regulations. Today there are more legal restrictions on the admission, production, and control of drugs than ever before, not to mention the increasing interventions designed to reduce the cost of health care. Protectionist ideas and their suppression of the national drug markets have been accompanied by mounting international competition (especially from U.S. and Japanese enterprises). This situation has been further aggravated by the decreasing marginal yields of research and development activities, which cannot go much farther using traditional technologies.

The Structure of the EC Pharmaceutical Industry

Although this discussion is concerned with the pharmaceutical industry of the European Community, it should be pointed out that the

TABLE 5-8

AREA, POPULATION, GNP, NUMBER OF DOCTORS, AND NUMBER OF
PHARMACIES IN EC COUNTRIES, 1987

Country	Area (sq. km.)	Population (millions)	GNP, 1987 (ECU million)	Doctors/ Pharmacies (thousands)
Belgium	30,507	10.0	123,048	30/5.2
Denmark	43,069	5.11	85,838	15/0.313
France	551,500	55.0	763,160	150/21.452
Greece	131,944	9.9	40,332	30/5.1
Ireland	70,283	3.5	25,353	5.5/1.126
Italy	301,225	57.1	657,399	250(190 active)/15
Luxembourg	2,586	0.37	—	0.7/0.072
Netherlands	33,491	14.4	185,407	—/1.403
Portugal	88,500	10.2	30,475	26/1.956
Spain	504,782	38.6	256,097	130(100 active)/ 18.1
United Kingdom	244,046	56.5	592,079	100/11.4
West Germany	248,624	61.0	972,280	223(171.5 active)/ 17.781

NOTE: Based on the 1987 exchange rate, ECU 1 = US$1.15 = DM 2.07.
SOURCE: EFPIA.

European Federation of Pharmaceutical Industries' Associations
(EFPIA) represents all the states of Europe that produce their own
pharmaceuticals—Belgium, Denmark, France, Germany, Greece, Ireland, Italy, the Netherlands, Portugal, Spain, and the United Kingdom within the European Community; and Austria, Finland, Norway, Sweden, and Switzerland outside it. Some statistics on the EC
industry are given in table 5-8.

Consumption. In 1987 the pharmaceutical market value of the EC
member countries (in exfactory terms) was approximately ECU 29
billion, with Germany, France, Italy, the United Kingdom, and Spain
accounting for nearly 90 percent of the market share (table 5-9). This
made the EC pharmaceutical market the second largest in the world,
behind the United States and ahead of Japan.

The percentage spent on pharmaceuticals indicates they play a
significant but not dominant role in health care. In most of the EC
countries (with the exception of Ireland, the Netherlands, Greece,
and Portugal), as in many other developed countries, pharmaceutical
spending accounts for 10–20 percent of total health care spending.
Public pharmacies dominate the distribution of pharmaceutical prod-

TABLE 5-9
Pharmaceutical Consumption within the European Community, 1987

Country	Pharmaceutical Market Value (ECU million)	Health Care Spending (ECU million)	Ratio of Pharmaceutical Spending to Health Care Spending (percent)	Pharmaceutical Consumption per Capita (ECU)
Belgium	947	8,715	16.8	96
Denmark	341	5,401	11.1	67
France	6,589	59,807	16.8	118
Greece	302	1,939	31.2	31
Ireland	149	1,712[b]	5.0[b]	43
Italy	5,926	41,353	17.7	103
Netherlands	835	15,715	9.2	57
Portugal	458	1,045	30.7	47
Spain	1,772	13,356	19.0	46
United Kingdom	3,939	34,946	13.0	69
West Germany	7,670	103,490[a]	12.24[a]	126
Total	28,928	287,479	10.06	89
Switzerland	798	11,175	13.1	89

NOTE: ECU 1 = U.S.$1.15 = DM 2.07.
a. 1985.
b. 1986.
SOURCE: EFPIA.

TABLE 5-10

LEGAL PHARMACEUTICAL CONSUMPTION WITHIN THE EUROPEAN
COMMUNITY, BY TYPE AND OUTLET, 1984

Country	Through Retail Pharmacies[a]	Through Hospitals	Over the Counter
Belgium	76	12	12
Denmark	70	15	15
France	78	13	9
Greece	83[b]	17	—
Ireland	80	15	5
Italy	79	13	8
Netherlands	—	—	—
Portugal	93[b]	7	—
Spain	88[b]	12	—
United Kingdom	67	13	20
West Germany	66	18	16
Total	74	14	12

— = not available.
a. Including dispensing doctors.
b. Including over-the-counter drugs.
SOURCES: EFPIA (1986–1987: 24–27), BPI (1988: 272–74), and Economists
Advisory Group (1988).

ucts (prescription drugs) to the consumers in all the EC states.
Hospitals (remaining prescription drugs) and OTC products account
for the remaining share (table 5-10).

Production and Foreign Trade. Europe is the world's largest producer
of medicines, and accounts for about one-third of the world market,
followed at some distance by the United States and Japan (table 5-11).
Within the European Community, Germany, France, Italy, the United
Kingdom, and Spain—in that order—are the largest producers.

Even though every EC state has a pharmaceutical industry, no
nation is completely self-sufficient. Consequently, the European
Community plays an important role in the European and worldwide
trade in pharmaceutical products. On average, the European countries export about 35 percent of their total output, 20 percent of which
remains within Europe. In other words, they claim more than two-
thirds of the global export business of pharmaceutical products. In
contrast, the United States exported barely 7 percent of its production
and Japan only about 2 percent.

Germany leads the nations of the world in pharmaceutical ex-

TABLE 5-11

PRODUCTION AND EXPORTS IN THE AREA OF PHARMACEUTICAL
PRODUCTS IN THE EUROPEAN COMMUNITY, 1987

| Country | Production | | Total Exports (ECU million) | Exports in EFPIA Countries (percent) |
	ECU million	Percent		
Belgium	1,079	2.7	957	72.6 (695)
Denmark	799	2.0	—	—
France	9,127	22.6	2,065	49.1 (1,014)
Greece	268	0.7	—	—
Ireland	337	0.8	—	—
Italy	7,315	18.1	1	48.8 (517)
Netherlands	1,020	2.5	831	64.5 (536)
Portugal	392	1.0	—	—
Spain	2,901	7.2	298	41.3 (123)
United Kingdom	6,967	17.2	2,395	50.3 (1,204)
West Germany	10,202	25.2	4,747	68.0 (3,228)
Total	40,407	100		
Switzerland	2,919		2,750	55.5 (1,525)
United States	32,100		2,210	—
Japan	28,990		585	—

— = not available.
SOURCES: EFPIA (1986–1987: 10–13), BPI (1989: 16).

ports, followed by Switzerland, the United States, Great Britain, and France, as well as Japan. Although Japan produces a great many pharmaceuticals of high quality, it supplies mainly the domestic market (dominating four-fifths of its home market), but is unimportant as an exporter. The German pharmaceutical industry was the leading exporter of pharmaceutical products even before World War II, with a 40 percent share of the world trade in pharmaceuticals. It regained its position in 1968 after the destruction and dismantling of parts of its production equipment during and after World War II. More than 65 percent of Germany's total exports of pharmaceuticals remain within Europe.

Even if economic integration is still far from a truly unhindered trade between the states, especially in the area of pharmaceuticals, the directives of the EC Council for the harmonization of existing legal and administrative rules have started the ball rolling. Of the ECU 10.6 billion worth of goods imported in the form of pharmaceuticals into the countries of Europe, only ECU 1.6 billion had their origin outside this region. It has been said that "one of the factors

TABLE 5-12

COUNTRY SHARES OF THREE PHARMACEUTICAL MARKETS, 1984

(percent)

	Market		
Country	European Community	United States	Japan
Belgium	4	<1	<1
France	17	<1	<1
Italy	8	<1	<1
United Kingdom	10	5	2
West Germany	22	4	4
Other EEC countries	5	<1	<1
Switzerland	10	8	3
United States	23	80	10
Japan	<1	<1	80
Other	1	<1	<1

SOURCE: Economists Advisory Group (1988: 75/41).

indicating the competitive strength of a national industry is the ability to gain market shares in other countries" (de Wolf 1988:238). By that definition, pharmaceuticals are doing fairly well. Table 5-12 shows the shares of important EC members, Switzerland, the United States, and Japan in the EC, U.S., and Japanese pharmaceutical markets in 1984. The EC market is dominated by EC firms (66 percent), followed by U.S. (23 percent) and Swiss (10 percent) firms.

The world's top fifteen drug companies, ranked by turnover in 1987, include some European enterprises: the German firms Hoechst and Bayer, and the British Glaxo within the EC, and the Swiss-based Ciba-Geigy, Sandoz, and Hoffmann La Roche outside the EC (table 5-13). The U.S. enterprise Merck & Co. heads the list. If one looks at the top sixty firms, European enterprises have the greatest share (25 percent), followed by the United States and Japan (figure 5-10).

Interdependence. "At first sight the pharmaceutical industry does not appear as highly concentrated as many others. Overall market concentration in any given country and, indeed, worldwide is relatively low. No single firm has as much as 5 percent of the world market or 20 percent of any major national market" (Organization for Economic Cooperation and Development 1985:12). A much higher degree of concentration is often found within single therapeutic categories.

Today the pharmaceutical industry has a strong international orientation; most of the large companies are organized on multinational lines, with foreign subsidiaries to import and repackage the products from the parent company, and sometimes with foreign production facilities as well. In the European Community, the manufacture of active ingredients is usually confined to a limited number of sites. Foreign companies with production facilities in the European Community are listed in table 5-14. Clinical and other development work is often dispersed, but basic and commercially sensitive research tends to be centralized (Economists Advisory Group 1988:39). The main center of research and development is normally in the firm's country of origin. National pharmaceutical industries are still largely dependent on their national home markets (table 5-15).

Research and Development. Numerous risks are attached to the development of innovative pharmaceutical products, and consequently R & D in this field is expensive. The success rate in the development of a new medication that will meet the desired standards of efficacy and safety is about 1 : 6,000. Some individual firms put the rate closer to 1 : 10,000. The costs associated with the development of a new active agent amount on average to about DM 250 million (about ECU 120 million), which includes the costs of unsuccessful research and development (BPI 1989:18).

Even when a substance appears to be marketable, it may not assert itself in the market, and the immense R & D expenses may not be recoverable. Innovative companies must therefore be internationally orientated; they have to distribute their products worldwide to cover the costs of innovation and to limit the risk of failure. Table 5-16 shows the R & D expenditure of the top ten firms in the world. Figure 5-11 compares the worldwide distribution of the leading 100 R & D companies in Europe, the United States, and Japan.

The European pharmaceutical industry spent ECU 5.9 billion on R & D in 1987 (table 5-17). This represented 13 percent of its overall production, "a proportion virtually unparalleled in any sector of manufacturing industry. Unlike other sectors, which benefit from state-funded research programmes, it is almost entirely self-financed" (EFPIA 1986–1987:19). Thus it is not surprising that the European pharmaceutical firms are strong competitors on the world market. Indeed, they supply about half of the top fifty drugs prescribed throughout the world.

One problem for innovative companies, however, is the relatively short life of the pharmaceutical patent in the European Community. Since 1965 effective life of such patents has declined from thirteen to

TABLE 5-13
TOP FIFTEEN PHARMACEUTICAL COMPANIES WORLDWIDE, 1987

Rank, Firm, and Nationality	Turnover (ECU million)[a]	Main Therapeutic Areas[b]
1. Merck & Co., United States	3,676 (83.5)	Cardiovascular, antirheumatics, ophthalmological
2. Hoechst, Germany	3,052 (17.1)	(Chemicals)
3. Glaxo, United Kingdom	2,934 (100)	Antiulcer, antiasthmatic, dermatological, other
4. Ciba-Geigy, Switzerland	2,757 (30.0)	Antirheumatic, cardiovascular, other (chemicals)
5. Bayer, Germany	2,574 (14.3)	Cardiovascular, CNS, other (chemicals)
6. American Home Products, United States	2,543 (58.2)	CNS, hormones, over-the-counter drugs (consumer products)
7. Takeda, Japan	2,383 (62.6)	

8. Sandoz, Switzerland	2,369 (45.3)	Cardiovascular, analgesic, other (chemicals)
9. Eli Lilly, United States	2,071 (65.4)	Antibiotics, other (agrochemicals)
10. Abbott, United States	2,029 (53.2)	Antibiotics, cardiovascular (hospital supplies)
11. Pfizer, United States	2,027 (47.4)	Antibiotics, cardiovascular, antirheumatics (agrochemicals)
12. Warner Lambert, United States	1,990 (65.7)	Cardiovascular, dermatological, over-the-counter drugs (toiletries, foods)
13. Bristol-Meyers, United States	1,928 (41.0)	Antibiotics, anticancer, other (toiletries)
14. SmithKline, Beckman, United States	1,874 (49.8)	Antiulcer, cardiovascular (scientific equipment)
15. Hoffmann La Roche, Switzerland	1,803 (40.1)	CNS, vitamins (fine chemicals)

a. Figures in parentheses denote percentage of total sales.
b. Other interests indicated in parentheses.
SOURCES: *Pharmazeutische Industrie*, 51 (1989: 606); Economists Advisory Group.

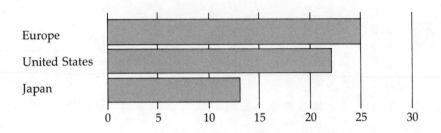

FIGURE 5–10
NATIONALITY OF TOP SIXTY PHARMACEUTICAL FIRMS, BY
WORLDWIDE SALES
(percent of world market)

SOURCE: EFPIA (1986–1987:21); and industry sources.

five years (figure 5-12). But the effective life of a patent for a new medication may be considerably shorter—in Germany the average is only 7.7 years—because the patent starts with the registration, which must take place soon after the discovery of a new substance to safeguard the property right. As a result, the original producer has much less time than was originally planned by the legislator to recover the high research and development costs and then turn a profit.

The European patent convention became effective on October 7, 1977, and the following year the European patent office began its work as an international authority. As before, located in Munich, the inventor can submit a national patent application at the patent office of his home country, but he can also apply for patent protection in the member states of the European patent convention. The European patent is treated as a national patent in the member states.

Present and Future Development of the EC Pharmaceutical Market

A number of steps have already been taken toward the development of a common pharmaceutical market, and several more are expected by the year 2000.

Current State of Affairs. The most progress toward integration has been made in the field of admission requirements. The same basic requirements have been laid down for all EC member states. At present, there is an EC application for admission that can be used in all the member states next to the national application for admission.

TABLE 5-14
FOREIGN COMPANIES WITH PRODUCTION FACILITIES IN EC COUNTRIES, 1988

Location of Facility	Nationality of Companies									
	Belgium	France	Greece	Italy	Nether-lands	Por-tugal	Spain	United Kingdom	West Germany	Total
Belgium		2	—	1	1	—	1	—	1	6
France	5	1	3	7	—	2	6	2	4	29
Italy	1	1	—		—	—	4	1	1	8
Netherlands	1	1	1	2	—	—	1	1	1	8
Portugal	—	—	—	1	—	—	—	—	—	1
United Kingdom	4	6	3	5	—	1	5	5	3	27
West Germany	1	5	2	10	1	2	10	19	14	36
United States	9	18	7	19	2	5	17	3	3	110
Switzerland	4	3	2	4	1	—	4	1	1	24
Other	—	—	—	—	1	—	2			5
Total	25	36	18	49	6	10	50	28	28	254

— = not available.

SOURCE: Economists Advisory Group (1988: 134–98).

TABLE 5-15

DEPENDENCE OF NATIONAL PHARMACEUTICAL INDUSTRIES ON NATIONAL MARKETS, 1984

(millions of European currency units)

Country	Total Sales	Imports[a]	Sales from Local Production	Total Production	Local Sales as Percentage of Production
Belgium	890	503	387	1,296	38
Denmark	379	180	199	873	22
France	5,634	280	5,354	8,577	62
Greece	448	96	352	408	86
Ireland	166	166		1,042	<1
Italy	4,465	475	3,990	6,338	63
Netherlands	665	490	175	1,056	17
Portugal	353	105	248	415	70
Spain	1,845	56	1,789	2,585	69
United Kingdom	3,535	691	2,843	6,648	42
West Germany	7,705	980	6,724	10,197	66
Total	26,090	4,022	22,068	39,435	56

a. Imports of finished pharmaceuticals (SITC 5417).
SOURCE: Economists Advisory Group (1988: 112/77).

TABLE 5-16
TOP TEN R & D FIRMS WORLDWIDE, 1987

| | R & D Expenditure | |
Rank, Firm, and Nationality	ECU million	As percentage of turnover
1. Bayer, W. Germany	578.1	22.5
2. Hoechst, W. Germany	471.9	15.5
3. Hoffmann La Roche, Switzerland	373.2	20.7
4. Sandoz, Switzerland	334.7	14.1
5. Glaxo, United Kingdom	327.7	11.2
6. Boehringer Ingelheim, W. Germany	323.1	20.0
7. Johnson & Johnson, United States	293.0	16.9
8. Bristol-Meyers, United States	279.6	14.5
9. SmithKline Beckman, United States	269.6	11.7
10. Rhone-Poulenc, France	253.0	15.7

SOURCE: *Pharmazeutische Zeitung* 31 (1989: 606).

Some EC directives identifying important principles and criteria in certain areas have also been established to provide guidelines for the preparation of national legislation.

As mentioned earlier, two admission procedures have been introduced to facilitate access to the common pharmaceutical market. These procedures coexist with the national procedures. One is the multistate procedure implemented by directives 75/319/EEC and 83/570/EEC. Its purpose is to help an already existing admission gain recognition in other EC member states. This is achieved by way of mutual recognition of the application of admission that has already been approved by the first authority. This procedure is used both for pharmaceutical products with a new chemical substance and for already known pharmaceuticals backed up by published documents in their application. But the latter drug is treated as a pharmaceutical specialty until an extension has been obtained on the directives on all finished pharmaceuticals. The Committee for Proprietary Medicinal Products plays a central role in this procedure (see figure 5-13).

The second method of admission, the high-tech concertation procedure was introduced on July 1, 1981, by directive 87/22/EEC (figure 5-14). This procedure was designed in part to address the problem of insufficient patent protection and safeguard against imitators, especially in the field of genetic engineering. At the same

141

FIGURE 5–11
NATIONALITY OF TOP 100 R & D FIRMS WORLDWIDE

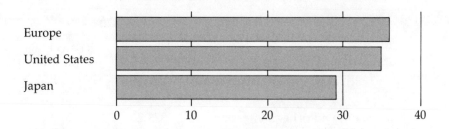

SOURCE: *Scrip Review* (1988: 11–12).

time, member states were aware of the difficulty of evaluating genetic engineering products. In order to strengthen the competitive position of the pharmaceutical industry, and to protect intellectual property, the EC Commission ruled that this procedure be followed before pharmaceutical products from genetic engineering and high technology apply for national admission. A medication that does so is protected against imitation in each member state for ten years. The guaranteed protection time begins only upon first admission in an EC state, after the successful termination of the concertation procedure.

Both procedures are intended to pave the way for the mutual acceptance of decisions of admission and of the results of experiments. Some opinions still diverge, however, especially in the final risk-benefit evaluations of the twelve national admission authorities. Medical schools are at the base of the problem in the admission of pharmaceuticals. They differ in their conceptions of certain diseases and of the therapeutic procedures required and therefore make it difficult to follow uniform regulations. Nonetheless, the concertation procedure contains elements of a supranational central admission authority.

Integration has not yet been tackled in other areas, such as prescriptions, pricing, and refund systems.

Expected Developments up to the Year 2000. Many differences still exist in the pharmaceutical regulations of the EC states. To complicate matters, few states can agree on how and to what extent these differences can be reduced, although they do recognize that existing national rules (conditions) need to be subjected to the competitive

TABLE 5-17

R & D Expenditure and Capacity for Innovation by Nation, 1987

(millions of European currency units)

Country	Expenditure	Capacity for Innovation
Belgium	116	Medium
Denmark	96	Medium
Finland	41	Low
France	1,031	High
Italy	635	Medium
Netherlands	135	Medium
Norway	31	Low
Spain	60	Low
Sweden	310	Medium
Switzerland	1,214	High
United Kingdom	954	High
West Germany	1,301	High
European Community only	4,328	
Total	5,924	

Source: EFPIA (1986–1987: 18), OECD (1985: 16).

process. Many also recognize that harmonization is a prerequisite for a common market, even though individual nations can be discriminated against under harmonization regulations that are too stringent, and that there are no objective operational criteria for the creation of concrete guidelines that correspond to the needs of the people in the European market.

Guidelines. Only unhindered competition of the national systems will guarantee that individual preferences will be adequately taken into consideration. Furthermore, competition between the systems creates an incentive to correct the individual system in an effort to achieve acceptance. Thus attention focuses on innovation.

The prerequisite for such competition—apart from the liberalization of goods, capital, and manpower—is that the people carrying political responsibility must have confidence in a market controlled system. Although such competition does not necessarily protect every system from intervention, it does give individual citizens more control over the quality of a given system. A great deal depends, of course, on the way in which decisions are taken, and this is what will determine the future course of the pharmaceutical industry in the European Community.

FIGURE 5–12
Reduction in Effective Patent Protection, 1965 and 1985

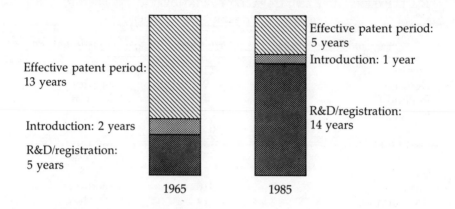

Effective patent period: 13 years

Introduction: 2 years

R&D/registration: 5 years

1965

Effective patent period: 5 years

Introduction: 1 year

R&D/registration: 14 years

1985

Source: De Wolf (1988).

Article 30 of the Treaty of Rome leaves room for exceptions from Article 36 if they are justified to protect the health and life of human beings, animals, and plants. But this regulation does not apply to pharmaceutical products. Therefore, each medication that is allowed admission into one EC country also is allowed admission into the other member states. In addition, discrimination against foreign pharmaceutical producers is prohibited.

Even though the pharmaceutical common market is supposed to be realized by 1992, this deadline probably cannot be met. One problem is that the national admission authorities are still reluctant to hand over sovereignty rights to an EC authority and are likely to remain so even after 1992. Nonetheless, some further harmonization concerning both admission and the definition of the term *pharmaceutical* can be expected. Some agreement may also be reached on the labeling, storage, and packaging of pharmaceuticals. In contrast, no agreement should be expected in the areas of price fixing and refund systems, which are closely tied to the social insurance systems in the EC member states.

At some point, attention will also have to be given to the task of integrating the European policy on pharmaceutical products into the overall framework of European industrial strategy. There will be special national regulations because of peculiarities in the fields of health and social policy, but they will have to be integrated into the

144

FIGURE 5–13
THE MULTISTATE SYSTEM OF PHARMACEUTICAL ADMISSION

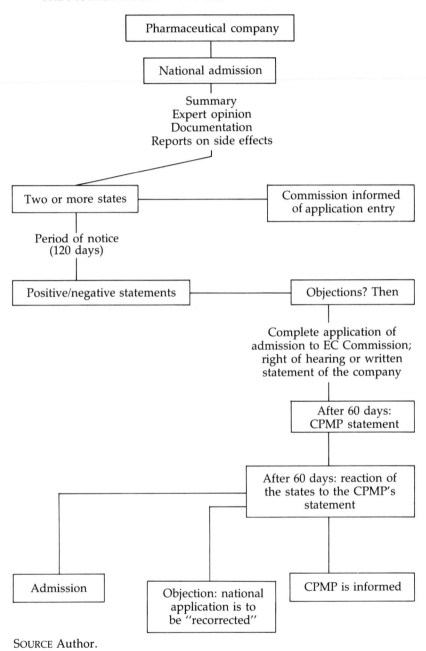

SOURCE Author.

FIGURE 5–14
The Concertation Procedure

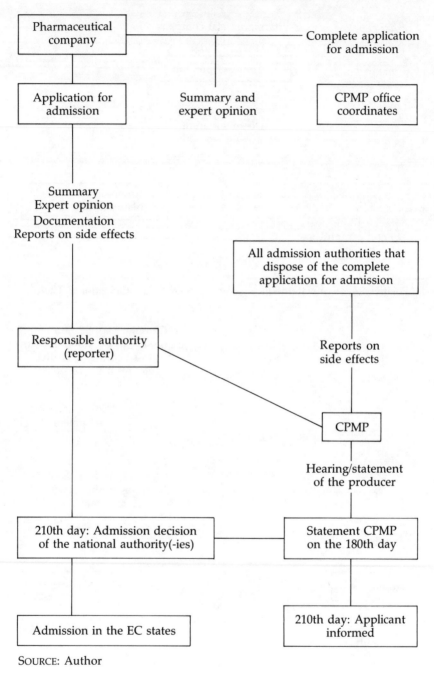

SOURCE: Author

TABLE 5-18

POTENTIAL AND ACTUAL SHARE OF OVER-THE-COUNTER DRUGS IN
SELF-MEDICATION IN SEVEN EC COUNTRIES, 1989

(percent)

Country	Potential Share	Actual Share
Netherlands	47	11
West Germany	37	16
France	35	19
Belgium	24	15
United Kingdom	22	14
Italy	13	12
Spain	9	7

SOURCE: Cranz (1989:29).

larger framework of European policy.

In addition, member states should reach an agreement on pre-scription drugs, at least on an obligatory list of prescription sub-stances that can be extended by the individual countries. An obliga-tory basic list of nonprescription substances will probably be drawn up as well. General obligatory guidelines concerning drug regulation will be enacted. Uniform ticketing, packaging, and patient and expert information can also be expected.

Self-medication. As table 5-18 shows, France is the leading country in self-medication (19 percent), followed by Germany (16 percent), and Belgium (15 percent). When the OTC potential is taken into account, the Netherlands leads with 47 percent, followed by Germany with 37 percent. In the United States and Switzerland, self-medication accounts for more than 30 percent of the pharmaceutical market and thus suggests that a huge area of the self-medication sphere in Europe remains to be explored. Self-medication can therefore be expected to increase in importance because all the national governments are concerned with reducing costs in the health care sector, especially in the area of pharmaceutical products. It should also be remembered that about 20 percent of the pharmaceutical production is sold outside of the European Community and therefore it is highly unlikely that the member states will be able to afford to follow a protectionist course after the completion of the Common Market.

When all is said and done, Europe is not likely to become a fortress, isolated from outside states. Nevertheless, as in all markets, certain problems will arise that can only be mastered on the scene. A useful strategy for American companies would be to enter the scene, by way of direct investments in Europe. They can invest in already existing companies or in new business and cooperative contracts with European producers of pharmaceutical products. In general, cooperation in the areas of research and development seems to offer the most new opportunities since, as has been shown time and again, innovation is the best way to tackle the up-and-coming challenges of complex systems such as the pharmaceutical industry

References

Abel-Smith, B., and A. Maynard. 1978. *Die Organisation, Finanzierung und Kosten des Gesundheitswesens in der Europäischen Gemeinschaft.* Brussels.

Bel, No. 1984a. "Künftige Regelung für den freien Verkehr mit Arzneimittelspezialitäten." *Pharmazeutische Industrie.* 46:129–34.

———. 1984b. "Zeithorizont 1990." *Pharmazeutische Industrie.* 46:1205–9.

Breitenbach v., G. 1989. "Europa 1992: Rahmenbedingungen und strategische Konsequenzen für die Pharmaindustrie." In *Wettbewerbsstrategien im Pharmamarkt,* edited by H. Simon et al. Stuttgart.

Bundesverband der Pharmazeutischen Industrie (BPI). 1979 *Pharma Daten '79.* Frankfurt (Main).

———. 1982. *Pharma Daten '82.* Frankfurt (Main). Bundesverband der Pharmazeutischen Industrie (BPI). 1983. *Basisdaten des Gesundheitswesens 1982/83.* Frankfurt (Main).

———. 1988. *Basisdaten des Gesundheitswesens 1987/88.* Frankfurt (Main).

———. 1989. *Pharma Daten '89.* Frankfurt (Main).

Commission of the European Communities. 1985. *Vollendung des Binnenmarktes—Weißbuch der Kommission an den Europäischen Rat.* Luxembourg.

Cranz, H. 1989. "EG-Binnenmarkt und Selbstmedikation." *Pharmazeutische Zeitung* 134, no. 24 (June, 15):29–31.

Cranz, H., S. Czech-Steinborn, H. Frey, and K.-H. Reese. 1982. *Selbstmedikation—Eine Standortbestimmung.* Kiel.

Davis, P. W. 1989. "Der amerikanische Pharmamarkt—Situation und Wettbewerb." In *Wettbewerbsstrategien im Pharmamarkt,* edited by H. Simon et al. Stuttgart.

Donnell, P. O. 1981. "Gegenseitige Anerkennung und freier Warenverkehr." *Pharmazeutische Industrie.* 43:826–29.

Dyckerhoff, G.A., and B. Weber. 1989. "Wachstum durch internationale Joint Ventures." In *Wettbewerbsstrategien im Pharmamarkt,* edited by H. Simon et al. Stuttgart.

Economists Advisory Group. 1988. *The "Cost of Non-Europe" in the*

Pharmaceutical Industry. Luxembourg.

Emmerich, V. 1980. *Staatliche Interventionen, Arzneimittelmarkt und EWG-Vertrag.* Baden-Baden.

European Federation of Pharmaceutical Industries' Associations (EFPIA). *EFPIA in Figures 1986–1987.* Brussels.

European Intelligence. 1989. *European Intelligence Document-Balance sheet of Measures in the Single Market Programme Those Adopted and Those on the Way to Adoption.* July.

Fuß, E.-W. 1981. *Der Beitrag des Gerichtshofs der Europäischen Gemeinschaften zur Verwirklichung des gemeinsamen Marktes.* Baden-Baden.

Huber, W. 1988. *Nachahmerwettbewerb bei Arzneimitteln.* Bayreuth.

Institut der Deutschen Wirtschaft. 1989. *Zahlen zur wirtschaftlichen Entwicklung der Bundesrepublik Deutschland 1989.* Cologne.

May, O. 1989. "Zulassungsverfahren in der EG." *Pharmazeutische Zeitung,* 134, no. 24 (June 15):12–16.

Mestmäcker, E.-J. 1979. *Vereinbarkeit von Preisregelungen auf dem Arzneimittelmarkt mit dem Recht der Europäischen Wirtschaftsgemeinschaft.* Baden-Baden.

Oberender, P. 1984. "Pharmazeutische Industrie." In *Marktstruktur und Wettbewerb in der Bundesrepublik Deutschland, Branchenstudien zur deutschen Volkswirtschaft,* edited by P. Oberener. Munich.

———. 1985. "Regulierungen und Handelshemmnisse innerhalb der Europäischen Gemeinschaft. Eine ökonomische Analyse zur Lage der deutschen pharmazeutischen Industrie." *Pharmazeutische Industrie.* 47:149–52.

———. 1989. "Arzneimittelforschung in Deutschland: Gefahren und Voraussetzungen für erfolgreiche Arzneimittelinnovationen." *Pharmazeutische Industrie.* 51:44–51.

Oberender, P., and G. Rüter. 1988. *Gefahren für Innovationen im Arzneimittelbereich. Eine ordnungspolitische Analyse.* Baden-Baden.

Organisation for Economic Co-operation and Development. 1985. *The Pharmaceutical Industry (Trade Related Issues).* Paris.

Riebel, P. 1959. "Das Rechnen mit Einzelkosten und Deckungsbeiträgen." *Zeitschrift für handelswissenschaftliche Forschung, Köln.* 11:237–38.

Ringenaldus, H. 1982. "Nichttarifäre Handelshemmnisse im Warenverkehr von Arzneimittelspezialitäten auf dem Markt der Europäischen Gemeinschaften." *Pharmazeutische Industrie* 44:128–32.

Sauer, M. 1985. "Analyse europäischer Pharma-Preise- und Arbeitsproduktivität." *Pharmazeutische Industrie* 47:380–83.

Schütz, S., and K.-H. Eichin. 1989. "Internationale Perspektiven der Pharmaindustrie." *Wettbewerbsstrategien im Pharmamarkt,* edited by H. Simon et al. Stuttgart.

Statistisches Bundesamt. 1962. *Statistisches Jahrbuch für die BRD 1962.* Stuttgart and Mainz. 1989.

Verband der Chemischen Industrie (VCI). 1989a. *Chemiewirtschaft in Zahlen 1989*. Frankfurt (Main).

———. 1989. *Jahresbericht 1988/89*. Frankfurt (Main) 1972–1971.

Vernon, J. M. 1972–1971. "Concentration, Promotion and Market Share Stability in the Pharmaceutical Industry." *Journal of Industrial Economics*, 19:246–66.

Wolf, P. de. 1988. "The Pharmaceutical Industry: Structure, Intervention and Competitive Strength. In *The Structure of European Industry*, edited by H. W. de Jong. Dordrecht.

6
Commentaries on Pharmaceuticals

A Commentary by Fred M. Scherer

Although Peter Oberender has provided an enormous wealth of detail about the European pharmaceutical markets, his chapter raises more questions than it answers.

Perhaps most notably, his table 5-15 reveals a remarkable degree of pharmaceutical supply autarky in many of the Common Market nations. In France, 95 percent of national pharmaceutical sales are supplied from local production; in West Germany, 87 percent; in Italy, 89 percent; in the United Kingdom, 80 percent. Yet if ever there was an industry in which one should expect a large amount of intraindustry trade—that is, with national producers cross-shipping differentiated products into each others' home territories—pharmaceuticals is it.

Front-end costs for research, development, and clinical testing are enormous, implying substantial dynamic economies of scale. Differences in the therapeutic properties of diverse chemical entities are often important for the consumer's welfare, so that, under the logic of optimal product variety, one should expect a wide variety of products to be offered. There are almost surely economies of scale in bulk production and, less significantly, in dosage size preparation and packaging. All this implies a tendency for the production of any given product variant to be centralized for sizable markets, with much transborder shipping if producers are scattered more or less evenly over the European map, as they appear to be. Yet this is evidently not the case.

The explanation no doubt lies in phenomena to which Professor Oberender has alluded: national preferences in the approval of new drug products, inclusion on formularies and national health plan reimbursement lists, and the procurement of drugs by state agencies. Professor Oberender states that Brussels is writing new laws on these matters. But students of regulation know that there is many a slip between issuing new regulations and actually changing behavior. Will the European Community's actions actually succeed in undermining national preferences and thereby create a truly common market in pharmaceuticals? Absent more solid evidence, I remain unpersuaded.

151

For pharmaceutical companies whose home base is outside the Common Market, there is a further problem. The statistics in Professor Oberender's chapter often make distinctions among companies, depending upon the headquarters location. Will similar distinctions be made in the Common Market's post-1992 regulations? That is, discrimination by government procurement agencies in favor of locally based suppliers and against firms whose home base is another EC nation may be discouraged, but will the even-handedness prevail also for companies having production facilities within the European Community but headquarters outside it? How will EC companies be defined—by the site of their production, their R & D, their place of incorporation, their headquarters location, or what? An EC representative at our session insisted that fears of discrimination against companies whose headquarters are outside the Common Market were groundless and perhaps even paranoid. But in Washington, paranoia is considered a healthy syndrome. If you don't suspect someone is out to get you, you've lost contact with reality.

Another conjunction of facts and assertions in Professor Oberender's chapter puzzled me. He suggests that the average cost of developing a new chemical entity in Germany has recently approached $150 million. Although there is some dispute as to how one does the accounting for such averages, this figure is of the same general magnitude as research, development, and testing costs in the United States. That in itself is surprising, because if I understand Oberender's discussion of West German law correctly, companies there do not have much in the way of efficacy to prove through their clinical trials, whereas in the United States a high level of proof is demanded, except in the case of life-threatening therapies such as those directed toward AIDS. The similarity of R & D costs is surprising, given what appear to be substantial differences in the burden of proof one must sustain.

Professor Oberender attributes the sharp rise in drug research and testing costs to "growing technical obstacles" and to "decreasing marginal returns of R & D activities as a result of the advanced opening of the traditional technological basis." This, too, I find less than intuitive. How can we be experiencing diminishing returns on the supply side at a time when there are great increases in our scientific knowledge of how drugs react with organisms of the human body? Some further explanation seems necessary. I suspect the answer lies more in rising requirements for proof of safety and efficacy and in the large number of worthwhile medications already available, making it increasingly difficult to find new drugs that provide a desired therapy more effectively. That is, the obstacles may lie more on the demand side than on the supply side.

Professor Oberender's analysis reveals astonishing differences in the organization of retail pharmacy markets in Europe, for example, in the regulations imposed by national authorities, in the degree of cartelization, and in some of the statistics. Thus, table 5-8 shows the number of retail pharmacies per thousand population to range from 31 in Denmark to 520 in Belgium. Furthermore, table 5-18 reveals sizable differences in the market shares of over-the-counter drugs. Why these differences exist is not made clear. And, at a deeper level, why is a prescription system needed at all for the consumer to obtain pharmaceuticals? In a recent issue of *Regulation* magazine, Sam Peltzman suggested that the absence of the prescription mandate, letting consumers decide for themselves what entities they would purchase, was not associated with significant differences in national mortality rates. Why aren't European economists asking similar questions about their regulations?

Still more generally, the wide differences among European nations in pharmaceutical industry regulations and institutions present European economists with a marvelous opportunity for learning more about how such institutions affect behavior. The diverse states of the United States and the provinces of Canada also exhibit large differences in formulary listing, cost reimbursement, generic substitution, malpractice liability, and other regulations affecting drug prescription and dispensing, and as such, they provide a kind of natural experiment for analyzing how such differences matter. This possibility has been exploited in richly revealing studies by Paul Gorecki, James McRae, and Francis Tapon in Canada and by Allison Masson, Robert Steiner, Mark Hurwitz, and Richard Caves in the United States. From some of the references in Oberender's chapter, it would appear that similar data sources exist in Europe. I urge European industrial organization economists to undertake comparable statistical analyses. From them, we may learn both the consequences of diverse regulations and whether changes in EC rules are having a material effect.

To sum up, Professor Oberender's chapter shows that there are large differences in pharmaceutical industry institutions among the EC nations, that many problems remain to be solved as the European Community moves toward 1992, and that many of these problems have not been thoroughly investigated by European economists. As always, much remains to be done before we can say that we really understand the situation.

A Commentary by Michael Hodin

The key question that needs to be asked is, What form of public policy is required to allow innovations of medicine to continue in Europe and, indeed, everywhere? We need a basic public policy that provides for innovations in new heart drugs, improved antibiotics, a cure for AIDS, and so forth. As innovation occurs worldwide— throughout Europe, the United States, and Japan—specific policies in the process of the integration of the European market are under consideration. The first policy issue is pricing. Nothing is being done in the European market with respect to the diversity of pricing throughout the twelve countries: twelve different countries have their own levels of pricing as a result of different levels of reimbursement. As a result of these differences in drug prices in Europe and the free movement of goods and services, a condition of "parallel trade" arises. That is, prices in Greece, for example, where reimbursement levels are very low, may be very low too. Germany and the United Kingdom have higher reimbursement pricing and higher drug prices.

A Pfizer antiarthritic pill might be reimbursed at roughly 30 cents in Greece and in the United Kingdom at a dollar. A firm in London could buy the product in Greece and distribute it in London at some price between 30 cents and a dollar, making money off the differential. This process, if left unabated, would obviously result in all drug products going to Greece and selling at Greek levels. This sort of parallel trade could cause a very serious problem within Europe and elsewhere.

Registration is another issue. The European Community might allow companies and innovators various routes to registration: a European "FDA," as it were, in Brussels; national registration; or mutual recognition.

The preference for more than one option, a policy route offered in a variety of areas, gives the maximum amount of flexibility and provides the greatest amount of opportunity for continued innovation in pharmaceuticals.

Essential to continued innovation in pharmaceuticals is patents. A great deal is going on in this area, and soon we will have what we refer to as "patent term restoration." When a researcher thinks he has discovered a new and useful drug, he files for a patent. The patent clock starts ticking. Under current U.S. law, that patent clock runs during the regulatory approval process, which may take anywhere from eight to twelve years.

Europeans, however, are considering giving back some of that time otherwise lost during the regulatory approval process. The details of this plan are still to be worked out, but it is a very positive development for encouraging continued innovation.

Mr. Oberender's chapter alluded several times to patent innovation. In the main, I believe, he alluded positively to innovation, but once he raised the question of the appropriate continued use of patents in the context of competition.

I have two points to make in response. First, if we want continued innovation, we need very strong patent policies, including patent term restoration.

Second, competition in the pharmaceutical area works quite differently from competition, for instance, in vacuum cleaners. Patents conjure up the notion of monopoly. In fact, though, in virtually any therapeutic product category, and for virtually any product save the absolute miracle discovery, any new product will be competing with a range of other products already on the market.

If twenty oral antibiotics are on the market and a new one with an incremental benefit is developed, it still has to compete with the twenty already on the market. Competitive factors, therefore, continue to operate. (Obviously, if someone found a cure tomorrow for AIDS, that would be a unique situation and one in which competition in this context would not prevail.) Of course, the price regulations that exist throughout each of these EC member states, except for the United Kingdom, which has profit regulation, would apply a kind of competitive pressure there as well.

Many other policies are being considered with application to the internal market in Europe—advertising, promotion, marketing, labeling, and the like. These ideas are being discussed and will probably proceed with some degree of harmonization. The pace at which individual countries will seek to harmonize whatever is done in Brussels is not likely to be fast. One notes, for example, that of the 280 *EC 1992* directives two-thirds have been put forth.

However, only fourteen have actually worked their way through the actual national process. So to go from proposal through Brussels and then to be properly harmonized by individual national government is a process that will take many years in the best of circumstances.

The height of trucks, for instance, is a fairly complicated issue, like pharmaceuticals; one can be extremely skeptical about the degree to which the process will result in a truly harmonized market.

A Commentary by Nancy Johnson

The EC-1992 debate has, without doubt, helped to raise U.S. consciousness about our economic relations with Europe. Debate and

155

action in response to this initiative have helped achieve a proper balance of praise and encouragement for the overall deregulatory effort, coupled with a careful monitoring of developments and their potential impact on U.S. businesses.

Furthermore, both U.S. business and the government have been willing to act forcefully when legitimate interests appear to be threatened. The result has been a healthy dialogue that helps keep both sides of the Atlantic honest.

Developments in Eastern Europe and the prospect of significant new markets there make it even more important for the United States and Europe to maintain this dialogue. Peter Oberender suggests the pharmaceutical industry, for example, will be difficult to penetrate in Europe, but for reasons that have little to do with Europe 1992. As he points out, on-the-ground solutions are needed. In other words, you have to be there to be a player. Du Pont's experience as a multinational company in Europe for some thirty years would support that fully.

At the same time, part of the solution to the fragmented pharmaceutical industry in Europe may lie precisely in initiatives such as EC-1992, with its emphasis on deregulation and harmonization. For the U.S.-based chemical industry, the harmonization of standards and certification of testing procedures are the main issues. We at du Pont believe that much progress has been made in these areas and that Europe is on a positive path there.

Many of us in du Pont also believe that the 1990s may be the decade of Europe. The impact on European economic integration of democracy breaking out all over Eastern Europe can, however, be overstated. These developments—the so-called DDEE, Dramatic Developments in Eastern Europe—seem to change on a daily basis. Nonetheless, new markets and new economic relations are going to be coming soon.

I would also point out that some integration has already been in place for many years—ever since Germany was divided in 1948, East Germany maintained special access to Europe through tariff-free entry into West Germany. As the European Community expanded from its original six members, new special trade relationships developed with the six original countries, with Yugoslavia and Hungary, and with the Lomé Convention countries.

Now, this trend is coming into focus and into fruition with relatively unfettered trade among some twenty-six countries in and near the European region. The 1990s should see the GDP of the core of Europe, the EC member states, grow from about $5 trillion to about $9 trillion.

Clearly, the United States will not be the center of the economic universe in the 1990s, and it would be misguided to think of that region as a market for U.S. products. Any company aspiring to be a global competitor has to stake a claim in Europe. It is the place from which to market to that region and to other important world markets.

Du Pont earns roughly one-third of its total $35 billion in sales in Europe. It is a European firm, albeit with U.S. heritage, or parentage. Its subsidiary headquarters in Switzerland oversees du Pont's sales and investments not only in Europe but also in the Middle East, Africa, Eastern Europe, and the Soviet Union.

Du Pont finds Europe an excellent place to operate in and to export from because European governments show few of the schizoid tendencies that it finds in the United States. They are more pragmatic about export controls, and they do not impose economic sanctions that damage only their domestic business concerns. They also provide more export credit. Moreover, their political leaders are willing to speak on behalf of businesses when they travel to third countries. Therefore, du Pont is there to stay, and looks forward to great prospects in the 1990s.

7

The European Telecommunications Equipment Market

Claude G. B. Fontheim

Most of the political and business leaders of Europe believe that a first-rate telecommunications industry and infrastructure are essential to the economic future of the European Community. Consequently, the European telecommunications market is expanding and changing greatly under the EC policies currently being implemented. These changes are being closely watched by the U.S. telecommunications industry, which has become intent on increasing its share of what appears to be evolving into a more open European market. In order to achieve an integrated market, however, the European Community may resort to a new external toughness—by creating a Fortress Europe. This chapter examines the many changes now under way in telecommunications policy, law, and regulation in the European Community; the American perspective on these changes; and the implications of these changes for U.S.-EC commercial relations.

The U.S. government is still "making up its mind" about the EC-1992 process in general, and EC telecommunications policy in particular, although it has designated the European Community a priority country, pursuant to the Telecommunications Title of the Omnibus Trade and Competitiveness Act of 1988 (see Spiegel and Hammonds 1988). The purpose of this action, however, was to indicate that U.S. telecommunications products and services continue to have limited access to the European market, not to pass judgment on the direction of the European Community's telecommunications reforms. For their part, EC trade negotiators have refused to address the question of market access in the context of the Telecommunications Title. They have instead relegated the question to the GATT Government Procurement Code negotiations, GATT Uruguay Round negotiations, and existing telecommunications forums.

Background

The importance of the international telecommunications market to the United States and Europe cannot be overstated. Global spending on telecommunications equipment increased approximately 7 percent per annum during the 1980s (*London Financial Times* 1989). Total spending increased from $83 billion in 1986 to about $113 billion in 1990. The EC Commission has declared telecommunications a basic infrastructure industry and estimates that it now accounts for 3 percent of the Community's GDP, which is likely to climb to 7 percent by the end of the century. According to figures issued by the U.S. Department of Commerce, U.S. exports to the European Community increased from $788 million in 1988 to approximately $1.2 billion in 1989. EC exports to the United States increased from $370.3 million in 1988 to $384.3 million in 1989. Although a change in the tariff classification system makes for an imperfect comparison between 1988 and 1989, the growing importance of the industry is clear.

The EC market for telecommunications equipment is also expanding. It was already close to $20 billion in 1989 and since then appears to have increased by almost 50 percent. In contrast, the U.S. market increased by only 13 percent during that same period, and the total world market by 34 percent. By 1995, the increase in the EC market is expected to reach 67 percent, in comparison with 23 percent for the U.S. market and 59 percent for the total world market. It is easy to see why U.S. equipment manufacturers want increased access to the European market—they need to retain an adequate share of the international market in order to develop and market successive generations of infrastructure equipment.

American telecommunications companies have come to view trade barriers as their principal problem in most European markets (as in those of Japan, Korea, and Canada). The U.S. industry has thus turned to political means to gain greater access to the markets of Europe, particularly those of France and the Federal Republic of Germany, and to other markets of the leading manufacturing countries. These two developments have sparked commercial and political conflict. Although the United States deregulated its telecommunications market and thus greatly increased competition there, no equivalent effort has been made to liberalize the principal foreign markets (that is, those of Europe and Japan). Many in the United States believe that this has had an adverse effect on the U.S. industry, as is reflected in trade statistics.

In particular, manufacturers would like to retain or capture a substantial share of the international market in switching equipment. Sales of terminal equipment earn smaller margins and are considered "loss leaders" for the sale of related services. To develop the current generation of digital switching equipment reportedly cost each company involved approximately $1 billion. The next generation will cost an estimated $2–2.5 billion. Many in the United States thus believe that the European Community has been willing to liberalize its market for terminal equipment and not for infrastructure equipment in order to protect this market and allow indigenous European manufacturers to earn monopoly profits. The most resistance to liberalization is said to be coming from France and Germany.

The U.S. industry's political efforts to open foreign markets and possibly close the U.S. market were sparked by the declining balance of trade in telecommunications products, especially consumer goods, after the market was deregulated and opened up to foreign competition. The U.S. surplus in these products had fallen from $802.6 million in 1980 to $275 million in 1982 and then plunged to a deficit of $2.6 billion in 1987. Many in the U.S. industry sought support for their strategy in the U.S. Congress because the Reagan administration was thought to be wedded to free-trade policies and reluctant to take tough action. U.S. manufacturers and labor unions first focused their attention on the so-called Japanese onslaught. In response to their efforts, the Reagan administration negotiated a series of market liberalization agreements with Japan. The industry then shifted the pressure for market access agreements to Europe.

The market-oriented sector-specific (MOSS) talks with Japan were initiated in January 1985, after a Reagan-Nakasone summit meeting. These talks produced bilateral agreements, which Japan implemented through various liberalization measures (for example, the certification of U.S. telecommunications products is to be based on tests performed in U.S. laboratories). Although most U.S. manufacturers concede that these agreements have eliminated the formal barriers to entering the Japanese market, some are wondering why there appears to have been little change in the U.S.-Japan balance of trade in telecommunications products.

Soon after initiating the MOSS talks, the United States began a series of less formal fact-finding talks with the governments of Korea, Germany, France, Spain, the Netherlands, Sweden, Italy, and the Commission of the European Communities. U.S. industry and labor leaders were notified that these discussions would be used quietly to apply political pressure on these governments to open their telecommunications markets. Market unification is one of many complex factors that U.S. officials must take into account in their efforts to open European telecommunications markets.

U.S. government policy toward the EC telecommunications market is now largely shaped by the provisions of the Telecommunications Title of the 1988 Omnibus Trade and Competitiveness Act. The Telecommunications Title mandates negotiations between the United

States and priority countries in order to gain increased access for U.S. telecommunications products and services. It also requires trade retaliation against these countries in the event that the United States is unable to enter into such agreements. This mechanism was intended to correct what the U.S. Congress perceived to be an imbalance between an open U.S. system, created by telecommunications deregulation, and the protected markets of most other industrialized countries.

The U.S. trade representative must consider the following criteria in selecting priority countries that deny U.S. companies adequate access to their markets: (1) the nature and significance of the acts, policies and practices that deny mutually advantageous market opportunities to telecommunications products and services of U.S. firms; (2) the economic benefits (actual and potential) accruing to foreign firms from open access to the U.S. market; (3) the potential size of the market of a foreign country for telecommunications products and services of U.S. firms; (4) the potential to increase U.S. exports of telecommunications products and services, either directly or through the establishment of a beneficial precedent; and (5) the measurable progress being made to eliminate the objectionable acts, policies, or practices. The European Community was one of only two priority countries designated under these criteria.

Many in the United States attribute the high level of protection in the European telecommunications market to the procurement policies and standards of the EC countries. But the size of the market and its rate of growth offer enormous potential for increasing U.S. exports of telecommunications equipment, thus making the European Community a prime target under criteria two, three, and four above. Finally, U.S. trade officials have been frustrated in their attempts to open the European telecommunications market through such means as the GATT Agreement on Government Procurement. Under criterion five above, the lack of progress in these continuing negotiations is a reason for designating the European Community.

Consequently, they are now focusing on three other initiatives: (1) the EC-1992 process, in which the U.S. government has sought a "seat at the table"; (2) implementation of the Telecommunications Title of the 1988 Omnibus Trade and Competitiveness Act, under which the European Community has been designated a priority country and is now subject to market access negotiations;[1] and (3) renegotiation of the General Agreement on Tariffs and Trade Agreement on Government Procurement (Government Procurement Code), in which U.S. negotiators are seeking to extend the disciplines of the code to European telecommunications administrations (TAs).

161

The European Community's plan for implementing the EC 1992 program in the telecommunications sector was set forth in the 1987 Green Paper on the Development of the Common Market for Telecommunication Services and Equipment (Commission of the European Communities 1987, 1988a; Goldberg 1988). The Green Paper was to be the basis for unifying the European market for telecommunications and computer services and equipment. It was widely believed that the European Community needed to strengthen its telecommunications infrastructure in order to achieve an EC-wide market for goods and services and to make the European economies more competitive.

The stated purpose of the Green Paper was to start a "common thinking process" and thus to be the basis for new policies, laws, and regulations that would govern the integration of Europe's telecommunications industries. Its authors endeavored to identify and analyze common positions and objectives and to agree on the means for achieving such objectives. They gave special attention to the external problems posed to all member states by the rampant evolution of the international telecommunications market. To resolve these problems, the Green Paper recommended following the changes in Europe's telecommunications regulatory scheme:

• Telecommunications administrations (TAs) should retain their rights to monopoly provision of the network infrastructure and the provision of certain basic services. Value added services will be competitive, and the TAs will be able to join in that competition.

• TAs should equip the providers of competitive services with an interconnect capability.

• A competitive, European market for terminal equipment should be accelerated.

• Regulatory and operational functions of the TAs should be separated.

• A common set of standards should be established by a newly created European Telecommunications Standards Institute (ETSI).

The European Community has thus embarked on an ambitious program of reforming its telecommunications market at the same time that the United States has launched an aggressive campaign to influence the telecommunications policies of foreign governments (and thereby increase access for U.S. exports).

Trends in U.S.-EC Telecommunications Trade

The recent trends in U.S. telecommunications trade have by no means been entirely negative. The U.S. trade deficit in telecommunications equipment remained relatively stable in 1988, at about $2.6 billion.[2] That year witnessed the smallest annual increase since the beginning of the deficit in 1983. Perhaps more important, the rate of U.S. export growth had increased from 13 percent in 1987 to 25 percent in 1988. At the same time, the rate of import growth had declined from 19 percent in 1987 to 15 percent in 1988.

The U.S. trade deficit in telecommunications equipment fell an additional $83 million during the last half of 1989, in comparison with the same period for 1988. If this pattern continues, it will be the first annual decrease since 1983. The rate of export growth continued in 1989, increasing to 27 percent, while the rate of import growth slipped to 13 percent.

Although the United States maintains a surplus in its telecommunications equipment trade with the European Community, it runs an overall deficit because of the unfavorable balance in its trade with Japan, Canada, Hong Kong, Korea, Singapore, and Taiwan. The bilateral balance of trade with the European Community is not a criterion for setting priorities for negotiations pursuant to the Telecommunications Title, which now shapes U.S. telecommunications trade policy. Many in the United States view the German telecommunications market as both the most impenetrable and potentially the richest market among the EC member states. In 1988, Germany's market for telecommunications equipment (including fiber optics) was $7.5 billion, compared with $6.3 billion in 1987. The rate of growth slowed in 1989, but was still close to $7.8 billion. This market is expected to experience continued growth up to 1992, at an average annual rate of approximately 5 percent (and should amount to $8.8 billion by the end of this period).

The Bundespost (Germany's telecommunications authority) accounted for approximately two-thirds of all telecommunications purchases in Germany in 1988. Its total investment in 1989, according to its official budget, was $11 billion; $4.5 billion of this amount was invested in telecommunications equipment and fiber optics. Access to Bundespost procurement is thus extremely important to U.S. telecommunications equipment manufacturers.

Germany's principal equipment manufacturer, Siemens, has a close procurement relationship with the Bundespost. Siemens has greatly expanded its international operations, primarily through acquisitions, which have placed it in a strong position throughout Europe and in North America.

Germany manufactured $8.7 billion worth of telecommunications equipment in 1988. Of this amount, approximately 37 percent was exported. German imports of telecommunications equipment from the United States amounted to $254 million in 1988. Although the Bundespost has no official policies favoring German manufacturers, U.S. industry and government officials believe that in practice it has an overwhelming preference for German manufacturers, wherever possible. They are also worried about the international expansion of European manufacturers and about their own ability to compete in the long run if those manufacturers have the benefits of a protected home market (including the monopoly profits that derive from such protection).

To cite one example, Siemens acquired most of IBM's Rolm telecommunications unit in December 1988. The remainder of Rolm Telecommunications was folded into a joint venture between IBM and Siemens. This marked a retreat by a substantial American competitor from the international telecommunications market and a significant advance for Siemens in its efforts to expand internationally, particularly in the United States. Also in 1988, Siemens launched its first attempted hostile takeover, of Plessey PLC, in tandem with Britain's General Electric Company. In addition, it acquired France's IN2 and Bendix Electronics.

In contrast to the German market, the British market has changed considerably in the past five years after being privatized by the Thatcher government. Up to 1984, British Telecommunications was a public utility (an official telecommunications authority) and had a statutory monopoly on domestic telecommunications. Cable and Wireless, another government-controlled company, handled the international network. Cable and Wireless has been allowed to compete with British Telecom by establishing Mercury Communications as an independent domestic network. British Telecom itself was privatized and is now a publicly owned corporation.

U.K. investment in telecommunications network equipment is currently $5.8 billion per year. Many in the United States consider the British market to be the most open of the large European markets. British Telecom has, however, maintained a close relationship with the indigenous British telecommunications equipment manufacturers: General Electric of Britain, Plessey PLC, Thorn EMI, STC, and Pye. Although British Telecom is a privatized entity, systems are generally purchased through negotiation, in accordance with the EC procurement guidelines. U.S. equipment is generally purchased at the module and subsystem level. U.S. manufacturers hold approximately 30 percent of the U.K. import market (in contrast to 12.7 percent in Germany).

Legal and Regulatory Reform in European Telecommunications

Many directives arising from EC 1992 apart from those dealing specifically with telecommunications will affect U.S. companies operating in or exporting to Europe. Directives are binding on the EC member states and must be implemented through enabling legislation passed in each of the member states. Directives regarding such matters as competition policy and intellectual property protection will obviously affect the European telecommunications market and U.S.-EC trade in telecommunications equipment. This chapter, however, deals principally with the series of directives and other measures directed specifically at telecommunications products. These directives may, depending on how they are implemented, have a substantial effect on commercial relations between the United States and the European Community.

The EC action plan for the development of an information services market, which has been adopted by the EC Commission, is intended to promote the use of advanced information services within the Community (*Journal of the European Community* 1988). This action plan provides for the funding of pilot and demonstration projects. The EC Commission has also decided to make more uniform the standards governing information technology and functional specifications for the services offered over the public telecommunications network for the exchange of information and data. The proposed directive on trade in electronic interchange systems would be the first step in standardizing electronic data interchange among users in business, industry, and government (*Journal of the European Community* 1987). These actions regarding telecommunications services will indirectly affect Europe's telecommunications equipment market.

The EC Commission has made a public recommendation to the member states that the TAs coordinate the introduction of pan-European cellular digital land-based mobile communications in the EC. The Council has also approved a directive requiring member states to reserve certain frequency bands for this purpose (*Journal of the European Community* 1987b).

Certain EC directives, if they are enacted and fully implemented, will directly and fundamentally change the European market for telecommunications equipment. These directives are discussed below.

Procurement Procedures in Telecommunications. The proposed directive on public procurement in the field of telecommunications

(Commission of the European Communities 1988b) would, for the first time, take an important step toward opening procurement of the European TAs (Commission of the European Communities 1988b). This proposed directive mandates more open procedures for procurement within the European Community and allows the TAs flexibility in their method of procurement. Firms established entirely outside the Community would be prohibited from participating. As mentioned previously, the domestic content requirements of this directive would obviously restrict access for U.S. exporters.

This directive will force the most entrenched TAs (such as the Bundespost) out of their closed procurement procedures. This may be a first step toward a greater opening, perhaps even accession to the Government Procurement Code. Whether the directive will go far enough to satisfy the requirements of the Telecommunications Title of the 1988 trade act remains to be seen. This will depend, in part, on how the U.S. trade representative construes the standard that "priority foreign countries should agree to provide "mutually advantageous market opportunities" for trade in telecommunications products and services. It will aso depend on what the U.S. trade representative hears from the U.S. telecommunications industry regarding its ability to compete effectively in the European market.

The procurement directive states that "any offer may be rejected when more than half of the price offered represents the value of products or services performed outside the Community." It does not require the rejection of these "non-Community offers," but grants a 3 percent price advantage to competing "Community offers."

EC trade officials argue that local content requirements and price preferences are common in public procurement law and that the U.S. industry benefits from similar preferences under U.S. law. "Buy America" laws require 50 percent local content and provide a 6 percent price preference on some government purchases. But the U.S. industry does not benefit from this local content requirement to the same extent as European manufacturers do because most procurement of telecommunications equipment in the United States is in the hands of private entities (principally the regional holding companies, or RHCs).

European TAs may choose between open, restricted, and negotiated procedures for making procurement decisions. The EC Commission has stated that "it would not be a great surprise if the open procedure were mainly used for purchasing standard off-the-shelf items and the negotiated procedures were applied in the cases of complex and sensitive projects." Because most network products are complex systems that have to be custom-made, most tenders will be handled according to the negotiated procedure. Many in the U.S. industry are concerned that the directive does not apply stricter limits on the use of the negotiated procedure and does not favor competition more strongly. As a result, they fear that too many tenders will be excluded from the competitive process that this directive is intended to promote.

The procurement directive also includes the following provisions:

• European, rather than national, standards will be used where they exist.

• Reciprocal access to procurement opportunities must be negotiated in non-EC countries.

• The Commission of the European Communities favors specific remedies for injured firms (these remedies would be implemented by the member states).

The procurement directive was to go into effect by December 31, 1989. Once the directive is approved, implementation may be a problem, because previous reforms in this area have been widely ignored by the EC member states. An additional directive covering means of redress is to be issued in the near future.

Competition in Telecommunications. The terminal equipment directive (*Journal of the European Community* 1988c) incorporates several principles that are vital to market liberalization.

1. Transparent technical specifications and type approval. The preamble to the terminal equipment directive requires member states to adopt transparent procedures for type-approval and technical specifications. Member states are called upon to formalize and publish such specifications and type-approval rules and to provide notice of such new regulations in draft form. The preamble also states that the monitoring of type-approval specifications and regulations cannot be entrusted to competitors in the terminal equipment market in view of the obvious conflict of interest.

Responsibility for preparing type-approval specifications and regulations must be assigned to a body independent of the operator of the network (the TAs) and of any other competitor in the market for terminal equipment in order to eliminate the conflict of interest. Such conflicts are inherent in the regulatory systems of most member states today. The commission did, however, provide for a two-and-a-half-year transition period for the implementation of these rules.

2. Exclusive rights prohibited. Member states are directed to ensure that no special or exclusive rights are granted to any public or private body for the importation, marketing, connection, or maintenance of terminal equipment. Measures must be taken (for example, the introduction of draft legislation) no later than three months after the effective date of this directive. This prohibition is based on the premise that such grants of special or exclusive rights are contrary to the purposes of the European Community's agreement on competition and that such grants of special or exclusive rights are inherently anticompetitive. The preamble to the terminal equipment directive acknowledges that the European market is governed by a system that allows competition to be distorted. This constitutes an infringement of the competition rules laid down by the Treaty of Rome.

3. Connection to the network: termination points. The preamble to the terminal equipment directive emphasizes that access to the network must be available at the network's "termination points." To ensure that users will have access to the terminal equipment of their choice, it is necessary to know and to make transparent the characteristics of the termination points of the network to which the terminal equipment is to be connected. Member states must see that the characteristics of such termination points are published so that users will have access to these termination points.

The requirements regarding termination points are somewhat similar to the so-called network information disclosure obligations placed on telecommunications carriers in the United States. The Federal Communications Commission requires the carriers to publish such information regarding new or changed services that could affect the connection or interoperation of customer premises equipment (CPE) and the carriers' network services. This requirement reflects the need for compatibility between terminal equipment and network equipment.

In the United States, carriers are required to make available information regarding deployment, availability, pricing, and other factors related to new or revised services, in addition to providing the related technical information. CPE manufacturers require such information because of the interdependence between the equipment and the telecommunications services with which it is used.[3] The necessary information must be made available reasonably in advance of a new or revised service so that terminal equipment can be designed or modified and produced to connect to and interoperate with such services.

An important question regarding this directive is whether U.S. companies, through negotiations, will receive treatment equivalent to that afforded EC companies. The directive sets out schedules for submitting drafts of technical specifications, including network termination characteristics and type-approval procedures, to the commission.

The definition of "termination points of the network" is of particular concern to the U.S. industry. The Federal Communications Commission has adopted a policy requiring the termination points to the network for all services to be at the interface with the transmission facility. In allowing customer equipment to be directly connected to analog services as well as to all present and future digital services, this policy has given rise to an intensely competitive and highly innovative CPE market in the United States. Although users in most EC member countries can choose much of the analog equipment used with telecommunications services, the digital equivalents of such equipment (digital data sets) are provided almost exclusively by the monopoly TA as a part of the regulated service.

The directive now requires customers to connect to digital services through TA-provided devices located on their premises; they are not allowed to choose the device for direct connection to digital transmission facilities. In the view of the U.S. industry, this severely restricts competition in the digital equipment and systems markets and inhibits innovation in the terminal equipment utilized with digital services. In contrast, the equipment used with digital services is provided by the customer. Various features and capabilities of the available equipment enable users to manage and control "private" data communications networks (consisting of user-provided equipment and regulated transmission services). Much of this equipment was developed so that it could be used within integrated network management systems that give users end-to-end control of all aspects of their private data communications networks and thus enable them to operate their businesses more efficiently. Many of these networks are becoming international in scope and must interconnect user locations within both the United States and foreign countries.

Before integrated solutions could be applied to an international network (encompassing the United States and Europe, users in the European Community would have to be able to use equipment that provides an interoperational capability. These users would also have to be able to select and directly connect equipment of their choice. Procompetitive legislation governing terminal equipment appears to have been enacted in the United Kingdom. In part because of the pressure of U.S. business concerns, Germany is adopting legislation requiring the deregulation of terminal equipment. Although France and Italy seem to be dragging their feet, it is believed that they will soon attempt to carry out the provisions of the directive. Several other countries, including Belgium and Italy, have reportedly petitioned the EC Commission requesting an extension of the implementation schedule outlined in the terminal equipment directive. The commission's response to these requests is unknown.

A global approach to technical specifications, testing, and certification. The European Community recently established the European Telecommunications Standards Institute in Nice, France, to take over the standards-setting functions performed by the TAs (*Journal of the European Community* 1985). ETSI's role has not yet been fully defined, however, and it is not clear whether the institute will be independent from the TAs. The U.S. government and industry are concerned that the telecommunications regulatory authority will not be truly separated from the TAs, as called for in the Green Paper.

Telecommunications equipment manufacturers in the United States view the standards resolution as an important market-opening measure. Uniform standards will be welcomed by European and non-European manufacturers alike, who will no longer have to adhere to twelve different sets of standards. The level of transparency of this standards-setting process, however, is still an open question. Another critical issue that needs to be settled is the mutual recognition of type approval. Otherwise, products tested in the United States and found to meet European standards will have to be reapproved in the European Community.

Standardization of information technology. The European Community has also established EC standards for information technology systems and functional specifications for information and data services provided over public telecommunications networks (*Journal of the European Community* 1987c). These standards do not apply specifically to telecommunications equipment, but to equipment (principally computers and "peripherals") and software that are linked to the telecommunications network.

Information technology is defined as "systems, equipment, components, and software required to ensure retrieval, processing, and storage of information . . . which generally requires the use of electronics or similar technology." The objective is to promote the preparation and application of standards throughout the European Community that are deemed necessary to ensure that information and data will be exchanged and that systems will be interoperable, with a view to expanding the market for member states' products and services. The decision covers private information technology systems as well as services offered over the public network (value-added services).

This council decision calls for the following measures:

• Priority standards should be determined on a continuing basis.

• European standards institutions and specialized technical bodies should be required to establish European standards or prestandards.

• The application of these standards and specifications should be facilitated by coordinating member states' verification and certification of conformity.

• European standards and international standards should be referred to in public procurement orders of the member states valued at $115,000 or more.

Mutual recognition of type approval for telecommunications terminal equipment. The proposed directive on mutual recognition of type approval for terminal equipment would establish standards for information technology and telecommunications (*Journal of the European Community* 1986). This proposal also requires that EC standards conform with international standards to the extent possible.[4] Furthermore, the approval of a product by any member state must be recognized by the rest of the member states.

The type-approval directive is seemingly on its way to being implemented. Efforts are now under way to define a common type-approval process and to prepare for the harmonization and mutual recognition of the required specifications and standards. The European Postal & Telecommunication Authorities (CEPT) has issued two recommendations outlining the procedures for type approval and three standards for CPE type approval, called NETs (Normes Européenes de Telecommunications). In 1988, the responsibility for NETs moved to ETSI, where three more NETs are being formulated.

At this time, all CPE must be approved in EC laboratories. The European Community has, however, agreed to negotiate mutual recognition of approval. The U.S. government is working with the Community to set up a trial involving three laboratories in Europe and three in the United States.

U.S. Industry and Government Perspective

Telecommunications equipment manufacturers in the United States appear to have reached a consensus regarding several principal policy objectives for the European market: (1) reduction of the European content requirement in the public procurement directive, (2) a liberal definition of what constitutes "an EC company," (3) a liberal and transparent type-approval process, (4) acceptance of tests from foreign laboratories for standards purposes, and (5) an open and transparent process for setting standards. A limited definition of what constitutes an EC company might exclude from TA procurement even the most substantial and long-established European subsidiaries of U.S. firms. It might also exclude such European subsidiaries from the process of formulating standards.

U.S. trade officials would not like to give up "something for nothing." Some believe that U.S. telecommunications equipment manufacturers may already be so well established in Europe, or soon will be so that they will be in a position to take full advantage of intra-Europe liberalization without having to negotiate for additional concessions. Nonetheless, many in the U.S. industry are concerned that European operations—whether in manufacturing, research and development, or marketing and distribution—may not confer treatment equal with indigenous European firms.

Many in the U.S. industry view the European Community as the market most deserving of U.S. government action under the terms of the Telecommunications Title. They argue that the Community meets the Telecommunications Title criteria because of the size of its market and the lack of bilateral or multilateral agreements providing for access to this market. By contrast, the government of Japan has entered into several bilateral agreements providing for U.S. access to its telecommunications market. The U.S. government and industry consider no other markets to have more promise in the short term than those of Japan and Europe.

In accordance with the Telecommunications Title, the U.S. government's general objectives in its negotiations are (1) to obtain multilateral or bilateral agreements (or the modification of existing agreements) that provide mutually advantageous market opportunities for trade in telecommunications products and services between the United States and foreign countries; (2) to correct the imbalances in market opportunities resulting from reductions in barriers to the access of telecommunications products and services of foreign firms to the United States market; and (3) to facilitate the increase in U.S. exports of telecommunications products and services to a level of exports that reflects the competitiveness of the U.S. telecommunications industry.

The Telecommunications Title also provides for specific objectives to be pursued in negotiations with priority countries. The following list summarizes these negotiating objectives and the EC acts, policies, and practices to which they would apply:

• National treatment for telecommunications products and services that are provided by U.S. firms. Various EC policies and directives, including the procurement directive with its EC content requirement, discriminate between U.S. and EC telecommunications companies.

• Most-favored-nation treatment for products and services. EC telecommunications policies and directives do not discriminate between the United States and other non-EC telecommunications firms.

• Nondiscriminatory procurement policies for products and services and the inclusion under the Government Procurement Code of all telecommunications products and services. European TAs are not subject to the Government Procurement Code.

• The reduction or elimination of customs duties on telecommunications products. European customs duties on telecommunications equipment have not been raised by the U.S. industry or government as an issue affecting market opportunities in the European Community.

• The elimination of subsidies, violations of intellectual property rights, and other unfair trade practices that distort international trade in telecommunications products and services. Adequate and effective intellectual property protection has generally not been a problem in the European Community.

• The elimination of investment barriers that restrict the establishment of foreign-owned business entities that market such products and services. U.S. telecommunications equipment manufacturers have already invested heavily in the European Community.

• Assurances that any requirement for the registration of telecommunications products that are to be located on customer premises for the purposes of attachment to a telecommunications network in a foreign country and for the marketing of the products in a foreign country should be limited to the certification by the manufacturer that the products meet the standards established by the foreign country for preventing harm to the network or network personnel.

• Transparency of, and open participation in, the standards-setting processes used in foreign countries with respect to telecommunications products. The level of transparency and openness to non-EC companies to the standards-setting process to be administered by ETSI remains to be seen. At present the TAs are both manufacturers and regulators. As a result, the systems are neither open nor transparent.

• Assurance that telecommunications products located on customer premises can be approved and registered by type, and, if appropriate, that procedures will be established between the united States and foreign countries for the mutual recognition of type approvals. The terminal equipment directive provides for liberal type approval, but this directive has not yet been implemented.

• The nondiscriminatory procurement of telecommunications products and services by foreign entities providing local exchange telecommunications services that are owned, controlled, or, if appropriate, regulated by foreign governments. Procurement by the European TAs remains perhaps the principal problem of access to the EC telecommunications market in the view of the U.S. government and telecommunications equipment manufacturers. Coverage under the Government Procurement Code is an objective of U.S. trade negotiators.

The United States has several broad concerns regarding changes in EC telecommunications regulations. In a press release of October 20, 1988, the EC Commission announced a policy of "reciprocity," under which "the community reserves the right to make access to the benefits of 1992 for non-EC firms conditional upon a guaranty of similar opportunities or at least non-discriminatory opportunities in those firms' countries." EC officials view this policy as a means of increasing access for European products and services to foreign markets. They hope to use the inducement of access to what will be the world's largest market as leverage to gain new trade concessions. In the United States, this is considered an unfair tactic because the U.S. telecommunications market was opened unilaterally through deregulation, without insisting on reciprocal trade concessions.

In exchange for making European TAs subject to the Government Procurement Code, European negotiators have asked the United States to make the following concessions: (1) make regional holding companies subject to that code, (2) make procurement by the state governments subject to that code, and (3) make all U.S. federal government procurement of telecommunications subject to that code. U.S. trade negotiators have serious difficulties with the first two demands because RHC procurement is already open (they cite substantial purchases of imported telecommunications equipment by the RHCs as evidence). To impose the Government Procurement Code on the RHCs, they argue, is an unnecessary burden that may, in any case, be politically infeasible. The imposition of the code on state governments raises serious constitutional questions.

U.S. negotiators have few concessions to give regarding access to the U.S. government market for telecommunications equipment. Most telecommunications infrastructure equipment (principally switching, transmission, and media equipment) is purchased in the United States by the regional holding companies, which are prohibited from manufacturing. The market for terminal equipment has been deregulated and has thus been opened to domestic and foreign competition.

The U.S. trade representative requested that the International Trade Commission study EC government procurement initiatives affecting "excluded sectors," including telecommunications. The report therefrom is being used by the government's interagency 1992 task force to develop U.S. government policy.[5] In addition, telecommunications policies of the European Community are in a state of flux, and certain of the telecommunications directives are still under development. Thus the extent to which the EC-1992 process will open the European telecommunications market to non-Europeans remains to be seen.

It now appears to many in the U.S. industry that the European market for terminal equipment will be open to non-European manufacturers. Some concerns remain, however, regarding the terminal equipment market and the regulations for type approval and acceptance of product tests performed outside of the European Community.

The principal concern within the U.S. industry revolves around the European market for infrastructure equipment, which is composed primarily of the TAs. Unless the European TAs can be brought within the scope of the Government Procurement Code, TA procurement is likely to remain by and large closed to telecommunications equipment manufactured outside of the European Community. As a result, non-European manufacturers could lose sales, whereas the European manufacturers would have a long-term competitive advantage because they would continue to earn monopoly profits in their home markets. Such monopoly profits could then be used to finance the enormous development costs of subsequent generations of infrastructure equipment.

The proposed EC directive on telecommunications procurement requires 50 percent domestic content before a telecommunications product can be considered an EC product eligible for procurement by the TAs. This will obviously limit the access of U.S. telecommunications firms to the European market.

Many in the U.S. business community have also expressed concern regarding the efforts of the European Community to redefine the term "EC firm." Pursuant to Article 58 of the Treaty of Rome, free market access is afforded to "companies or firms formed in accordance with the law of a member state and having their registered office, central administration or principal place of business within the community." A move is now under way within EC governing institutions to apply this provision more narrowly than in the past, which would thus limit the access of many U.S.-based firms.

The U.S. government may pursue independent discussions with one or more of the EC member states in order to facilitate a market access agreement with the European Community. The Telecommunications Title imposes statutory deadlines for the completion of these negotiations and provides for trade sanctions in the event that no market access agreement can be reached. On the one hand, the threat of such sanctions may provide the necessary leverage to gain concessions from the European Community; on the other hand, they may simply harden the EC position.

Although the liberalization of the telecommunications market will ultimately benefit the European economy, it may not be able to achieve such openness on its own. Whether the firms based outside Europe will benefit will depend, in large part, on the extent to which their business strategies anticipate the consequences of the reform process and effectively convey their views to European policy makers.[6] The efforts of the U.S. government and industry to engage in a dialogue with the European Community should be helpful (whether or not the Community formally acknowledges the mechanism established by the Telecommunications Title). The Telecommunications Title may, however, limit the flexibility of U.S. trade negotiators and cast too much political attention on these issues, which may make it difficult to achieve a compromise with the European Community.

Trade sanctions against European Community would obviously cause a serious breach in economic relations between the United States and Europe. The European Community would almost certainly retaliate and charge that such action is inconsistent with U.S. GATT obligations (depending on the nature of the sanctions). The result would likely be another intractable trade dispute between the United States and Europe (similar to the disputes over agricultural policies, which seem to defy solution). Although such trade sanctions can be kept in the background as a credible alternative, an all-out effort should be made to achieve an acceptable understanding with the European Community. On balance, the process it is going through should lead to substantial liberalization of the European telecommunications market. Liberalization is a relative term, however. Thus, the extent to which the countries of Europe can overcome the political inclination to retain substantial elements of protectionism in the telecommunications sector remains to be seen.

References

Commission of the European Communities. 1987. "Towards a Dynamic European Economy—Green Paper on the Development of the Common Market for Telecommunications." COM (87) 290, June 30.

———. 1988a. "Towards a Competitive Community-wide Telecommunication Market in 1992—Implementing the Green Paper on the

Development of the Common Market for Telecommunications Services and Equipment." COM (88) 48, February.

―――. 1988b. "Proposal for a Council Directive on the Procurement Procedures of Entities Operating in the Telecommunications Sector." COM (88) 378, October.

Goldberg, H. 1988. "A U.S. Observer's View of the Green Paper." *Telematics* 5 (5).

Journal of the European Community. 1985. "Council Resolution on a Global Approach to Technical Specifications, Testing, and Certification." OJ C 136, June.

―――. 1987a. "Council Decision of 5 October 1987, Introducing a Communications Network Community Program on Trade in Electronic Data Interchange Systems (TEDIS)." No. 87/499/EEC, OJ L285, October.

―――. 1987b. "Council Directive of 25 June 1987, on the Frequency Bands to be Preserved for the Coordinated Introduction of Public Pan-European Cellular Digital Land-Based Mobile Communication in the Community." No. 87/372/EEC, OJ L 196, July.

―――. 1987c. "Council Decision on Standardization with Field of Information Technology." OJ L 36.

―――. 1988. "Directive on Competition in the Telecommunications Terminal Equipment Market." OJ L 181/88, April.

8
Commentaries on
Telecommunications Equipment

A Commentary by Michael Skarzinski

I would like to comment on Claude Fontheim's chapter in the context of Japan, as opposed to the European Community. The U.S. telecom discussions with Japan have fallen into the Section 1377 area; hence, discussions of different parts of the trade act are every bit as animated as discussions with the European Community, even in a different context. The United States has some rather firm ideas and positions on telecom issues with Japan that are important to bear in mind.

If ever an industry were a global industry, telecommunications is one. If ever a technology traveled quickly, here is one. And if nations and corporations have sought to maximize their self-interest, we see it in this industry.

The global telecommunications industry has many suppliers of the actual telecommunications switch equipment. The largest in the world is AT&T; the second largest is Alcatel, which recently bought the ITT Corporation switch business. U.S. companies must grapple with many complex trade issues: acquisitions, antitrust problems, finding the proper size of the company, and defining the role of a large company in the U.S. market. A competitor in the United States with telecommunications as his main business would get a rather jumbled picture of events. It is very difficult to figure out where one is at any given time, to know who is in charge of setting policy and exactly where the industry is headed.

AT&T and other corporations went through divestment in the 1980s and then found that some of the businesses that they thought they were in should be expanded to compete with companies they used to own.

A company created and fashioned in a deregulatory environment, in an area of new technological advances and in an area where certain services were made available, is likely to be extremely competitive and can move very quickly. When you snooze you lose in this game, and it takes a lot of work not only in the research labs and in the marketplace but also in the halls of Capitol Hill, of the executive branch, and of the judiciary to figure out where a company is placed and where that company is headed. And after one knows where his company is in the U.S. market, then he can go compete with European corporations. Things seem better today than they were previously for U.S. producers in this sense: there used to be twelve competitors and now there are fewer, and probably there will be fewer still because of future consolidations. ITT, for example, was subsumed by the Alcatel Corporation.

In determining what difference the nationality of a company makes, we see some preferences played out not simply in the research money and intellectual capital but also in market access. In understanding this, we must also acknowledge barriers to entry into the U.S. market. If, for example, Siemens decided it was in the best interest of its shareholders to buy one of the regional Bell operating companies, it could own only up to 25 percent of that company because of FCC laws that limit foreign ownership. Indeed, British Telecom has complained that since U.S. companies operate freely in the British market, owning cellular phone or paging businesses, British companies should be able to own more than 25 percent or so of American telecommunications firms. Furthermore, how could a corporation like Siemens sell to the U.S. market, to the seven regional Bell operating companies with whom AT&T has an entrenched position with the switch equipment through its historical relationship with these companies that were once an integral part of the AT&T operation?

In conversations about trade relations, the European Community has often been cited as an unfair trader in telecommunications. The European Community as a whole and specific member states pose certain obstacles to U.S. companies selling to these markets. It is a rather large set of background facts against which one begins this conversation. Even a cost accountant would find it difficult to calculate the profits to the Siemens Corporation in selling to the Bundespost certain equipment and services, just the way it would be difficult to calculate those same profits for AT&T from selling certain switches to regional Bell operating companies or providing certain long-distance services. It is a very complicated situation. What, then, can we do about it?

I can only state the U.S. government objectives in the telecom trade discussions both with the EC and with other partners: the U.S. position is that U.S. suppliers should be able to share in the benefits of EC telecom liberalization, just as EC suppliers benefit from U.S. liberalization and the AT&T divestment. Otherwise, EC manufacturers could subsidize their international sales from the high prices they

179

charge in their own domestic market.

The Trade Act allows U.S. trade negotiators to keep trade sanctions as a last resort and to seek an agreement with the EC on mutually advantageous market opportunities. We recognize that the EC is exerting effort in a process that should lead to telecom liberalization. We cannot rely solely on multilateral negotiations under the GATT as the EC would prefer, however, in the hope that it will address all our issues of access to the EC market. Completion of the Uruguay Round with GATT, including renegotiation of the government procurement code, remains the top trade negotiation priority of this administration. Certainly U.S. concerns about access to the EC market may not be adequately addressed in the multilateral negotiation forum. Multilateral procurement, for example, is unlikely to address sufficiently the detrimental effects of government subsidies, nondiscriminatory standards, or extension of the code to telecom sectors of certain countries, such as Greece, Spain, and Portugal, which have not yet acceded to the code. Likewise, the standards code is not likely to be revised to reflect such sector-specific objectives. Moreover, bilateral U.S.-EC negotiations under the telecom title of the Trade Act not only supplement but also support the multilateral negotiations.

The dialogue that we have between the United States and the EC is one approach to opening the procurement of private entities controlled or influenced by governments, and, as such, it is not suitable for the GATT negotiations on the procurement code.

U.S. manufacturers look to the U.S. government to press on every front, whether in bilateral or multilateral negotiations, to provide them the benefits of EC 1992 on terms similar to those of foreign companies' access to the U.S. market. We in the Bush administration seek to ensure that U.S. manufacturers will have the same opportunity to sell in the global marketplace as their European counterparts.

A Commentary by Christian Stoffaés

The French have loved the concept of strategic industry for many centuries. Why is the telecommunications industry a strategic one? I will first say something about being strategic, from the European and especially the French point of view.

Telecommunications equipment is a strategic industry because it is the key to the information economy. We are already in an information economy, since about two-thirds of the working population in modern countries works in information production and processing.

180

What is at stake is the modernization of this information economy. It is industrialization. And, of course, the telecommunications network will be the core infrastructure of the modernization of the information economy. That is why it is strategic. It may not constitute a large part of the GNP—with about $100 billion a year of markets, it is a small share. But it is strategic because it has a role similar to that of the steam engine at the beginning of the industrial revolution. That was not a large part of the GNP, but everything in the economy was shaped around the technology of the steam engine.

First, consider how much telecommunications equipment commands. The industry of telecommunications services, which has already fallen by $1 billion per year, is four times smaller than the equipment market itself. International sales of services have been considered more of an investment than a trade, because selling services abroad means sending people abroad to sell them. Of course, things will change with the integration of the telecommunications network worldwide. Instead of sending people abroad to sell services, you will market them directly from your own country. Thus, very important sectors such as advertising, accounting, broadcasting, financial services, movie making, insurance, and even manufacturing will be exported and made tradable by telecommunications development.

A second reason why telecommunications is strategic is that it is key in the global information technology industries war. In France we have called this concept *"fillaire* electronics." *Fillaire* means integration, and it is clear that telecommunications are increasingly interlinked to computers and other information technologies. Large mainframe computers and large switching equipment are merging and becoming increasingly hard to distinguish.

Telecommunications networks command the links between computers. Of course, the question of the standoff in communications is a key to the compatibility of the computers. Fiber optics, television standards, and consumer electronics—all parts of the information technology industries—are linked more and more closely to terminal equipment.

Telecommunications equipment is a part of this complex of electronic and computer industries and is linked to networks that are still national monopolies. Adding information technology industries and information services together amounts to about $1,000 billion per year.

Telecommunications equipment is also a strategic industry for the United States. It is not by chance that telecommunications equipment has been targeted as a major trade issue by the U.S. government, and as a war by U.S. society and industry in the past years.

It is an area where U.S. industry is still very strong, at least in infrastructure equipment. In terminal equipment Southeast Asia and Japan have taken the lead, but switching equipment and transmission equipment still constitute a stronghold for American technology. There is a very high potential for economic growth, technological innovation, and the deregulation process in the United States.

The idea behind deregulation is to dismantle the vertical integration between telecommunications equipment and telecommunications services. The deregulation process in the United States has important potential gains in technology for American manufacturers, but also potential fragilities, because it opens up the U.S. telecommunications equipment market for competition.

In summary, electronics and information technology development is a strategic industry, and more precisely a strategic complex of industries for the future. But Europe is lagging behind Japan and the United States in this industry, especially in two vital areas—namely, computers and information services, related to computers, microchips, and electronic competence.

The European market is flooded by imports from the United States and increasingly from Japan, and the domestic industry in Europe is largely American. There is one exception to this tragic weakness of Europe in electronic and information technology industry. That is in telecommunications.

In telecommunications equipment, Europe is still in the first ranks, a position it shares with the United States, at least quantitatively. The United States still leads in informatics and computers, but Japan leads in consumer electronics and in chip memories. In robots and in microcomputers, Japan is a challenge to American industry, and the battle is going to be increasingly fierce in the years to come. The field of Europe is to be the battlefield of Japanese and U.S. competition in strategic industries in the 1990s.

The United States already has a trade surplus in telecommunications equipment with Europe. The problem of the deficit of the U.S. balance of trade is not with Europe but with Southeast Asia and Japan. With an increasing surplus in telecommunications equipment between the United States and Europe and an increasing deficit between the United States and Southeast Asia and Japan, the fact that the U.S. administration is focusing upon European telecommunications equipment policy and deregulation is an index that Europe is going to be the battlefield between Japan and the United States.

Europeans believe that the telecommunications equipment industry can be the stronger of the bases for the conquest of lost positions in information technologies and related industries, because it is protected by public procurement. Consider the example of Siemens. Siemens was almost nonexistent in electronics twenty years ago. Now it is very strong in telecommunications, and it is using telecommunications to develop diversification in other areas of electronics. Siemens is becoming a champion of microchips and electronic components, of robots, and of computers. It is divesting from the electric industry, or "strong current," as the technicians would say, to invest in the "weak currents."

Telecommunications equipment is still a fragmented industry compared with high-tech industries such as aerospace and computers. In other words, there are probably too many competitors in the telecommunications equipment industry, and these will be restructured in the coming years. This is owing to the skyrocketing cost of research and development. To develop the next generation of switching equipment will cost tens of billions of dollars of research and development programs, and only a very limited number of manufacturers can do it. We fear that the main victims of this worldwide restructuring will be in Europe. We have several major manufacturers, including Ericsson, Siemens, and IT&T, and smaller ones. If we want to have an idea of what is coming in the restructuring, we just have to look at what happened to the British telecommunications equipment industry, which is fragmented and threatened by acquisitions from abroad.

Finally, there is a fair monopoly effect in telecommunications equipment. Telecommunications is almost a case study of antitrust legislation because it generates enormous scale economies. The dismantling of the Bell System has been a controversy and a good illustration. It is an industry that has to be regulated in order to avoid monopoly effects. In the related industries such as mainframe computers, IBM has been suspected several times in the past two or three decades of abuse of monopoly powers. There have been lawsuits in the United States; there have been lawsuits in the European Community that have finally been abandoned. These lawsuits suggest a suspicion that telecommunications and computers might lead to abuse of monopoly powers, especially by the users of standardization of linkage.

So the argument is that deregulation of telecommunications services should not lead to the creation of monopolies in manufacturing industries. The dismantling of monopolies in one sector—namely, the breaking up of the vertical integration between telecommunications equipment and telecommunications services—should not lead to worldwide monopolies in manufacturing and in technology.

A Commentary by Sidney Topol

This commentary will address three topics: cable and satellite communications, globalization, and East-West trade in telecommunications.

Cable and Satellite Communications. Cable television and satellite communications are both American phenomena. The industry of satellite communications and cable television is no more than fifteen or twenty years old, but the United States has an enormous investment in cable television and satellite communications that goes back to the space program and the initiation of the Communications Satellite Corporation. This program led to Intelsat and to the entire investment made in launching satellites.

Probably one of the most significant outgrowths of the U.S. investment in space has been satellite communications and synchronous satellite communications. A satellite launched 22,300 miles above the equator will rotate in synchronism with the earth, with a fixed antenna. One of the early problems in satellite communications was the concern about distance and voice communications. Today we have symetric communications, with which we are able to send more information in one direction than in another.

Symmetric communications means voice communications, and fiber and digital switches and central offices optimize it. If one person is talking, somebody has got to talk back to him. But in the fields of television and data, satellite communications has been optimal. Tremendous investments have been made in the United States. We took the whole industry, from one-hundred-foot to one-foot antennas. The marriage of satellite communications with cable television created a new industry in the United States. We have 90 million television households in the United States, more than 50 million of which are on cable, and probably three million of which are receiving a signal directly via satellite.

And for better or worse, we have invented the concept of multiple channels, allowing electronic journalism today to make in-depth analyses of various subjects that formerly only print journalists could analyze. So we are concerned that Europe recognize that we have reached economies of scale, of production quantities, and of systems engineering—first coaxial tree and branch systems and now fiber—in this industry. We want to make sure that that market is open to us in Europe, as the terminal market was open when we deregulated here in the United States. We would appreciate a truly open chance to compete, because we think we can compete in price, performance, and standards and of quality.

Early on, Europeans believed that perhaps the cable business would be an entree into an information highway, a two-way information system with banking and shopping. A big effort was made, particularly in the United Kingdom, to have a star switch system using fiber, but it was discovered not to be economically viable. One of the things we learned in the United States is that a system has to be economically viable; it can be subsidized for only so long, but in the end it has to make economic sense. We think we have done that with cable and satellite, and we are very anxious that we be treated fairly in that area as we go forward.

Globalization. The concept of globalization is one where Europe and the United States can completely agree. The agreement is, Don't sell the Europeans short on consumer electronics. For example, Thompson and Phllips between them have a tremendous market share, particularly since Thompson bought RCA and GE and bought 22 percent of the market share in the United States. The Europeans can be very proud of these two companies in their globalization process. We find that globalization is two-sided.

People discovered some years ago a global market for certain products—particularly high-tech, electronic, consumer telecommunications satellite products, including cable television. There is a sort of uniformity. Unfortunately, twenty-five years ago we damaged color TV standards, in the cases of NTSC and Pal. But over the years the standards issues have become less important than the manufacturing and marketing issues. A TV set can be made today with a switch in the back so that it can receive all three; that is fairly cost competitive.

But globalization inherently means foreign direct investment. It is highly unlikely that a company can access a global market from its own country completely, with all its manufacturing, its marketing, its human resources, and its financial resources. Foreign direct investment is the other side of globalization.

What really counts, in Europe as in the United States and in Japan, is that a company set up a complete entity, that is, including research and development and manufacturing. Again, the Europeans should be proud of Thompson and Phillips, who probably have more U.S. content in their color TV sets than Zenith has. In Knoxville, Tennessee, there are roughly 300 engineers and about 5,000 employees; in Briarcliffe, New Jersey, there is a research laboratory. Thompson and Phillips have gotten inside the infrastructure, particularly in the HDTV area, a huge worldwide battle of both production standards and transmission standards.

185

A number of people in the United States are fighting the wrong enemy. Everybody got nervous and became aggressive toward the Japanese. In actual fact, Thompson and Phillips and Zenith represent more than a 50 percent market share in color TV. Thompson and Phillips recognized early that what was needed in the United States was a uniquely American system; Americans were not going to bring HDTV to the United States via satellite, as the Japanese thought was the way to go. The Japanese introduced in the United States a Japanese system led by NHK, a Japanese company. This was a bad strategy. A proper global strategy was to introduce a U.S. system by U.S. engineers, with U.S. trademarks like RCA, GE, Magnavox, and Philco. Such a system needed to meet FCC requirements and to be upward and compatible, or friendly, to cable, satellite, and fiber in the future.

Globalization is, then, a way of life. We in the United States have to understand what an American company is, just as the Europeans are struggling to understand what a European company is. AT&T wants to be known as a European company in the European marketplace, and Thompson wants to be known as an American company here, and all of that is possible.

East-West Trade. The third area I will discuss is East-West trade. I am nervous about the United States using Eastern Europe as a supplier of telecommunications equipment. It is a tremendous opportunity for the United States, but it will require a partnership between government and business and industry. The telephone system in Eastern Europe is a shambles; this is true of the local telephone systems, of the number of telephones per hundred people, and particularly of the long-distance system across Eastern Europe and to the Far East. The Soviets are interested in building a long-distance fiber network of the quality that we would build in the United States or the Europeans would build in Europe, and they have approached us about it. I think this would give us an opportunity to have an immediate impact on the trade balance, if the United States were to do something unique—such as putting together a consortium of manufacturing companies that would be responsible for both the local telephone system and the long-distance fiber system. It should be proposed as something feasible; the hardware installation, operation, and maintenance of a complete American telephone system in Eastern Europe would be financed by the United States. This would require certain modifications of current regulations.

In summary, there is a strong cable television and satellite business in the United States that we would like to bring to Europe.

We understand the globalization process, and we support companies that move in either direction, create complete entities, and become part of the system. We think that the United States should get aggressive in communications equipment in the East European countries; otherwise, Siemens will build a plant in East Germany next week and then the ball game will be over.

A Commentary by Dominique Bocquet

Telecommunications, along with agriculture and financial services, ranks among the few subjects that are high on the GATT agenda and that also raise several systemic questions. So it is important to determine how open the various markets are and to examine more closely some of the points Claude Fontheim has raised.

First, I want to say a word about the European process of liberalizing markets. In fact, the European Community intends to liberalize *all* aspects of telecommunications. This includes not only terminal equipment, but also infrastructure equipment. The liberalization is also aimed at services, but that side of the process is beyond the scope of this workshop.

A guideline on terminal equipment was issued in 1988 and there will soon be one on infrastructure equipment. I want to emphasize that public procurements are one of the main subjects of 1992. The European economy has suffered greatly from market segmentation, especially in the area of telecommunications equipment. The Cecchini report, published in 1987, reminded us that there were no less than eleven producers of telecommunications infrastructure equipment in Europe, whereas in the United States there were only two.

This situation has had an adverse effect on European competitiveness and on Europe's economy. Two problems have been to blame. First, each country of the region had only one producer and therefore faced no competition. Second, producers were not large enough to benefit from economies of scale. Thus we have the drawbacks of concentration without its advantages.

Note, too, that an important decision has recently been made in Brussels concerning telecommunications infrastructure equipment. The European Council has decided to open public procurements to competition in the fields of energy, transport, water supply, and telecommunications. Consequently, contrary to what many in the United States appear to believe, the European Community is not altogether unwilling to liberalize its markets for infrastructure equipment.

With regard to the trade in telecommunications equipment, Claude Fontheim pointed out that deregulation in the United States created a kind of unilateral opening of the market. It should be added that the main imports consisted of terminal equipment, not switching equipment. Moreover, most of this terminal equipment came from Japan and East Asia, not from Europe. So if there was a natural opening of the American market, Europe did not benefit from it.

But, as Fontheim also mentioned, this situation cannot deprive Europe of the, I would say, honor of being selected a priority country under the provisions of the 1988 trade act. The focus of debate should now be on the way the deregulation is carried out in Europe. There is no serious disagreement between the United States and Europe on terminal equipment, and I thank Fontheim for suggesting that the 1988 European guidelines satisfy the main U.S. criteria for an open market.

An issue that needs to be discussed further, however, concerns the technical specifications for connection to the network. It is true that, in the American approach, public authorities have only to make sure there is no "harm to the network," whereas the Europeans are a bit more demanding; they want the international standards of inter-operability to be implemented. There is some disagreement on this point.

On the one hand, you could say that the Europeans are being a bit restrictive; on the other hand, many in Europe fear that private standards could also limit access to the market. For instance, a large company could develop noninterworking systems to prevent smaller competitors from entering the market. I think this is the basis for the European position.

Another slight difference between the American and the European points of view has to do with the special rules for public procurement. The Americans argue that only public authorities should be submitted to these rules, according to the provisions of the Buy American Act. But the Europeans say that every company with special rights or a monopolistic position should be submitted to these rules and that the European directives on public procurements should also apply to companies such as British Telecom, although it is a private corporation.

The European argument is based on two factors. First, these firms are actually retaining monopoly positions and they are not operating in a completely competitive context. Second, many of them have special connections with equipment producers. So this is yet another matter that should be discussed in the GATT negotiations.

A Commentary by Harmon Schweitzer

Claude Fontheim's chapter gives a fairly clear description of the differences between the telecommunications industry in the European Community and the United States. Without question, we are in an extremely competitive global market. We face a large and increasing development cost to stay in this business, and our equipment customers have also made a large investment in their embedded base. Whether they are a public or a private enterprise, they need to continue to increase that embedded base and to ensure its consistency and stability. Both in the United States and in Europe, our customers are fundamentally local monopolies for regulated local service.

On both sides of the Atlantic the public administrations have been historically linked to their suppliers. Any vendor in this business has to find a way to retain or increase his market share. All of us need volume to recover the immense development cost to stay in the business. The alternative is to consolidate with other vendors to achieve the same effect, as we have seen on the European continent.

The public telegraph and telephone companies of the world, however, must find a way to provide additional value-added services to their business customers and sooner or later to their end customer, in addition to sustaining their basic telephone service. To me, this is the most important issue concerning the effect of 1992. If in fact the local monopoly is maintained, then the vendor who can provide the equipment will enable the Postal, Telegraph, and Telephone authorities (PTT) or the regional holding company to increase its revenue stream beyond a stable embedded base. That is really the competition under discussion. It is very difficult for any telecommunications service provider to change immediately the supplier that he has been acquainted with and has done business with over a period of years. I believe that deregulation or privatization puts greater pressure on the PTTs to generate their own revenue stream. In spite of their local monopoly position—whether they are a private or a public company—they will be in competition with each other. The pure competitive nature of the PTT business will, I think, give the best supplier the opportunity to meet those needs.

I do not believe that vertical integration in and of itself is bad, but I am confused that the argument is used on both sides of the Atlantic to make the same point. Either we seen the benefits of vertical integration, or we do not. We cannot argue against it when we would like to have market entry and argue for it when we would like to have market protection. I believe the U.S. suppliers really desire opportunities similar in openness to what foreign corporations receive when they enter the U.S. market: that is, equal access to the local networks to allow them to provide value-added services, uniform and reasonable standards and testing procedures that enable free and open competition, and, finally, limited practical definitions of corporate structure and local content. For instance, our strategy in Europe has been to attract local participation and local European partners because we need people close to the marketplace who can contribute to the growth of the business. As for local content, three significant decimal places worth are not really the issue here. I know of no major company that has not put significant investment into the countries they are committed to working within. To me, local content is just a fact of doing business. I don't believe a percentage needs to be applied. The marketplace will define the amount.

Finally, continued discussion among the parties is always the best solution. From my company's perspective, it truly is a global marketplace. It is not only a strategic challenge but a strategic imperative to participate in that global marketplace. I think the view of this approach is similar to that of the European Commission. We recognize that there will always be a close relationship between an incumbent supplier and a telephone administration, whether it is public or private. Any company that wants to displace the established supplier, then, has to be extremely good and has to offer substantial inducements.

I believe that we should continue the multilateral and bilateral discussions on trade and that significant progress has been made. I believe the GATT process would be a fine approach. The real key here is whether we believe another country has reacted in a protective fashion.

Deregulation has proved a valuable lesson in the United States, where it has increased competition. Our market share has also suffered as a result of deregulation and other industry changes, however.

A Commentary by Robert G. Rogers

My fascination with the subject of Claude Fontheim's chapter—the EC-U.S. conflict over trade in telecommunications equipment—is with the premises that normally attend its discussion. After all, how this conflict is finally resolved is going to hinge on how well these argumentative building blocks are defined and agreed upon. What's needed, therefore, is to set the stage correctly and fairly.

The Americans, as plaintiffs, and the Europeans, as defendants, need front-row, center seats—not slanted views from the corner, balcony box of a particular competitor. If we set the stage in this way, we will recognize some of the dangerous assumptions we are making on this side of the Atlantic. Let me list some that have occurred to me.

We assume the Bell System breakup opened the floodgates to foreign competition in this country and thereby gave us our telecommunications equipment trade deficit. Yet it is simply not so! In fact, our telecommunications equipment trade deficit reached its peak in the two-year period preceding divestiture. Since divestiture, the deficit has been reduced each year.

We tell ourselves the Bell System breakup completely opened the U.S. market for infrastructure equipment—particularly central office switching systems. But at most, it opened—if, indeed, "opened" is the right term—75 to 80 percent of this market. The bulk of the remaining market share, a market share every bit as significant as that of any European PTT, continues to be supplied on a captive basis by the manufacturer—the *one* manufacturer—that is vertically integrated with the service providers who make up this remaining market share.

We are being somewhat presumptive in our rush to demand that others adopt the kind of industry restructuring Judge Greene imposed on us. Six years after the fact, according to a recent profile of Judge Greene in the *New York Times*, the idea of the Bell System breakup is as unpopular a decision in this country as it has ever been. Misery may love company. But just because *we* got a divorce—and apparently are not happy that we did—does not justify our imposing one on our friends and neighbors.

It is misleading to imply telecommunications equipment is telecommunications equipment is telecommunications equipment. It is not. At a minimum, we should distinguish terminal equipment from network equipment. Otherwise, we will be misleading both ourselves and our listeners and will reach erroneous, oversimplified conclusions.

We love to paint the picture of Bell Atlantic, Ameritech, and the other Bell operating companies (BOCs) backing their trucks to the piers of ocean freighters to pick up foreign-made central office switching systems. That is wrong. What the BOCs buy here, virtually without exception, is researched, developed, manufactured, and sold here—in America, by Americans.

The word *export* is something of an oxymoron in the business of selling central office (CO) switching systems. For a variety of legitimate reasons—ranging from protection against currency fluctuations for the manufacturer to stable sources of supply for the customer and national security—local manufacture is a reality of the central office switch business. Telephone service providers in the world's large industrialized nations simply do not import central office switching systems to any appreciable degree. Nowhere is this truer than in the United States. Even the fledgling governments of Eastern and Central Europe appear intent on having homegrown sources of supply for CO switches. So, if it is exports we are after, fine, but let's recognize the futility of looking to the CO switch business to satisfy this goal.

Also in the oxymoron category is our penchant for applying us-versus-them rhetoric to the central office switching market, a global market that, by most estimates, is quickly whittling down to four, five, or six players. A Northern Business Information analyst, speaking at another EC-92 conference last week, predicted a shakeout to three central office switch makers by the end of the 1990s! Those of us in the central office switching business recognize that we live in one world. It is one market and we are all in it together, everywhere. Us-versus-them thinking just does not fit.

And let's be clear about what we are trying to protect in our discussion of central office switching systems. It is not U.S. manufacturers. Nor is it the U.S. telecommunications equipment manufacturing industry. By conventional measures, there is only one U.S. central office switching system manufacturer. And one company does not an industry make.

We say we want to negotiate, but that we don't want to give up anything—because we might be giving up "something for nothing." If this is the case, then I suddenly realize why my mail is so filled with ads for how-to-negotiate tapes, books, and seminars. The nation's bargaining skills have apparently gone the way of its youngsters' Scholastic Aptitude Test scores. Agreements do not exist without consideration. There is no free lunch. Not even for bullies.

We say we have done nothing to seek reciprocity for the trade concessions inherent in deregulation and divestiture. How soon we forget! We forget the Federal Communications Commission's leadership, which, not long after divestiture, did some effective—and arguably jingoistic—saber-rattling over the FCC's ability to drag its feet on the terminal equipment registration applications of companies that come from certain countries. Likewise, we forget the FCC backed all of official Washington into a corner by adopting rules to compel telephone companies to reveal the nationality of the firms from which they bought central office switching systems. The telcos, you may recall, told the FCC in no uncertain or respectful tones what it could do with its rules. Ultimately, an embarrassed White House—through its Office of Management and Budget—told the FCC likewise.

Needless to say, I feel compelled to offer some personal observations in response to Claude Fontheim's rather damning claims about the role of my company's parent in the German market for central office switching systems.

First, to talk of the Bundespost is inaccurate and telling. The telecommunications service provisioning arm of what was the Deutsches Bundespost has been essentially privatized and is now known as DBP Telekom. To disregard this point belies either an awareness or appropriate appreciation of the tremendous liberalization effort that has occurred in the German telecommunications industry.

Fontheim's chapter subtly condemns my company's parent on two unconnected counts: having a "close relationship" with the Bundespost, and expanding internationally, "primarily through acquisitions." What can I say? All right, I admit it. The Bundespost—now DBP Telekom—is a good customer, and we try to be as responsive as possible to it, as well as to all other of our customers. Insofar as expanding internationally is concerned, I merely commend readers to recognize the incredibly high stakes involved in staying competitive in the central office switching systems business and, thereby, to recognize that the markets for such systems are truly global. We are doing what we have to do—and what all other remaining central office switch makers are doing—staying in the game.

Fontheim states that U.S. industry views the Bundespost as having an overwhelming preference for German manufacturers, most notably Siemens. Well, yes, the Bundespost apparently does have such a preference. But so do the Bell operating companies and other U.S. telecommunications service providers have a commensurate preference for American-made central office switching systems. Let there by no mistake: U.S. telephone companies do *not* buy foreign-made central office switching systems. Not at all! The truth of the matter is that about 33 percent of the Bundespost's lines are served by central office switching systems installed by a "German" central office switch manufacturer that was owned lock, stock, and barrel—until a few years ago—by a U.S. company. Siemens switches serve about 57 percent of the Bundespost's lines.

The benefit Siemens might enjoy, *arguendo*, from a protected home market is no greater—indeed, it may pale in comparison—than the commensurate benefit the U.S. central office switching system manufacturer reaps by virtue of the apparently sole-source supply arrangement it has with its vertically integrated telecommunications service provisioning entity, the dominant provider of long-distance services in the United States.

Rolm neither manufactures central office switching systems, nor is a factor in the international market for such equipment. Fortheim's discussion of Siemens's acquisition of Rolm, therefore, is irrelevant and immaterial to the subject at hand.

There is no question that U.S. economic growth and the welfare of U.S. citizens hinge on the success of our government's efforts to eliminate and reduce unfair foreign trade barriers. The extent to which the government is successful in this quest with regard to telecommunications equipment, however, will depend to a large extent on its going to the bargaining table willing to bargain and committed to making proposals based on a 20–20 perspective of the realities of the central office switching systems market and the dynamics of the U.S. market for this kind of equipment.

PART THREE
Services

9
Telecommunications and Information Services

Jonathan D. Aronson

The June 1985 EC White Paper, "Completing the Internal Market," is the focal point of Europe's plan to usher in a new age of vitality, marked by the creation of a single, integrated market by December 31, 1992 (Commission of the European Communities 1987b). The White Paper identified almost 300 measures needed to remove remaining barriers, and it established a timetable for their implementation. As of February 1990, 184 of these measures had been adopted by the European Community's Council of Ministers (Commission of the European Communities 1989b). The twelve members of the European Community have pledged to harmonize existing national laws and policies and have agreed to transfer a significant portion of their regulatory and policy authority to the European Community from the member states. The program was bolstered when the Single European Act entered into force on July 1, 1987, streamlining the European Community's decision-making process. For the first time most legislation could be passed by a majority vote of member states. Unanimity was no longer required (U.S. Department of State 1988: 2). Taken together these events amounted to "nothing less than the redistribution of sovereignty between Brussels and the members states (Goldman 1988: 24). Even these momentous events were upstaged by the democratic revolution that swept through Eastern Europe in 1989, which vastly complicated the situation and heightened the need to consider the implications of the fast-paced changes transforming the European economic and political landscape.[1]

This chapter focuses on the implications of European unification for Atlantic relations in the area of telecommunications and information services (Aronson and Cowhey 1988; Cowhey, Aronson, and Szekely 1989: 5–78). The market for communications and computer equipment is linked to services and ideally should be considered in conjuction with services.[2] In this instance, however, telecommunica-

I thank Claude Barfield, Geza Feketekuty, and especially Peter Cowhey for their comments on an earlier version of this chapter.

tions equipment is the subject of another chapter in this series (Fontheim 1991).[3] Important issues arising in the broadcast realm also are excluded from consideration here.[4] There is not much included here about satellite communications either, mainly because the long-delayed EC Satellite Directive has not been issued even in draft form as of mid-1990.[5]

The question at the core of this chapter is, Will European economic unification result in increased or diminished opportunity for U.S. providers of telecommunication and information services? Two follow-up questions immediately suggest themselves. First, in the absence of bilateral or multilateral telecommunications negotiations involving Brussels and Washington, which service subsectors will be likely to grant non-European, and specifically U.S. firms the widest (or narrowest) latitude to compete for market share and profits? Why? Second, what sorts of rules, regulations, and principles might be negotiated bilaterally between the European Community and the United States, or within the context of the negotiations on trade in services that may yet move forward in the Uruguay Round multilateral trade negotiations? Which outcomes would most likely guarantee that foreign telecommunications and information service providers will be able to compete on a level playing field for international and domestic customers in Europe during the 1990s?

This chapter is divided into four sections. The first defines the telecommunications and information services treated here, surveys the structure of the market for these services, and forecasts the rough pattern of growth of these services in the 1990s. The second reviews the evolution of European thinking about telecommunications services during the 1980s and puts European Community-92 telecommunications-service plans into context. The third explores the implications of the proposed changes for non-European corporations that wish to provide services in Europe. The fourth summarizes U.S. government and business goals and strategies in seeking principles, rules, and procedures to govern trade in telecommunications and information services in bilateral and multilateral forums, assesses the likelihood that these positions will promote agreement, and considers the implications of successful or failed negotiations.

Definitions and Market Structure

Definitions and distinctions involving telecommunications services are ambiguous and evolving. It frequently is unclear whether a specific service should be classified as basic or enhanced. The long-term utility of the distinction between basic and enhanced, stressed in the FCC's Computer Inquiry II of 1980, is heatedly debated.[6] The problems are compounded as communications, computer, and broadcast technologies intertwine and new services that span these market segments emerge.[7] Even the distinction between services and equipment is becoming less distinct.[8]

Nonetheless, at least tacit agreement on definitions is important, because without rough agreement negotiations are impossible. Indeed, a favorite tactic of countries wishing to undercut negotiations is to demand that agreement on definitions and classifications be reached before any substantive negotiations occur. A better approach, if progress is desired, is to begin with an imperfect definition or classification and ensure that negotiators can alter the definitions as time and experience reveal appropriate adjustments.

Telecommunications Services—A Sixfold Breakdown. This chapter borrows a sixfold breakdown of telecommunications and information services without rehashing all the debates about definitional distinctions and precision (Aronson and Cowhey 1988: 61–110; Cowhey 1990a: 217–18).

• Network facilities. Facilities include equipment that permits the provision of services over networks open to all users.

• Basic public services. Three types of services are distinguished: (1) telephone services, including local, long-distance (and international) services; (2) simple document transmission, including telegraph and telex services and, for some authorities, simple fax transmission as well; (3) basic transport and leased circuit services. These services involve no manipulation of the content or format of a message. No potential customer can be excluded from networks that deliver these services, and these networks may be obliged to provide universal service.

• Enhanced (value-added and information) services. Voice, data, and video services, involving substantial manipulation of format or content, may be offered on public or private networks. Electronic mail combined with electronic-data-interchange provides both content and format manipulation. Voice services may become enhanced services when provided through voice mail systems.

• Overlay (mobile and radio) facilities and services. New mobile and radio technologies give rise to selective new network facilities and services. Overlay facilities may provide basic or enhanced services, such as cellular telephone, mobile data and fax services, remote pager systems, and air-to-ground telephone and navigation systems.

• ISDN and IBC (Integrated Services Digital Network and Integrated Broadband Communication). ISDN provides a mix of voice, data, and video within the limits of its bandwidth, speed, and technical design, using a narrower bandwidth than IBC, the "second generation." IBC will include items such as switched video that required larger bandwidth. In many ways, ISDN and IBC are closer to an architecture than a service.

• Private networks. Regulatory authorities often allow a single user, for example a large transnational company, to establish a private internal network to provide all services within the firm. These networks often are global.

These definitions are important because the U.S. business community remains divided about how much to seek in the initial agreement. Should the United States seek an agreement for enhanced and overlay services alone or push for a more ambitious, wide-ranging agreement?[9]

Market Structure. Until the 1980s telecommunications technology and regulatory policy progressed at an orderly pace. Capacity increased gradually and prices decreased just as gradually in the absence of major competition in most sectors. The 1980s were characterized by revolutionary technological and regulatory changes. Capacity surged, new services were introduced almost weekly, and, except for local telephone services, prices fell rapidly.[10]

The causes driving these changes is disputed, but there is near unanimity that the leverage of large corporate users has increased dramatically, at least in industrial countries. It is no accident that the United States, the United Kingdom, and Japan, the three countries with the most important financial markets in the world, are also the three countries most committed to telecommunications liberalization and competition. Combinations of liberalization, competition, deregulation, privatization, and corporatization are being implemented in numerous countries, including developing countries.[11] Since the tumultuous events in Eastern Europe, signs indicate that momentous communication changes can be expected in Socialist countries as well.[12]

Since the 1980s European telecommunications has evolved at breakneck speed (Ungerer and Costello 1988; Foreman-Peck, Haid, and Muller 1988; Roobeeke 1988: 297–28). An often repeated forecast is that telecommunications and information industries, broadly defined to include computers and office equipment, will account for 7 percent of European GDP in the first few years of the twenty-first century; they accounted for a bit more than 2 percent in the mid-1980s. If this projection is in the ballpark, it would mean that the EC telecommunications market, broadly defined, would increase from

TABLE 9-1
EC TELECOM MARKET IN 1986 AND 2000
(billions of dollars)

	EC 12 in 1986	EC 12 in 2000	Percent Increase
Telecom services	84[a]	277	330
Voice	74	190	157
Enhanced and overlay	6	88	1,367
Telecom equipment	25[a]	47	88
Computing equipment[b]	30	138	360
Total	139	462	224

a. Figures are for 1987, including telex and telegraph.
b. Integrated office equipment and software.
SOURCE: Peter Cowhey, "Telecommunications," Gary Clyde Hufbauer, ed., *Europe 1992: An American Perspective* (Washington, D.C.: Brookings Institution, 1990), p. 165.

almost $139 billion in the mid-1980s to about $740 billion in the year 2000. Table 9-1 suggests that growth rates for the aggregated portions of the market are likely to experience dramatically different growth patterns. Telecommunications services should continue to account for about 60 percent of total revenues. New services will increase at a far more rapid pace than traditional voice services, however, more than quadrupling their share of the total services until they account for approximately 32 percent of total services ten years from now. Simultaneously, computing equipment, including software, should increase its share from about 21.5 percent to just under 30 percent. Telecommunications equipment will grow more slowly. Its share of total telecommunications revenues in the European Community is expected to drop from just under 18 percent to about 10 percent of the total.

EC Telecommunications Services Policy

The 1980s witnessed major changes in national economic and regulatory policies for telecommunications in Europe, the United States, and Japan. Other countries are now reforming their own systems. Without detailing continuing developments in specific countries, this section summarizes some overarching patterns of change.[13]

Early in the 1980s it became evident to officials in most Postal, Telegraph, and Telephone authorities (PTTs) in Europe that the top echelon of the Commission of the European Communities and many national leaders in business and government saw PTTs as extreme nationalists and overtly protectionist. Their long-term positions and prerequisites were reconsidered. One index of their diminishing mandate was the increasingly common use of the term Telecommunications Authorities (TAs) rather than the former, more far-reaching name, Postal, Telegraph, and Telephone authorities.

National Experiences. Except in Britain, all the European TAs are fighting to hold on to their monopoly on network facilities and basic public services, which continue to account for the bulk of their revenues. Recognizing that some competition was inevitable, most TAs initially agreed to introduce competition in the provision of pure information services and to open parts of the terminal equipment market for competition. To satisfy demands for greater innovation and a wider variety of enhanced services, they promised to speed up the creation of a broadband ISDN system linking all of Europe. Many critics believed that the TAs were trying to migrate into the enhanced and overlay markets themselves, preempting potential competitors.

Foreign firms that wished to provide enhanced services in Europe or to operate their own corporate networks raised a variety of concerns. They worried that TAs would hold on to their monopolies on certain services. Foreign enhanced-service providers feared that European TAs might use their monopoly on underlying facilities and basic telephone services to cross-subsidize their own enhanced-service offerings or to discriminate against their competitors.[14] They were concerned about whether competition would be permitted in the provision of overlay facilities and services and whether new American satellite competitors of Intelsat would be licensed. Foreign firms feared they might be exluded from forums involved with setting tariffs and designing future networks and standards, or from new EC-wide research consortiums such as the Research and Development in Advanced Communications Technologies for Europe (RACE). And foreign enhanced-service providers wondered whether the licensing arrangements proposed by the TAs would be fair and efficient; while regulatory and operating authorities remained linked in many countries, foreign providers reasoned they might be unfairly treated if disputes arose (Cowhey 1990a: 221; Atlantic Council 1990).[15]

Different EC members embraced change in telecommunications with varying degrees of enthusiasm. In the United Kingdom, where British Telecom's network was antiquated and deteriorating and its work force woefully bloated and unproductive, Margaret Thatcher instituted a major shake-up that introduced privatization, duopolistic competition between British Telecom and Mercury (a subsidiary of

Cable & Wireless), allowed for significant rate rebalancing, and permitted British Telecom to tap capital markets for investment funds. Oftel, a new independent regulatory body "with teeth," vigorously set out to stir the competitive environment. When Mercury, the officially sanctioned competitor, failed to penetrate the marketplace as rapidly as Oftel wanted, Oftel licensed radio, cable, and ultimately satellite companies to offer new services.

The Netherlands, which separated its telecommunications and postal activities in early 1989, and Denmark cautiously edged toward a more liberal position on the scope of competition during the 1980s. Belgium, to promote Brussels as the commercial center of a post-1992 Europe, is belatedly showing interest in a rapid modernization as well.[16] The most marked changes came in Germany. After the Witte Commission report was filed in 1987, the *Bundespost*, pushed by the minister of communications, Dr. Christian Schwarz-Schilling, surprised most outside observers by beginning to transform itself from the most conservative PTT in Europe to one of the two leaders of the liberal forces in the European Community (Witte 1988; Haid and Müller 1988).[17]

At the other extreme, France, Italy, and to varying degrees the other six members of the European Community, formed a block of eight countries that wanted to move toward competition slowly and on as narrow a basis as was politically feasible. France, for example, boasted about the rapid digitalization of its network and the success of Transpac, its packet-switched network.[18] France also basked in the positive publicity it received from its Minitel experience, which generated thousands of information services for consumers; but this hoopla masked the question of Europe's generally poor performance in the provision of value-added networks. Moreover, France has been particularly conservative in promoting competition in other parts of its market, and foreign providers of basic and satellite services have found working with France particularly difficult.[19]

The Evolution of EC Policy. The commission's role in telecommunications evolved in two stages during the 1980s. Initially it was a catalyst for Europe-wide cooperation. It tried to build bridges among the member countries in the name of European unity and prosperity. Later the commission became a more aggressive player. In the context of EC 92, the commission increasingly asserted its authority over TAs and even, on occasion, over national governments. The commission and particularly two of its directorates—DG-XIII, which oversees the telecommunications and information industries, and DG-IV, which holds the competition (antitrust) portfolio—asserted an independent role and started to force the TAs to alter their protectionist posture and accept greater competition in a wider variety of areas. This second process was helped along by increased lobbying from large users within the community, who were concerned that individual European countries and companies would lose in head-to-head competition with foreign firms without an internal market.[20]

Building cooperative bridges. For almost twenty years the European Commission has argued that the opening of public procurement in telecommunications equipment was a prerequisite for future development in the sector. The member states were slow to agree. "Telecommunications was one of the three sectors excluded from the application of the 1976 EC Directive on the opening of public procurement supply contracts."[21] But by the late 1970s there was a growing consciousness that new information technology represented an opportunity and challenge for Europe. A major breakthrough was the commission's establishment of the Task Force on Information Technology and Telecommunications.[22] In 1979 and 1980 EC Vice-President for Industry Etienne Davignon asked his newly created Information Task Force to prepare proposals on telecommunications and information within the European Community.[23]

Momentum began to increase at the June 1983 meeting of the EC council in Stuttgart. The commission requested that member governments appoint senior officials to discuss the formation of telecommunications policy for the European Community. The council approved this request in November 1983. The resulting Senior Officials Groups on Telecommunications (SOG-T) met six times between November 1983 and March 1984 to hammer out lines of action for the Commission to pursue on telecommunications policy (Sandholtz 1990: 20).[24] A first result, in May 1984, was a commission statement setting out a plan to develop a consistent program in telecommunications. A Senior Official Group on Information Technology Standards and a senior advisory group on the information market also were formed. By July 1984 the commission signed agreements to cooperate with the European Conference of Postal and Telecommunications Administrations (CEPT).

During this formative period, Davignon was the driving force with the European Community on European telecommunications cooperation. In 1983 Davignon launched the pilot phase of the European Program for Research and Development in Information Technology (Esprit). The stated goal of Esprit was to promote precompetitive intra-European technological research technology projects with commercial applications. The not-so-hidden agenda of Esprit and of the RACE project that followed it was to get European industries into the habit of working with one another and not just with U.S. or Japanese partners. The commmission hoped that as cooperation developed, a strong Europe-wide industry-users group would emerge that would be willing to espouse European positions that contrasted sharply with stated TA policy.[25]

Between autumn 1984 and the end of 1987, the Council of Ministers, following proposals by the commission, adopted twelve directives, decisions, regulations, and recommendations on telecommunications. These decisions covered such areas as the implementation of a common approach in the field of telecommunications and, further, the instituting of a program for the development of less favored regions of the community. The program would entail improved access to advanced telecommunications services, standardization in the field of information technology and telecommunications, the coordinated introduction of ISDN in the European Community, the coordinated introduction of public pan-European digital mobile communications in Europe and RACE, and an EC program in the field of telecommunications.[26]

The commission as player. The commission and DG-XIII became more central to the telecommunications scene when the push for a European internal market was given weight by the 1985 White Paper. They gained an important ally when DG-IV for competition took an active interest in trying to open the telecommunications market during the mid-1980s (Utton 1988). The pivotal precedent was created on March 29, 1985, when the European Court of Justice supported DG-IV in a case involving British Telecom. A private British message-forwarding agency charged that prohibitions by the U.K. Post Office and, after 1981, by British Telecom were unfair and anticompetitive; they prohibited the forwarding of telexes between continental Europe and North America and the forwarding in telex or telefax form of messages received via computer connections. In late 1982 the commission, under the authority granted it by Article 90(3) of the Treaty of Rome, concluded that the prohibitions constituted an abuse of a dominant position, but the Italian government appealed the case to the European Court of Justice. The court dismissed in its entirety the Italian complaint, confirming the commission's view that competition rules of the Treaty of Rome do apply to telecommunications administrations. The court in effect narrowed the permissible monopoly rights of TAs and signaled that they would disapprove attempts by the TAs to extend their monopolies into new technological services when they arise (Ungerer and Costello 1988: 167–68).[27] In addition, the successful use of Article 90(3) in the British Telecom case gave the commission a still-contested mechanism to issue a directive without council approval, thus partially insulating EC decision makers from the TAs' domestic political clout.[28]

The basic strategy of the commission with regard to telecommunications was laid out in a Green Paper issued on June 30, 1987 (Commission of the European Communities 1987a).[29] The Green Paper distinguished between "reserved services"—basic services redefined but probably still including telephone and telex services—and "competitive services." Reserved services would continue to be provided exclusively by government-owned or controlled telecommunications monopolies, mainly on the basis of universal access. Competitive services would cover what in the United States is often called value-added and information services. The Green Paper proposed to allow the TAs to participate in the competitive services market and to retain their regulatory authority and their monopoly in the reserved services market (Cooney 1989).

In addition, the Green Paper proposed that TAs should continue to control and operate the network infrastructure, except in the case of two-way satellite systems that might be allowed to compete on a case-by-case basis. Users should be free to choose their own terminal equipment, including Receive Only Earth Stations.[30] The Green Paper proposed the establishment of strict standards for network infrastructure and services for all providers including TAs, strict continuous review of all commercial activities of TAs with particular regard to cross-subsidization of services and manufacturing,[31] and strict continuous review of all private providers in newly opened sectors to avoid the abuse of dominant positions. It urged that all requirements imposed by TAs on providers of competitive services for use of the network be clearly defined and fully transparent. More specifically, the Green Paper proposed a unified agreement on standards, frequencies, and tariff principles to promote EC-wide competition, and called for the creation of a European Telecommunications Standards Institute (ETSI) to create common standards. To help achieve these ends, the Green Paper urged that telecommunications regulatory and operating functions be separated in countries where they still are unified.

The Green Paper pushed for greater liberalization while attempting not to completely alienate the TAs. It was a step toward liberalization, but still it left control over basic services, more than 85 percent of TA revenue, with the individual countries. In addition, the Commission states that both the prohibition of voice resale and the form of tariff for leased lines must remain the prerogative of the TA in each member state (U.S. Department of State 1987: 5). Moreover, some provisions regarding technical standards and the protection of the network might be interpreted to limit non-European competitors.

By mid-1988 the European Community was willing to go further. The Council of Ministers formally resolved that the development of a common market for telecommunications equipment and services should be part of the EC-92 program.[32] Significantly, the ETSI, proposed in the Green Paper, began operation in April 1988.[33] The ETSI is meant to create the Europe-wide standards for telecommunications services and equipment that did not emerge from CEPT. The TA-controlled CEPT will take part in ETSI deliberations, but will no longer have full control over these activities. Membership has been thrown open to more than 100 members, including telecommunications manufacturers. The net result should be to make standards and the standard-setting process more transparent and accessible.

Two Key European Commission Directives. At the heart of the internal market program envisaged for 1992 are the directives and related decisions and proposals. A surprisingly large number of these actions are related to telecommunications.[34] In chapter 7 Claude Fontheim describes and analyzes the key directives, resolutions, and decisions related to telecommunications equipment. The two main directives related to telecommunications services are described and analyzed as follows.

Draft commission directive on competition in the markets for telecommunication services. In late June 1989 the EC Commission put forward draft directive COM(89)475 under Article 90(3) of the Treaty of Rome, cutting back the monopolies over telecommunications services maintained in most states in Europe. In its original form the directive would have abolished monopolies for all services to the general public except voice telephony, but member states would still be allowed to regulate such services under objective, nondiscriminatory commercial rules. Publication of technical interconnection data needed by operators would be mandatory by the end of 1990. During a transition period, current prohibitions on the resale of leased line capacity that might be used to compete with public data services could remain in effect until January 1993. All restrictions on processing signals before or after their transmission via the public network would be abolished, regulatory powers of telecommunications organizations would be separated from operational activities, and measures would be taken to allow termination of existing long-term contracts.[35]

The commission's staff sought regulations based on objective, nondiscriminatory commercial rules. France, supported by a majority of EC members, initially opposed liberalizing data services. They also made certain that, as initially formulated, the directive did not apply to the telecommunications network itself—the traditional telephone lines, fiber optic lines, microwave and satellite links, radio telephony, and cable television networks.[36] Moreover, TAs could retain exclusive rights to operate voice telephony even after the introduction of an ISDN (Telecommunications Reports 1989, July, 27–28).[37] Ultimately France offered a counterproposal to allow competition in the provision of basic services, with the proviso that member administrations could impose licensing requirements, such as requiring competitive providers to offer nationwide, universal service. The liberal faction led by West Germany worried that licensing restrictions could discourage competition by unnerving potential entrants.

Another tactic to undercut the directive on procedural grounds was taken by Belgium, which indicated that it might "ask the European Court to find that the commission lacks authority to restrict telecommunications monopolies on its own—that such action must be taken by the Council of member nations rather than the commission's non-elected professional staff" (Telecommunications Reports 1989, November, 23).

To overcome their differences the council of EC telecommunications ministers met in Brussels on December 7, 1989. A compromise was reached that bridged the differences between the main liberalizers (Germany, the United Kingdom, the Netherlands, and Denmark) and the majority, which favored permitting national administrations to maintain their monopolies over a wider array of services. The ministers adopted a framework for opening all but voice telephony and the network infrastructure to competition. All value-added services were liberalized when the directive entered into force in 1990. The commission's new proposal backed away from the late June 1989 proposal designed to abolish monopolies for all services offered to the public except voice telephony. Basic data services would be opened to competition on January 1, 1993. The commission also may consider prolonging the transition period during which simple resale of leased line capacity may be prohibited by any individual member state from the end of 1992 until the beginning of 1996, if it can demonstrate that its network for packet-switched data transmission services has not advanced sufficiently.[38]

The compromise also permits national licensing provisions, but only if they are approved in advance by the commission. The commission would review proposed licensing criteria to make certain they are appropriate to the applicant companies and that they do not go beyond what is "absolutely necessary to safeguard the public service obligations of the national TA in question." After 1992 special licensing provisions would apply only to basic packet-and-circuit swtiched-data-transmission services, since the EC liberalized all value-added services when the directive entered into force in 1990.[39]

Draft commission directive on open network provision. In December 1988 the commission put forward a preliminary proposal for a directive on "open network provision" (ONP), which will determine the conditions of access to European networks, a task central to the implementation of the Green Paper. The stated goal of ONP is to create "an open, efficient, and harmonized environment for the development of non-reserved services in the Community, in particular for the so-called value-added services" (Commission of the European Communities 1988a). It was, in effect, designed to ensure competitive service providers access throughout the European Community to public network infrastructure needed to provide their services and also to ensure interoperability across national borders. ONP is Europe's equivalent to Open Network Architecture (ONA), which is being developed in the United States.

In late June 1989 the commission adopted a revised proposal for a directive to implement ONP in a single EC telecommunications market that incorporated some modifications sought by the EC Parliament (Commission of the European Communities 1989b, 1989a). The main modification concerned the scope of the ONP requirement. The European Community made its changes to clarify that the directive applies to both public and private telecommunications organizations to which a member state grants special or exclusive rights and covers services for which no exclusive rights have been granted. This provision was viewed as necessary to guarantee efficient access to, and use of, public telecommunications services such as switched data, which rely on the public network infrastructure. Nonetheless, the most liberal member states were concerned that ONP requirements for cross-border "harmonization" would create entry barriers to small companies and could limit competition.

As part of the compromise to move the telecommunications services directive along, at the December 7, 1989, meeting of the council of telecommunications ministers, a general agreement was reached to make compliance with ONP standards voluntary, but with a presumption in favor of compliance. The European Community's Council of Ministers approved the December compromise on February 5, 1990, and issued a statement of their common position on May 11, 1990. Service providers who comply with ONP standards will be able to provide their services on an EC-wide basis. ONP will be phased in in stages. Areas for which ONP conditions may be drawn up will be selected from the following list of six: (1) leased lines, (2) packet- and circuit-switched data services, (3) ISDN, (4) voice telephony service, (5) telex services, and (6) mobile services, as applicable (Council of the European Communities 1990). The European Community, however, retains the authority to enforce ONP conditions if it appears that voluntary approaches are not producing the desired effect of harmonizing service availability across the European Community. Specific service directives will follow, beginning with a directive covering the two services over which the TAs will be allowed to retain their monopolies—leased lines and voice telephone service. By January 1992 the staff of the commission hopes to obtain council approval for proposals for technical interface specifications, usage conditions, and tariff principles for other services, such as packet-switched data-transmissions and the ISDN.[40] ONP conditions are likely to be issued in the form of recommendations by mid-1991 for packet-switched data transmissions, and by the beginning of 1992 for the ISDN.

Under the compromise the ministers apparently sided with the competition directorate, DG-IV, by agreeing despite opposition from some member states that it was legal to use Article 90(3) to implement the services directive. The commission made two key concessions on the ONP directive, however: "(1) members states may establish licensing conditions for private basic data communications operators provided they are non-discriminatory and are reviewed by the commission; and (2) exclusive provision of basic telephony, telex and data switching may be exempted from the 1993 expiration deadline until 1996 where member states are able to demonstrate to the commission that their public services are at risk" (Transnational Data and Communications Report 1990: 5). In essence the ministers agreed to go forward on services for nonmonopolists but to give it a much lower order of priority. In effect this policy will delay implementation several years. When implementation does take place, it is promised that only the minimum standards needed to guarantee interconnectivity will be required.

One additional European telecommunications initiative deserves comment. In November 1990 the European Commission issued a Green Paper on satellite communication that urged the liberalization of the earth segment in all member countries (France dropped its opposition in mid-1990 and only Belgium remains outspoken in its opposition). It is likely that a directive that formalizes this recommendation will be issued in late 1991 or early 1992. How the European Community will approach the more complicated and controversial problem of reforming the space segment is not yet clear. Significantly, competition to the national carriers in the provision of satellite services already has emerged in the United Kingdom and Germany and is likely to spread to other countries by the mid-1990s. It also is possible that the terms of the Eutelsat convention that "prevent the establishment of rival European cross-border satellite systems where these would cause the organization 'economic harm' " could be relaxed. Intelset already has taken this step (Fin. Tech. Telecom Markets 1991: 2–3).

As with all significant innovations, the ultimate impact of the two Green Papers and the services and ONP directives will be unclear until some time after they are implemented and operating. U.S. firms express different levels of concern about potential future problems. For example, some worry that if ONP usage conditions are applied to value-added service providers and other users, the impact on U.S. business interests could be negative. Cost of compliance could be high, and proprietary communication systems that were expensive to develop might be compromised. Several issues relevant to U.S. business prospects are explored in the next section (U.S. Department of Commerce 1990).

Implications of EC 92 for Foreign Service Providers

General U.S. Industry Concerns. Many of the problems identified by U.S. firms wishing to supply or purchase telecommunications services in Europe are potential rather than existing difficulties. Since many competitive services are not yet offered in many European countries, firms are not really certain how they will be treated in Europe. As opportunities widen over the next few years, U.S. firms will work to make sure their interests and needs are taken into account.[41]

Obviously the interests of U.S. firms differ, so there is ongoing consultation and negotiations among them in forums such as the U.S. Chamber of Commerce to try to identify the important issues and to formulate advice on appropriate strategy and tactics for U.S. negotiators. Nonetheless, during 1990 a sharp division emerged. One group, composed of large users, value-added and information-service providers, and some computer firms, favored an aggressive push to press the TAs into a corner, curtailing the scope of their monopoly services and simplifying licensing and standard-setting procedures as much as possible.[42] Their goal was to establish a broad, general right to do business and to nip possible discrimination by TAs in the bud. They were especially concerned that any agreement should cover private leased line networks that were used to transmit basic services. Otherwise they feared that any telecommunications agreement could turn into "a bill of rights for the telephone administra-

211

tions and others who seek restrictions on usage of the network (Nugent 1991: 13).

By contrast, AT&T and a few other firms favored a more limited approach that kept basic services off the agenda of negotiations.[43] They worried that putting basic services on the negotiating table would overload the negotiations, threaten the TAs too much, and stiffen their resolve to oppose any agreement. If coverage were to extend to basic services, AT&T worried that negotiations would too quickly become complicated and collapse under their own weight. They also worried that inclusion of basic services would improve the bargaining position of foreign monopoly service providers at their expense. The Office of the U.S. Trade Representative (USTR), which wanted an agreement, usually leaned in this direction as well. In August 1990 AT&T, MCI, U.S. Sprint, and others wrote to U.S. Trade Representative Carla Hills demanding that the U.S. government adopt this approach. The pressure worked. USTR began openly advocating AT&T's position as its own.

Despite their differences, all concerned U.S. firms and the U.S. government want to make certain that as the EC Green Papers are modified and implemented by the services, ONP, and other directives, U.S. firms will be able to provide a large variety of services and compete on a level playing field in Europe. In general the Green Papers and the directives are applauded as representing significant steps toward addressing U.S. government objectives and industry concerns. U.S. suppliers of value-added and information services want reassurance, however, that the United States will support their rights in future negotiations and disputes as they compete in partially or fully liberated markets, often in competition with TAs. Their priority objectives with regard to seeking the freedom to compete in the value-added and information services arena can be summarized as follows. According to the U.S. Chamber of Commerce Telecommunications Trade Task Force, these are the essential elements for the provision of value-added and information services and intracorporate use:

- clear boundary between monopoly and competitive services
- nondiscriminatory availability of reasonably priced, flat-rate leased circuits
- safeguards to ensure a competitive marketplace
- freedom to handle and move all types of information subject to the exceptions granted with respect to reserved services
- no mandatory requirements for interconnection, use of CCITT standards, or RPOA status
- minimal uniform licensing standards

212

- domestic transmission available to providers of international value-added and information services as well as intracorporate use
- freedom to attach equipment to the network
- right to establish a commercial presence

As long as some EC TAs are not overseen by separate regulatory bodies, there is a real chance that licensing procedures could become cumbersome or discriminatory or that they might have to reveal their business plans to their chief competitors. This concern is magnified because there is so far no EC directive on the separation of operations and regulatory functions of the TAs. Firms heavily dependent on leased lines fear the move to cost-based pricing in general, but they particularly worry that countries such as France and Germany might levy discriminatory surcharges on leased line usage and discriminate against those that need access to and require use of the public telecommunications transport network. Value-added and information service providers and users also want to try to guarantee that they will be granted access to and use of public telecommunications services on a nondiscriminatory basis. These firms hope to commit foreign TAs to permit bypass of the public network through use of leased lines, to open up the ownership and operation of satellite earth station equipment. An additional concern is that TAs may create European consortiums to offer nonreserved services that could dominate the market and decimate potential competitors before they can become viable.[44]

Concerns about the Services and ONP Directives. U.S. firms have raised some specific worries related to the services and ONP directives. The services directive is applauded by most U.S. firms because it explicitly limits the TA's monopoly provision of services to basic services, probably just voice and telex. Ambiguity remains, however, about the definition of key terms, how much paperwork will be involved in registering or licensing new service offerings, how individual services not addressed specifically in the directive such as telex, paging, radio-telephony, and satellite services will be handled, how promised nondiscriminatory treatment will operate, and how the timing of implementation of the various directives will work.

The industry wants as much clarification and precision as possible to minimize wiggle-room for the TAs.[45] They want to minimize bureaucratic obstacles that might delay or prevent them from offering such services as they deem reasonable. If possible, they want assurance that U.S. firms will be free to provide services throughout the European Community on the same basis as European firms and TAs.

213

The industry hopes that the sequencing of implementation will not be crafted to allow the TAs to get a jump on their competition in the enhanced-services market.

Naturally, U.S. firms, particularly users and enhanced-services providers not already integrated into the process, want transparency and the ability to provide appropriate inputs into the standard-setting and decision-making processes involving telecommunications.[46] They also want assurances that the services directive will in fact require the TAs to provide basic services offered over the public network infrastructure to all providers of competitive services on an equal basis. When TAs compete in these markets they should derive no special benefits from their own networks.

U.S. firms with the most ambitious agendas for negotiations urge the U.S. government to press the European Community for safeguards to prevent TAs from abusing their control over their networks to discriminate against foreign competitors. Firms heavily dependent on leased lines argue that even though the issue is not treated explicitly in the directives, the European Community should be persuaded to ensure the availability of flat-rate leased circuits on a non-discriminatory basis or at least that tariffs on leased lines should be cost-oriented. There should be no access charges for private leased-line interconnection to the network. Guarantees of flexible interconnection are sought that would commit the European Community to explicitly recognize the right of competitive service providers to use proprietary protocols and to make independent interconnection decisions without government interference.

Issues Addressed during the Uruguay Round Negotiations. Throughout the 1980s the United States argued that one of the critical goals for the GATT Uruguay Round of trade negotiations should be the extension of the trade regime to cope with the consequences of emerging issues—particularly services, intellectual property, and trade-related investment measures. For services and telecommunications services, which are at the core of the services negotiations, a prime strategy was to examine whether and to what extent concepts applicable to trade in goods might also apply to services. The specific arguments that swirled around telecommunications services during the Uruguay Round negotiations are discussed in the next section. Here, several key principles flagged at the November 1988 Montreal midterm review of the Uruguay Round negotiations are examined and their possible application to telecommunications services are discussed (Group of Negotiations on Services of the Uruguay Round 1988).[47]

Transparency. In its simplest form, transparency means that relevant laws and regulations are published and easily available to all interested parties. The United States seeks advanced notification of laws and regulations. Many other countries see this as a needlessly onerous burden and an impingement on their sovereignty. U.S. firms would like to be able to comment on proposed laws before they are set and to participate in administrative and regulatory proceedings. Others object, seeing this as an incursion on their rights.

U.S. telecommunications-services providers favor the timely publication of regulations and policies and want to participate in the process. Specifically, they want to ensure that transparency applies to items such as the terms and conditions for access to and use of exclusively provided services, the pricing of all exclusively provided services, the licensing requirements for the provision of competitive telecommunications services, and the processes for establishing telecommunications standards.

National treatment. If foreigners are granted national treatment, they are treated just like domestic entities providing the identical service or making the identical use of a service. National treatment in a monopoly sector depends on achieving market access and is threatening to countries that fear that if they accept this principle, they might not be able to prevent foreigners from offering telecommunications services in their markets. Therefore, countries almost certainly will reserve some services from national treatment.

Providers of value-added and information services want to provide services on the same terms and conditions as the national entities. Users want assurances that there will be no discrimination between foreign and national firms. Signatories to an agreement might make the same information available to foreigners, allow them to participate in the regulatory process, sell them services at the same prices, hold them to the same standards, and apply identical licensing conditions to them as to domestic firms. They also might make available exclusively provided telecommunications services equally to foreign and domestic entities.

Most favored nation (MFN) and nondiscrimination. These concepts are central to the GATT. Unconditional MFN would commit all contracting parties not to discriminate among the service providers of other parties. The European Community, for example, argues "that no country should be made to open its basic telecom market, but should it choose to do so, it must do so on an MFN basis and remain within a multilateral framework." They continue to support unconditional MFN for telecommunications, and suggest that an MFN exemption could undermine multilateralism (Pirzio-Biroli 1991: 10). In the context of telecommunications services most U.S. firms and USTR believe this practice is probably unworkable. They favored linking MFN with market access to force countries to exchange commitments in good faith. Ultimately, some form of conditional MFN probably will need to be negotiated that will extend MFN to all signatories of any agreement. Indeed, the adoption of conditional MFN might induce some countries to sign the agreement to guarantee their benefits. U.S. negotiators and firms, however, want to allow interested parties to enter into even more ambitious bilateral or regional agreements that would generate greater liberalization than is probable in the context of the GATT.

Market access. Market access for services is a large part of what the services negotiations are about and is the most innovative, complicated, and controversial aspect of the negotiations. Market access for providers of competitive telecommunications services is the ultimate goal of supporters of the telecommunications-services annex.[48] Service providers, whether or not they are established in a territory, want to be able to market their services directly to customers and to be free to establish or not establish in a territory, and still market services deemed to be competitive.

Safeguards and exceptions. Countries will want to protect their national security and cultural and other goals and interests, including perhaps the stated obligation to provide universal service. Exceptions and safeguards are inevitable, but the goal of U.S. negotiators is to draw them as narrowly as possible so they do not undermine commitments to seek progressive liberalization.

Regulatory situation and fair competition. National regulatory prerogatives must be respected, but if the separation of regulatory and operational responsibilities in the telecommunications sector can be achieved, countries might more credibly ensure that access to and use of exclusively provided telecommunications services are provided on a nondiscriminatory basis. The need for regulatory oversight might also be minimized by the introduction of competition in network facilities and basic public services.

Reciprocity. One additional issue not included among the Montreal principles needs attention. Some believe that global reciprocity could emerge as an important element of EC external trade relations after 1992. The proposed second banking directive released in February 1988 generated widespread concern that the European Community was poised to create "Fortress Europe." If a similar formulation was implemented for telecommunications, the results would certainly be highly protectionist.[49] As first drafted, the second banking directive provided that non-EC banks would receive the same benefits as EC banks only if banks from EC member states received the same amount of access to the foreign country's market as the foreign banks enjoyed in the European Community. Fears that reciprocity would be used to create a Fortress Europe were fanned in July 1988 when former EC Commissioner Willy de Clercq suggested that the economic advantages of opening up the European market might not be automatically extended to the European Community's trading partners (Library of Congress 1989: 30).

The U.S. government and industry objected strongly to this formulation. They argued that reciprocity should not be used as a trading principle and that it was an inappropriate principle for granting third countries access to newly liberalized sectors in Europe. Global reciprocity would have forced other countries to alter their domestic regulatory practices and mirror EC laws and regulations in order to have equal access to Europe's internal market. Thus legitimate differences in national regulatory schemes might be used to justify discrimination against foreign firms. U.S. Treasury officials warned that "reciprocity that seeks to achieve identical commercial privileges in countries with different regulatory regimes will almost inevitably result in discrimination. In short, reciprocity that seeks identical treatment in different countries is a retreat back to protectionism. The United States would prefer, therefore, to use national treatment as an instrument to avoid discrimination and preserve open markets.[50] In response, on April 13, 1989, the EC Commission modified the second bank directive, substituting national treatment for equivalent access at its core. The commission still stressed the desire to achieve reciprocity. But, it no longer contended that the absence of reciprocity was enough to deny foreign firms access to the integrated European market (Library of Congress 1989: 30).

Telecommunications and Trade Negotiations

The future prospects of U.S. telecommunications firms in Europe might be improved or their fears might be allayed if U.S. bilateral and multilateral trade negotiations are successful. This final section explores the results of bilateral telecommunications negotiations with the European Community mandated by the Omnibus Trade and Tariff Act of 1988. It examines what might emerge from an agreement covering trade in telecommunications services within the context of the still stalled Uruguay Round.

Bilateral Negotiations. Access by the U.S. telecommunications industry to EC member countries varies widely on such items as standard-setting procedures and the provision of value-added services. In late 1988 pressure mounted to name the European Community or some of its member states priority countries under the Omnibus Trade and Tariff Act of 1988. The European Community argued that bilateral negotiations were a waste of time. They contended that as Europe implemented the Green Paper and the directives, the European market would be opened to foreign competition. Moreover, the European Community complained that bilateral telecommunications negotiations might undercut the multilateral GATT negotiations.

USTR under pressure from U.S. industry, however, was quite concerned about potentially restrictive French standard-setting procedures, the rules for interconnection of customer premises equipment to the French network, and extended delays in equipment approvals. To a lesser extent they focused on problems in Germany, Italy, and Spain.[51] U.S. firms also sought more participation in national and Europe-wide standard-setting exercises and in the formulation of the EC-92 directives. Ultimately, USTR decided that it was inappropriate to target individual member states, but that the European Community was the appropriate entity to target.

In late February 1989, U.S. Trade Representative Carla Hills, after reviewing the activities of thirteen U.S. trading partners, acted to comply with section 1374 of the Omnibus Trade and Competitiveness Act of 1988 by identifying the European Community (and South Korea) as "priority countries" for trade negotiations on telecommunications products and services. USTR found that "the combination of commercial interest in the U.S. market, market size, potential for U.S. sales opportunities, and the seriousness of the barriers were such as to warrant their inclusion on the initial list for negotiations." To prompt action by the executive branch, Congress mandated under the 1988 act that unless sufficient opening of the European market were achieved, the United States was required to retaliate before February 1990. An escape clause gave the president enough leeway, however, to defer retaliation until 1992. Predictably, given progress toward 1992 and the continuing Uruguay Round negotiations, as the deadline for retaliation neared, USTR declared sufficient progress had been achieved and promised to review the situation again in 1991.

The USTR announced its intention to address telecommunications issues in future bilateral and multilateral negotiations. The prospect of negotiating these issues in the context of the Uruguay Round was particularly appealing because "the schedule for certain negotiations under the GATT closely matches that envisioned in the law for resolution of telecommunications market access problems" (Telecommunications Reports 1989, February, 26–27).

GATT Negotiations. The Uruguay Round was launched at a ministerial meeting in Punta del Este, Uruguay, in September 1986. In late 1988 a ministerial midterm review fell apart over disagreement on agriculture. In April 1989 an interim compromise allowed negotiations to continue. The round was scheduled to close with a two-week meeting of ministers in Brussels from November 26 to December 8, 1990. Again the negotiations faltered on agriculture. The developing countries walked out of all negotiating groups when the European Community refused to budge on agriculture. In early 1991 frantic efforts to revive the Uruguay Round continue. Europe signaled that it might be willing to bend. U.S. Trade Representative Hills asked Congress to extend "fast-track" negotiating authority for two more years. Despite substantial opposition in Congress led by Democratic Senator Fritz Hollings of South Carolina, it seems probable that the administration will win an extension. The final compromise agreement now seems likely to emerge in early 1993.[52]

As part of the original bargain that put services on the Uruguay Round agenda, services negotiations were organized under a Group of Negotiations on Services (GNS) that operates separately from the rest of the negotiations.[53] The consistent goal of services supporters was to negotiate a general framework agreement that could be applied to a broad range of services. Individual service sectors would be treated in greater detail in separate sectoral codes or annexes.[54]

Early in the process it became evident that telecommunications services would be central to any services agreement.[55] In March 1987, barely six months after the Round was launched, the Services Policy Advisory Committee (SPAC) to USTR recommended that rules governing monopoly behavior be placed within the general framework agreement. The free flow of information also was a priority.[56] By mid-1988, OECD discussions among industrial countries identified market access as "the central principle" for trade in telecommunications-network based services (Organization for Economic Cooperation and Development 1988a: 9). A year later negotiators were discussing the applicability of specific trade principles and concepts to telecommunications.[57]

By late 1988 negotiators focused on the "Montreal principles": transparency, progressive liberalization, national treatment,[58] most-favored-nation treatment nondiscrimination market access, and the concept of increasing participation of developing countries. In October 1989 the United States tabled a proposal that presented in formal legal terms a set of obligations countries might assume under a services agreement.[59]

In November 1989 the United States Council for International Business issued a sweeping statement that advocated liberalization of telecommunications services and the protection of the rights of competitive service providers and of users.[60] It proposed a more aggressive stance, particularly toward coverage of basic telecommunications services, than the position taken by USTR and supported by AT&T.[61] The paper argued for an agreement that covered access to and use of monopoly-provided telecommunications services and the provision of competitive telecommunications services. It also favored specific rules that would commit TAs to make leased lines available at cost-based, flat rates. Even for services that countries reserved for themselves, the council argued that national administrations should grant access to their networks and infrastructure in a timely, reasonable, and nondiscriminatory manner. Providers should offer users flexible access without burdensome restrictions.[62]

With deadlines looming, meetings became more frequent. On December 15, 1989, a heavily bracketed text of a General Agreement on Trade in Services (the framework agreement) emerged. On March 31, 1990, the United States tabled a proposed annex for telecommunications services that would be attached to the framework agreement.[63] Although it conformed more closely to AT&T than to the U.S. business council's vision, it still provoked criticism at home.[64] Abroad, other countries wondered why the United States focused so much on guarantees related to use of the network instead of focusing more on telecommunications per se. Within months the European Community and Japan tabled their own proposal for an annex. Serious discussion of the telecommunications annexes began in July 1990.

The initial annex proposed by the United States contained four articles. Article 1 stated that its purpose was to elaborate on the framework agreement "as it applies to access to and use of 'services of public telecommunications transport networks' " (public telecommunications transport services). Article 2 spelled out the scope and definition of the annex. USTR accepted that countries have the right to reserve services that would not be covered on the agreement. The U.S. goal was to limit these reserved services to voice telephony, telex, and network infrastructure. Article 3, the heart of the annex, suggested rules to cover access to and use of public telecommunications transport services. Article 4 called on parties to any agreement to adhere to the provisions for transparency spelled out in the framework agreement. The United States was particularly concerned about transparency in telecommunications. It wanted the fullest possible disclosure.

Article 3, the core of the U.S. proposal, focused on *access to and use of public telecommunications transport services*. The United States hoped to clarify the rights and obligations of private firms when they worked with or competed against "a monopoly provider of a service" or an "exclusive service provider."[65] The United States sought guaranteed access to services provided over the public network, but U.S. firms also wanted to retain the right to choose whether they were willing to provide their services to any particular customer. The United States wanted its firms to have the freedom to choose and use their own equipment and to make use of their own specialized protocols and standards except insofar as mandated standards were technologically required to affect interconnection. They also sought a wide array of guarantees that would ensure that they could run their leased lines networks efficiently, frequently providing services in competition with the TAs.[66] The initial proposal also asked for guarantees of the free movement of information across national borders.[67] In essence, U.S. firms asked for everything that they needed to be secure and certain that they could compete with public monopolies or exclusive providers of telecommunications services. Other countries, not surprisingly, pointed out that the United States was asking for access to their networks when they wished it, but did not want to be forced to use those same networks if they did not wish it.

More broadly, signatories need to be able to sign an agreement without locking themselves in permanently. TAs need to be able to reserve services to themselves, to guarantee that "what is theirs is theirs."[68] But the regulatory and competitive environment is changing so rapidly that the agreement must be flexible enough to allow interested parties to extend its scope. Indeed, any agreement should be sufficiently dynamic to evolve over time. It is not enough for an agreement to manage the situation as it was in 1986; it must be equally applicable to 1996 or 2006. One possibility is continuous negotiations. Representatives of signatory countries might meet twice or more a year to address continuing issues and controversies and furthr develop and refine existing agreements.[69]

The situation for telecommunications became more confused on four different levels as the Brussels ministerial meeting approached. First, when the decision was made to seek a telecommunications annex to the services framework instead of a separate code, the stakes were raised. It was no longer possible for reluctant countries to acquiesce to the services framework but refuse to commit themselves to telecommunications liberalization. Therefore negotiators needed

221

to water down the telecom annex in part to preserve the framework agreement. Second, the debate over MFN divided the United States and Europe, making unified action on telecommunications harder to achieve. Third, AT&T's strong push at the last moment to recast the U.S. position caused the U.S. government position to swing toward AT&T but divided U.S. industry. U.S. trade negotiators were less likely to make a telecommunications annex a high priority, if U.S. interests could not agree on it. Other countries recognized that U.S. negotiators were likely to be less vigorous in the absence of a united industry. Fourth, when the developing countries, many of which still oppose a services agreement, submitted their own restrictive language for a telecom annex, the GATT secretariat tried to put together a composite document instead of formulating its own compromise proposal.[70] As a result the bracketed text that emerged was contradictory and so complicated that it was probably doomed to die under its own weight. Even had the Brussels ministerial meeting not broken down over agriculture, it is likely that negotiations would have amputated the telecom annex in order to save the general services framework. Predicting what will finally emerge is impossible, but it seems likely that a reasonable framework agreement for services will be signed by a large number of countries. The fate of the telecom annex is more problematic. The delay may give supporters time to reformulate their positions. Though they differ on form and content, the United States, the European Community, and Japan all want an agreement. There could be some compromise that would allow a short, seemingly bland annex to go forward. It almost certainly will be less detailed than the proposed U.S. annex, but it could go some way at establishing principles of transparency and market access in the enhanced telecommunications sphere. Future negotiators would have something to start from as they work to flesh out more details in bilateral, plurilateral, or multilateral forums.

Future Prospects for U.S. Service Providers

The greatest opportunity for U.S. telecommunications service providers in the European Community is likely to be in the fast emerging markets for value-added and information services (especially VANs) and advanced radio communications.[71] Telephone companies, which have so far failed to make major inroads into the enhanced-services market, are likely to flourish in the cellular and other overlay markets. The RBOCs also have sought cable franchises in Europe that are cheaper than comparable franchises in the United States.[72] The RBOCs, however, are hampered in their effort to compete on the U.S.

end because they are not allowed to interconnect to their home networks.[73] By contrast, the market for basic voice and telex services that still accounts for the vast bulk of TA revenues is likely to continue to be dominated by the TAs for the foreseeable future. Although pressure may build from Eastern Europe's demand for cheap satellite technology, so far the European Community has moved cautiously in the satellite realm, not wanting to undermine the regional monopoly of Eutelsat, its regional public satellite organization. Similarly, the TAs do not want users to be able to bypass them and interconnect with private satellite networks.

Confrontation is most likely at the moving boundary that separates reserved and nonreserved services markets. The TAs can be expected to try to push the definition of reserved services into previously uncharted territory. U.S. firms will try to enlist the U.S. government, the EC Commission, and emerging national regulatory bodies to make certain that the TAs do not dominate markets for anything beyond the most basic of services, and that they do not use licensing, standard setting, or cross-subsidization from their protected turf to discriminate against new domestic and foreign service providers.

These skirmishes are important because they will shape the competitive playing field of tomorrow in telecommunications and other sectors. Which companies win and lose depend on the rules and standards that are ultimately accepted. But the general trend is already clear: "The PTTs have lost the war" (Calingaert 1988: 115).

The newly emerging TAs will retain significant power, but European, U.S., and other users and providers will all gain ground.

References

Aho, C. M., and J. D. Aronson. 1985. *Trade Talks: America Better Listen!* New York: Council on Foreign Relations.

Aronson, J. D., and P. F. Cowhey. 1988. *When Countries Talk: International Trade in Telecommunications Services.* Cambridge, Mass.: Ballinger.

Atlantic Council. 1990. Working Group on Telecommunications. *The U.S. Telecommunications Services and Equipment Sector and the European Community Unified Market—1992.* Policy paper.

Bruce, R. R. 1988. *The Telecom Mosaic.* Salem, N.H.: Butterworth Legal Pubs.

Bruce, R. R., J. P. Cunard, and M. D. Director. 1986. *From Telecommunications to Electronic Services: A Global Spectrum of Definitions, Boundary Lines and Structures.* Salem, N.H.: Butterworth Legal Pubs.

———. 1989. "Telecommunications Services and a Multilateral Agreement on Trade in Services: Problems, Issues, and Prognosis." Paper prepared for International Institute of Communications Forum, Dec. 14–15, New York.

Calingaert, M. 1988. *The 1992 Challenge from Europe: Development of the European Community's Internal Market.* Washington, D.C.: National Planning Association.

Commission of the European Communities. 1984. *Television without Frontiers: A Green Paper on the Establishment of the Common Market for Broadcasting, Especially by Satellite and Cable.* COM(84)300 final (June 14).

———. 1987a. *Towards a Dynamic European Economy: A Green Paper on the Development of the Common Market for Telecommunications Services and Equipment.* COM(87)290 final (June 30).

———. 1987b. Office for Official Publications of the European Communities. *Europe without Frontiers: Completing the Internal Market.* Per. 4/1987. Luxembourg.

———. 1988a. *Telecommunications: Progress on the Definition of Open Network Provision (ONP).* Short status report, draft. COM(88)718 (December 13).

———. 1988b. *Completing the Internal Market: An Area without Internal Frontiers.* COM(88)650 final, November 17. The progress report required by article 88 of the treaty.

———. 1988c. *Towards a Community-wide Telecommunications Market in 1992—Implementing the Green Paper on the Development of the Common Market for Telecommunications Services and Equipment—State of Discussions and Proposals by the Commission.* COM(88)48.

———. 1988d. *Telecommunications in Europe.* European perspective series. Report prepared by H. Ungerer and N. Costello.

———. 1989a. *Revised Proposal for a Council Directive on the Implementation of Open Network Provision (ONP).* COM(89)325 final—Syn 18 (August 10). Brussels.

———. 1989b. *Report Drawn on Behalf of the Committee on Economic and Monetary Affairs and Industrial Policy on the Proposal from the Commission to the Council (COM/88/825-C2-318/88) for a Directive on the Establishment of the Internal Market for Telecommunications Services through the Implementation of Open Network Provision (ONP).* Doc. A2-122/89 Syn 187 (April 27).

Cooney, S. 1989. *EC-92 and U.S. Industry. See* National Association of Manufacturers.

Council of the European Communities. 1990. *Common Position Adopted by the Council on 11 May 1990 with a View of Adopting a Directive on the Establishment of the Internal Market for Telecommunications Services through the Implementation of Open Network Provision.* Annex 1 (May 11) 4078/90. Brussels.

Cowhey, P. F. 1990a. Telecommunications. In *Europe 1992: An American*

Perspective, ed. G. C. Hufbauer. Washington, D.C.: Brookings Institution.

―――. 1990b. "The International Telecommunications Regime: The Political Roots of Regimes for High Technology." *Int. Organ.* 44 (Spring): 169–200.

Cowhey, P. F., J. D. Aronson, and G. Szekely. 1989. *Changing Networks: Mexico's Telecommunications Options.* La Jolla, Calif.: Center for U.S.-Mexican Studies, Univ. of Calif., San Diego.

CSI Reports. 1989. Coalition of Service Industries Newsletter. December.

Dodsworth, T. 1988. "EC Seeks to End Parochialism in Telecommunications." *Financial Times.* July 11.

European Telecommunications Research. 1988. *West Germany: Deregulation Set to Open Up Telecommunications Market.* West Sussex.

Federal Republic of Germany. Government Commission for Telecommunications. 1988. *Restructuring of the Telecommunications System.* Chairman: Witte, E. Heidelberg: R. Decker's Verlag, G. Schenck.

Feketekuty, G. 1988. *International Trade and Services: An Overview and Blueprint for Negotiations.* Cambridge, Mass.: Ballinger.

―――. 1989. "The New World Information Economy and the New Trade Dimension in Telecommunications Policy." Mimeo.

Fin. Tech. Telecom Markets. 1991. 169: January 24.

Foreman-Peck, J., A. Haid, and J. Muller. 1988. *The Spectrum of Alternative Market Configurations in European Telecommunications.* Study by the Commission of the European Communities, the Anglo-German Foundation, Alcatel N.V., and the German Ministry for Research and Technology. Berlin-Newcastle: Deutsches Institut Für Wirtschaftsforschung in collaboration with the Centre for Research in Public and Industrial Economics of the University of Newcastle upon the Tyne. April.

Goldman, C. N. 1988. *Europe 1992.* Report prepared for the Joint Economic Committee of the Congress of the United States. 100th Cong., 2d sess. (S.Hrg. 100-1008).

Group of Negotiations on Services of the Uruguay Round. 1988. Ministerial statement on services. MIN-6.DOC (December 12).

―――. 1989a. *Agreement on Trade in Services, Multilateral Trade Negotiations, the Uruguay Round, Group of Negotiations on Services.* Communication from U.S. government. October 17. Geneva: GATT Secretariat.

―――. 1989b. Note on the meeting of 5–9 June 1989. MTN.GNS/23 (July 11).

―――. 1989c. *Trade in Telecommunications Services.* MTN.GNS/W/52; companion doc., MTN.GNS/W/51.

Haid, A., and Muller, J. 1988. "Telecommunications in the Federal

Republic of Germany." In *The Spectrum of Alternative Market Configurations in Telecommunications. See* Foreman-Peck 1988.

Library of Congress. 1989. *European Community: Issues Raised by European Integration.* Report prepared for the Subcommittee on International Economic Policy and Trade of the House Committee on Foreign Affairs. June. Washington, D.C.: Congressional Research Service.

Los Angeles Times. 1990: June 19.

Meyers, R., and D. E. Harper. 1989. "Opportunities Growing in EC Telecommunications." *Europe 1992* 1:20 (October 25).

National Association of Manufacturers. 1989. *EC-92 and U.S. Industry—A NAM Report on the Major Issues for U.S. Manufacturers in the European Community's Internal Market Program.* February. Washington, D.C.

New York Times. 1989: December 10, October 24.

Noam, E. 1988. "International Telecommunications in Transition." In *Changing the Rules: Technological Change, International Competition, and Regulation in Communication,* ed. R. Crandall and K. Flamm. Washington, D.C.: Brookings Institution.

———. 1991. *Telecommunications in Europe.* New York: Oxford Univ. Press.

Nora, S., and A. Minc. 1980. *The Computerization of Society.* Report to the president of France, 1978. Cambridge: MIT Press.

Nugent, P. Michael. 1991. "A Telecom User's Perspective." In *Is There Life after GATT?* January 24. Washington, D.C.: Center for Strategic and International Studies. International Communications Studies Program.

Organization for Economic Cooperation and Development, Committee for Information, Computer and Communications Policy. 1985. *Trade in Telecommunications Services: The Current Institutional Framework and the Potential for Change.* ICCP 85:12 (September).

———. Secretariat for the working party on telecommunications and information services policy. 1988a. *Trade in Telecommunications Network-based Services.* DSTI/ICCP/TISP/88.2 (June 1). Paris.

———. Committee for Competition Law and Policy. 1988b. *Competition Policy and the Deregulation of Telecommunications.* Working paper no. 2 on competition and deregulation. Prepared by M. A. Utton, AFFE/RBF/WP2/87-12 (February 9). 1st revision.

Pipe, G. R. 1988. *How the EC Plans to Conduct External Trade Relations after 1992.* August 18. Washington, D.C.: Transnational Data Reporting Service, Inc.

Pirzio-Biroli, C. 1991. In *Is There Life after GATT? See* Nugent 1991.

Roobeek, A. J. M. 1988. Telecommunications: An Industry in Transition. In *The Structure of European Industry.* 2d ed., ed. H. W. de Jong. Boston: Kluwer Academic Pub.

Sandholtz, W. 1990. "New Europe, New Telecommunications." Paper prepared for annual meeting of the American Political Science Association. August 30–September 2, San Francisco, Calif.

Services Policy Advisory Committee to U.S. Trade Representative. 1987. *Telecommunications and Information Services in Trade in Services Negotiations.* March 20. Washington, D.C.

Snow, Marcellus S., ed. 1986. *Marketplace for Telecommunications: Regulations and Deregulation in Industrialized Democracies.* New York: Longman.

Telecommunications Reports. 1990: February 19. 1989: December 18, November 20, July 3, April 17, February 27.

Telephony. 1990: January 22. 1989: December 18, December 11.

Temin, P., and L. Galambos. 1987. *The Fall of the Bell System.* New York: Cambridge Univ. Press.

Transnational Data and Communications Report. 1990: April, January.

Ungerer, H., and N. Costello. 1988. *Telecommunications in Europe. See* Commission of the European Communities.

U.S. Council for International Business. 1989. *U.S. Industry-proposed Approach for a General Agreement on Trade in Services (GATS) Applicable to the Telecommunications Sector.* Statement of the Council. November. New York.

U.S. Department of Commerce. 1990. *EC 1992: A Commerce Department Analysis of European Community Directives.* Vol. 4. Washington, D.C.: International Trade Administration, March.

U.S. Department of State. 1987. "Analysis of the European Community Green Paper on the Development of the Common Market for Telecommunications Services and Equipment."

———. 1988. *The European Community's Program to Complete a Single Market by 1992.* July 5. Regional briefs on Western Europe.

———. 1990. *Eastern Europe, Please Stand By.* Report of the task force on telecommunications and broadcasting in Eastern Europe. Washington, D.C.: Advisory Committee on International Communications and Information Policy. Spring.

Utton, M. A. 1988. "Competition Policy and the Deregulation of Telecommunications." *See* Organization for Economic Cooperation and Development. Committee on Competition Law and Policy.

Wildman, S. S., and S. E. Siwek. 1988. *International Trade in Films and Television Programs.* Cambridge, Mass.: Ballinger.

10
Commentaries on Telecommunications and Information Services

A Commentary by Geza Feketekuty

What we really need is an assessment of how far Community policy has come in relation to U.S. policy and what gaps remain in a transatlantic context. It is important to recognize, for example, that the gap between the United States and the European Community has been significantly reduced as a result of the EC Commission's efforts in connection with EC 92. Gains have also been made in individual member states as a result of pressure from American businesses and, of course, the large European firms.

Germany is a case in point. It used to be at the tail end of reform and now is in the vanguard of reform. The involvement of both the European and the American business community in the policy-making process has been critical to this outcome. We have thus come much closer to each other. It would have been helpful if Jonathan Aronson had reflected on this movement somewhere in his chapter.

The United States and the European Community have converged not only in the area of policy substance, but also in the policy-making process. Take the involvement of the courts. The courts are playing an increasingly important role in Europe in ensuring competition in telecommunications. This is an important step forward in developing parallel processes in the United States and Europe.

We should also recognize that Europe is opening up the standards-making process. The users are now included locally—foreign firms that are established in Europe are being included. There is also more open discussion of the new regulations. Because of this progress and EC 92, we can actually contemplate reaching a fairly good telecommunications agreement in the context of the Uruguay Round. Otherwise, we might never have reached this point in our negotiations.

As long as the United States and the Community can agree, I am sure we can bring along the other developed countries and the most advanced developing countries. The transatlantic debate has therefore been critical to the development of a global consensus.

But we must also recognize that some important directives have not yet been issued by the EC Commission—directives that will spell out the detailed policy guidelines on leased lines (including the conditions under which leased lines are to be made available), satellite policy, the rights and obligations of value added networks, and, of course, the obligations or monopolies with respect to competitive suppliers of value added services.

The European Community is expected to issue more detailed directives in each of these areas, which is where some of the differences between the United States and the Community will emerge. My informal discussions with commission officials suggest that the directives, when they come out, will represent further substantive progress. Even so, the Community will clearly not go as far as we would like toward open competition in these areas.

One of the most important of these issues concerns the rules for shared use and resale of leased lines, and, of course, joint user groups. The Community is moving ahead in each of these areas. The question is when will it be ready to take specific steps and how far is it prepared to go in making the environment more competitive?

Another critical issue concerns cost-based pricing. Community members are now saying that their long-term goal is cost-oriented pricing, but exactly what do they mean by this? This is also going to be an important subject of transatlantic discussion.

The policy on communication satellites raises the question of how the down-link and the up-link are going to be treated. The EC Commission appears to be prepared to allow companies to establish their own down-link—that is, to give private users, private networks, the right to link into a local earth station from a leased satellite circuit. Up-link—that is, establishing a link from a cable station to a satellite—is going to create far more problems, and this is where the Community may not agree with us. Establishing an up-link involves frequency allocation and other equally touchy issues.

Another issue that must be addressed has to do with the competitive safeguards required when monopolies participate in competitive markets. It looks as though this question is going to be fought out in the antitrust arena, both in the context of national antitrust laws and the EC competition rules. During recent conversations with an official from the Competition Directorate, I did get the impression that it plans to issue a general directive or guidelines on competitive behavior at some point.

This is clearly an issue that will be discussed in detail in drafting a Telecom Annex to the services framework agreement in the Uruguay Round. The Telecom Annex will need to establish basic principles with respect to the relationship of the monopoly suppliers of telecom transport services and competitive suppliers of telecom services not covered by the monopoly. Issues such as cross-subsidization, full transparency of internal accounts, the use of monopoly power to put competitors at a disadvantage must be addressed as well.

The rights and responsibilities of value added networks will be a particularly rough subject to tackle. We have said our networks should have the right to use private protocols and to have no obligations whatsoever, while the monopolies have all the obligations. From the European point of view, that is not going to sell. The Europeans will argue that a competitive value-added network supplier could exploit a dominant position and that dominant suppliers of such services will have to assume certain obligations in providing access; and that although they should have the right to their own protocols, they should also have to make it possible to interconnect on the basis of standard protocols.

What Aronson has demonstrated is that in negotiations on trade in services, the key issue is regulation; that national treatment is not as simple a solution to the question of ensuring market access to services as it is in the area of goods. The United States has made it clear to the Community and others that, in telecommunications, national treatment cannot ensure market access because current rules restrict access to that market.

Interestingly, we have argued just the opposite when it comes to financial services. We have said that national treatment is adequate, whereas the Community has argued that it is not. In general, however, national treatment is not a sufficient standard in services. Thus the key issue in the liberalization of trade in services is to what extent underlying domestic regulations have to be adjusted to ensure effective market access.

A Commentary by Werner Hein

Three issues should be addressed: (1) Will the European Community in the 1990s provide more or less opportunity for U.S. firms? (2) Where should the U.S. government and U.S. businesses place the emphasis in their market-opening drive? and (3) How can Eastern Europe be gotten off on the right track?

In response to the first question, I think opportunities for U.S. firms are to be expected. Just two years ago, for example, monopolies were prominent in all twelve nations except the United Kingdom. Practically all business opportunities were occupied by monopolies.

Now, in countries like the United Kingdom, Germany, and the Netherlands, the telecommunications monopolies should be limited to voice traffic, public switched-voice traffic, and network. But competition should be possible in the overlay services, in mobile, cellular radio, and satellite.

Indeed, several of these countries are more liberal than the United States. U.S. companies, for instance, may invest in cellular operations in the United Kingdom and Germany without any limits on their share holding, whereas in the United States the Communications Act prohibits more than 20–24 percent for foreign participation. So here other countries took a leap, certainly to their advantage, because the technology and the knowledge in this area particularly are concentrated in the United States.

Sometimes when we criticize the Europeans, we should reflect first on how the situation is for foreign companies in this country. It is a checkered picture.

How did these European countries liberalize? The United Kingdom took the lead; then Germany followed and then the Netherlands. Those major industrialized countries served as a catalyst for all of Europe. The EC Commission since then has proposed regulations for the whole telecommunications area. Fortunately, the commission took, in most of the areas, a liberal attitude. Without U.S. pressure, though, Europe would not have gone so far.

Now the question is, Where should we in the United States put the emphasis in the future? I believe that pressure on Europe is required and should continue. Perhaps, though, we should gradually move from a bilateral approach to a multilateral approach. The war, so to speak, for the liberalization in Europe has already been won. The emphasis should really be put on the industrial blocs outside the Community. I would like to see the U.S. government encourage multilateral negotiations in GATT.

From my practical experience, I have found that working from the inside means that investors can move things much faster than many of the diplomatic efforts or government plans can.

An example that comes to mind is mobile radio. The United Kingdom, like Germany, issues private licenses. The licensees can procure for themselves all the system technology, the switches and the transmission equipment, and what-have-you. Basically, the license is a gate for additional U.S. equipment exports, for U.S. system technology. U.S. involvement brought pressure on the monopolies, which now seek not only subsidized but also cost-effective equipment procurement.

We must also consider the issue of the target conflict in Europe: that is, liberalization harmonization. Harmonization will certainly benefit foreign businesses as well as domestic because these companies do not want to face different standards in different individual countries. Whereas it is important to find the common denominator for liberalization, we have to make sure that harmonizing the EC rules is not done on the least common denominator.

Once a kind of "liberalized island" exists, where the U.S. companies, for instance, can invest, liberalization will spread within Europe very fast because various financial and industrial centers will compete to become the economic hub for Europe. The governments and the monopolies, as well as the regulators, will see that to get most of the economic benefits, they will have to liberalize. Again, here I see a great need for U.S. business to work from the inside.

Of course, we all share the concerns over the broad licensing discretions of national regulatory agencies, over cross-subsidization, and over the abuse of network control. And while we should always raise those points, we are unlikely to nail them down very specifically. We will probably have to go to Europe to do the work and operate from the inside.

There, the individual countries have antitrust rules that apply to telecommunications. In Germany and the United Kingdom, for instance, is abuse of network control.

As for Eastern Europe, it deserves great attention in this historic time. The economy, including telecommunications, requires a complete overhaul. Eastern Europe faces the danger, as those countries now try to switch over from forty years of government monopoly in all social, individual, and economic life, of another kind of state monopoly. In fact, Western Europeans just emerged from such a monopoly in telecommunications.

It is important right away, I think, to get Eastern European countries on the right track. Just as the United States pointed Western Europe in the right direction after World War II, with its free market economy, perhaps the United States should come into Eastern Europe now.

Western Europe, because of its transition from a state monopoly to a free market approach in telecommunications, might not be the best teacher here.

Investors, however, are needed for liberalization of private business. I think it would be a lost opportunity if, because of attention to other areas of the world, we failed to invest in Eastern Europe and allowed those countries to lapse into state monopolies again.

A Commentary by Claiborne H. Johnson, Jr.

Jonathan Aronson has pulled together many important details to remind us of the complexity of international relations. Let me now comment from a more personal perspective, although the viewpoint appears to be fairly widespread.

My company is Electronic Data Systems and my responsibility has been to provide the communication services our customers need to do their business. Our contribution, in general, has been to integrate complex information systems and to help manage those systems. We are not a carrier, certainly not a common carrier in the communication sense, and we do not provide any basic or commodity communications except insofar as they are embedded in other things. Actually, we are more like a giant user and in some ways are not too different from the U.S. government.

As a user, we are embedded in the business operation of our customers and whatever they are doing. That means we are already present in Europe and in many other places in the world—as good citizens, we hope, because we are trying to make the companies that hired us more productive and to create jobs. This gives us some license to speak, in a nonthreatening way, to the governments of the countries that we are talking about.

This is not to say that I am not completely in favor of competition, open networking, cost-based pricing, and the like. Such things help us get the communications that we need to integrate into other information management systems. But they are not all equally important to us and, as Aronson points out, we should not ask for the kitchen sink.

What seems of primary importance from a giant user's perspective is that the basic building blocks are there. Without them, it makes no sense to even contemplate integrating into other things. These blocks include the right technology with the right lead times, and at something approaching the right price, although that is not as critical as having the functionality. And, of course, the open-network philosophy must be present, for all the obvious reasons.

We need these things not so that we can use them to compete with their suppliers, but so that we can do something else with them. And if the building blocks are not readily available, we then need the permission to "make" (in the make-versus-buy sense) them ourselves—again, not as a public competitor but as a private representative of our customers.

In general, I would characterize what we need, and what any big user needs, as the freedom to become partners with the basic suppliers of these building blocks. Those basic suppliers can be the telecommunications administrations (TAs) or they can be competitors of the TAs. Frankly, it does not make any difference to us. We are not trying to compete with either group.

Since we are only adding value and are doing so privately—we are not doing it for everybody, but for our customers—and since the added value is in areas such as network management and new functionality, firms like ours do not affect the business volume of the supplier of the basic things, whether this happens to be the TA or some competitor of the TA. That is another reason why the user should be less threatening to the establishment.

All this translates into a priority list that starts out with the terminal equipment directive, which contains the essential ingredients that enable you to connect things to the network, regardless of whose network it is. One must be able to work under the philosophy of open network provisioning. You need that to provide all the functions, to integrate them, and to operate on a global level. As an intelligent user, you need to be plugged into the planning and the standards setting. That is part and parcel of the openness.

At the same time, some aspects of the service directive could be relaxed where the user is concerned. Remember that we are not trying to compete fairly, just to obtain fairly. Experience shows, of course, that without competition fairness soon disappears from the side of getting things. So the competition is fine. It's just that if you have to back off from something, from my perspective it is more important to retain the availability than protect the competitiveness.

A Commentary by Warner R. Sinback

The telecommunications industry is important not only in its own right, but also for its contribution to economic growth and social progress. Consequently, telecommunications policy is receiving considerable attention from the European Community as it charts its economic course for 1992 and after. Several principles have already been defined to guide activities in the area of telecom services.

First, the member states will endeavor to choose competition over monopoly supply when, from an economic standpoint, it is a viable alternative. They recognize that a competitive market adjusts better and more rapidly to technological change; that a competitive environment produces new services faster and is more responsive to market and customer needs; and that industry exposure to free market competitive forces is more apt to create pricing structures that reflect the true economic costs of providing specific services, and thus to give correct pricing signals to the marketplace. In this way states can avoid basing new services on false economic premises, such as the uneconomic bypass.

Second, the Community recognizes the importance of creating a forum for industry views as a part of the process of developing policy. These would include the views of users, value added service providers, basic (monopoly) service providers, and equipment suppliers.

Third, the Community is willing to hear complaints of unfair treatment from any party and if, on investigation, it finds them legitimate, it will use its influence to obtain correction.

The EC Position in 1980. In 1980 all telecommunications services in the EC countries were provided through a monopoly, although not always a monolithic one. Service providers ranged from public agencies under direct ministerial control to government-owned corporations and regulated companies with varying amounts of public and private ownership. Some countries combined telecom services with postal, radio and broadcasting, and related financial, savings, and payment services. This provided opportunities for covert cross-subsidization. In other countries, the telecom monopoly was fragmented into functional monopolies or regional monopolies run by different organizations.

Thus, Europe came to have a diverse array of structures, with the German monolith at one end of the spectrum and Italian diversity at the other. What was monopolized also varied from country to country, with variations in the provision of user terminal equipment, PABXs, modems, telex terminals, and also in equipment installation and maintenance. Even where the provision of equipment was allowed to be competitive, technical approval procedures and regulations could be used to manipulate national standards and protect national manufacturing interests. Similarly, they could be used to delay the introduction off newer technology. The introduction of fax equipment could be delayed, for example, to protect the provision of telex terminals and services.

Tariff structures had failed to adjust to the changing costs of service provision resulting from the increased productivity generated by new technologies. Growing revenues were often used for cross-subsidization, disguised taxation, or artificially to preserve employment levels in obsolescent activities.

Commercial and industrial users with a need for internal communications, private-use networks, or external communications to

235

their trading partners were frustrated by the restrictive and outdated practices, patricularly those that kept international services from entering their nations. Even the limited value added services available at the time were considered a threat rather than a means of promoting, developing, and enhancing the use of the monopoly infrastructure. There was obviously no European Common Market in the telecommunications industry, which behaved as though the Treaty of Rome had never been signed.

The well-worn phrase "European PTT" was only meaningful if defined in a national context, and even there the differences were greater than the similarities. As each nation rushed to the defense of its telecom structure, it implied that the other EC members had the wrong kind. Meanwhile, consumers were more concerned about the service products and their quality than about structure. And more users were being introduced to the information technology terminal as it invaded the workplace in industrial firms.

Changes since 1980. From 1980 onward, a number of EC countries began independently to revise their telecommunications laws, organizational structures, and national practices. The purpose of some of these changes was to liberalize monopoly practices and remove restrictions on value added services. Others recognized that where the government has been the watchdog of public interest, the regulator, the decision maker on pricing, the manager of the infrastructure, the vendor of services and equipment, and the technical judge and jury, a monolithic structure is impractical. Activities that should be performed separately become a confused web and the complexity of making ddecisions under such circumstances is so great that the legislature begins to lose control.

Probably the most extensive changes have been made in the United Kingdom, which has transformed a government-managed post office monolith into a structure consisting of independent divisions. Ministerial and industrial policy is in the hands of the Department of Trade and Industry, and the monitoring of behavior in the marketplace, cost-controlled pricing, and the first channel of recourse for the consumer is provided by OFTEL. The infrastructure monopoly has been broadened to a duopoly, with other public operators licensed for satellite services and the newer specialized services. Under its director general, Sir Brian Carsberg, OFTEL has developed a control mechanism for managing fair play between the consumer and the interconnected but increasingly competing duopoly of British Telecom and Mercury. In 1989 even the restriction on national "speech bypass" or "simple" resale was removed and value added services made unrestricted. The extent to which the local network of British Telecom is under attack from alternatives such as cellular radio, PCN, and other technology remains to be seen, but in this respect Mercury is a limited competitor.

Although other countries have retained their infrastructure monopolies, they have made various degrees of progress toward liberalizing services provided through the infrastructure. But this has always stopped short of the resale of live-voice (non-value added), and it continues to be difficult to change fifty-year-old structures. In the Federal Republic of Germany the legal and political processes were completed in 1989, and the new market environment for value added service delivered via the monopoly infrastructure is beginning to take shape.

It was not until June 1987, with the publication of EC Commission's landmark Green Paper (COM/87)290 on the development of the common market for telecommunications services and equipment, that the process of collective change was launched. Since then, Community members have become more aware of the need for competition law to check the behavior of monopolies—even government monopolies—in providing services to the consumer. They also recognize that tariff or technical barriers to the provision of services and equipment between member states can also distort the market.

Nonetheless, the commission's Green Paper did not propose to reduce the monopoly power of the infrastructure or of Public Service Live Telephony and defended the national governments' prerogatives in these fields. Nor did it propose that the monopolies be deprived of the right to provide value added services, but it did permit other value added services vendors to use the infrastructure on a "level playing field basis," without prohibitions, discriminatory pricing, or artificial technical barriers.

In its proposal for open network provision (ONP) the commission did not define value added services, except insofar as they are services supplied outside the infrastructure entry and exit points but not within it. It did recommend that EC countries remove the barriers created by the lack of common technical knowledge, disparate usage conditions, and discriminatory tariff structures. Although these proposals were welcomed by the user community and government economists, the telecommunications administrations in some countries resisted them and were in a strong position to delay the changes without openly opposing them.

As a result, progress in this direction has been slow, and attempts to liberalize terminal and value added services using Competition Law (Article 90.3) have been delayed by court appeals based on procedural grounds. The user community is alarmed and hints that the resistance is not "just" the result of procedural concerns inasmuch as the Council of Ministers could have, but did not, implement the changes.

When it became clear that the 1992 single market might not include telecommunications, a compromise was negotiated in the Council of Ministers, and firm timetables for several aspects of open network provision were agreed. Many outside the Community charged that it was building a Fortress Europe with respect to telecommunications, but this was strongly denied. The debate will no doubt continue during the GATT negotiations.

The Future EC Environment. The current political consensus within the European Community is that member states should continue to decide on the way in which their basic infrastructure for telecommunications is provided and that a national monopoly for this may be retained. Moreover the provision of "live-voice" services may also be retained as a monopoly, or "reserved," service. The extent to which the provision of telecommunications via cable or radio frequencies is monopolized or limited by the issuing of a restricted number of operating licenses per country will vary.

To compensate for failing to include a provision on competition, the Community will create national regulatory bodies, which are independent of the monopoly providers, with statutory obligations to represent consumer and industrial interests. In addition, European law (specifically, Articles 85 and 86 of the Treaty of Rome) protects against the abuse of a dominant position. As a guardian of the treaty, the Competition Directorate of the commission is responsible for promoting compliance.

Although it will be regrettable if court action is needed to end abusive practices, after a few precedents resistance should wane. The ONP process will ensure that the infrastructure, although it does not provide for competition, will give users through the European Community access to a set of universally available standards on similar and converging quality and contractual conditions.

Value added services can be expected to be deregulated, and the market should expand in a competitive environment. But since the new telecom environment spelled out in the Green Paper will ultimately depend on the implementation of local laws and regulations, different rates of progress can be expected in the various countries.

11
U.S.-European Air Services in the 1990s

Daniel M. Kasper

As the world enters the seventh full decade of commercial international air service, three important developments have become clear to careful observers of international aviation. First, the underlying economics of modern airline operations—particularly in an increasingly deregulated international marketplace—will give rise to a relatively small number of global airline networks that will compete with each other in markets around the globe. Second, this globalization combined with the drive toward European integration already has eroded beyond repair the foundations of the postwar international aviation regime. Third, the resulting struggle to shape a new world aviation order is likely to create turbulent aviation relations over the coming decade, particularly between the United States and the members of the European Community (EC). This chapter examines the economic factors promoting globalization and their effects on the international aviation regime. It also provides some suggestions for constructing a new set of aviation agreements to replace the existing bilaterally based regime.

Deregulation and Globalization

Aviation developments in the United States have traditionally had an impact far beyond its national borders. Thus, it should come as no surprise to those familiar with the history of civil aviation that, when the world's largest aviation market and leading aviation power reversed its forty-year-old policy of economically regulating the airline industry, the reverberations of that change would be felt around the globe. Indeed, in important respects, commercial aviation in the 1980s can be best understood as the struggle of U.S. airlines to cope with deregulation and the struggle of the rest of the world's airlines—and governments—to cope with deregulated U.S. airlines (for a more detailed examination of these issues, see Kasper 1988).

Deregulation eliminated governmentally imposed restrictions on entry, pricing, routing and other aspects of airline competition that had prevented or impaired competition in U.S. domestic airline markets. Freed of the control of the Civil Aeronautics Board (CAB), airlines radically realigned their route structures, explored new pricing strategies, adjusted their aircraft fleets, developed new approaches to marketing and distributing their services, and consummated a rash of mergers and acquisitions. The airline industry that has emerged from the first decade of deregulated competition is characterized by a relatively small number (four to eight) of national— and increasingly international—single-carrier air transportation systems. The route networks operated by the surviving airlines typically consist of multiple, interconnected hubs, each served by frequent "feeder" flights from a large number of destinations. It has been possible to manage and coordinate the activities necessary to sustain these increasingly far-flung networks by the use of a variety of powerful, computer-based information systems. The resulting U.S. airline networks appear to produce substantial economies of scale and scope comparable to those that characterize other multiproduct firms (Bailey and Freidlander 1982; Levine 1987).

Deregulation also had important effects internationally. The restructuring precipitated by deregulation made U.S. airlines stronger than their foreign competitors, particularly in the competition for traffic to and from the United States. Since foreign carriers generally lack the right to serve points behind their U.S. gateways (and, in most cases, could not economically provide such service even if they had the legal right to do so), they have relied traditionally on connecting services provided by U.S. airlines for access to nongateway traffic in the United States. Before deregulation, U.S. domestic airlines were precluded from serving international markets, and U.S. international carriers had only limited rights to serve the domestic market. As a result, U.S. domestic carriers had an economic incentive to feed traffic to foreign carriers and permitted those carriers to compete effectively with U.S. international airlines for nongateway traffic.

But deregulation significantly changed the incentives of U.S. carriers to provide foreign airlines with connecting traffic from interior points and, as a direct result, weakened the competitive position of foreign flag airlines serving the United States. It did this by providing U.S. airlines with unfettered access to the entire domestic market, which in turn made it possible for those airlines to serve many new markets. U.S. airlines quickly discovered, however, that only by adopting hub-and-spoke route systems could they provide economically viable service to the vast U.S. domestic market. Once they had established domestic hubs, it was a simple step for U.S.

240

carriers to add service (that is, new "spokes") to international markets using traffic collected at their hubs from the hundreds of U.S. cities. As a result, U.S. domestic carriers that had previously been happy to carry passengers to New York, Los Angeles, and other gateways for connections to foreign airlines now sought to carry those passengers abroad on their own flights. Deregulation and the economic logic of hubbing had made international expansion by U.S. carriers virtually inevitable.

Deregulation also heightened the competition among U.S. airlines to attract and maintain the patronage of travelers, particularly frequent (that is, business) travelers. Because the rapid expansion of international trade and the trend toward globalization in other sectors of the economy have stimulated the demand for international travel, an airline's ability to provide international service has become an increasingly important competitive factor, even in domestic markets, where a frequent traveler's choice may be affected by a desire to accrue mileage in a single frequent-flier program. Furthermore, deregulated U.S. airlines have sought expanded access to international markets because both traffic and profitability are expected to grow at faster rates than in domestic markets.

U.S. deregulation has put foreign airlines under increasing competitive pressure from more, larger, and increasingly efficient U.S. airlines. Plagued by small domestic markets, restrictive international agreements, and often inefficient airlines, other governments have adopted—sometimes reluctantly—market-opening measures affecting their domestic and international markets in an effort to replicate the efficiency and competitive benefits experienced by the deregulated U.S. airline industry. Thus, since 1978, numerous governments—including those of Canada, the United Kingdom, Japan, Australia, Taiwan, Korea, and even China—have taken significant steps to deregulate or substantially liberalize their domestic and, in some cases, international aviation markets. In addition, the European Community is now in the midst of a phased program that could substantially deregulate airline competition throughout the huge internal EC market.

Meanwhile, foreign airlines in general and European airlines in particular have scrambled to keep pace with their U.S. counterparts, principally by means of either acquisitions or strategic alliances with other airlines. To date, most of the acquisitions have been national: British Airways (BA) has acquired British Caledonian; Air France has taken over two French carriers, UTA and Air Inter; and Lufthansa has sought control of the former East German carrier Interflug. In contrast, some partial acquisitions have moved across borders. These include KLM's substantial minority stake in Northwest Airlines; SAS's equity stake in Continental; a three-way cross-ownership arrangement involving SwissAir, Delta, and Singapore Airlines; and Iberia's purchase of a large position in Aerolineas Argentinas. Although less active than European airlines, Pacific rim carriers have also taken equity positions in other carriers, including two in the United States—Japan Air Lines (JAL) in Hawaiian and the Australian carrier Ansett in America West. In addition, the Australian carrier Quantas holds a significant stake in Air New Zealand.

European airlines have also been active in forming strategic alliances across national boundaries. SAS has taken the lead by entering a variety of such alliances, including agreements with airlines in the United States, South America, Europe, and Asia. British Airways and United have entered a major "marketing" agreement that provides BA with improved access to interior points in the United States. (That agreement has been jeopardized by United's subsequent acquisition of Pan Am's rights to serve London.) Other examples of such alliances include the arrangement among SwissAir, Delta, and Singapore; code-sharing agreements between TWA and Austrian Airlines and American and Quantas; and other such agreements too numerous to mention.

The Withering Away of the Postwar Regime

International air services are governed today by the legal and institutional arrangements developed in the 1940s, beginning at the Chicago Conference on Civil Aviation in 1944. Like the General Agreement on Tariffs and Trade (GATT) for goods, the existing regime for international air services arose piecemeal because nations were unable to agree on a more comprehensive, multilateral system. As a result, air services throughout the world have been controlled by bilateral agreements between the nations concerned. The Bermuda Agreement negotiated by the United States and the United Kingdom in 1946 established what was then regarded as a relatively liberal pattern for the exchange of economic rights, but many of the agreements subsequently negotiated by other nations have been significantly more restrictive.

Following the adoption of an explicitly competitive international aviation policy in 1979, the United States began to use its economic clout and the promise of access to additional U.S. cities to negotiate significant liberalization of existing bilateral agreements. These U.S. efforts were particularly successful in Europe, where the "carrot" of access to large, economically attractive markets and the threat of traffic diversion to carriers whose governments had signed market-opening agreements with the United States were sufficient to produce a series of new and substantially more liberal bilateral agreements.

But European carriers soon discovered that the strength of U.S. carrier hubs undercut the Europeans' ability to compete for nongateway traffic. They also made two additional discoveries: first, beyond a certain number, the value of access to additional gateways in the United States diminishes because many cities generate insufficient traffic to sustain direct service; and, second, in order to compete with U.S. carriers for traffic to and from such interior points, foreign airlines might have to provide connecting services at their U.S. gateways to numerous interior points. Given the expense of acquiring and operating a fleet of aircraft, it would be economically infeasible to establish the capability to provide such connecting service unless the aircraft could also be used to serve the U.S. domestic market. In short, foreign airlines may need the right to serve the U.S. domestic market in order to compete effectively for international traffic to and from the United States. Because most national markets outside the United States are geographically small enough to be served effectively through a few gateways, U.S. carriers do not face a mirror image of this problem in serving most foreign markets. U.S. carriers face other, equally significant problems abroad, however, as discussed below.

Foreign carrier access to domestic traffic poses significant political and economic issues. To begin with, the United States and most other nations have enacted regulatory prohibitions against cabotage—that is, against the carriage of domestic traffic by a foreign carrier. Even if these legal restrictions were eased to permit such access to be negotiated, the negotiators would still face formidable problems.

As described earlier, deregulated competition in the United States has demonstrated the importance of operating a widespread network of hubs, each supported by an array of feeder flights. Under deregulation, foreign carriers given access to the U.S. domestic market would be free to establish operations in the largest domestic market in the world, a market large enough to sustain operations on an economically efficient scale. U.S. carriers, in contrast, would typically receive access to foreign domestic markets too small to support efficient operations. Although the United States could in theory negotiate rights to carry traffic between pairs of European states, as a practical matter it would be impossible for the United States to negotiate bilaterally, for example, a set of agreements that provided U.S. carriers with significant access to internal European traffic. Moreover, unless European internal and domestic markets had been deregulated, U.S. carriers would be severely restricted in their ability to establish and sustain viable services in those markets.

Hence, conflicting domestic regulatory systems combine with small national markets to create a significant problem for U.S. and European negotiators under a regime based on bilateral agreements: Although the internal EC market is roughly equivalent to the U.S. domestic market, providing U.S. carriers with access to the internal EC traffic is beyond the power of any single member state to grant. Thus, even if U.S. negotiators could grant access to the U.S. internal market, no single foreign government would be in a position to provide equivalent access for the United States.

Relations between the European Community and the United States

The increasing divergence in the scale and scope of economically efficient airline markets and those defined by national boundaries has heightened interest—both in Europe and the United States—in the European Community's efforts to establish a barrier-free internal market for air services. After all, if part of the air services problem lies in a disparity in market size between the United States and the rest of the world, can that problem not be addressed by aggregating a group of smaller markets into an equivalent bloc?

Although EC member states have continued to negotiate bilateral air service agreements, they have done so in the absence of a Community air transport policy. Hence, the adoption of such a policy would undermine the rationale for continuing bilateral negotiations between individual EC member states and third countries. As in the case of trade negotiations under the GATT, where the Commission of the European Communities already represents the member states, both the logic and the effective operation of a barrier-free internal air transport market ultimately require a common front for negotiating with third parties.

In fact, the commission's second package of liberalization measures (Commission of the European Communities 1989) already contains most of the elements of a common air transport policy. It also contains a number of elements that substantially increase the likelihood that the commission will become directly involved in air service negotiations with the United States and probably other countries as well.

The second package specifically recognizes, for example, that a common EC air transport policy has "important implications for relationships between Member States and third countries" and reiterates earlier statements that relations between the Community and third countries need to be based on the "principle of reciprocity" defined as "a guarantee of equivalent, or at least non-discriminatory, opportunities." In this context, the commission specifically noted that "it does not seem to the Commission that existing concessions to third countries in respect of fifth freedom between Member States (Community cabotage) are balanced by similar advantages abroad for Community air carriers." The impression that this comment appears to be directed primarily at the United States is reinforced by the remarks of a number of EC officials who regularly refer to an "imbalance" in the number of European cities served by U.S. airlines compared with the smaller number of U.S. cities served by European carriers. In view of these implications, as well as the potentially significant impact of third-country bilaterals on the internal EC market, the commission announced its intention to seek a mandate to negotiate with third countries "in appropriate cases."

The second aspect of the package that is likely to precipitate greater Community involvement in air service negotiations with the United States involves fares. The commission indicated that "it appears appropriate" to extend the commission's fare regulations to cover domestic and third-country fares, as well as fares for services between member states. Although not yet proposing such an extension of its jurisdiction, the commission has pointedly noted that the European Court specifically affirmed the commission's jurisdiction over such fares in the *Ahmed Saeed Flugreisen* case decided by the European Court on April 11, 1989.

The commission's assertion of jurisdiction over fares will inevitably precipitate negotiations between the commission and the United States (and possibly other states) because—if member state jurisdiction over fares to and from the United States is supplanted by the European Community—it would call into question existing pricing articles negotiated by the United States with various member states. Since the United States negotiated those pricing articles in exchange for valuable routes and other rights, it is unlikely to accept changes in them without either additional compensation or a reduction in other rights enjoyed by Community airlines.

Third, the proposed definition of a "community airline" in the second package specifically includes some carriers that are neither owned nor effectively controlled by nationals of member states, thus permitting some—but not other—non-EC citizens to control existing airlines based in the Community. Such discriminatory treatment is likely to antagonize nations whose citizens are excluded.

Fourth, the commission has indicated that the citizenship and control provisions of existing bilateral agreements among member states are null and void with respect to citizens of the Community.

245

(These provisions require that airlines designated by a signatory state be owned and controlled by citizens of that state.) Moreover, the commission has "requested" that member states "take the necessary steps" to ensure that third-country bilaterals conform with the requirement in the Treaty of Rome that the Community eliminate internal market barriers based on nationality. The stated intent of the commission is to ensure "the right of establishment" throughout the European Community for its nationals.

The commission's efforts to amend the citizenship and control provisions of agreements between member states and third countries are also certain to precipitate negotiations with the United States. Since amending these provisions to meet the commission's objectives would make it possible for any community airline to operate air services to the United States from the territory of any of the twelve member states, U.S. negotiators are likely to require compensation before making such changes, a move that will trigger negotiations either directly with the Community or with its member states as a group. In light of the difficulties encountered by the United States in dealing with a large group of European nations in the European Civil Aviation Conference (ECAC) negotiations, U.S. negotiators may well conclude that American interests would be best served by negotiating directly with the European Community (Kasper 1988 75ff.).

Where We Go from Here

The second package of air transport proposals signifies an increasingly aggressive effort by the commission to push European air transport toward a barrier-free market by the beginning of 1993. As a result of that effort, the odds are increasing that the Community will reach its goal by the mid-1990s if not by 1993. Even without the second package, however, the recent European Community decisions involving external fares as well as citizenship and control have substantially increased the likelihood that the United States and other non-EC nations will find it necessary to negotiate directly with the Community on air service matters. Indeed, the commission is already preparing for air service negotiations with the countries of the European Free Trade Association (EFTA) and then with the other European states. Community aviation officials clearly expect (and want) the initial negotiations to involve first the EFTA states, followed by "other European" nations (for example, other ECAC member states) and then the United States and other third countries. EC officials seem to believe that by sequencing negotiations in this fashion they will be able to put together a broader bloc of European nations and thereby strengthen their position in negotiations with North America and Asia. They seem particularly anxious to prevent the United States from launching a divide-and-conquer strategy in Europe.

The commission appears to have in place at least the rudiments of a strategy for dealing with the United States in the air transport sector. That strategy can be summarized as follows:

- force a rationalization of the European airline industry by increasing the level of competition
- negotiate first with non-EC nations to create both a European-wide aviation market and a larger economic bloc for negotiating with the United States (and Asia)
- use the EFTA-EC negotiations to build the commission's expertise and to develop mechanisms for using the aviation expertise that exists in the members states
- convert internal EC and, if possible, European routes into cabotage routes that can be exchanged for additional traffic rights in negotiations with the United States and Asia
- use the leverage from a common European front to gain more access to the United States or to restrict U.S. access to Europe

It is thus a matter of when—not whether—air service negotiations will take place between the United States and the European Community. The more interesting question is whether either party will take the initiative in precipitating those negotiations or whether they will be forced into negotiations by pressures arising from the rapid changes under way in the airline industry.

In my view, a strategy of waiting would be a mistake—for both Europe and the United States. By reducing the economic pressure on Europe to move rapidly toward liberalization, a wait-and-see approach may strengthen the hand of those in Europe who are opposed to a more open, competitive regime for air services. Without the threat of U.S. effort to further liberalize air services (and divert traffic from the airlines of illiberal nations), liberalization could be slowed not only across the North Atlantic but within the European Community as well.

Moreover, waiting for Europe to attain a common market is almost certain to delay U.S.-European liberalization past 1992 and may make European nations less willing to pursue such a course in air services. The explanation for this is straightforward: It is simply not realistic to expect Europe to engage in substantial market-opening negotiations with the United States on the heels of bruising internal EC negotiations. And even if the European governments were willing, they might find it extremely difficult to muster domestic support for trades with the United States that effectively unraveled compromises struck as part of the internal EC negotiations. Thus, by waiting for Europe, the United States, the Community, and the world could be faced with a second, equally odious CAP—for aviation policy rather than agriculture—by 1995.

Whether or not policy makers in the United States and Europe are prepared to act, recent events have significantly increased the likelihood of major changes in aviation policy. War in the Persian Gulf coupled with a recession have dealt a crippling blow to the world's airline industry by simultaneously raising airline costs while driving down traffic and revenues. The result has been to accelerate the already strong pressures toward greater industry consolidation—both in the United States and Europe. Since the outbreak of war in the Persian Gulf, two of the large U.S. airlines have sought the protection of the bankruptcy courts and another, Eastern, has ceased operating entirely. In Europe, the commission has adopted some temporary measures designed to help Community airlines cope with the economic downturn. Even so, Air Europe has ceased operations and virtually every other major European airline has announced draconian measures to cope with the deteriorating economic conditions.

Although EC competition policy officials have stated they intend to "avoid the U.S. mistakes" in dealing with airline mergers, the liberalization of EC air transport regulation is certain to consolidate the European airline industry. The current level of mating activity among European airlines suggests that most have already accepted the likelihood of significant liberalization in the internal EC market and are now acting on the (entirely reasonable) expectation that liberalization will lead to further consolidation in the industry.

Since Europe starts the process of liberalization with substantially fewer airlines than did the United States, however, the prospect of increased concentration in the EC air transport market poses difficult problems for the Community's competition policy. EC officials seem prepared to acknowledge that the existence of significant economies of scale and scope will lead to some concentration. Indeed, many believe that European airlines must become larger to compete effectively with American and Asian carriers in a global market.

But EC officials should also be troubled by the possibility that European airlines might use the specter of U.S. giants to create a tight oligopoly that would dominate the internal market to the detriment of European consumers. A number of recent and prospective agreements among European airlines should be particularly worrying to those interested in fostering a more competitive European aviation market. It remains to be seen whether the commission will sacrifice a competitive industry structure in the pursuit of European champions.

EC officials should soon become aware—if they have not already—that, if reduction in the number of European airlines is inevitable, it may be more desirable from the perspective of competition policy for some of the smaller European airlines to be acquired by non-Community airlines. Yet, under the proposed definition of a "community airline" in the second package, an airline from an EC member state cannot now be acquired by a carrier from a third country without losing its rights and privileges within the Community.

At the same time, policy makers in the United States face their own dilemma. Although the efficiencies of large networks can explain much of the consolidation that has taken place in the U.S. airline industry, the effects of the recession, the war, and inflation in fuel costs have been particularly devastating for several U.S. airlines that had previously undertaken leveraged buy-outs or other highly leveraged financings. As a result, the United States must now deal with a situation in which the best way to preserve and enhance competition in its airline markets may be to permit foreign acquisition of weaker U.S. air carriers.

The United States appears to have recognized the potential of foreign investment. On January 23, 1991, U.S. Secretary of Transportation Samuel K. Skinner announced a significant easing of restrictions on foreign ownership of U.S. airlines. In approving investments in U.S. airlines by SwissAir, KLM, Ansett, SAS, and JAL, the department has also demonstrated some sensitivity to the importance of foreign investment and has shown that a more liberal policy on foreign investment and control would not necessarily permit U.S. airlines to dominate the world industry. At a minimum, U.S. approval of European investments in U.S. airlines should mute opposition to comparable U.S. carrier investments in EC airlines. Should a U.S. airline seek to obtain more than a 25 percent interest in an EC airline, however, opposition could increase because of the 25 percent limitation on foreign ownership contained in the U.S. Federal Aviation Act.

Conclusion

For liberalization to proceed in the air services, substantial changes will be required both in *how* negotiations are organized and *what* is included in those negotiations. Neither change is likely to come easily.

The problem of disparate market sizes and domestic regulatory systems cannot be overcome without some aggregation of smaller markets into larger bargaining entities. The GATT is an obvious vehicle for reaching such an agreement, but certainly not the only one. Moreover, the application to air services of the GATT principles, including unconditional most-favored-nation and national treatment, would impede rather than promote further liberalization.

A more promising approach would be to focus on securing a liberal agreement among an initially small group of air service powers with competitive airlines and market-oriented economies—in other words, to aim for a trageted multilateral agreement. Such an approach is far more likely to produce a truly liberal regime for air services than is an approach based on the GATT (Kasper 1989: 93ff.). Because such an agreement could cover a large share of existing airline traffic, it could heighten the pressure on more restrictive countries to accept liberalization and reduce the ability of protectionist governments to dilute liberalization to the lowest common denominator.

For a variety of airline and political reasons, an agreement between the United States and the European Community is the most likely starting point for a targeted multilateral agreement. Both have large, well-developed internal air service markets. Moreover, as mentioned earlier in the chapter, recent EC initiatives are likely to require direct air service negotiations between the United States and the Community sooner rather than later.

Although U.S.-Community negotiations will not be easy, they will be far simpler than would talks among a larger, more diverse group of nations. Even here, governments will be required to make difficult, sometimes wrenching, changes in long-standing policies. In particular, they will be required to put on the negotiating table items that they have traditionally excluded. They will find it necessary to give foreigners broad access to domestic and interregional markets. Governments will also have to accept the inevitability of acquisitions, mergers and the multinationalization of airlines formerly viewed as national flag carriers and, in some cases, as extensions of the state. Furthermore, these changes will force governments to eliminate their subsidization and, eventually, ownership of airlines.

Despite the formidable challenges facing U.S. and European Community negotiators, not moving ahead with liberalization could be costly. If the United States and the Community cannot act quickly enough to replace the existing air services regime with one more suited to current and future conditions, the forces of change already at work in the world airline industry will surely find the "fault lines" in the existing regime and cause the industry to be restructured along the path of least resistance; such a restructuring is likely to be neither as efficient nor as open as a regime negotiated along the lines I propose.

Air service negotiations between the United States and the European Community are inevitable and the existing international regime governing air services cannot long survive. The United States and the Community are in the best position to negotiate a replacement regime that can provide a sound basis for the continued expansion of international air services. Under the circumstances, there is no valid excuse for either side to be unprepared for the task at hand.

References

Bailey, E., and A. Freidlander. 1982. "Market Structure and Multiproduct Industries." *Journal of Economic Literature*, vol. 20 (September), p. 1024.

Commission of the European Communities. 1989. COM(89), 373 Final (September 8).

Kasper, Daniel M. 1988. *Deregulation and Globalization*. Cambridge, Mass.: AEI-Ballinger.

Levine, Michael. 1987. "Airline Competition in Deregulated Markets: Theory, Firm Strategy and Public Policy." *Yale Journal on Regulation*, vol. 4 (April), p. 393.

12
Commentaries on Air Services

A Commentary by Frederick Sorenson

Whenever the air transport policy of the European Community is discussed, it is usually under the heading of "deregulation." This is misleading. The main aim of our aviation policy is to remove the barriers between the member states and to create a common aviation policy. The driving force here is the movement toward the internal market. Thus, the removal of national barriers means liberalization.

Our aviation policy is designed to promote not only liberalization, but also harmonization and external policy. Liberalization refers to the dismantling of the bilateral regulation and, to some extent, to the introduction of the necessary Community-wide regulations. Harmonization means that Community-wide regulations will replace different national regulations, where useful. External policy may lead to liberalization or to regulation, but only time will tell, because it will depend on our partners in the rest of the world. Whatever controls remain or are created, their basic intent will be to eliminate unfair advantages.

Liberalization

Liberalization will be promoted in four main areas: airfares, market access, capacity control, and competition rules.

Airfares. The Council of Ministers has agreed that beginning on January 1, 1993, the Community will follow a system of double disapproval. This means it will still be possible to intervene in the presence of excessive or predatory prices. The purpose of these controls is to prevent unfair practices among air carriers. Between now and 1993 a transitional system will be in effect. It will be based on the existing zonal system with automatic approval for certain fares and double approval for the fares that are not covered by the zones. The zones will be less restrictive than the existing ones, however, and will be entirely devoted to the normal economy fares.

Market Access. After January 1, 1993, the European Community will

252

recognize full third-, fourth-, and fifth-freedom traffic rights, multiple designation, and cabotage. The third- and fourth-freedom traffic rights will be introduced before that time, and the fifth-freedom right will only be allowed for up to 50 percent of the capacity of the service concerned. Cabotage will not be introduced until January 1993.

Rules will also be established for the licensing of air carriers in each member state. The so-called right of establishment will apply in every state. This means that the citizen of any state will have the right to set up business in another member state. Under these conditions, the present monopolies should disappear. The Council of Ministers has decided that licensing rules must be established by July 1, 1992. Air routes will be decided on as well. The Community rules to be established will affect the relations between a member state and its own carriers (that is, carriers established on its territory).

Capacity Control. No bilateral capacity control will remain after January 1993. Until then, a member state will be entitled to 60 percent of the capacity shared by itself and another member state. In addition, a member state may increase its present capacity share a year earlier by 7.5 percentage points. This means that a member state with 63 percent of the capacity may increase its share to 70.5 percent. Some states may run into difficulties here, however, since the European Community is not a union, and it may be forced to reorganize its air transportation. In that case, a freeze may be imposed for a year or two, while the reorganization takes place, but then the market will have to be opened up for competition again.

Competition Rules. The antitrust rules in the Treaty of Rome are already being applied and a fine-tuning will be carried out this year. This fine-tuning will redefine the rules for cooperation between airlines.

Harmonization

Harmonization is taking place in a great many areas, one of which is accident investigation, where cooperation and the exchange of expertise have already been going on for ten years.

Rules to limit noise were also introduced ten years ago, and now all aircraft operating within the Community are reguired to meet at least the Chapter 2 requirements of the International Civil Aviation Organization. We have also forbidden the importation of aircraft that do not meet Chapter 3 requirements, and a nonoperation rule for aircraft that do not meet these requirements will be introduced in the near future.

In August 1989 we introduced a code of conduct for computerized reservation systems. Its purpose is to prevent the distortion of competition to the detriment of air carriers and consumers alike—another example of our campaign against dirty tickets.

A code of conduct for the allocation of slots is under development. Again, the purpose is to avoid distorting competition through unfair advantages. Common licensing requirements are also being developed and will be introduced before January 1993. The same is true for flight-time limitations.

Common airworthiness requirements are being developed not only for the Community but for the whole of Europe. The aim is not only to remove unfair advantages, but also to ensure the free circulation of aircraft between national registers. In other words, if an aircraft has been certified in one member state, then this certification will be valid in all member states. This means that air carriers will not need to modify aircraft when they are moved from one register to another, and leasing companies will be in a better position to operate across the Community. The airworthiness requirements will cover not only construction but also maintenance.

Most of the harmonization that I have been describing involves safety in one way or another. We do not believe that air carriers should be given a competitive edge by relaxing the rules of safety. In addition, we intend to harmonize denied boarding compensation. Of course, this is being done to protect consumers, and air carriers are not too happy about the prospects. Furthermore, we expect to introduce common rules setting up regular consultation between airports and users. These rules will seek to ensure the best possible use of scarce facilities, but will also emphasize cost-effectiveness for airport charges.

We shall also take a hard look at air traffic control (ATC). Economic integration, along with the liberalization of existing bilateral constraints, has increased traffic considerably and put a strain on existing ATC capacity. Various groups are trying to resolve this problem and are working with the Community to integrate the operation of air traffic control in Europe. Another solution in many places will be to provide better equipment and more and better-trained air traffic controllers. This should be achieved in about four years. By that time, airport capacity will clearly be a serious concern, which is why we are developing a code of conduct for slot allocation now.

External Relations

Although internal barriers between our member states are disappearing, barriers still exist in our agreements with other countries in the world. Thus, we have also put together some proposals concerning external relations.

The most important of these proposals is to set up a procedural framework to cater to the relationships with third countries in aviation matters. Another proposal asks for a mandate to open negotiations with the countries of the European Free Trade Association.

At present, some 700 bilateral air services agreements are in force between individual Community member states and third countries. These agreements are based on the Chicago convention. They regulate the air services between the states and provide general criteria and procedures to fix the level of tariffs and capacity, the designation of airlines, consultation, and information procedures.

In view of this large number of relations, it is impossible for the Community to take responsibility for all the negotiations at once. Therefore a transitional period is envisaged in which member states may continue to conduct negotiations under certain conditions. Gradually, the Community will become responsible for the external aviation regulations. The existing bilateral framework will have to be replaced by air services agreements concluded between the Community as a whole, on the one hand, and a third country or third countries, on the other.

In certain areas, however, the Community must take immediate responsibility, as in the case of fifth-freedom traffic rights exercised by carriers from third countries within the Community. These rights are a Community asset and should therefore only be granted by the Community as a whole. This does not mean that the Community is closing in on itself. On the contrary, existing agreements will be respected and new fifth-freedom rights will not be excluded, but will have to be considered on a Community basis.

Attention will also be given to situations in which third countries might take advantage of the lack of Community unity. Using a divide-and-conquer strategy, some third countries have been able to gain advantage that are not fully justified by the market. The Community hopes to piece the playing field level, however, and to bring about a better balance—better from our viewpoint, of course.

In general we hope to achieve better results for our member states than they could obtain individually. In particular, we intend to obtain the same market opportunities for our airlines irrespective of where they are established in the Community. In doing so, we expect also to increase market opportunities for airlines from other parts of the world.

In principle, international relations in aviation can also be organized on a multilateral rather than a bilateral basis. Some argue that, in view of the complexity of the existing bilateral framework and many specific sectoral features, a multilateral approach to trade in air services is difficult—if not impossible—to achieve. Indeed, recent discussions on trade in services in Geneva suggest that we are still far from a breakthrough on a multilateral approach to worldwide aviation. Even so, we must recognize the global nature of air transport services, which are being produced and sold more and more on a worldwide scale. This is not surprising in view of technological developments such as CRS distribution systems and increasing worldwide economic integration.

The surprising element is that the international aviation business is still regulated predominantly on the basis of a bilateral system built on the classical concept of reciprocity—that is, an eye for an eye and a tooth for a tooth. Whether this fits well with the basic characteristics of the air transport industry is doubtful. Our concept of reciprocity has more to do with market opportunities (that is, traffic potential) than with the notion of 50 percent for you and the rest for me.

It is not my intention to criticize the Chicago Convention. This system has substantial merits and will continue to be the cornerstone of international aviation. But we should remember that the air transport of the 1990s is not the same industry that existed in 1944. Consequently, we should at least begin opening our minds to the possibility of establishing a multilateral approach to international aviation.

The European Community has started gradually replacing the traditional bilateral framework with a multilateral approach to traffic rights, fares, and many other issues. Why not extend the basic elements of this model, which is producing encouraging results, to a larger geographical area? This does not necessarily have to be the whole world, of course. But countries and regions finding themselves in a comparable situation regarding their overall economic philosophy, should reflect on how they might arrive at multilateral rules on the economically relevant aspects of international aviation. There is certainly room for improving the regulatory situation to the benefit of all participants.

What we in the European Community can offer in this context— apart from our willingness to discuss this subject—is to make available our own technical, economic, and political experience. I am convinced that such an open-minded discussion could produce highly beneficial results, as long as we avoid overly ambitious objectives.

A Commentary by James R. Tarrant

I am happy to report that the U.S. government has taken the initiative in dealing with the still evolving aviation developments in Europe, although not in precisely the way Daniel Kasper recommends. We are in no way taking a "wait-and-see" attitude. In reality, our objectives are constrained by the difficulties of engaging a Europe and a European Community that are in the midst of a vast internal transition. Nonetheless, we are moving ahead on a number of fronts in our aviation relations with Europe as part of our effort to liberalize international aviation worldwide.

Some of our current efforts are designed to implement Secretary Skinner's cities initiative, liberalize bilateral agreements, strengthen multilateral discussions, and mobilize public interest awareness.

The Cities Initiative. On January 30, 1990, Secretary Skinner issued a final order entitled "Expanding International Air Service Opportunities to More U.S. Cities"—the so-called cities initiative, or Skinner proposal. One of the factors leading up to this proposal was the widespread recognition that aviation has become vital to a broad range of U.S. trade and travel interests. In other words, it is part of the lifeblood of a modern, international economy.

Our bilateral aviation partners all have markets that are smaller than ours. But because of the legislative mandate that there be a "balance of benefits" in our traditional bilateral agreements, foreign carrier access to the U.S. market has been limited. A number of U.S. cities that could serve as commercially viable international gateways have been denied the international service they desire to support economic growth in their regions. Secretary Skinner's proposal is designed to allow foreign carriers to provide this needed service in certain cases.

Simply stated, carriers must meet two main criteria to qualify under this new program: (1) there must be no existing nonstop or one-stop service offered by a U.S. carrier on the proposed route; and (2) there must be a pro-competitive bilateral agreement in place, such that a U.S. carrier could provide the service competitively if it chose to do so.

When foreign carriers meet these and other criteria, they can initiate service without going through the formal bilateral negotiating process; that is, they will be able to bypass traditional restrictive bilateral agreements. Since the policy was issued, a number of foreign carriers have asked to serve new U.S. cities. The Department of

257

Transportation is now evaluating their proposals and inviting public comment to ensure that they meet the necessary criteria.

Bilateral Agreements. For more than forty years, nations have operated international air service by virtue of the rights agreed to in bilateral air service agreements. The system is not ideal and does not meet the needs of today's sophisticated world economy. Until we get something better, however, this is what we have to work with.

There is little doubt that liberal bilateral agreements are the most beneficial to an economy as a whole. Take the example of the German and Italian markets between 1977 and 1988. In 1977, U.S. airlines carried more passengers between the United States and Italy than between the United States and Germany. Then we signed a generally liberal agreement with Germany, while the Italian agreement remained highly restrictive.

By 1988, our airlines carried almost three times as many passengers to and from Germany as they did to and from Italy. In Germany, we went from one U.S. passenger airline in 1977 to five in 1988. In Italy, we still have only two airlines, the same as in 1977. In 1977, we had three nonstop routes to Italy but only one to Germany. In 1988, there were fifteen nonstop routes to Germany, but such routes to Italy actually declined to two. There are other factors at work, of course, but the implications of these trends for trade, tourism, and local economic development are obvious.

To maximize international opportunities for U.S. airlines, many of which are highly competitive in world markets, and to expand the economic benefits of liberal air services for both sides, the United States made some dramatic new offers to our largest European partners last fall. We offered "open skies" agreements to Germany, France, and the United Kingdom. Such agreements would remove virtually all restrictions on airline operations between and through our respective countries. None of these countries has yet responded positively to the offer, although some possibilities remain. We are now considering whether to extend the offer to some of our other aviation partners who may be more interested.

Our message should be clear: The United States is seeking liberal aviation agreements and the mutual benefits that flow from them. We intend to make deals where we can get them and continue down the same policy road. We recently signed a new agreement with Japan that will increase the number of routes between our countries by nearly half. This is the most significant expansion in the U.S.-Japanese aviation market since 1952. And just last month we made considerable progress toward liberalizing our aviation relationship with the Italians. Over the next few years, numerous new routes will be opened and three new U.S. carriers will begin to serve the market. I am hopeful the U.S.-Italian market will regain the prominence it once had.

Multilateral Discussions. Airline operations need greater flexibility if they are to achieve maximum efficiency. Aviation is a global industry. It makes sense to establish aviation rights in multilateral forums.

As might be expected, our primary multilateral focus is on Europe, although we are evaluating other multilateral organizations around the world for those that could serve as forums for aviation liberalization.

The European Community is establishing its competence in CRS, airport slot allocation, pricing, and other areas, and will eventually be dealing in route rights. We have been talking to the EC Commission all along as its competence has grown. Our dialogue with the European Commission will increase as member states implement Phase II of the aviation program. We are also considering the possibility of holding talks with the European Civil Aviation Conference (ECAC), a broader group of European countries, but with a more limited mandate.

Public Interest Awareness. Most people, including many in the business community, are surprised to learn that international trade in aviation services is highly restricted, to the detriment of a variety of trade, tourism, and economic development interests. Aviation is a prime component of modern economic development, and we need to raise the awareness of the vital public interests involved in aviation policy, both here and abroad.

U.S. cities and their congressional delegations are becoming more vocal in demanding that our international aviation policy take fuller account of their needs—as it should. Secretary Skinner's cities initiative is an important step toward meeting those needs. In addition, we are inviting these cities to become involved in our deliberations on aviation policy and are encouraging their efforts to be heard. We are also calling on the tourist industry, both here and abroad, to participate in the development of aviation policy.

We would like the tourist industries in Germany, France, and the United Kingdom, for example, to recognize the economic benefits that would come from an open skies aviation policy and then to let their governments know in clear terms what they want.

Within the U.S. government, we are working with U.S. industry and interested parties to build a consensus for new initiatives in international aviation. Assistant Secretary of State Eugene McAllister and Transportation Assistant Secretary Jeff Shane recently met with U.S. airlines and U.S. city and airport representatives to get their input on international aviation policy. They in turn met with labor, tourism, and other interested groups.

Our Challenge to Europe. Let there be no misunderstanding about our view of aviation policy developments in Europe. We applaud the efforts of the European Community to liberalize internal air travel. We believe in the broadest availability of air travel. People should not be kept off airplanes because of artificially high prices caused by government interference in the market. Now, our firm hope is that the European Community will extend its recognition of the benefits of liberalization to relations with third countries.

As I noted earlier, we are seeking a broader exchange with the European Community on aviation matters. In the process, we will continue pressing for more liberal bilateral agreements with European countries. In all of these efforts, our objectives are the same: to end the artificial restrictions that constrict international aviation, to free airlines from the sometimes heavy hand of government so that they can make their own rational and competitive commercial decisions, and to bring the benefits of aviation liberalization to all sectors of our economies.

Our message to Europe is simple. We are prepared to make the market across the North Atlantic the most efficient and economically beneficial international aviation market in the world.

13

Insurance Trade between the United States and the European Community

Robert L. Carter

The insurance industry plays an important economic role that is all too often overlooked. It provides the producers of other goods and services risk-bearing services and capital with which to increase their efficiency and competitiveness in domestic and international markets.

Risk Transfer and Risk Spreading

Insurance is primarily a mechanism for transferring risks: it enables individuals and organizations, in return for the payment of an agreed premium, to transfer to an insurer the risk of financial loss arising from the occurrence of specified uncertain loss-producing events. If the risks are too large for an individual insurer to accept without imperiling its solvency, the required insurance may be provided through the participation of a number of insurers. Risk may be spread in several ways:

• *Co-insurance:* Several insurers can participate directly in the insurance, each co-insurer being separately responsible to the policyholder for its agreed share of any loss.
• *Layers:* The coverage, usually for liability risks, can be arranged in layers with different insurers; the first layer covers losses up to a certain amount, the second layer covers an amount in excess of the first, and so on.
• *Reinsurance:* A direct insurer can transfer a part of the risk(s) it has accepted to a reinsurer, which, in return for a premium, undertakes to meet an agreed part of any claims that may arise on the original insurance(s) (Carter 1983). The reinsurer in turn may reinsure part of its liabilities so that very large risks are spread among insurers worldwide.

It has long been the practice of insurers to spread large risks internationally. Today enormous values are often at risk. They include

261

the potential losses from natural disasters and man-made catastrophes that arise from technological, demographic, economic, legal, and social developments. To supply the amount of insurance required to cover these risks, national insurance industries have a continuing, and frequently increasing, need to tap the additional underwriting capacity available from international insurance and reinsurance markets. Even the American insurance market, which writes almost a half of the world's non-life premiums, is not self-sufficient for the insurance of very large individual risks such as aviation liabilities, offshore oil installations, or petrochemical plants. Thus, although the Piper Alpha oil platform was owned by a consortium of mainly American companies, after allowing for claims recoveries from international reinsurers, American insurers will have to meet only about 5 percent of the total insured losses (excluding workers' compensation) of US$1.2–1.5 billion (Mercantile & General Reinsurance 1988a). The U.S. market is also unable to handle losses that may be caused by natural and man-made disasters, particularly earthquake and hurricane losses in the main exposure zones and pollution liabilities. In a 1986 study of the effect of two major hurricanes striking the Gulf and Atlantic coasts of the United States, it was established that more than one-third of the total estimated insured losses of $14 billion would be recovered from foreign insurers and reinsurers (All-Industry Research Advisory Council 1986).

Despite the increasing need to spread risks internationally, the internationalization of insurance services has not progressed at the same pace as other financial services. Indeed, in some areas it has regressed in relation to the total business written.

Savings and Investment

In both the United States and in most countries of the European Community, life insurers have diversified away from pure protection and moved into the provision of savings-type contracts, most of which require the policyholder to pay premiums at regular intervals over ten or more years. Consequently, they are in competition with other institutions in the market for personal savings. Also, the assets held by life insurance companies to meet the claims of policyholders place them among the largest groups of institutional investors and make them an important source of funds for capital markets (table 13-1). Many of the large insurance groups, particularly life insurers, in both the United States and Europe have diversified into other financial services, and some have developed into, or become parts of, financial conglomerates.

TABLE 13-1
ASSETS OF SELECTED FINANCIAL INSTITUTIONS, DECEMBER 31, 1987

Type of Institution	United States (billions of U.S. dollars)	United Kingdom (billions of pounds)
U.S. institutions		
FSLIC-insured institutions	1,250.9	
FSLIC-insured federal savings banks	284.9	
Savings banks	259.6	
Credit unions	169.1	
Life insurance companies	1,044.5	
U.K. institutions		
Life insurance companies		173.4
Pension funds		196.3
Building societies		158.4
Unit trusts		33.2
Investment trusts		14.4

NOTE: Credit unions, March 31, 1988.
SOURCES: United States: *Federal Reserve Bulletin* (April 1989: table A26/27); United Kingdom: *Financial Statistics* (January 1989: tables 7.7, 7.11–13).

The Economic Aspects of Production

The production and distribution of insurance services has traditionally depended on a combination of financial, human, and intangible resources.

Capital Resources. The amount of capital required by an insurance company to operate efficiently and to provide adequate protection for its policyholders depends on a number of factors. At the minimum, it must meet the capital and solvency requirements enforced by the supervisory authorities of the countries in which it operates. Financial prudence may dictate, however, that it maintain a higher level of capitalization in order to minimize the risk of insolvency inherent in its chosen underwriting, reinsurance, and investment policies.

A company's level of capitalization also affects its competitive strength because brokers and knowledgeable buyers judge the security of an insurer by the strength of its capital base, which also determines the size of risk, the amount of business it can underwrite, and its ability to provide continuous coverage for clients in periods of

263

heavy losses. Consequently, although the EC solvency regulations require nonlife insurers to maintain surplus funds of less than 18 percent of their net premium incomes, the leading U.K. companies, like their U.S. counterparts, endeavor to achieve a capital:premium ratio of 50 percent or more.

Human and Other Resources. The efficiency, security, and competitive ability of an insurance company depends on the quality of its personnel; an information system able to provide detailed information on the clients, products, and area of operation; and an appropriate network for distributing the product. An insurer or reinsurer that wishes to write overseas business must be prepared to invest in acquiring knowledge of the markets concerned, their methods of operation, the nature of the risks involved, and local economic, legal, and social conditions bearing on those risks. Many companies that have failed to do so—such as the Instituto de Resseguros do Brasil (Hill 1986) and the Korean Reinsurance Corporation (Wasow 1986)— have incurred large losses over a short period of time.

Highly trained, experienced managers and senior staff are required in all of the key areas of an insurer's operations. Underwriters must have the knowledge and skill to evaluate the risks presented for insurance. Sound claims management is needed to engender good client relations and to contain claims costs, which usually account for two-thirds or more of an insurer's total costs. And only by expert financial and investment management and access to well-developed capital markets can an insurer hope to maximize the investment return on its funds—and so keep its premium rates competitive.

Information Technology. Over the past twenty years, information technology has substantially transformed the production and distribution of insurance services. Today technology plays an important role in product design, risk evaluation, marketing, and investment management. The development of expert systems is likely to bring further changes before the end of the century (Rajan 1987). Note, however, that technology has supplemented rather than replaced skilled human resources.

Distribution and Pre- and Post-Sales Servicing. Before an insurer can sell its products, it needs to acquire sufficient information to decide on the price and terms. Afterward, it must provide an efficient claims service. Therefore, like suppliers of other financial services, insurers generally require some form of local presence in a country in order to write a substantial volume of business, particularly personal and small trade insurances. The free movement of labor across national boundaries is therefore vital for transacting insurance internationally (Bhagwati 1987; Walter 1988).

Economies of Scale and Scope. The nature and size of the economies available to insurers is a matter of debate because of the problems of defining output and measuring costs in a multiproduct industry. Most studies, however, have shown total average cost curves to be L-shaped, with significant economies of scale being exhausted at premium income levels that are low relative to total domestic premiums in almost all countries (Geehan 1986). Sales and administration costs are influenced by differences in the distribution systems, and an insurer specializing in a narrow product range may be able to obtain some economies of scope by diversifying into other lines of insurance or possibly into other financial services.

Competitive Behavior and Market Regulation

Like the markets for other financial services, insurance markets can be defined in terms of the client, arena, and product (Walter 1988). Clients can be categorized into corporate and private (including both individuals and small traders) on the basis of their product-related attributes and consumer protection needs as perceived by governments. Corporate clients differ so greatly in their risk characteristics that they require individual underwriting and premium rating. In contrast, personal and small trade insurance is rated by classifying clients into broadly homogeneous groups.

Individuals and small firms have more need for regulatory protection than corporate clients. Not only do the latter have access to information and expert advice not available to most individuals, many also possess substantial bargaining power. Only a small number of insurers in the United States and Europe are capable of putting together for multinational corporations the global insurance programs that will accommodate the client's own risk-retention capabilities and captive insurance company.

Arenas. The boundaries of market arenas can be wider or narrower than national boundaries, according to regulatory and monetary sovereignty, market practice, client needs, and other factors. Whereas the American insurance market enjoys the unifying advantage of a common currency and language, it is fragmented by having the states responsible for supervising the insurance business. State laws require residents to place their insurance with insurers licensed to operate within the state, and insurers must be licensed by every state in which they wish to trade. Although the 1992 program ultimately will permit EC residents and insurers to trade freely across EC state boundaries, differences in language, culture, and currencies will continue to fragment the European market for personal and small trade insurance into twelve arenas.

Products. As noted earlier, many insurers do not limit their activities to supplying the widely varying range of insurance services. They provide other financial services, too. In the United States and most countries of Europe, regulatory controls make it necessary to separate life from general insurance business. An insurer that wishes to supply its clients with the whole range of insurance products must therefore adopt a group-holding structure.

The resources required to compete effectively in each market cell are beyond the means of all but a small number of companies worldwide. The majority of insurers limit their activities to certain lines of insurance, clients, and territories.

Competitive behavior between insurers is strongly influenced by the need to fix premiums at the inception of each contract before the ultimate claims costs can be known. Such uncertainty tends to induce both collusion between insurers in determining minimum premium rates and regulatory control by government supervisory agencies, whose aim is to ensure that premiums are neither inadequate nor excessive and discriminate fairly between policyholders. The less regulated the insurance markets, the greater the tendency toward premium rate and profit instability, with an accompanying higher risk of insurer insolvency.

The Single European Market

Since the decision was taken in 1985 to form a single internal market by December 31, 1992, considerable progress has been made in removing the remaining nontariff barriers to trade that will create a unified trading bloc of some 320 million people. It is hoped that the ensuing increase in competition and the reorganization of European industry will generate substantial efficiency gains and faster economic growth (Cecchini 1988). It should also strengthen Europe's international trading position.

How far the rest of the world will benefit (or lose) from Europe 1992 will depend upon the Community's external trading policies. European integration could provide the catalyst for wider trade liberalization, or the Community could become Fortress Europe, possibly erecting new trading barriers against the rest of the world, or at best removing existing barriers only through bilateral agreements based on strict reciprocity. The direction in which Europe moves is of particular importance for insurance services that for the past thirty years have been subjected to increasing trade barriers, particularly, though not exclusively, by the developing countries (Carter and Dickinson 1979).

In 1989 the European Community initialed an agreement with Switzerland that will bring it into the single European insurance market, allowing its insurers to establish in any EC member state or to supply insurance services across national frontiers on the same conditions as a Community insurer. Therefore, Switzerland has been treated as part of the European Community in this discussion.

Insurance in the U.S. and European Economies

Individual European countries have a small share of total world insurance premiums in comparison with the United States (which produces about 40 percent of world premiums) and Japan (with 22 percent) (see table 13-2). With integration, however, the insurance business of the European Community will immediately obtain a 24 percent share of world premium income.

Expenditure on Insurance. Measured in premiums per capita and as a percentage of gross domestic product, expenditure on insurance is higher in the United States than in any European country other than Switzerland (table 13-3). At the same time, over the past twenty years expenditure on insurance has been growing faster in most European countries than in the United States (Swiss Reinsurance 1987).

The insurance market is at considerably different stages of development in the northern and southern countries of the European Community. Although levels of expenditure on both life and nonlife insurance in the southern countries is far lower than in the north, the less developed markets of southern Europe are now growing significantly faster than in the north and are expected to continue to do so after 1992 (Farny and Schmidt 1989).

International Insurance Activity. The integration of insurance markets will give the European Community the largest share of international trade in insurance services. With few exceptions (for example, Greece and Portugal), the European insurance industries are more heavily involved internationally than the American industry, although in all countries foreign business is confined to a relatively

TABLE 13-2
WORLD SHARES OF GROSS DOMESTIC PREMIUMS, 1987
(millions of U.S. dollars)

Country	Life Business		Nonlife Business	
	Premiums	World share (%)	Premiums	World share (%)
United States[a]	165,414	30.34	241,238	45.96
Japan[b]	178,344	32.71	62,725	11.95
Switzerland	8,877	1.63	7,128	1.36
European Community				
Belgium	1,972	0.36	4,710	0.90
Denmark	1,903	0.35	2,987	0.57
France	21,236	3.90	28,764	5.48
Greece	203	0.04	427	0.08
Ireland	2,517	0.46	1,538	0.29
Italy	4,270	0.78	15,471	2.95
Luxembourg	66	0.01	195	0.04
Netherlands[a]	7,083	1.30	8,188	1.56
Portugal	135	0.02	918	0.17
Spain[b]	4,175	0.77	6,681	1.27
United Kingdom	40,155	7.37	23,665	4.51
West Germany	36,391	6.67	44,962	8.57
EC total	120,106	22.03	138,506	26.39

a. Net premiums.
b. March 1987–1988. Excluding recargo externo; including primas unicas.
SOURCE: *Sigma* (1989: 3: 18–21).

TABLE 13-3

PREMIUM EXPENDITURE IN THE UNITED STATES AND THE EUROPEAN
COMMUNITY, 1987

(U.S. dollars)

	Total Premiums ($ million)	Premiums per Capita		Total Premiums as % of GDP
		Life	Nonlife	
United States	406,652	678.6	989.6	9.07
Japan	241,069	1460.7	513.8	6.43
Switzerland	11,352	1,257.3	1,089.9	8.02
European Community				
Belgium	6,682	198.9	474.8	4.17
Denmark	4,890	371.0	582.2	4.30
France	50,000	381.7	517.1	5.06
Greece	630	20.3	42.8	1.24
Ireland	4,055	711.0	434.5	12.24
Italy	19,741	74.4	269.9	2.35
Luxembourg	261	178.4	527.0	3.35
Netherlands	15,271	483.2	558.5	6.29
Portugal	1,053	13.0	88.7	2.69
Spain	10,856	107.5	172.1	3.31
United Kingdom	63,820	705.8	416.0	8.35
West Germany	81,353	594.9	735.0	6.40
EC total	258,612	371.0	427.8	5.80

NOTE: See table 13-2.
SOURCE: *Sigma* (1989: 3: 22–23).

small number of large companies (and in Britain, also to Lloyd's of London).

The United Kingdom is unique within the Community, being, like Switzerland, a large net exporter of insurance services through both the establishment of British insurance companies abroad and through cross-border insurance trade. In 1987 overseas business accounted for 47 percent of the total premium income of the Swiss insurance and reinsurance companies. U.K. companies obtained approximately 44 percent of their worldwide net (of reinsurance ceded) nonlife premium income and 16 percent of their life premium income from abroad, and Lloyd's of London obtained two-thirds of its premiums from abroad (Carter and Diacon 1989). The overseas earnings of the U.K. insurance industry (including insurance brokers) from overseas establishments and cross-border trade and from overseas portfolio investment income accounted for 60 percent of the United

Kingdom's total 1988 net overseas invisible earnings *(United Kingdom Balance of Payments 1989)*.

International business, mainly transacted by foreign subsidiaries, also accounts for a substantial part of the total premium income of the major insurance companies in most other EC countries. For example, overseas premiums make up one-third of the total premium income of the German company Allianz (Europe's largest insurer) and more than one-half of the total premium incomes of the AGF Group (France), Generali (Italy), and Nationale-Nederlanden.

A little more than 1 percent of the 5,800 U.S. insurance companies are established outside North America, and only about a dozen of those are extensively involved in overseas business. The International Insurance Advisory Council estimates that the foreign gross premium income of American insurers and reinsurers is less than 3 percent of domestic premiums, but the Office of Technology Assessment (1986a) calculated that in 1984 U.S. insurance affiliates abroad had premium revenues of US$5.4–5.5 billion for life and health insurance and US$7.3–7.5 billion for property/casualty insurance in comparison with total domestic premium revenues of US$134.8 billion and US$121.9 billion, respectively. The Office of Technology Assessment (1986b) also estimated that in 1984 U.S. insurance exports were in the range US$2.8–3.7 billion against imports of US$4.8 billion: virtually all of the exports and imports of insurance and reinsurance services would be connected with property/casualty business. There are no published estimates of the net earnings of U.S. insurers' foreign affiliates, but estimates of cross-border insurance transactions show that the United States is a net importer of insurance services, largely because of its imports of foreign reinsurance (tables 13-4 and 13-5).

Insurance and Financial Services. In both the United States and Europe, the activities of insurance companies interface with other parts of the financial services sector. The Bank Holding Act of 1956 and its various amendments generally preclude American banks from carrying on any insurance business within the United States or owning insurance companies (other than in respect of banking-related insurances). In some European countries (notably Greece and Spain) there have long been ownership and operating links between banks and insurers. With the recent developments in the markets for financial services, new links are being forged throughout the European Community. In Britain, for example, the first life insurance company subsidiary of a major retail bank was established in 1965. Following the Financial Services Act of 1986, there has been substan-

TABLE 13-4

U.S. Insurance Exports and Imports, 1986–1988

(billions of U.S. dollars)

	1986	1987	1988[a]
Insurance Exports			
Direct insurance			
Premiums received	2,800	2,823	2,756
Claims paid	1,200	1,227	1,445
Net	1,600	1,596	1,311
Reinsurance			
Premiums received	1,715	2,009	1,972
Claims paid	1,269	1,320	1,719
Net	446	689	253
Insurance imports			
Direct insurance			
Premiums paid	954	1,083	1,193
Claims received	477	531	591
Net	477	552	602
Reinsurance			
Premiums paid	6,264	7,331	7,822
Claims received	4,538	4,714	5,644
Net	1,726	2,617	2,178
Net balance	−157	−884	−1,216

a. Provisional.
SOURCE: U.S. Department of Commerce (1989b).

tial restructuring of the personal savings market. The majority of the banks and building societies have become tied agents of insurance companies for the selling of life insurance, and they are forming an increasing number of joint-venture life insurance companies. The banks and building societies also sell nonlife insurance, mainly to personal clients, and the Royal Bank of Scotland has pioneered the direct telephone selling of motor insurance through its own nonlife insurance subsidiary. Approximately fifty life insurers own unit trust management companies; leading insurance groups (Prudential, General Accident, and Royal) have acquired extensive real estate agency chains; and Confederation Life is proposing to establish its own deposit taking bank.

Many French banks own life insurance companies, and now banks and the leading insurance companies are coming together to exploit the banks' branch networks for the selling of insurance. Banque Nationale de Paris and L'Union des Assurances de Paris, for

TABLE 13-5
U.S. DIRECT PROPERTY AND CASUALTY INSURANCE AND REINSURANCE PREMIUMS, 1981–1988
(millions of U.S. dollars)

| Year | Gross Direct Premiums | Written by U.S. Companies | Reinsurance Premiums | | | |
| | | | Ceded abroad | | Received from abroad | |
			($ million)	As % of (1)	($ million)	As % of (3)
1981	100,973	6,989	2,109	2.09	953	45.2
1982	105,035	7,469	2,538	2.42	983	38.7
1983	107,817	7,698	2,872	2.66	1,150	40.0
1984	121,879	8,637	3,486	2.86	1,243	35.7
1985	151,817	11,255	4,625	3.05	1,327	28.7
1986	184,838	15,102	6,264	3.39	1,715	27.4
1987	199,478	15,151	7,331	3.68	2,009	27.4
1988	207,260[a]	13,355	7,822[a]	3.77	1,972[a]	25.2

a. Provisional.
SOURCES: Gross direct premiums: Insurance Information Institute, New York, *Insurance Facts*. Reinsurance premiums of U.S. companies: *National Underwriter*, June 19, 1989. Reinsurance premiums ceded and received from abroad: U.S. Department of Commerce (1989a, 1989b).

example, have entered into 10 percent cross-shareholdings, and Groupe des Assurances Nationales proposes to increase its shareholding in Credit Industriel et Commercial from 34 percent to 51 percent.

In Germany, the Deutsche Bank has formed its own life insurer, and the Allianz insurance group, has entered into a marketing agreement with the Dresdner Bank for the joint marketing of their respective products. And the Aachener und Munchener Insurance Group, which owns a building society, has purchased the trade union Bank fur Gemeinwirtschaft.

Italian leading insurance brokers have entered into insurance distribution agreements with banks, the British insurance group Guardian Royal Exchange has purchased three Italian insurers in partnership with Instituto Bancario San Paolo di Forino, and the Allianz subsidiary RAS has announced that it will open its own bank.

Spain's third largest insurance group, Mapfre, has purchased the Oviedo Bank, Allianz has taken a holding in Banco Popular Espanol, AGF has acquired a 5 percent holding in Banco Atlantico, and in 1988 Metropolitan Life and Banco Santander formed a joint venture life and pension insurer.

Market Structure. Large numbers of domestic and foreign insurance companies operate in both the American and European insurance markets (table 13-6). The total numbers of companies in these markets has been falling, whereas the numbers of foreign and foreign-owned companies has been rising. In Europe the 1973 Non-Life and the 1978 Life Insurance Establishment Directives, by removing the legal and administrative obstacles to Community insurers establishing in other member states, provided both the stimulus and the means for Community insurers to extend their activities to other parts of the Community. By extending the same rights to the EC incorporated subsidiaries of foreign insurers, the directives also provided an incentive for American and other insurers to establish subsidiaries in one or more Community states.

Table 13-7 gives an indication of the sizes of the leading companies on both sides of the Atlantic relative to their domestic markets, although the percentages tend to overstate the degrees of market concentration because company premium incomes include both domestic and foreign premiums, whereas the total market premiums relate only to insurance written in the country. In particular, the figures shown for the largest British, Dutch, and Italian companies substantially overstate their domestic market shares because of their large foreign interests. Nevertheless, two facts stand out: (1) the

273

TABLE 13-6

NUMBERS OF DOMESTIC AND FOREIGN INSURERS OPERATING IN THE U.S. AND EUROPEAN MARKETS, 1985

Nationality	Belgium	Denmark	France	Greece	Ireland	Italy	Luxembourg	Netherlands	Portugal	Spain	United Kingdom	West Germany	United States
Nonlife insurance													
Belgium	151		20	2	2	1	10	2			1	7	1
Denmark		154	2	2				3			2	1	2
France	16	2	245	5		2	3	10		1	8	15	3
Greece				37									
Ireland					10								
Italy	8	1	11	5	2	136		6	1	2	5	8	3
Luxembourg	1						8						
Netherlands	9	4	9	5		1		224			3	6	1
Portugal			1	1				1	18	1			
Spain	1		4						2	570	1		1
United Kingdom	38	30	45	32	21	18		32	14	9	446	41	17
West Germany	21	1	20	7		10	2			3	5	310	8
United States	4	3	4	7		6		10		4	9	6	3
Other countries	22	16	29	7	1	7	3	34	1	4	24	19	32
Total	272	211	393	148	41	181	26	324	36	594	508	414	3,543

Life insurance

Country of incorporation	Belgium	Denmark	France	Greece	Ireland	Italy	Luxembourg	Netherlands	Portugal	Spain	United Kingdom	West Germany	United States	Total
Belgium	80		4							1			7	1
Denmark		22												
France	5		73	37		1		2		3	3	1	2	4
Greece				10										
Ireland			2											1
Italy			1	48		6								
Luxembourg	1													
Netherlands	2	1	1					61						
Portugal									12					
Spain	1								3	156				1
United Kingdom	1		2	9				4		1	253			1
West Germany			2		1			1			1	98		
United States	1		6		2			2		1	5		2,048	
Other countries	4	1	7	2	3		2	3	3	3	12		6	61
Total	94	24	89	47	22	53	19	72	18	165	273	106	2,109	

NOTE: Companies are classified by company of incorporation, not by country ultimate holding company. Composite companies (that is, companies that undertake both nonlife and life business) are included in both parts of the table.

SOURCE: *Sigma* (November/December 1985).

TABLE 13-7

LARGEST INSURANCE COMPANY GROUPS WITH HEAD OFFICES IN THE UNITED STATES AND IN EUROPEAN COUNTRIES, 1986

(life and nonlife premium income, millions of U.S. dollars)

	West Germany	United Kingdom	France	Italy	Nether-lands	Bel-gium	Spain	Den-mark	Ire-land	Por-tugal	Greece	United States
Largest	9,894	5,122	4,478	5,770	5,422	957	1,050	589	627	113	89	19,367
Percentage of total	16.6	8.7	9.6	39.9	44.0	18.9	13.4	14.0	27.8	14.6	19.0	5.2
Fifth	1,647	3,476	2,049	762	554	337	330	330	121	76	31	11,080
Percentage of total	2.7	5.9	4.4	5.3	4.5	6.7	4.2	7.8	5.4	9.8	6.7	3.0
Tenth	996	1,914	968	468	204	178	159	141	75	18	7	6,131
Percentage of total	1.7	3.3	2.1	3.2	1.7	3.5	2.0	3.4	3.3	2.3	1.6	1.7

NOTE: Percentage of total = percentage of total premiums written in the country, including for the United Kingdom the business transacted by Lloyd's of London.

SOURCES: Mercantile & General Reinsurance (1988b); *Best's Review* (August 1987, July 1987); *Sigma* (May 1988).

premium incomes of the largest American insurers far exceed those of the leading European insurers, and (2) the U.S. insurance market taken nationally is less concentrated than the domestic markets any of the EC member states (although the levels of market concentration in some parts of the United States may be significantly higher). Although the combined premium income of the approximately 400 underwriting syndicates that constitute Lloyd's of London is larger than that of the largest U.K. company group shown in table 13-7, the syndicates compete both between themselves and against the companies.

Market Shares of Foreign Insurers. Although European insurers have acquired several American companies over the past ten years, foreign companies still write only about 3 percent of American direct domestic insurances (table 13-8). Foreign insurers' market shares in the EC member states vary from one-fifth or more in Portugal, Spain, and the Benelux countries to less than 10 percent in France, Germany, and Italy.

Competitive Behavior. The ability of the large companies to dominate the insurance markets of the United States and of Europe is limited in various ways.

First, because economies of scale are exhausted at relatively low levels of output, the large companies do not enjoy significant cost advantages over the smaller, often more specialized, companies. Although the large companies may enjoy some marketing advantages from being able to supply lines of insurance and, possibly, other financial services, company market shares vary between lines of business, with smaller, more specialized insurers sometimes achieving larger shares than the leading groups. In the United Kingdom, for example, the specialist provident associations dominate the health insurance market, and in 1987 a relatively small company, the Orion, wrote the largest aviation account.

Second, dominant domestic companies are exposed to competition from powerful foreign groups established in their markets and, in those countries whose market entry barriers are relatively low, they face the threat of potential new competition from the entry of other large foreign groups.

Third, in order to mobilize the underwriting capacity needed to provide the insurance required for the large industrial and commercial risks, companies usually need to secure the cooperation of many insurers. In those markets where co-insurance is practiced, only a small number of insurers may be competing for the position of the

TABLE 13-8
GROSS DIRECT INSURANCE BUSINESS WRITTEN IN THE REPORTING COUNTRY, 1986
(percentage of total gross premiums)

Country	Life				Nonlife			
	Domestic companies	Foreign controlled	Branches/agencies of foreign	Total	Domestic companies	Foreign controlled	Branches/agencies of foreign	Total
United States	96.9	3.1	—	100.0	98.3	1.4	—	100.0
Belgium	73.0	15.9	11.2	100.0	56.9	28.3	14.8	100.0
Denmark	92.3	5.9	1.8	100.0	86.4	8.7	4.9	100.0
France	—		2.9	100.0	—		5.6	100.0
Germany[a]	93.0	3.3	3.6	100.0	92.2	3.7	4.1	100.0
Greece[a]	81.4	0	18.6	100.0	82.8	0	17.2	100.0
Ireland	75.6	0	24.4	100.0	69.6	0	30.4	100.0
Italy	—			100.0	—			100.0
Luxembourg	—			100.0	—			100.0
Netherlands[a]	78.6	11.4	10.0	100.0	75.6	15.6	8.7	100.0
Portugal	58.7	6.3	34.9	100.0	80.5	10.7	8.7	100.0
Spain	66.8	24.9	8.2	100.0	70.9	19.8	9.3	100.0
United Kingdom[a]	—			100.0	—			100.0

— = not available.

a. Based on net premiums, including reinsurance business (non-life for Germany is based on gross direct premiums).

b. The U.K. market shares of foreign-controlled companies are estimated to be 18 percent for nonlife insurances and 14 percent for life insurance.

SOURCE: Organization for Economic Cooperation and Development (1989).

leading insurer who decides the premium and contract terms, but before that the insurance can be fully placed, the successful leading insurer must obtain the support of a sufficient number of following insurers (Carter and Diacon 1989). Moreover, an insurer that acts as a recognized leader for some types of risk may be content to act as a follower for others. If a large risk is not co-insured, then the insurer must obtain the support of sufficient reinsurers.

Supervisory Control. In most countries, competition between insurers is restricted to some degree by state supervision of the insurance business. Universally, governments have legislated to regulate both the entry of new companies to the market and the financial standing and behavior of existing insurers. In the United States, as noted above, state regulation of the insurance business fragments the industry into fifty-one separate markets; although some insurance companies operate nationwide, they must adhere to each state's regulatory rules governing the conduct of business.

Insurance business in the Community is still conducted almost entirely through the twelve national markets. Market behavior and competition in each of the countries remains subject to national regulations of varying degrees of stringency. At the one extreme are the liberal regulatory regimes of the Netherlands and the United Kingdom, in which insurers are by and large free to determine premiums and contract terms according to commercial considerations. At the other extreme are the highly regulated markets of France, Germany, and Italy, whose regulatory authorities exercise close control over such matters and over the investment of insurers' funds. Consequently, there are considerable differences between the cost of similar insurance sold in the various EC countries, as shown in table 13-9. Some of the differences may be explained by intercountry variations in loss expectancies, but conservative premium rating controls exert a marked influence on premium levels in many European countries. For example, the lower discount rate and population mortality tables that Belgian insurers are required to use in the calculation of life insurance premiums are responsible for most of the difference between the risk premiums (that is, the premium before the loadings for insurers' expenses) Belgian insurers charge for short-term temporary life insurance and the premiums U.K. insurers, free from such restrictions, are able to charge (Carter and Morgan 1986). Similarly, consumers in the highly regulated German life and automobile insurance market pay considerably more for their insurances and have less product choice than U.K. consumers, but enjoy no significantly greater security from insurer insolvencies (Finsinger et al. 1985).

TABLE 13-9

COMPARATIVE "PRICES" OF INSURANCE SERVICES IN VARIOUS EUROPEAN COUNTRIES, 1988

(European currency units)

	Belgium	Denmark	Spain	France	Italy	Luxem-bourg	Nether-lands	United Kingdom
Term insurance	380	225	294	285	392	355	195	150
House insurance	118	144	135	195	253	220	164	266
Motor insurance	494	436	758	413	942	671	354	316
Commercial fire and theft	1,296	2,023	1,765	3,587	4,896	1,204	1,412	1,797
Public liability	968	1,257	1,364	1,852	1,508	934	714	798

NOTE: Term insurance: average annual cost. Motor insurance: annual cost of comprehensive insurance, 1.6-liter car, driver ten years experience, maximum no claims bonus. Commercial fire and theft: annual coverage for premises valued at ECU 387,240 with stock and contents at ECU 232,344. Public liability: annual premium for engineering company with twenty employees and annual turnover of ECU 1.29 million; includes employer liability.
SOURCE: Price Waterhouse (1988).

Trade in Insurance Services

International trade in insurance can be defined as insurance services "produced by factors of production whose ownership resides in one country and [is] sold to residents of another, often through some sort of direct presence of the supplier in the client's country" (Walter 1988). Thus, it embraces both conventional trade in the form of services supplied across national borders, and the supply of services based on direct investment by insurance producers and intermediaries in production and distribution outlets in foreign markets.

The internationalization of insurance services began in the Middle Ages with marine insurance. By the beginning of the nineteenth century, British insurance companies were appointing agents to represent them in North America and Europe, and by the end of the century many of the companies had set up branch offices throughout the world (Dickson 1960; Supple 1970).

As argued earlier, an insurer cannot compete successfully without some form of local presence in the market in which it seeks to transact a substantial volume of business. It will not only need to obtain detailed client, risk, and market underwriting information, but will also have to provide an efficient claims service. Moreover, an insurer may also have to overcome consumer prejudice against dealing with a foreign company, particularly if it is not easily accessible. Many insurers therefore prefer to enter a foreign market by acquiring and continuing to trade under the name of a local company. Although Lloyd's of London operates only on a cross-border basis, its underwriting syndicates are able to rely on accredited brokers and loss adjusters established in, or visiting, countries of risk to service its business.

U.S.-European Trade in Insurance. Extensive, long-standing insurance trading links exist between most EC countries (and Switzerland) and the United States. Insurers and reinsurers from both sides of the Atlantic trade across borders and from local establishments in each other's territories. Lloyd's of London is unique in that although direct insurances and reinsurances of American risks account for half of its premium income, all of its business is underwritten in London. Since the 1930s it has been an admitted licensed insurer in the states of Illinois and Kentucky, but it still conducts no underwriting there (U.S. Department of the Treasury 1989).

Reinsurance Business. The U.S. Department of Commerce (1989a) statistics on reinsurance cross-border transactions show that European Community and Swiss insurers account for about 40 percent of both U.S. reinsurance premiums ceded abroad and of net reinsurance premiums received from abroad by U.S. insurance companies (table 13-10). In addition, the fifteen U.S. subsidiaries of Community insurers listed in the Reinsurance Association of America's 1987 survey accounted for some 8 percent of the total net reinsurance premiums written by all property-casualty reinsurers domiciled in the United States (table 13-11). The Munich Reinsurance Company's U.S. subsidiary was the fifth largest (measured by net written premium income) reinsurer on the American market in 1987, and the Swiss Reinsurance Company ranked sixth.

Until recent years, American reinsurers were content to concentrate their activities on serving their large domestic market, but since the 1970s they have been looking abroad for business expansion. But foreign premiums still account for a smaller share of the major companies' business than for the leading European reinsurers. For example, in 1987 the General Reinsurance Corporation, which is America's largest and the world's third largest reinsurer (after Munich Reinsurance and Swiss Reinsurance) obtained only 5 percent of its premiums from abroad, whereas overseas business accounted for 79 percent of the nonlife premiums and 63 percent of the life premiums of Britain's largest reinsurance company, the Mercantile & General, and more than 90 percent of the premium incomes of Swiss reinsurers come from abroad. Most of the large American companies, however, are now established in Europe, mainly in London, Zurich, and Brussels, and they see 1992 as an opportunity for further expansion (in 1989, for example, Employers Reinsurance Corporation acquired the Danish company Nordisk Reinsurance). Table 13-12 records the 1987 premium incomes of American reinsurers established on the London market.

Direct Insurance. Trade in direct insurance between the United States and the European Community takes place through cross-border trade and through the establishment of U.S. insurers and their subsidiaries in Europe and of European insurers in the United States.

Cross-border trade. In cross-border trade in reinsurance, the United Kingdom is America's largest trading partner in Europe, followed by the Benelux countries, France, Germany, and Italy, with the balance of trade in favor of the European Community (see table 13-13).

EC establishment in the United States. The leading U.K. insurers have had branches and subsidiary companies operating in the U.S.

TABLE 13-10
REINSURANCE TRANSACTIONS OF U.S. INSURANCE COMPANIES WITH REINSURERS RESIDENT ABROAD, 1981–1988
(percent)

Year	Net Premiums Ceded					Net Premiums Assumed			
	Total ($ US million)	U.K.	Rest of European Community	Switz-erland		Total (US $ million)	U.K.	Rest of European Community	Switz-erland
1981	2,109	30.5	15.5	4.3		953	24.9	20.2	4.8
1982	2,538	30.4	13.2	5.0		983	21.9	21.9	2.6
1983	2,872	25.6	14.1	4.8		1,150	20.6	22.0	2.3
1984	3,486	22.6	13.8	6.5		1,243	16.1	27.7	1.7
1985	4,625	24.0	12.4	6.3		1,327	18.5	21.5	1.7
1986	6,264	27.8	11.9	5.9		1,715	21.7	18.0	1.7
1987	7,331	26.0	11.3	5.8		2,009	22.7	16.7	1.8
1988	7,882[a]	23.3	9.9	5.1		1,972[a]	24.6	17.2	2.0

a. Provisional.
SOURCE: U.S. Department of Commerce (1989a).

TABLE 13-11

NET REINSURANCE PREMIUMS OF U.S. RESIDENT REINSURERS, 1987

Rank	Company	Country of Holding Company	Net Reinsurance (US $ million)	Premium Written Share of Total (%)
1	General Re. Group	United States	2,235.8	16.5
2	Employers Re. Corp.	United States	1,251.7	9.2
3	American Reinsce Co.	United States	1,002.8	7.4
4	Prudential Re. Group	United States	692.4	5.1
5	Munich Re. Group	West Germany	679.1	5.0
6	North American/Swiss Re.	Switzerland	647.5	4.8
26	Scor Re.	France	103.1	0.8
27	Winterthur	Switzerland	100.1	0.7
28	M & G America	United Kingdom	80.1	0.6
	Twelve other European Community companies		231.8	1.7

a. Cie Financiere et de Reassurance du Groupe AG has shareholdings in United Reinsurance Co. of New York (20 percent) and Translantic Reinsurance Co. (4.1 percent).

SOURCE: Reinsurance Association of America (1988).

TABLE 13-12

U.S.-OWNED PROPERTY AND CASUALTY REINSURERS AUTHORIZED TO
TRANSACT INSURANCE BUSINESS IN THE UNITED KINGDOM, 1987

Company	Ultimate Holding Company	1987 Net Written Premium Income (US $ million)[a]
Allstate Reinsurance Co.	Sears Roebuck	78.0
American Re. (U.K.)	Aetna Life & Casualty	43.1
CIGNA Re. (U.K.)		58.1
Continental Re. (U.K.)	Continental Corp.	32.5
Unionamerica		94.2
CNA of London Re.	CNA Management	208.7
Employers Re.		0.6
Fremont Insurance (U.K.)		22.5
General Re.		17.9
Highlands (U.K.)	Halliburton Co.	15.1
Kemper Re.		21.6
Le Rocher (U.K.)	Prudential of America	0.3
Meadows Indemnity	Gould Inc.	49.6
Metropolitan Re. (U.K.)		9.0
Reinsurance Corp., N.Y.		8.5
Security Insurance (U.K.)	Orion Capital Corp.	6.9
Terra Nova	Aetna, CIGNA, Travelers	224.3
Transatlantic Re.		4.6

a. Converted at end-of-year exchange rate of US$1.88 = £1.00.
SOURCE: Returns to the Department of Trade and Industry.

property and casualty insurance market since the nineteenth century
(Dickson 1960; Supple 1970). Many of them incurred large underwriting losses from the 1970s onward and have either drastically pruned
or, in some cases, closed down their U.S. operations. In 1988 however, the U.K. conglomerate BAT Industries expanded its large insurance and financial services division by taking over the Farmers
Group, the seventh largest American property and casualty insurer.

At the same time that U.K. insurers were scaling down their
American nonlife operations, the Legal and General led the entry of
U.K. insurers into the American life market with the purchase of the
American life insurer Government Employees Life Insurance Co. in
1981. In 1986 the largest U.K. life insurer, the Prudential Corporation,
acquired Jackson National Life, and since then several other U.K.
insurers have begun writing life business in America. Other European
insurers have also entered the American market through the acquisition of U.S. insurers; in 1982, for example, the Winterthur Insurance

285

TABLE 13-13
U.S. Direct Insurance Transactions with Nonresident Insurers, 1986–1988

| | Net Paid Abroad | | | Net Received from Abroad | | | |
Year	Total (US $ million)	United Kingdom	EC(6)[a]	Rest of European Community[b]	Total (US $ million)	United Kingdom	EC(6)[a]	Rest of European Community[b]
1986	954	47.6	2.2	0.1	2,800	5.0	4.3	0.7
1987	1,083	54.2	1.5	0.2	2,823	5.1	4.3	0.7
1988	1,193[c]	51.0	1.8	0.2	2,756[c]	3.4	4.3	0.7

a. EC(6) = Belgium, Luxembourg, France, West Germany, Italy, and the Netherlands.
b. Canada accounts for almost 40 percent of direct insurance premiums received from abroad by U.S. insurers, but for ony 2 percent of U.S. premiums paid abroad.
c. Provisional.
Source: U.S. Department of Commerce (1989b).

TABLE 13-14

EUROPEAN INSURERS (EXCLUDING REINSURERS) WITH U.S.-ADMITTED
SUBSIDIARIES, 1987

(millions of U.S. dollars)

Company	Country of Holding Company	Net Premium Income 1987 Nonlife	Life
Allianz of America[a]	West Germany	474	1,107
AMEV Holdings	Netherlands	242	—
AXA-Midi	France	32	—
Commercial Union	United Kingdom	1,110	54
General Accident	United Kingdom	1,363	—
Guardian Royal Exchange	United Kingdom	197	—
Legal & General	United Kingdom	—	40
Nationale Nederlanden	Netherlands	679	493
Prudential	United Kingdom	—	1,349
Royal	United Kingdom	2,313	60
Standard Life	United Kingdom	—	132
Sun Alliance	United Kingdom	406	—
Union des Assurance de Paris	France	75	6
Winterthur	Switzerland	579	32
Zurich	Switzerland	1,417	58

NOTE: Aachener & Munchener (Germany) took a 20% interest in Academy Insurance Group Inc. in 1983. Assicurazioni Generali SpA (Italy) has an interest in Aegen Int Inc.

a. Allianz Group also received $316.2m in net reinsurance premiums from the United States.

SOURCE: *Best's Review* (1988).

Group (Switzerland) acquired Republic Financial Services Inc., and more recently Nationale-Nederlanden acquired Southland Life, and Irish Life acquired Inter-State Assurance. The 1987 American business of European insurers is shown in table 13-14.

U.S. company establishment in Europe. American insurers have entered European markets through a gradual process of organic growth and acquisition, although the pace of new entry has increased since the 1970s. Between 1976 and 1985, for example, twenty-six U.S.-owned companies obtained authorization to transact insurance business in the United Kingdom.

Table 13-15 records the premium incomes of American-owned companies established in the United Kingdom. For some companies,

TABLE 13-15

U.S.-OWNED INSURERS AUTHORIZED TO TRANSACT INSURANCE BUSINESS IN THE UNITED KINGDOM, 1987
(millions of U.S. dollars)

Company	Ultimate Holding Company	Net Premium Income 1987 Nonlife	Net Premium Income 1987 Life
Aetna Life	Aetna Life & Caslty.	—	97.8
Albany Life	Metropolitan Life	—	296.1
American Intnl. Underwriters	American Intnl.	50.7	—
American Life	Group	—	96.3
American Family		5.5	1.5
Anglo-American Insurance	Calfed Inc.	135.8	—
Atlantic Mutual of New York		n.a.	—
Cannon Assurance	Lincoln National	—	100.6
Crusader		—	186.3
Insurance Co. of North America	CIGNA Corp.	43.8	—
CIGNA Europe (London branch)		107.2	—
Citibank General	Citicorp	109.9	—
Citicorp British National Life		4.6	—
City Insurance (U.K.) Co.	US Intnl. Re.	9.1	48.1

Company	Parent		
Combined Insurance of America		13.7	57.3
Continental Insurance Co. (U.K.)	Continental Corp.	22.9	—
FM Insurance	Factory Mutual	7.1	—
Harbour Assurance	Navistar Intnl.	5.5	—
London & Edinburgh (inc. Excess)	ITT Corp.	630.9	—
Ludgate	MMI Cos.	28.2	
Pan Atlantic Insurance		51.1	59.0
Regency Life	Transamerica Corp.	—	—
St. Katherine	⎫ St. Paul Group	68.2	—
St. Paul Fire & Marine	⎬	69.2	—
San Francisco Insurance (U.K.)	⎭	0.3	
Transatlantic Re		4.6	
USAA Ltd.	United Services Auto.	n.a.	
Wausau (U.K.)	Employers of Wausau	4.0	
World-Wide Reasce. Co.	American Express	—	50.7

n.a. = not available.

— = not transact that class of business.

NOTE: Excluding property/casualty reinsurers shown in table 13-12. Converted at end-of-year rate of $1.88 = £.00.

SOURCE: Returns to U.K. Department of Trade and Industry.

however, the net (of reinsurance ceded) premiums substantially underreflects the volume of business being written in the United Kingdom; for example, the 1987 net written premium incomes of the London branches of CIGNA Europe and the American International Group's subsidiary the New Hampshire were approximately only one-third and one-tenth, respectively, the size of their gross premiums.

Both Aetna Life and American International Group entered the U.K. life market in the mid-1980s to transact unit-linked life business, and Citicorp extended its U.K. insurance interests with the acquisition of British National Life. In 1986, however, the ITT Corporation disposed of its 51.8 percent shareholding in the U.K. insurer Abbey Life, although it retained its ownership of the London & Edinburgh Group. In 1987 American-owned companies controlled approximately 9 percent of the net nonlife direct and reinsurance premiums and 2.5 percent of the life premiums written in the United Kingdom (excluding Lloyd's).

Table 13-16 lists U.S. insurers (and reinsurers) established in other EC member states. The two main U.S. international insurers, CIGNA Corporation and AIG, are either already established in, or plan to expand into, most of the member states of the European Community; CIGNA is the third largest insurer in Belgium and AIG is the sixth largest company in Greece. Kemper Property & Casualty, with subsidiaries in Belgium, France, and the United Kingdom, has formed a joint-venture company with Union des Assurances de Paris to write highly protected risk insurance. In 1986 American companies and their affiliates operating in Germany had a 0.1 percent market share in life business and 0.7 percent in property and casualty (Gesamtverband der Deutschen Versicherungswirtschaft 1988), and in Ireland they controlled almost 4 percent of the non-life market (Department of Industry and Commerce).

Lloyd's of London. Although American brokers handle the majority of the surplus line (that is, direct) insurance and reinsurance that is placed with Lloyd's, all of the business has to be channeled through authorized Lloyd's brokers, who alone are permitted to deal with Lloyd's underwriters. Consequently, in the 1970s several large American brokers acquired leading firms of Lloyd's brokers to give them direct access to the Lloyd's market (for example, Marsh McLennan acquired the Bowring Group and Alexander & Alexander acquired Howden).

Freedom of Establishment and Services

The Treaty of Rome, which established the European Economic Community in 1957, contains two articles that set the framework for

TABLE 13-16

U.S. INSURERS OPERATING IN SELECTED EC MEMBER STATES, 1987

Company	Bel-gium	Den-mark	France	West Germany	Ire-land	Italy
Allstate Re.			X			
American International Group	X	X	X		X	X
American Re.			X			
Chubb			X			
CIGNA	X	X	X	X	X	X
Combined					X	
Continental		X	X	X		X
Employers Re.			X			
Federal Insurance			X			
Hartford				X		
Kemper	X		X			
National Union of Pittsburgh			X	X		
Nationwide				X		
PanAtlantic					X	
Transamerica			X			
Travelers			X			
Unity Fire & General			X			
Vigilant			X			

NOTE: In its 1988 annual report, American International Group stated that it is preparing its "operations in Europe to function continent wide in concert with the 1992 integration of European Community trade" and that its French subsidiary is in the process of licensing in other EC countries and Switzerland.

SOURCES: Company annual reports: Germany, *Die deutsche Versicherungswirtschaft*, Jahrbuch 1986 des Gesamtverbandes der Deutschen Versicherungswirtschaft; Ireland, Department of Industry and Commerce, *Insurance Annual Report*; and Italy, *Annuario Italiano delle Imprese Assicuratrici*.

the dismantling of trade barriers within the Community. These articles deal with the freedom of establishment and freedom of services:

> Restrictions on the freedom of establishment of nationals of a Member State in the territory of another Member State shall be abolished . . . such abolition shall also apply to restrictions on the setting up of agencies, branches or subsidiaries. . . . Freedom of establishment shall include the right to take up and pursue activities as self-employed persons and to set up and manage undertakings . . . under the

conditions laid down for its own nationals by the law of the country where such establishment is effected (Article 52).

Restrictions on freedom to provide services within the Community shall be progressively abolished . . . in respect of nationals of Member States who are established in a State of the Community other than that of the person for whom the services are intended (Article 59).

The treaty also sets out the basic principles for the creation of a single internal market, including the institution of a system to ensure that competition is not distorted and to ensure the approximation of the laws of member states to the extent necessary for the proper functioning of that market. The common market in insurance was to be accomplished by 1969.

It was agreed from the outset that trade liberalization for insurance should proceed in two stages. First, freedom of establishment was to give an insurer incorporated and authorized to transact insurance in any member state the right to establish an agency, branch, or subsidiary anywhere in the Community and to undertake business on the same conditions that apply to the nationals of the country in which the establishment is effected.

Once freedom of establishment had been achieved, the second stage of the program, that is, freedom of services, was to be implemented to give Community insurers the right to sell their services across state borders to the residents of other states without having an establishment there.

Reinsurance Business. Both freedoms were implemented for reinsurance transactions by the reinsurance directive of 1964. It granted Community insurers free access to the insurance markets of each member state and virtually freed reinsurance business from insurance supervision, except in the country in which the reinsurer has its head office.

Direct Insurance. In the reinsurance business, both parties to the contract are usually well informed regarding market practice and contract terms. In contrast, the contracting parties in direct insurance are (a) an insurer and (b) an individual or organization whose knowledge and understanding of insurance principles and practice and of available markets may vary greatly. Therefore, issues of consumer protection and the harmonization of supervisory law to ensure fair competition between insurers were more difficult to resolve.

Freedom of establishment for direct insurance. The Non-Life Establishment Directive was not adopted until 1973, and it was not fully implemented until 1976. The Life Establishment Directive issued in 1979 became effective in 1981. Both directives coordinated the financial and other conditions that an insurer must fulfill in order to obtain authorization to set up an establishment; the minimum solvency margin that it must thereafter maintain and the rules for its calculation, the regulations requiring insurers to maintain, in each country in which they carry on business, sufficient assets to cover the technical reserves. Any rules relating to the valuation of assets and responsibility for the monitoring of an insurer's solvency remained the prerogative of the supervisory authority of the country in which an insurer's head office is located. The Life Directive prohibited the formation of new composite companies wanting to carry on both life and nonlife business and the opening of new branches in other countries by existing composites.

If a Community insurer meets the required conditions, the supervisory authority of another member state cannot withhold authorization for it to set up an establishment there, and no deposit or other security can be required. A condition of the right of establishment is that an insurer must comply with the laws of the country concerned. Thus, for example, although decisions on premium rates and insurance contract terms are matters for commercial judgment and negotiation between the two parties in the United Kingdom, a British insurer that sets up an establishment in, say, France or Germany will have to submit its operations there to official supervision in such matters, in accordance with local laws.

An insurer with a head office in a third country that wishes to establish an agency or a branch in a Community member state must fulfill the same conditions for authorization as a Community insurer. It must also appoint a general representative, maintain within the country assets of a prescribed value, and maintain a prescribed solvency margin for both its worldwide business and its business carried on within the Community. If it operates in more than one Community state, the supervisory authorities may agree to supervise it on a pan-European basis so that it does not have to contend with separate rules on the maintenance of minimum guarantee funds and solvency in each state.

The authorization of a third-country insurer to set up a branch or agency in a member state is left to the discretion of the supervisory authority in question, although that is not an insuperable barrier to entry. If instead of seeking authorization to set up an agency or branch a third-country insurer chooses to operate through a subsidiary company incorporated in a member state, that company will be subject to the same conditions for authorization and solvency requirements as any other Community insurer, and having been authorized to transact business in one member state, it will then be entitled to open branches in other states.

Freedom of services for nonlife insurance. The ability of an insurer established in another member state to sell its services across national borders poses more problems for consumer protection and fair competition between insurers than does freedom of establishment. Differences in insurance contract law between member states, for example, mean that the consequences for a policyholder of his or her failure to disclose to the insurer prior to the inception of the contract all of the facts that may be deemed material to that contract vary considerably. Therefore, if a British insurer sold insurance in France subject to the more stringent U.K. law on duty of disclosure, not only may the French policyholder later find himself in a worse claims recovery situation than if the insurance had been purchased from a French insurer, but the British insurer could afford to sell at a lower price than its French counterpart.

The attitudes of Community members toward consumer protection also vary widely. Whereas the British and Dutch governments have been content to regulate the entry of insurers to their markets and to supervise their solvency, the German government has believed that an important additional element of consumer protection is market transparency. Consequently, German insurers have been required to charge virtually identical premiums for identical contracts. To get around these problems, the introduction of freedom of services for direct insurance was to be conditional not only on the prior introduction of freedom of establishment, but also on the simplification of procedures for the reciprocal enforcement of judgments and the coordination of insurance contract law. To date, the last item has still not been achieved.

In 1978 the Coinsurance Directive was issued to permit industrial and commercial risks "which by their nature or size call for the participation of several insurers for their coverage" to be insured with two or more insurers established in different member states. Although less of an issue here, some member states put a restrictive interpretation on the directive. As a result, little business was so conducted and eventually the EC Commission instigated proceedings in the European Court of Justice against the Danish, French, German, and Irish governments.

In some respects, the judgments of the court delivered in December 1986 were helpful in promoting freedom of services. It ruled that the leading insurer on a Community co-insurance contract could be based in any member state and that a member state could not prohibit its citizens from using an intermediary when placing risks with an insurer established in another Community country. Although the court held that there was less need to protect the policyholder in the case of large industrial insurance, it was of the opinion that smaller firms and individuals are in need of legal protection and that pending the further harmonization of supervisory and insurance contract laws, a member state may require insurers who offer cross-border insurances to its citizens to be authorized to do so and may impose on such insurers national requirements such as the constitution and investment of technical reserves and general policy conditions. Nevertheless, the court's decisions did enunciate a set of principles on which the EC Commission could proceed with implementing the program of freedom of services.

The Second Non-Life Insurance Directive adopted in June 1988 provided for the phasing in from July 1, 1990, of free cross-frontier trade in marine, aviation, transport, credit, suretyship, and other large risks (that is, after December 1992, the risks of companies that satisfy two out of three size criteria: 250 employees, an annual turnover of ECU 12.8 million, and an annual balance sheet total of ECU 6.2 million). The directive also permits the insurances of mass risks (that is, the insurances of firms smaller than the thresholds set to qualify as large risks, and all personal nonlife insurances) to be placed across frontiers, but subject to the regulations of the country of the policyholder and other restrictive conditions. Thus, little if any such business will be transacted on a services basis, and further directives will be needed to bring about freedom of services for the mass risks.

Freedom of services for life insurance. A study undertaken for the European Commission in 1986 showed that many supervisory, tax, and other obstacles remained in the path of freedom of services for life insurance (Carter and Morgan 1986). In December 1988, the commission, taking advantage of the 1986 decision of the European Court of Justice, produced the draft Second Life Insurance Services directive, which was finally adopted in November 1990.

The directive implicitly accepts that if an insurer wishes to market its products in another member state without having an establishment there, then generally the policyholders of that state are entitled to the protection of the same laws that apply to transactions with established insurers. Therefore, a member state may require a Community insurer not established there to obtain authorization to supply cross-border insurance, and to impose its own laws on the conditions of insurance and the financial soundness of the insurer.

The commission did, however, accept that no special protection is required for informed consumers who are prepared to act on their own initiative. Therefore, the directive provides for freedom of services for individuals who on their own initiative seek out a life insurer established in another member state and who are prepared to sign a declaration waiving their rights to the protection afforded by their country of residence. A local broker may be employed to arrange the insurance (although member states will be able to delay the implementation of this provision for three years after the directive becomes operative in May 1993). The directive also grants freedom of services for group life and other employer related life insurances.

The directive still leaves untouched the overwhelming majority of individual life insurance. Furthermore, because of the close relationship between private pension and the social security arrangements (which differ between member states), pension schemes are excluded from the directive.

The framework directives. In 1990 the EC Commission published two new proposed directives for direct insurance business: the *Nonlife Framework Directive* and the *Life Framework Directive.* These directives will change the provisions of the current establishment directives by requiring a Community insurer to obtain authorization only from the member state in which its head office is located, although if it wishes to sell its products to the residents of other member states, it will need to obtain the approval of its home state's supervisory authority. The insurer will then have the right to market in such other member states through either local establishments or across frontiers, the full range of insurance products for which it is authorized, subject only to its home country regulations. Both directives propose that member states will be prohibited from requiring the systematic notification or prior approval of either policy wordings or premium rates. Eventually competition based on the remaining differences between the regulatory systems of member states will probably lead to a more or less uniform system of supervision throughout the Community.

U.S.-European Trade Issues

The volume of trade in insurance services that flows between the European Community and the United States indicates that neither trading bloc possesses overwhelming advantages in the availability and cost of the factors (including the technology) required for the production and distribution of insurance services. The United States may possess an advantage over the lesser developed members of the Community. But its resource advantages can be matched in most member states of the Community and in Switzerland, where, as in the United States, some firm-specific advantages are enjoyed by Lloyd's of London and a small number of companies that have become international insurers and reinsurers.

Why the balance of trade is in favor of Europe can be explained in part by the large difference in the size of the domestic markets of the two trading blocs. American insurers have for many years enjoyed access to a large domestic market with a wide geographic spread and a growing premium expenditure, so that only a few companies have felt any need or ambition to exploit their specific advantages by trading internationally, particularly by establishing abroad. Conversely, European insurers that have wished to grow and achieve wider geographic spread of the risks they insure have been far more constrained by the size of their domestic markets and so have had to seek that growth abroad.

The progress being made toward a single internal EC market is inducing some structural changes in its insurance industry and also making Europe a more attractive market for some third-country insurers, but neither development as such will change U.S.-European trading positions to any degree in the short term. The factors that could profoundly influence the future of U.S.-EC insurance and reinsurance trade are regulatory control and trade policy, and both of those are still in a state of flux.

International Competition. The prospect of a single European insurance market is influencing the corporate strategies not only of EC insurers and of those third-country insurers already established in the market(s) of one or more of the member states, but also of other third-country insurers. Provided high entry barriers are not erected to protect the post-1992 EC market from external competition, some third-country insurers will see its size and growth potential as an opportunity to expand their business internationally. According to a recent survey, EC insurers expect the main interest in entering the market to come from Japanese (41 percent), American (37 percent), Swedish (9 percent), and Swiss (7 percent) insurers (Farny and Schmidt 1989). It is not only EC-owned insurers, but all insurers established in the European Community that face a threat of potential new competition from third-country insurers, particularly for the business of corporate clients for whom the single market will become effective from mid-1990.

The threat of new competition from both within and outside the EC has already induced some defensive merger activity among European insurers. For example, the French market has been substantially

FIGURE 13–1
THE LARGEST INSURERS IN EUROPE IN TOTAL BUSINESS, 1988
(billions of U.S. dollars)

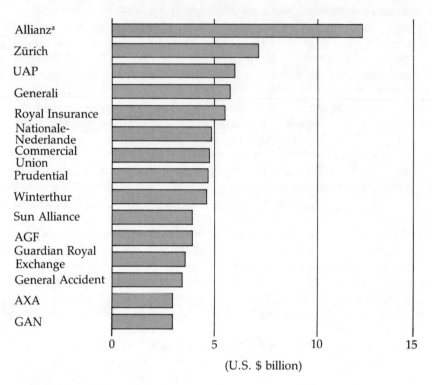

(U.S. $ billion)

a. Includes RAS.
SOURCE: *Sigma* (1989: 2, 21).

restructured through the creation of a small number of groups—
notably AGF, AXA-Midi, GAN, and UAP—which now rank among
the largest European insurers (figure 13-1). Also many companies
have entered into arrangements involving cross-shareholdings or the
taking of strategic shareholdings (such as the UAP's 31.1 percent
shareholding in the large Belgian insurer Royal Belge). Not all of the
action has been purely defensive. The leading European insurers,
including the large French companies plus Allianz, Generali, Royal,
and Winterthur, have also been responding to the opportunities of
1992, seeking to develop the extent of their European interests to
become pan-European insurers through the acquisition of insurers
established in other member states. Nevertheless, the newly enlarged
European insurers still remain much smaller than the leading Ameri-

FIGURE 13–2
THE LARGEST INSURERS WORLDWIDE IN TOTAL BUSINESS, 1987
(billions of U.S. dollars)

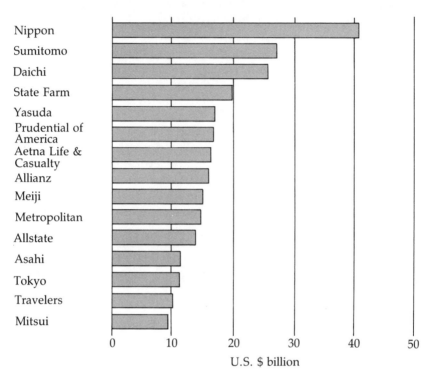

SOURCE: *Sigma* (1989: 2, 20).

can and Japanese insurance groups (figure 13-2).

Some of the American insurers currently established in the European Community also have expanded their European activities. For example, AIG has expanded into Spain with the purchase of the AB Group, and the St. Paul Group has acquired in the United Kingdom Minet Holdings and St. Katherine Insurance Co. How many other American companies will eventually wish to enter Europe is a moot question. American insurers have been accused of being slow to plan for 1992 (Henderson 1989), and a survey of more than 150 U.S. life, health and property, and casualty insurers confirmed that a clear majority are unlikely to enter Western European markets in the next ten years (Arthur Andersen & Co. 1988). Therefore, the main threat of new entry from abroad would appear to be coming from

Japan, although a few insurers from other countries may see a future in Europe, too; for example, in 1989 the Australian Mutual Provident substantially extended its U.K. activities through the acquisitions of London Life Association and Pearl Assurance.

The leading Japanese insurers exceed in size both the largest American and European insurance groups (figure 13-2). Currently the small amount of business they conduct in Europe is largely written on the London market, although they do have subsidiaries elsewhere (notably in Belgium, France, Germany, and the Netherlands). From their operations in the highly regulated, profitable Japanese market, they have accumulated vast financial resources that could be used to finance new entry, either through direct investment in branches or subsidiaries or through the acquisition of established EC insurers.

In the past, they have been handicapped by their lack of knowledge of, and insufficient number of staff experienced in, the workings of European markets. Recently, however, several Japanese insurers have made moves into Europe: Asahi Mutual Life has acquired a 5 percent holding in the Belgian Groupe AG; Dai-Itchi Mutual Life is to cooperate with Victoria Leben in group life; Sumitomo has entered into a cooperation agreement with the Italian La Fondiaria Group and has set up facilities to write industrial insurance in Spain; Taisho has entered into a cooperation agreement with Generali; Tokio Marine and Fire has entered into a joint venture with Allianz in Italy; Yasuda has formed a joint venture in France with the French insurer GAN, which will give it the knowledge and experience required for successful entry on a larger scale; and Yasuda Europe is to begin writing industrial insurance in Spain. In 1988–1989 a number of the Japanese companies increased the capitalization of their U.K. subsidiaries in order to finance their expansion into Europe.

The EC insurers questioned by Farny and Schmidt indicated that they expect non-EC companies to control 12 percent of the total EC premiums generated by corporate clients and 6 percent of the premiums for individual insurances by the end of the century. What actually happens will depend not only on the conditions on which foreign insurers will be allowed to enter the European Community, but also on how they perceive trading conditions there. Until now competition in those national markets has been constrained by stringent regulatory rules, but with competitive pressures increasing, the opportunities for profitable new entry are diminishing. Moreover, since the generally preferred route for entry into foreign markets is through the acquisition of an established insurer (Schroath 1988), the costs of new entry have risen sharply. The mergers and acquisitions that have already occurred have so reduced the numbers of European insurers that are both available and suitable for acquisition that the price expectations of owners have risen to levels that now make them unattractive targets for many potential bidders, whether European or foreign (Trade and Industry Committee 1989: par. 581).

The Restructuring of the European Market. EC insurers are having to make strategic decisions regarding their future roles in an integrated European market. Some small- to medium-size companies will choose to remain national insurers, relying on continuing differences in culture, customs, and language and the loyalty of their customers to provide some protection from increasing competition from the emerging pan-European groups. Others will become niche players in the national or wider European market, and some will seek the security of some form of involvement in larger groups capable of competing in most, if not all, Community countries.

The number of insurers operating in the single European market is expected to decline (Farny and Schmidt 1989) and competition to increase as a small number of large pan-European companies—based mainly in Britain, France, Germany, Italy, Netherlands, and Switzerland—gain control of an increasing share of national markets. The larger European companies will then be better able to withstand the competition from the leading American and Japanese companies, both in Europe and in world markets, although the managerial and financial resources that European insurers are expending on securing their positions in the Community may mean that in the near future their expansion plans will be focused there rather than on other territories.

A special feature of the market for personal insurances is that insurers will have to secure their distribution channels. Consequently, the links that are either already in place or are being formed between banks and insurers in the Community will make entry by foreign insurers that much more difficult.

An increase in the size of companies has implications for reinsurance business in that larger companies are able to retain for their own accounts more of the risks they insure. Thus, the total demand for reinsurance by Community insurers is likely to decline, with some replacement of proportional reinsurance that generates a high volume of premium income for reinsurers by an increase in demand for high-level risk and catastrophe excess of loss reinsurances (Mercantile & General 1988b; Hammick 1989). That change in demand will both intensify competition within reinsurance markets and spill over into the demand for reinsurance supplied from the United States and elsewhere. The most significant response has been the merger of the French reinsurers SCOR and UAP Re to create a powerful new company with a premium income of approximately Fr 9.5 billion (= US$1.7 billion).

Reciprocal Trading Conditions. The future pattern and extent of U.S.-EC insurance trade will also depend on the post-1992 trade policies yet to be agreed by both parties. In 1988 the European Commission criticized several of the provisions of the U.S. Trade Bill as being protectionist. The Americans in turn have been critical of the Community's proposals for trade reciprocity in relation to services.

Article 9 of the proposed Second Council Directive on Freedom of Services for Direct Life Insurance published on February 15, 1989, required member states to refer to the EC Commission any request from a foreign company to establish a subsidiary or to acquire a controlling interest in an EC insurer. Any decision would then have been deferred until the commission had investigated whether all Community insurers enjoyed "reciprocal treatment" in the third country in question and, if not, until negotiations had secured such treatment. The article did not indicate whether reciprocal treatment was to be mirror-image treatment (which would allow an insurer to do in a host country whatever it may do in its home country), or national treatment to enable a foreign insurer to operate under the same conditions as indigenous insurers.

Given their differing degrees of involvement in international trade, the Community's national insurance industries and their governments differ in their attitudes to trade reciprocity. Some apparently see it as providing "a cloak for the protection of domestic industries" from new competition from foreign institutions (Trade and Industry Committee 1989: par. 86). Conversely, the British financial service industries in general, and the insurance industry in particular, knowing that of all the EC national industries they have most to lose from any trade war in services, share the view of the U.K. government that reciprocity provisions at best are unnecessary and at worst are likely to provoke retaliation. The fear of possible retaliation was reinforced by the representations made to the commission by the American and Japanese governments and the knowledge that the U.S. government had been preparing retaliatory measures should the need arise. Therefore, the U.K. government was urged to press for the amendment of the reciprocity provisions in the Second Life Directive and in all of the remaining draft directives on financial services, to bring them into line with the revised reciprocity provision in the draft Second Banking Directive issued in April 1989, which made two substantive changes to the previous proposals.

First, "reciprocal treatment" was reframed in terms of "national treatment." Second, instead of the automatic case-by-case referral of applications from non-EC banks, the commission was instructed to carry out before the directive comes into force a general examination of how third countries treat EC credit institutions. If the commission then finds that a third country is not providing national treatment for EC banks, it can suspend the granting of a license to a non-EC bank from that country until effective market access has been negotiated for all Community banks. Furthermore, such monitoring of conditions will be a continuing process (Trade and Industry Committee 1989: par. 87).

In December 1989 the Council of Ministers agreed to substitute the revised banking directive reciprocity provision for the original Article 9 of the Life "Services" directive, which now brings EC trade reciprocity provisions for insurance services into line with U.S. trade policy.

EC Insurance Regulatory Rules. The U.S. insurance industry and government may object to two features of EC insurance supervisory law in particular.

First, EC member states have some discretion over the establishment and licensing of agencies and branches of third-country insurers. Although that obstacle can be surmounted by forming an EC incorporated subsidiary, that does not meet the objective of the International Insurance Advisory Council (which represents the leading U.S. companies with large overseas interests) that U.S. companies wishing to trade abroad should be free to choose their form of organization (Parker 1986). European insurers who might wish to trade through a branch in the United States, however, would encounter similar obstacles there.

Second, some EC member states (including France, Germany, and Italy) restrict residents from insuring abroad with nonadmitted insurers. Although the implementation of freedom of services eventually will entitle all EC residents to place their insurances with an insurer established in another Community country, individual member states will retain the right to continue to restrict the placing of insurances with nonadmitted third-country insurers. Again, the American states impose similar restrictions on nonadmitted insurance and reinsurance.

The one fear is that further progress toward completing the internal EC market for insurance may depend on the member states with the more liberal supervisory regimes accepting more regulation of their markets, including further restrictions on foreign insurers that wish to trade through agencies or branches, or across Community borders. That risk is, however, receding.

One reason is that the EC Commission is pressing for a less regulated, more competitive insurance market based on home-country control. The terms of the two proposed framework directives recognize that insurance is part of a financial services industry that is becoming international in character and operations. Furthermore, the imposition of new trade restrictions would run counter to the Community's stance in the Group of Negotiations on Services (GNS) in the Uruguay Round of the GATT.

U.S. Discrimination against Foreign Insurers. The U.S. insurance industry would have nothing to fear from an EC insistence on reciprocal treatment if foreign insurers were not subject to discriminatory treatment in regard to either establishment or cross-border trade. But they are!

Barriers to establishment. A serious problem for foreign insurers that may wish to enter the U.S. market is the complexity of the state system of insurance regulation, which can operate as an entry barrier, as a B.A.T. Industries spokesman has explained:

> It is a highly complex marketplace to enter and to obtain authorisation. It is a very successful takeover block, if you wish to have one, to have an insurance company registered in the United States, because it takes forever to get an authorisation. My own company undertook an aggressive, hostile takeover in the United States last year. It took us over a year from the point at which we launched it, and a great deal of money in terms of legal costs State by State to eventually win. This was the Framers Insurance Company, which we acquired at the beginning of this year. The process, and therefore the protectionism that is inherent in the system in the United States is very very offputting except for the most determined and deep pocket (Trade and Industry Committee 1989: 104).

To the extent that state regulatory rules do not discriminate, either explicitly or in regulatory practice, against foreign or foreign-owned insurers that wish to establish and operate in the United States—either by the acquisition of a U.S. insurer or otherwise—but treat them exactly the same as American-owned companies, then such barriers to entry do not work against national treatment principles. It is immaterial from a trade policy standpoint that the regulations constrain competition by raising market entry costs or by curtailing commercial freedom of action, as long as they equally affect both indigenous and foreign companies.

An investigation of the regulatory requirements of California, Illinois, Massachusetts, and New York did, however, find that foreign insurers are subject to some discrimination in capitalization and surplus requirements regarding state licensing and admission rules and in taxation (U.S. General Accounting Office 1982). For example, unlike domestic insurers, foreign insurers must renew their licenses annually to operate in New York, and in New York and Illinois they are taxed 1–2.6 percent more than domestic companies. There are statutory bans in some states on the licensing of state-owned insurers that catch a few EC insurers.

Barriers to cross-border trade. The United States discriminates against cross-border trade with foreign insurers in two significant ways: through federal excise tax and nonadmitted insurance and reinsurance. Premiums remitted abroad to foreign insurers for the insurance of American situs risks are subject to federal excise tax, currently payable at the following rates: direct life insurance, 1 percent of the gross premium; direct property and casualty insurance, 4 percent of the gross premium; and reinsurances of U.S. risks, 1 percent of the gross premium. Insurance contracts placed with foreign insurers and reinsurers located in some countries, including some members of the European Community are either totally (as in the United Kingdom) or part (as in Germany) exempted from payment of the tax under the provisions of tax treaties with the United States.

Since the Tax Reform Act of 1986 raised the federal tax burdens of U.S. insurers and reinsurers, the Reinsurance Association of America (RAA, which represents the leading U.S. reinsurers) has campaigned for an increase from 1 percent to 4 percent in the rate of tax payable on reinsurance premiums and for the ending of the tax treaty exemptions. The RAA has argued that because foreign reinsurers are not subject to U.S. income taxes, they have an unfair advantage in competing for the reinsurance of U.S. risks. That argument ignores the fact that European reinsurers are subject to comparable domestic taxes payable on the whole of their incomes, whether derived from the reinsurance of domestic or foreign risks. The U.S. General Accounting Office (1989) has pointed out that any restriction on the supply of foreign reinsurance could harm U.S. consumers, that a change in the tax could be "perceived by U.S. trading partners as a barrier to entry to the U.S. market," and that the European Community "could reciprocate by erecting barriers against U.S. companies."

U.S. state insurance supervisory regulations impose additional

305

capital financing costs on foreign nonadmitted insurers and reinsurers that wish to accept the insurance and reinsurance of U.S. risks. Normally, when a U.S. insurer is calculating its surplus for the purpose of demonstrating compliance with solvency regulations, it can claim credit for liabilities passed to its reinsurers. No such deduction can be made in respect of reinsurance placed with foreign nonadmitted reinsurers unless the reinsurer either deposits cash or marketable securities in a trust account with a U.S. bank, or maintains an irrevocable, clean letter of credit with a U.S. bank (or a non-U.S. bank if confirmed by a U.S. bank), in favor of the ceding insurer and for an amount sufficient to cover the reinsurer's unearned premium and outstanding claims reserves in respect of the ceding insurer's reinsurance.

Since the 1960s, the state of New York has introduced other regulations that have made it administratively more costly for brokers to place surplus-line insurance and reinsurance with foreign nonadmitted insurers. Other states have followed suit.

Regulation 41, which regulates the activities of excess line brokers, prohibits the sale to New York residents of most lines of nonmarine insurance supplied by nonadmitted insurers, except to the extent that such insurance is unobtainable in whole or in part from authorized insurers writing such lines of insurance in the regular course of their business in New York State. Before a licensed excess lines broker can place a surplus lines insurance with an unauthorized insurer, written evidence must be obtained from, usually three, authorized insurers to confirm that they have declined to insure the risk; if authorized insurers are prepared to provide coverage for less than the full amount required, the broker may procure coverage from unauthorized insurer(s) only for the excess.

Before placing business with an unauthorized insurer, the broker must also ascertain that (1) the insurer is authorized in its domicilary jurisdiction to write such insurance; (2) that it handles its claims satisfactorily and is trustworthy, competently managed, and financially secure; (3) the insurer keeps on deposit in an American bank a trust fund in cash, readily marketable securities, or a clean, irrevocable letter of credit for an amount of not less than $1.5 million for the protection of its U.S. policyholders (for an association such as Lloyd's of London, the amount would be $50 million); (4) that its policies appoint the New York insurance superintendent as the attorney of the insurer in respect of any action brought by a policyholder; and (5) in the case of alien (that is, non-U.S.) insurers, the broker must obtain a financial statement from the insurer.

Regulation 91, which regulates reinsurance intermediaries, conferred special privileges on the underwriting syndicates of the then recently formed New York Insurance Exchange (which is no longer writing new business). A reinsurance broker placing reinsurance with the exchange's underwriting managers was relieved of the duty to supply the U.S. ceding insurer with various information, including, in the case of an unauthorized reinsurer, the requirement to inquire into its financial condition and to supply the ceding insurer with its most recent financial statement unless the reinsurer placed adequate funds with the ceding insurer.

State versus federal regulation. A legitimate concern of foreign governments in their negotiations with the United States is the right of the state governments to determine their own insurance regulatory policy. As noted above, not only may the sheer complexities of the state regulatory system be seen as an obstacle to trade, but it also raises the question of the ability of the federal government to enforce any agreement that involves regulatory changes.

U.S. Bilateral Trade Agreements. The U.S. government has used Section 301 of the U.S. trade act to persuade the government of the Republic of Korea to permit American insurers to have limited entry to its insurance markets. The first agreement concluded in July 1986 provided for the participation of two U.S. insurers (AIG and CIGNA) in the Korean compulsory fire insurance pool and for AIG to enter the life market. A new trade agreement concluded in 1989 permits five additional property and casualty insurers to enter the Korean market. An objectionable feature of those agreements is the lack of a most favored nation provision. As a result, third-country (including EC) insurers do not enjoy the same rights of market entry as U.S. insurers, so that Nationale Nederlanden had to employ its U.S. subsidiary to gain entry to the Korean market, and both it and Royal have employed the same device to enter Taiwan.

The Group of Negotiations on Services in the Uruguay Round of the GATT. The European Community shares the views of the United States on most of the issues that have been the subject of debate in the GNS, the aim of which is to produce a General Agreement on Trade in Services to bring about a progressive liberalization of trade in services through multilateral negotiations.

Liberalization through Multilateral Negotiations. Both the European Community and the United States recognize that access to markets through permanent establishments is an important element of trade in many types of services, including insurance, although many developing countries are still not willing to accept that permanent establishment should be covered by any agreement. Both also accept that an agreement should be based on the principles of transparency, progressive liberalization, market access, national treatment, and m.f.n./nondiscrimination. They accept, too, the possibility of sectoral negotiations and concessions for developing countries, recognizing their differing stages of development and needs.

Conclusions

Developments in the domestic markets of the United States and the European Community, including restructuring of the EC insurance industries and changes in the competitive forces in both markets, will undoubtedly play a major role in determining the volume of trade between the two trading blocs after 1992. At least some of those market developments will depend on government policy (including insurance supervision and trade policy).

In neither the fields of establishment nor of cross-border trade are there serious, insurmountable obstacles to trade between the United States and the European Community, as is evident in the current volume of trade. The European Commission says that the changes made to the reciprocal treatment provisions of the Second Banking and Life Insurance Directive show that it has no wish to turn the Community into Fortress Europe, but it does expect other countries to provide equally effective access to their markets for EC financial institutions.

Trade in financial services, including insurance, is just one part of the total package of trade issues that have to be resolved by the United States and the European Community. Therefore, in the event of conflict between the two trading blocs, the current obstacles to insurance trade in both the United States and the European Community—which in several instances are similar in nature (for example, the restrictions on nonadmitted insurance are similar in France, Italy, and the United States, and the French and U.S. regulations regarding deposits for nonadmitted reinsurance)—could be used as an excuse for retaliatory action. That would harm the interests of both the United States and the European Community, their insurance industries, consumers, and their negotiating positions in the GNS discussions for a General Agreement on Trade in Services.

Europe is the world's leading exporter of services. It would certainly not be serving its own interests by becoming a fortress. A wiser course of action would be to work with the United States, Japan, and other industrialized countries to promote the liberalization of trade in services, possibly through bilateral and plurilateral negotiations within the framework of a General Agreement on Trade in Services.

References

All-Industry Research Advisory Council. 1986. *Catastrophic Losses: How the Insurance System Would Handle Two $7 Billion Hurricanes.* Oak Brook, Illinois.

Arthur Andersen & Co. and Life Office Management Association. 1988. *Insurance Industry Futures: Setting a Course for the 1990s.* Chicago and Atlanta.

Bhagwati, Jagdish. 1987. "International Trade in Services and Its Relevance for Economic Development." In *The Emerging Service Economy,* edited by O. Giarini. Oxford: Pergamon Press.

Carter, R. L. 1983. *Reinsurance.* 2d ed. Brentford: Kluwer.

Carter, R. L., and Diacon, S. R. 1989. *The British Insurance Industry: a Statistical Review, 1988/89.* Brentford: Kluwer.

Carter, R. L., and Dickinson, G. M. 1979. *Barriers to Trade in Insurance.* London: Trade Policy Research Centre.

Carter, R. L., and Morgan, E. V. 1986. *Freedom to Offer Life Insurance Across EEC State Boundaries.* London: Economists Advisory Group.

Cecchini, P. 1988. *The European Challenge 1992: The Benefits of the Single Market.* Wildwood House.

Dickson, P. G. M. 1960. *The Sun Insurance Office 1710–1960.* Oxford: Oxford University Press.

Farny, D., and Schimdt, E. R. 1989. *Empirical Enquiry on the Single Insurance Market within the European Communities after 1992: Attitudes, Expectations and Appraisals of Insurers.* Geneva: Association Internationale pour l'Etude de l'Economie de l'Assurance and Institut fur Versicherungswissenschaften, University of Cologne.

Finsinger, Jorg, E. Hammond, and J. Tapp. 1985. *Insurance: Competition or Regulation?* London: Institute for Fiscal Studies.

Geehan, R. 1986. "Economies of Scale in Insurance: Implications for Regulation." In *The Insurance Industry in Development,* edited by B. Wasow and R. D. Hill. New York: New York University Press.

Gesamtverband der Deutschen Versicherungswirtschaft. 1988. *Die Deutsche Versicherungswirtschaft, Jahrbuch, 1986.* Karlsruhe.

Hammick, L. 1989. "Hands across Europe." *Post Magazine,* August 31.

Henderson, Donald B. 1989. "1992: Opportunities for U.S. in Europe." *National Underwriter,* July 10.

Hill, Raymond D. 1986. "Brazil: The Insurance Market Consolidation of the 1970s." In *The Insurance Industry in Economic Development,* edited by B. Wasow and R. D. Hill. New York: New York University Press.

Mercantile & General Reinsurance Company. 1988a. *Piper Alpha: The Insurance and Reinsurance Aspects.* London.

———. 1988b. *1992: The Implications for Insurance.* London.

Office of Technology Assessment. 1986a. *Services in the U.S. Balance of Payments, 1982–84, Documentation of OTA Estimates.* Industry, Technology and Employment Program, July.

———. 1986b. *Trade in Services: Exports and Foreign Revenues.* Special Report OTA-ITE-316. September.

Organization for Economic Cooperation and Development. 1989. *Statistics on Insurance: Comparative Tables of Insurance for 1986.* Part 2. Paris.

Parker, Henry G. 1986. "Insurance across National Borders: Problems and Solutions." Paper presented to the Summer National Meeting of the National Association of Insurance Commissioners. Washington, D.C.: International Insurance Advisory Council.

Price Waterhouse. 1988. *The Price of "Non-Europe" in Financial Services.* New York and London.

Rajan, Amin. 1987. *Services—The Second Industrial Revolution?* London: Butterworths.

Reinsurance Association of America. 1988. *Reinsurance Underwriting Review.* Washington, D.C.

Schroath, F. W. 1988. "Mode of Foreign Entry: An Analysis of the Property and Liability Insurance Industry." *Geneva Papers on Risk & Insurance* 13 (no. 49), October 1988.

Supple, B. 1970. *The Royal Exchange Assurance.* Cambridge: Cambridge University Press.

Swiss Reinsurance Company. 1987. "A Comparison of Insurance Markets in Europe and the USA." *Sigma* 4 (April).

Trade and Industry Committee, House of Commons. 1989. *Financial Services and the Single European Market.* HC 256. London: Her Majesty's Stationery Office.

U.S. Department of Commerce, Bureau of Economic Analysis. August 8, 1989a. *Reinsurance Transactions of U.S. Insurance Companies with Reinsurers Resident Abroad, 1981–1988.* Washington, D.C.

———. August 8, 1989b. *U.S. Direct Insurance Transactions with Non-Residents.* Washington, D.C.

U.S. Department of the Treasury. 1989. *Report to Congress on the Taxation of Income Earned by Members of Insurance or Reinsurance Syndicates.* Washington, D.C., February.

U.S. General Accounting Office. 1989. *Tax Policy: The Insurance Excise Tax and Competition for U.S. Reinsurance Premiums.* Briefing Report to the Honorable Fortney (Pete) Stark, House of Representatives.

310

GAO/GGD-89-115BR. Washington, D.C., September.

Walter, Ingo. 1988. *Global Competition in Financial Services.* Cambridge, Mass: Ballinger.

Wasow, Bernard. 1986. "Insurance in Korea." In *The Insurance Industry in Economic Development,* edited by B. Wasow and R. D. Hill. New York: New York University Press.

14
Commentaries on Insurance

A Commentary by Gordon Cloney

I would like my observations to complement Mr. Carter's chapter. I am glad to see these programs taking place in the United States. Mr. Carter's chapter reminded me of a comment made many years ago by a friend of mine, who is an Americanist, a demographer, and an anthropologist. We were talking about the discovery of America. He said, "Columbus did not discover America. The Indians knew it was there all the time; Columbus talked to the Indians." So, when I see Mr. Carter or Mr. Hindley and others from a cadre of people in London who have been thinking about some of these issues in a practical way for a long time, I think my friend's words are useful to keep in mind.

I will make some comments now on the EC and the liberalization side. The process of developing a harmonized or coordinated internal market insurance has been going on for a long time in Europe. It is not a recent phenomenon in the context of 1992; the premises were clearly set forth in the Treaty of Rome from the beginning.

Over the years, as Mr. Carter points out, major steps were taken to build the basis for a single market and for the standard for solvency, which is recognized almost universally in Europe; these were moves toward home country control. We hope to see more of that from the marketing point of view. I would also say, in light of some of the more recent developments, that some standards for regulatory procedures, discipline, and treatment are essential when going across borders. Those are some of the things in the collection of directives. In a regulatory sense, these data are important steps in Europe. The new framework will emerge from a market that was layered with living and nonliving businesses and that probably had some things in common with the U.S. market, such as operations via surplus lines and admission of most personal products to state markets.

By looking at the U.S.-EC insurance relationship, we know that the U.S. community shares the largest bilateral flow of the insurance business in the world. It is essentially a long-standing, stable relationship. British companies, for example, had an insurance relationship with this country that goes back almost to its founding. Britain has paid its dues by handling insurance claims from almost every wind storm that blows through the southern United States, and by being strong and welcome participants in the U.S. market.

Others in Europe have gradually entered that picture more recently. Some, however, have not paid their dues as the London market has. Bearing this in mind, however, European companies' participation is welcome in this open market, and I hope this does not change.

Movements forward and the reciprocity between markets depends on maintaining a standard of national treatment. If we slip from standards to qualitative judgments, we will be led into an intellectual debate that could become complicated and essentially destabilize this large and, heretofore, satisfactorily functioning, transatlantic insurance market. The United States would be concerned if a standard changed in Europe. Then we would question whether it should be changed in the United States, which would involve federal authorities and many state authorities that could evoke retaliatory capabilities. No one needs that. The trade balance favors Europe in insurance. So, it seems that to maintain a good business environment we must maintain a standard of national treatment.

In the future there will be much room, regardless of how things finally emerge in Europe, for additional regulatory cooperation. The two markets may be able to do things collectively over a period of time, thus making it easier to do business and to be more efficient.

Evident in the trade dialogue at the GATT and services level was sensitivity of regulators to the need of the United States to improve the system's internal efficiency without relinquishing state regulation. Toward that end, proposals, triggered in part by these trade talks, surfaced.

I think the Community's move forward in an area of comprehensive service talks, which might discipline both existing and future discriminations is disappointing.

For years the Community participants were vigorous and, at times, lecturing about the way in which things should move forward. Now that the rubber has hit the road, however, they are taking an extremely cautious approach that does not bode particularly well for a comprehensive services agreement. This is being fought out right now, but the approaches being taken by the United States and those being taken by the EC are quite different. They do not seem to be moving together—so far.

A Commentary by W. R. Rowland

Briefly, I would like to start with an important lesson from the history of the Royal Insurance Group, which was formed 145 years ago by Liverpool trading merchants, as perhaps the first truly international captive insurance company. It was formed not to insure U.K. risks, but international ones.

Within a year, it set up shop in South America and Singapore. Within three years, it established an insurance business in the United States, Australia, and Canada. But it took another nine years to get into Continental Europe. Why? The language? Culture? Custom? What was it about the European markets?

The answer to that question is not much different today. These markets still vary in size and nature. There are enormous differences in GDP. And marketing itself is handled one way here and another way there. The Italians, for example, do not seem to want direct marketing, but the Spaniards are starting to like it.

Fortress Europe has been overplayed and will not happen. National treatment as set out in a banking directive does seem to be the sensible way forward.

People in the United States, however, may want to watch some of their overzealous administrators and tax collectors. An attempt is being made in Washington to raise the federal excise tax on foreign reinsurers, on the grounds that we apparently front for captives and tax havens. I not only refute this, but would point out that such a tax on European reinsurers is not even in the best interests of U.S. insurance companies, domestically or internationally.

A better solution can be found closer to home. This unilateral approach could backfire on U.S. companies in Europe, and I strongly urge that common sense be applied if Americans do, indeed, want to avoid Fortress Europe. I agree with Gordon Cloney that we need to talk together about issues such as this.

On the European front, the most important steps being taken lie in the framework directives. They should cut through much red tape and bureaucracy and be in the interests of both consumers and suppliers.

The 1992 process is good for Europe and good for the world. It is opening up the marketplace. But remember the majority of customers will still want service in their home markets in the language and currency of their choice, with claims service on the spot. So we must go on studying and working in each market, as well as servicing across borders.

314

A Commentary by Stewart H. Steffey, Jr.

W. R. Rowland has made a good point. Europe will still be a local market to a degree. The services will be needed locally. So, for the insurance industry, a market-by-market approach seems appropriate. Whether an insurer is multinational, whether the risk is multinational or Euronational—loss control services, loss prevention, engineering, claims services and underwriting will still need to be provided on the ground in the cities of Europe, as well as the rest of the world.

One factor that may greatly affect the outcome of things, of course, is Eastern Europe. But I view it as an opportunity and not as a threat for the European Community. There are close to another half a billion people in those markets. The insurance opportunities there are real. They are already starting to happen for CIGNA, particularly in the reinsurance area. This seems to indicate that what is going on in Eastern Europe will broaden the opportunity, not change the course.

A Commentary by Oakley Johnson

Maybe we should be paying more attention to the forces that are changing the marketplace within Europe, both as a result of internal developments not yet mentioned and external pressures.

Consider, for example, the cross-subsidization practices between the personal lines of business (or mass risks) and the industrial lines of business (the so-called fire risks). These practices have considerable trade implications. If exporters from Europe are able to obtain services at a subsidized level because high profits from the personal lines are paying for the large losses on the nonpersonal lines, they are going to benefit substantially. They will have greater access to both local and worldwide markets for manufactured products and be better able to compete in them.

But some of these practices appear to be changing—at least, people are being more open about them. The German regulatory authorities are already pressuring companies to account for these practices publicly in their annual reports. Brussels itself will press for some kind of change as the European Community becomes more consumer-oriented. Some have said there's a need for a Ralph Nader in Brussels. Maybe there already is such a person.

Another force at work arises from the EC decision to impose a common standard of transparency in markets where the practices, rates, behavior of companies, losses, and profits are not particularly well known. Ultimately, these transparency requirements will come close to what we now see in the British market. This move should benefit not only the consumers, but also those of us who try to compete in this market and understand it on a day-to-day basis.

The same can be said for mergers and acquisition regulations. Many practices that exist are not in the laws and regulations of these countries. Business relations between entities, between boards of directors, and between families are deeply ingrained—they are part of the culture. And although they are going to remain paramount for a long time to come, Brussels is looking for a way that will allow the new authorities, whether they be pan-European or otherwise, to liberalize the access to mergers and acquisition opportunities in Europe, particularly for non-EC companies.

At the same time, home-country control may contribute to a greater understanding and a greater liberalization of the markets in Europe. As the French, the British, and others begin to compete across borders by providing cross services, particularly in the non-personal lines, there is going to be greater competition with lower rates driving down the profitability of companies, whether they be the pan-European galaxies that we've seen created in the past few months or non-European galaxies.

The East European countries will then want to deregulate or reregulate their insurance systems to accommodate what they see as an important alignment from a regulatory point of view, with Western Europe. As a result, the push toward home-country control may actually be slowed down a bit. It will be a natural reaction. Whether it will in fact occur, no one knows at the moment.

What this all means for the U.S. system also has to be considered. Of course, many domestic pressures in this country are going to resist change, whether it be toward universal financial services or whether it be toward a more unified state regulatory system. But what is occurring in Europe does hold out some lessons for the United States.

AIC has suggested that in due course home-state control might become a useful guiding principle in the United States. In this way, a commercial lines company domiciled in a particular state could be regulated by that state in the other forty-nine states, as long as there are minimal solvency and financial requirements and standards set for all states. This would certainly strengthen the competitiveness of our own industry, both domestically and in markets around the world.

Some people in this country are also worried about the fact that we don't have a unified way of operating and that this is going to present some difficulties in competing against Europe. We do indeed have a unique system, and it creates challenges for trade negotiations. But state regulation itself may not be as great a problem as the peculiarities that exist from state to state. As far as negotiations are concerned, there are internationally accepted ways to bind state obligations in international treaties. So we should be focusing more on getting federal people involved in these negotiations and maintaining a close dialogue with the state regulators. In other words, we, too, need to achieve some coordination on our side.

15

Financial Services in the European Community and the Implications for the United States

Paul M. Horvitz and R. Richardson Pettit

The post-1992 plans of the European Community call for the elimination of most restrictions on the movement of capital and the provision of financial services across borders. These changes will account for one-third of the total increase in GDP that the internal market is expected to generate across Europe (Commission of the European Communities 1988: table 10-2-1). Such changes obviously have profound implications for European banks and other financial services firms, and for European capital markets.[1] But changes of this magnitude will also significantly affect the ability of U.S. firms to compete in the European market, and may also affect domestic U.S. financial markets. The repercussions on U.S. financial markets and institutions are the subject of this discussion.

Individual EC countries currently have various legal and administrative barriers restricting the flow of goods and services into their markets. These barriers are greater in financial services than in most other areas. The EC initiative would remove most barriers to internal trade, but this obviously requires common restrictions on the entry of goods and services into the Community. The possible barriers to outsiders have Americans and other non-EC countries greatly concerned, although, of course, EC policy makers have been mainly absorbed with eliminating barriers inside the Community, and have treated the external implications as an "afterthought" (Wolf 1989: 1).

The main reason that the gains from the removal of barriers to the flow of financial services bulk so large in the GDP increases is that previous actions by the Community has already significantly reduced trade barriers on most goods and services in a region where the provision of financial services has traditionally been localized (for details, see Pavel and McElravey 1990). Thus, "for goods sold directly to private citizens, the customs union has already been successful. In

318

this respect, the additional benefits from 'completing the internal market' are small" (Wolf 1989: 16). Thus, attention will undoubtedly turn to exploiting any economies of scope in financial services, since up to now most countries have limited the ability of firms to provide a full variety of financial services (such as insurance and banking).

The EC Approach

The basic approach taken by the European Community is simple: financial institutions will be able to provide any combination of financial services (although only insurance companies can underwrite insurance, and combinations of financial and industrial activities may be restricted), firms chartered in any EC country will be able to branch freely throughout the Community, and supervision will primarily be the responsibility of the country in which the firm is chartered rather than the host country. This is an attractive approach from the point of view of American financial institutions now operating in Europe and others interested in such opportunities.

The principles behind the financial services directives are identical to those used for other goods and services: "mutual recognition" and "minimum harmonization." Mutual recognition of regulatory regimes is a significant liberalizing concept (see Key 1989). It means that any financial service or product that a bank in, say, Germany, is allowed to provide domestically, it can provide in France or Spain. Spain cannot prevent the German bank from providing this service on its territory any more than it can prevent the importation of Cassis de Dijon. It can, of course, prevent *Spanish* banks from providing this service, but that would put domestic banks at a competitive disadvantage. The pressures will be strong to allow domestic banks to do whatever foreign institutions could do. Although such a system, along with host country controls over credit and interest rates, could lead to an extremely complex tangle of regulations, ultimately, the most liberal regulatory regime will be the one that calls the EC tune.

This approach reminds some of what former Federal Reserve Chairman Arthur Burns called "competition in laxity," but that is not accurate. The EC program does call for some minimum harmonization of regulatory standards. The most important one, on bank capital, has already been agreed to, and includes the United States, Japan, and Switzerland, as well as the EC countries. EC policy makers recognize, in other words, that the Spanish consumer of French Cassis de Dijon is not harmed if its manufacturer goes bankrupt, but the Spanish buyer of an insurance policy issued by a French bank *is* harmed by bankruptcy. Responsibility for supervision does rest with

319

the home country, but procedures are envisioned to ensure that minimum standards are met.

An American bank that acquires a *subsidiary* in any EC country will have access to this large and liberalized market. But this does not necessarily apply to *branches* of American banks in the Community. Since no EC member is responsible for supervising the parent organization (the American bank), it appears that the host country will be so responsible. That is no different from the present situation, but the competitive position of the American bank with respect to European banks may change significantly.

At present, the Paris branches of an American bank and a British bank are both subject to supervision by the French as well as by their home countries. After 1992, that will still be true of the American branch, but the British branch will be subject *only* to supervision by the British authorities. This has implications not only for the competitive position of American banks (and the structural form of their entry into the European Community—that is, branch versus subsidiary), but also for the United States as a financial center. Italian and Spanish banks can establish branches in, say, Frankfurt, without any additional supervisory and administrative costs, whereas their branches in New York must pay the costs of dealing with the American authorities.

The main concern of American firms is that the licensing of non-EC firms to operate within the Community will be based on "reciprocity." The concept sounds rather straightforward—a bank from a non-EC country will not be allowed to operate in the Community unless EC banks are allowed to operate in that bank's home country. That concept is open to other interpretations, however. The United States for example, admits foreign banks, but they must abide by U.S. banking laws. Accordingly, they cannot operate branches across state lines, and they cannot provide a full range of investment banking and insurance services. The proposed EC rules would allow a non-EC bank to branch everywhere within the European Community and to provide all these services. The question now being debated is whether current U.S. law represents sufficient "reciprocity" to meet the European conditions.

Although some would disagree, the reciprocity issue is far from being settled and may continue to be a problem for some time to come. The central concern here, however, is not how the Community will finally resolve this problem, but what effects its actions might have on U.S. financial institutions and U.S. financial markets. Would current U.S. law, even if deemed acceptable under EC reciprocity standards, leave U.S. banks at a disadvantage in competing with foreign banks in the United States, in the European Community, and in third markets? And what would happen to U.S. markets and institutions if U.S. law was changed to mirror the changes that will take place in Europe?

Although many in the United States have strongly criticized EC authorities for considering a rigid definition of reciprocity, neither economic theory nor the theory of public policy leads to a rejection of reciprocity on principle. Reciprocity may be used either to open markets or to protect them. Each country will decide on the basis of national interest the extent to which such a device will be used. If the Community is insisting on reciprocity with a view to opening financial markets, criticism from the United States is unwarranted.

U.S. financial markets are subject to substantial government-imposed restrictions. Despite being the focus of much publicity, actual deregulation at the federal level has been modest, and even some of that has been reversed by the recently enacted Financial Institutions Regulatory Reform and Enforcement Act (FIRREA). Yet a substantial body of evidence indicates that American consumers of financial services would benefit from the removal of restrictions on interstate banking and from allowing affiliation among commercial banks, investment banks, and insurance companies. The evidence indicates that such changes in U.S. law would not represent an increase in the risk of failure of financial institutions, but might reduce that risk. It is possible that EC insistence on strict reciprocity may lead the United States to amend the Bank Holding Company Act (including the Douglas Amendment), the McFadden Act, and the Glass-Steagall Act. We do not attempt to predict the likelihood of such a response, but we do discuss its costs and benefits. First, we must look at the concept of reciprocity and its alternatives in more detail.

Reciprocity as Opposed to National Treatment

Almost every country considers its financial sector to be a particularly sensitive area of the ecomomy. Special rules have therefore been formulated to cover the operations of financial institutions (particularly banks). These rules have been concerned with issues ranging from the concentration of financial power and the relationship of banking to monetary policy to the allocation of credit, the safety of depositors' funds, and potential foreign control.

Some countries have restricted the operations of foreign banks or prohibited foreign ownership of domestic banks. Such considerations are a familiar part of U.S. financial history: "The strongest objection raised against the renewal of the charter of the First Bank of the United States . . . was the large holdings of the bank's stock abroad (Holdsworth and Dewey 1910: 75).

The Bank of the United States was not recharted when its original charter ran out in 1911, and the foreign issue in banking did not resurface for many years. From the early nineteenth century right up to the 1970s, there was relatively little foreign investment in U.S. banking. Japanese and Canadian banks did set up operations on the West Coast in the 1870s, and the Hong Kong and Shanghai Banking Corporation began operations in San Francisco in 1875. The first states explicitly to permit foreign banking were Massachusetts in 1906, Oregon in 1907, California in 1909, and New York in 1911. A boom in foreign banking occurred in the 1920s, when foreign securities found a ready market in the United States, but that terminated with the stock market crash of 1929.

After World War II, foreign banks again expanded their operations in the United States. In 1961 New York permitted branches of foreign banks, in reaction to threats of retaliation against the overseas expansion of New York banks in Japan, Brazil, and elsewhere. In 1970 fewer than 100 U.S. offices (subsidiary banks, branches, and agencies) were owned by foreign banks. By 1988 that number had reached 532.

Foreign bank operations in the United States were subject to state law, but there was no federal law until the International Banking Act (IBA) was passed in 1978, in response to the rapid growth of foreign banks that had begun in the mid-1960s. The IBA firmly embraced the principle of "national treatment"—meaning that foreign banks and domestic banks would receive equal regulatory treatment. More specifically, foreign banks were to receive such treatment even if their country did not afford equal access (or any access) to American banks.

This decision was not uncontroversial. Some states had long imposed their own reciprocity rules. New York, for example, did not allow foreign banks to establish branches in the state if their governments did not allow New York banks to branch in their country. This restriction had affected Canadian banks in particular. Nevertheless, most large U.S. banks supported the national treatment approach. Some feared that too tough a policy on reciprocity might antagonize countries in which they were operating. Also, some U.S. banks had negotiated special entry rights in other countries, and they were not anxious to see the value of their charter reduced by opening those markets to other U.S. banks.

In most countries, national treatment represents a substantial liberalization of the treatment of foreign banks. That was not the case in the United States because, prior to enactment of the IBA, foreign banks received *better* than national treatment. For example, foreign banks could operate in more than one state (which American banks could not, at that time), foreign bank branches were not subject to reserve requirements, and foreign banks could operate a somewhat wider range of nonbank activities than domestic banks (most important of these involved securities subsidiaries operating in New York under state law).

Even after the IBA was adopted, a substantial body of opinion in Congress and the banking community continued to argue that the United States should do more to ensure equal treatment of American banks abroad, or that the United States should adopt a reciprocal approach to liberalization of U.S. law regarding the operations of foreign banks. The IBA did require that the Treasury investigate the treatment of U.S. banks by foreign governments. This evolved into a comprehensive study of the treatment of American banks abroad, but it did not lead to any changes in the IBA.

Discussion of the IBA did not suggest that foreign banks should be barred from operating in the United States. Congress has thought about imposing restrictions on foreign acquisitions of U.S. banks, however, and actually placed a moratorium on such acquisitions for a time. Acquisitions of domestic banks have long been controversial, and not just in this country. As the Treasury study (1979: 432) pointed out,

> A large number of countries, including many with otherwise liberal entry policies . . . take a more restrictive approach to foreign acquisition of domestic banks. In some of these countries, acquisitions of equity interest in indigenous banks is prohibited or strictly limited to less than a controlling interest by law, many other by unwritten policy.

It is interesting to note that despite recent liberalization of entry restrictions on foreign banks by Japan, many observers believe that Japan would not allow the acquisition of a large Japanese bank by foreign interests.

Whereas national treatment is fairly easy to define, reciprocity is not. Reciprocity could mean that country A will allow a bank from country B to do in country A only what banks from country A are allowed to do in country B. Or it could mean that country A will allow a bank from country B to do in country A whatever domestic banks can do, provided that banks from country A are allowed to do in country B whatever domestic banks are allowed to do in that country (reciprocal national treatment, or reciprocity of opportunity). Finally, it could mean that country A will allow a bank from country

323

B to operate in country A only if banks from country A are allowed to do in country B whatever they can do at home (mirror-image reciprocity).

The economic issues relating to the international provision of financial services, or entry by foreign financial institutions, are not different from those connected with international trade in goods generally. National treatment, like trade without tariff or other barriers, benefits the United States, and hence makes economic sense regardless of what other countries do. Nevertheless, it is also true that, like bilateral or multilateral trade negotiations, efforts to pressure other countries to lower barriers may also benefit the United States. Because the U.S. market is a large and attractive one, other countries may be willing to make concessions in order to gain entry for their nationals. If reciprocity is a useful tool in such negotiations, we would not reject its use.

Exactly the same argument can be made from the point of view of the European Community. Consumers of financial services in Europe will benefit if American and Japanese banks are allowed to compete freely within the market. But it is not unreasonable for the Community to insist on reciprocal treatment for EC banks in other countries.

EC policy on the issue of national treatment versus reciprocity is still uncertain. The original proposal for a second banking directive, issued in February 1988, contained a reciprocity provision that raised considerable concern both within and outside the Community. The reciprocity provision would have made the entry of outside banks into the single market dependent on whether all EC banks received reciprocal treatment in the outside country. Under that provision, when a bank from a non-EC country seeks an EC banking license, the application would be suspended until the EC Commission determined that "all credit institutions of the Community enjoy reciprocal treatment . . . in the third country in question." The precise meaning of "reciprocal treatment" was unclear.

Despite the openness of the U.S. banking market, existing U.S. law might not satisfy a strict EC reciprocity requirement. Entry into the single market would allow U.S. banks to operate anywhere within the market without having to satisfy additional administrative requirements. EC banks are now generally limited to operations in one state in the United States, unless state laws allow interstate operation. Entry into the market would allow U.S. banks to sell insurance and to engage in securities activities, although EC banks cannot do either in the United States.

A strict reciprocity requirement has received support in Europe from those who believe it would increase EC leverage in opening foreign markets (perhaps in Japan more than in the United States). It has also been supported by those who expected such a provision to restrict foreign entry, and hence "reserve some of the potential benefits of the single market for EC-owned banks . . . and would protect EC-owned banks, at least partially, from the potential, increased competition from non-EC institutions" (U.S. International Trade Commission 1989: 5–10).

At the same time, some Europeans fear it would have protectionist effects and moreover would transfer additional power to the EC institutions in Brussels. In response to both internal and external pressure, new language on reciprocity was proposed by the EC Commission in April 1989 and incorporated in the Second Banking Directive.

The amended language appears less ominous, but it remains ambiguous. The automatic suspension is replaced with a notification requirement, providing that member states inform the EC Commission of any "general difficulties" that EC banks have in engaging in banking activities in any outside countries. Also, the member states must inform the commission of any applications for entry from outside banks.[2]

If the EC Commission finds that a country is not granting EC banks "effective market access and competitive opportunities comparable to those accorded by the Community to credit institutions of that third country," it may submit proposals to the EC Council "with a view to achieving such comparable access and competitive access through negotiations."

The term "reciprocal treatment" was deleted, although the new provision is entitled "reciprocity." But "effective market access" and "comparable competitive opportunities" are terms that are subject to differing interpretations, and are not necessarily any clearer than "reciprocal treatment."

If the EC Commission concludes that effective national treatment does not exist in an outside country, it may direct member states to "limit or suspend their decisions regarding requests for new authorizations and acquisitions" by banks from that country. This suggests that simple national treatment may not be sufficient, although some suggest that the intent is to see that EC banks receive national treatment that works in practice, recognizing that many banking supervisory matters are handled on an informal basis. If this is the standard, American financial firms have nothing to fear from the banking directive, since the United States does provide effective national treatment.

It is widely believed that EC statements on reciprocity have been aimed more at Japan than the United States. The Report of the U.S. International Trade Commission (1989: 5–15) notes that "in meetings with USITC staff in April 1989, many public and private sector officials in the EC indicated that Japan was the target of the reciprocity provisions." This is consistent with the emphasis on "effective" national treatment. Japan's banking laws provide for national treatment, but some observers question their effectiveness. The earnings performance of foreign commercial and investment banks in Japan has been poor. Several bankers report difficulty in obtaining business from Japanese firms, who seem to prefer Japanese banks. One might conclude that the Japanese market is not truly open to foreign banks, but there is no obvious solution. At the extreme, effective national treatment may be interpreted to mean reciprocity of results. It is not likely that the Japanese government would (or should) force private firms to deal with foreign banks against their will.[3]

These differences in the opportunities available to foreign banks exist within regulatory regimes that may both offer national treatment. The United States does not set any arbitrary limit on the number of foreign banks that may enter. Japan does impose limits. In fact, the head of international banking at Dai-Ichi Kangyo Bank stated last year that "if every member of the EC insisted on reciprocity, for every banking license granted to Japanese subsidiaries, at least 12 banking license applications would have to be accepted by the Japanese government. . . . [That] would be an extremely inequitable situation. (Yasuhiko Ikeuchi, quoted in *American Banker*, October 24, 1988). Actually, the European Community is likely to deny licenses to Japanese applicants if *any* EC bank is denied entry into Japan. This suggests that the U.S. interpretation of reciprocity is a liberal one, whereas the Japanese may be considered rigid or inequitable.

The right to operate within the EC single market has considerable value. There is no reason to expect that the Europeans will give away that right if there is an opportunity to gain something in exchange. With respect to Japan, gaining entry may be a sufficient quid pro quo. But European banks already have access to the United States on a national treatment basis. The European Community may reasonably expect some additional benefit.

An interesting analogy can be drawn with the negotiations between Canada and the United States regarding their free-trade agreement (FTA): "Canadian bankers are clearly frustrated by what they perceive as the FTA's imposition of an unfair playing field. Under the FTA, U.S. bankers will be able to freely enter Canada's deregulated banking environment while Canadian bankers are afforded entry to a U.S. market where the Glass-Steagall Act, for one, limits the scope of banking powers" (Bierman and Fraser 1988: 21). The Canadians apparently concluded that other parts of the treaty provided sufficient benefits to justify the agreement. This suggests that European bankers will compare the value of what they are giving with what they may gain.

A final issue that seems to have been resolved in the Second Banking Directive is whether any reciprocity provisions would be applied retroactively to any American banks already operating within the European Community. According to the Investment Services Directive, modeled on the Second Banking Directive, "the reciprocity regime does not apply to existing investment businesses already established in the Community." Although this seems to resolve the question for those American firms already operating in the European Community, it removes these firms as active participants in seeking to make the EC treatment of outside firms as liberal as possible. In fact, those already grandfathered as EC firms may seek to restrict entry by other American firms.

The literature coming from the Community clearly indicates that the main concern of those involved in creating the single market is to eliminate internal barriers. Although some attention has been devoted to the appropriate external barriers, this question has been of less interest. Views on this issue may change over time. It would not be surprising if some trading takes place among those who view the issue of external barriers as mere bargaining chips with which to debate the more important internal issues. But that would not mean the issue of reciprocity has been put to rest and that American financial firms need no longer be concerned.

This interpretation of the reciprocity issue is not without its critics. In April 1990 the European Commission issued a report that has been called "the latest challenge by the European Commission to what it views as unfair U.S. banking practices" (Kraus 1990: 14). The article goes on to report that "Federal and state banking laws impose undue hardships on overseas banks and in some instances are discriminatory, the European Commission has charged. . . . The commission cited restrictions on securities activities as among the most burdensome and discriminatory. . . . The commission said in its report that geographic restrictions in the United States also impose severe handicaps on foreign banks." It still remains to be seen what sanctions the European Community will be willing to use in seeking to eliminate these U.S. restrictions.

American policy makers hope that Europe will not insist on rigid

327

mirror-image reciprocity—on a requirement that EC banks be allowed to do in the United States all that they can do at home. That is the position of American commercial bankers who do not want to risk being excluded from the European Community and government officials who want to minimize conflict with our European allies. Certainly, American bankers are competent to determine their own interest. But it is possible that the United States would benefit from a restrictive EC reciprocity policy, if it led to the easing of domestic U.S. restrictions on competition in financial markets.

Implications of Possible EC Actions for the United States

It is widely believed that current U.S. policy regarding foreign institutions is an even-handed national treatment that will pass muster under any reciprocity requirement that is likely to emerge.

Reciprocal National Treatment. In this section we ask what might happen if the European Community was to adopt such a reciprocal policy. How would it affect the competitive structure of U.S.-based financial services and what opportunities would American financial firms have to compete abroad?

Competitive position of U.S.-based financial firms. The ability of U.S.-based providers of financial services to compete in an integrated European community ultimately depends on three things: (1) the magnitude and nature of the demand for financial services; (2) the relative success of U.S. institutions in producing and delivering desired services (the relative marginal costs of production); and (3) the regulatory environment, which determines whether institutions from within and outside the Community will be able to provide services (the relative marginal costs of the regulatory structure).

We assume that the third point is resolved in favor of reciprocal national treatment and analyze the first two. But we raise questions concerning the implementation of this regulatory structure when it seems likely to have bearing on the competitive environment. For example, we ask whether *each* application for entry is to be evaluated for compliance with equal access to the entrant's home country.

One of the most economically important expectations for Europe in 1992 is the growth of its financial sector. This growth will emanate from the direct expansion of demand in an industry that has been overregulated and overprotected in at least some geographic areas. Since the elasticity of demand for some services (such as consumer and real estate lending) is likely to be high at the current level of output, some lines of business expect a broad increase in demand as the costs of regulation to both consumers and producers decline. Since retail banking is the business sector that has been most effectively insulated from entry and competition, it will experience the greatest increase in demand.

In addition, changes in the nature of production and delivery of goods and services in the Common Market should increase the demand for financial services in general. Moreover, firms will find that they need different productive facilities and working capital with changes in underlying firm-specific demand. As a result, significant restructuring of financial contracts will take place. Some firms will expand and others will consolidate, but only with commensurate changes in firm financial structure.

Demand is also likely to be affected by the significant changes now taking place in Eastern Europe. Increases in the movement of people and goods, in joint ventures, and in direct investment would create a demand for the financial services of institutions with a physical presence in Europe. The demand could be enormous not only because of the potential number of people involved, but also because banking services are not widely available in Eastern European economies for financing consumption and productive operations. Obviously, whether and how financial needs develop and economic relations change remains uncertain—but it is a possibility that any producer of goods and services must begin planning for.

Indirect shifts in the demand for financial services also are likely to be significant, although the direction of their effect cannot be predicted. European business firms normally find it more difficult to tap local financial markets than do their counterparts in the United States.[4] This is true for both public equity and debt markets. As a result, firms receive a smaller portion of their long-term financial needs from issues of publicly traded debt and equity securities and a larger portion from private sources—including individual arrangements with banks and other financial entities. This had undoubtedly resulted in an increased cost of capital to all but the largest of European producers.

Changes in the debt and equity markets in Europe, although not as far along as in banking, should help to improve the access these firms have to low cost sources of funds. Assuming this happens, the question becomes whether this effect will, at the margin, take business away from some traditional banking operations. There is at least the possibility that this will lead banks to shift toward more fee-oriented activities (investment banking, mergers, securitization) and away from their traditional role as lenders. Such a change would be especially important for U.S. banks under some forms of reciprocity since they may be prevented from engaging in activities in Europe currently prohibited by Glass-Steagall. Even if that does not happen and national treatment holds, U.S. and Japanese banks may not have the necessary localized expertise to operate in these areas, since they do not provide these services in their domestic markets.

There is little reason to believe that the demand for financial services within the European market will be a function of the supplier's domicile. Consumer and business nationalism is not expected to be important. Indeed, the success that economic integration has experienced in Europe thus far is due to the general indifference of the consumer regarding the nationality of the producing firm. This in turn is due in part to the superregional nature of many European firms (if not their banks, to this point) and in part to the view that everybody will gain if economic nationalism is kept at bay. This tendency is likely to extend beyond the boundaries of the European Community if regulations themselves do not prevent equal market access. In other words, the issue is not whether consumers of financial services are willing to buy from "outside" suppliers, but rather whether "inside" producers are able to persuade the EC Commission that ease of entry cannot be justified.

In wholesale banking services, in particular, the long-time presence of U.S. banks clearly implies that customer preference will not depend on whether the producer is or is not domiciled in the United States. This issue is perhaps not as clear with regard to Asian banks. Although large business customers in Europe will obviously be willing to contract with Japanese or Hong Kong banks, smaller business customers and consumers may not. In some markets, the Asian banks may find it necessary to overcome the uncertainty of dealing with institutions that have not traditionally been present.

In sum, it is reasonable to expect a significant growth in the demand for financial services at both the wholesale and retail levels. But we can also expect important changes in the components of that demand beyond the traditional product lines currently offered. How these demands are met will depend on the cost structures faced by banks operating in Europe.

The ability of U.S. financial institutions to enter the EC market also will depend on their success at production and delivery of services that are directly related to capital position, economies of scope and scale, and branch structures.

As international standards for bank capital become more homogeneous, a considerable thorn in the side of cross-border banking is removed. In theory, at least, international standards will make it difficult for foreign banks to be denied entrance into the European

TABLE 15-1
CAPITAL RATIOS OF THE 500 LARGEST BANKS
IN THE WORLD, BY COUNTRY, 1988
(percent)

Country	Capital Ratio
Spain	6.68
Greece	6.48
Portugal	6.43
Italy	6.33
Denmark	6.30
United Kingdom	6.23
United States	6.14
Switzerland	6.02
Canada	6.00
Hong Kong	4.43
Netherlands	3.93
Luxembourg	3.58
Belgium	3.49
France	3.44
West Germany	3.21
Japan	2.87
Austria	2.55

SOURCE: *Euromoney* (July 1989).

Community because of confusion over measurement of capital. This will reduce, if not eliminate, many of the cost-of-capital arguments that suggest some banks have an advantage over others simply because of their domicile.

The problem will not go away entirely, however, since the risk-based nature of capital requirements leaves some room for interpretation. In particular, the actual risk present in a portfolio of loans and investments cannot be measured without error, regardless of the system used to measure it, as loans to developing countries and for commercial real estate development pointedly demonstrate. In the end some institutions may be able to gain a cost-of-capital advantage over others, although at a clearly diminished rate.

The 1988 capital positions of the 500 largest banks in the world, are given in table 15-1 by country of domicile. Because the figures reflect only the largest banks, they cannot easily be generalized to all banking markets in the European Community. Moreover, the largest of the U.S. banks (the ones currently in Europe) have capital positions that are less than the 6 percent cited in the table (figures for the largest banks are closer to 4.2 percent according to Baer and Mote 1989). Thus, it would seem that U.S. banks are in a strong competitive position, able to spend money in the development of business in an integrated Europe. Two factors exert a strong equilibrating force on these reported figures, however.

First, adjustments for unreserved loans to developing countries would reduce the capital positions of U.S. banks. Although the adjustment would strike the large U.S. banks the hardest—reducing the capital position of these banks by more than 1 percentage point according to one estimate (Baer and Mote 1989)—other money center banks would be affected to a lesser extent.

Second, unrealized capital gains on stock market holdings of Japanese banks, in particular, are large and positive. Realizing these gains would significantly increase the capital positions of Japanese banks, even after adjustments for taxes and needed LDC reserves. Although unrealized gains on securities are not capital for some purposes, it is nevertheless true that these banks would not view themselves to be short of capital for purposes of determining the extent to which they can enter the EC market. Conversely, of course, recent declines in Japanese stocks and real estate have had a significant negative effect on the unrealized gains themselves. The illiquid form of this capital and its recently diminished value will somewhat restrict the entry of Japanese banks through subsidiaries, where specific independent capital positions must to be maintained. In other words, in comparing the positions of U.S. and Japanese banks, the specific allocation of (realized) capital for the formation of subsidiary operations in Europe does not give Japanese banks nearly as much of an advantage as was originally suggested by their enormous equity positions they hold in 1989.

In view of these complexities, we conclude that there is not a great deal to choose from, in terms of capital positions, between European, Japanese, and U.S. banks. European banks generally have lower capital positions, but that is probably offset by their lower marginal costs to entering banking markets in Europe (given that they can operate within Europe on their existing bank license) than those faced by non-European institutions. Japanese banks still have more capital, but a large portion of it is in a form that is less liquid and therefore less easily transferred to a European subsidiary.

The second key production issue is concerned with economies of scope and scale. The EC Commission has issued directives that clearly envision banking markets with a great deal of competition and little explicit regulation over who enters and with what services. If that objective is implemented through reciprocal national treatment, then

U.S. financial institutions clearly have the option of entering EC markets in the manner they find optimal. Important to their choice are the costs and benefits associated with different banking structures, including subsidiaries or branches, wholesale or retail operations, and specialized versus general product offerings.

Some have argued that if reciprocal national treatment is the regulatory structure of choice, the market will evolve in favor of a relatively small number of well-capitalized universal banks, the rationale being that significant economies of scope and scale exist in serving these banking markets. This conclusion implies that the entry possibilities for U.S. banks may be limited, given the large resource requirements necessary to becoming universal European banking firms.

In some markets (such as those of France), however, past banking regulations have spawned a system made up of various categories of financial institutions with some degree of specialization. If universal banks are to become the predominant type of institution, at least some European competitors will enter the 1990s without the universal bank structure, and on a similar basis as U.S. and Japanese banks. The present situation seems to be changing rapidly as more banks are beginning to offer a larger variety of financial products and services.

Whether these issues push the industry in the direction of universal banks will depend on the existence of economies of scope and scale in banking in Europe. It will also depend on whether those economies can be captured by non-EC financial institutions.

Economies of scope exist whenever the joint production of banking services pushes costs below those for the same level of production undertaken by independent organizations. Such efficiencies may arise from two sources. First, technological factors in the production process may permit the employment of otherwise partly or wholly unused capacity (economies in production). Second, customer needs may be more effectively met when services are delivered from a single producer (economies in delivery). It is this delivery benefit that the industry traditionally has considered important in meeting the needs of its business and individual customers. Within the *scope* of the bank's operations, economies of scale relate only to whether costs are lower as the level of output increases.

Empirical studies of economies of scope in the production of financial services (unlike those relating to economies of scale) have not found definitive and important effects. This is not surprising given that firms select their mix of output on the basis of the cost and revenue structures they face. Moreover, the lack of data (especially revenue and cost data by product line) has severely limited the generalizations that can be made. Even so, there are many reasons for expecting economies of scope to have an important effect on financial services and thus on the structure of the European banking industry.

One question of concern to U.S. banks seeking competitive positions in Europe is whether economies of scope are limited to closely associated products and services. There is little reason to believe that economies in delivery extend beyond broad customer classes. The added convenience of a single bank producer being able to meet the various financial needs of its customers declines as the difference between the core product and the other financial needs grows wider. Although a bank may find it efficient to offer both lending and business acquisition services for large business customers, little further benefit may be gained by also offering securitization services to other financial institutions or retail services to individuals. Put simply, economies in delivery are not likely to extend beyond the needs of the customer.

In contrast, economies in production may extend beyond specific customer needs, since the source of the efficiency relates to the manner in which the product or service is produced. Most production processes in banking, however, are separable and not joint activities. Retail and wholesale banking involve different people and different assets. Cost centers in banking, in other words, correspond rather closely to well-defined customer groups. To the extent this is true, there would be no reason to expect economies of scope in production to differ markedly from those for delivery. Thus, economies of scope in banking production also may not easily extend beyond the needs of the bank's customers.

There are a few significant exceptions to this conclusion. Foreign exchange services and letters of credit used for foreign trade, in terms of volume, are primarily wholesale banking services. Yet the marginal net benefit associated with providing those services for individual clients (if not at the retail banking level) may be significant. Note, too, that management talent is often viewed as being sufficiently malleable that an extension of the production process, when excess capacity in managment exists, may bring significant gains. No one, as far as we know, has been able to document empirically that this feature is an important part of banking operations.[5]

For U.S. banks entering Europe, these points suggest, first, that entrants need not offer all services to all customers. Purely on the basis of economies of scope, it should not be necessary for U.S. banks operations in Europe to be in the form of a universal bank, even if

European banks are of that form. Second, however, it will be necessary to offer goods and services that meet the various financial needs of the customer base the bank decides to serve. This, of course, raises the question of whether U.S. banks can compete for wholesale business without offering both debt- and equity-based investment banking services. And third, because of the selective nature of economies of scope, entry decisions will be affected by the bank's current scope of business. A superregional retail-oriented bank in the United States is unlikely to find it easy to enter the European wholesale market.

A second important question for U.S. firms is whether non-European institutions have the same economies of scope and scale in Europe as those domiciled in Europe? To a degree, this question asks whether products and services offered in Europe are the same (with the same cost and revenue structure) as those offered in the United States.

As a banking organization expands from one geographic sphere (say the United States) into another (Europe), the variations in customer needs or in the production process can significantly alter its costs and revenues. In the framework of economies of scope or scale, retail banking in Europe may constitute a different service from retail banking undertaken in the United States. Whether U.S. banks can be competitive depends on the presence of economies of scope (if the services are different) and scale (if they are quite similar). If changes in products and services and in the demanded method of delivery are slight, then the extent of economies of scale will determine the ability to compete. It is possible, of course, that economies of scope and scale are present in banking markets but cannot easily be extended from one sector of the world to another. Historically, regulatory prohibitions and significant regulatory costs have been important in limiting entry. In addition, familiarity with the organization and with the products offered is often important to entry success. The importance of the first of these factors should be substantially reduced under a regime of reciprocal national treatment. The clear signal from the adoption of reciprocal national treatment is that competition is the goal, and equal access will be fostered.

Less is known about the importance of the familiarity factor, but there are several reasons to think that it will not be overwhelmingly important in the European Community. In most European banking markets, economic nationalism is unlikely to affect U.S. institutions and their European competitors differently. A U.S. bank and a German bank should face the same underlying customer demand functions in Spain—although those faced by a Spanish bank might be different.

Customer demand functions for wholesale banking services are even less likely to be a function of the domicile of the bank—unless the domicile affects the willingness or ability to offer some services. Wholesale banking in Europe has a rather strong international tradition, with large European organizations having effective access to a variety of services currently offered by the large U.S. and European banks. This access has grown stronger with the process of integration, in general, and with the success of the Eurocurrency markets, in particular.

Another question to consider is what effect economies of scope and scale might have on operations in Europe. The basic issue here is whether the level of output of a given service, along with efficiencies of scope, imply that only the largest of (universal) banks will survive. If so, the level of consolidation required in Europe would be enormous. Moreover, in this case, only the four or five largest U.S. institutions would have the capital base to compete efficiently with their European and Japanese counterparts.

The production functions for the generation of banking services are not likely to be such that universal banks would have a significant cost advantage over other banks. Empirical evidence in domestic markets strongly suggests that costs per unit of output level out at moderate levels of output. Moreover, there is nothing in international banking to suggest that potential access to lower-cost deposit markets, export and import business, or foreign currency operations—all necessary parts of international banking operations—leads to such efficiencies that only banks offering all banking services at significant levels can survive.

Branch versus subsidiary structure also may be a key determinant of success at entry. Under reciprocal national treatment, branches will be supervised by the country in which the branch is located when the domicile of the bank is outside the European Community. But subsidiaries licensed in one country can operate offices in any EC country under the supervision of only the country in which they are headquartered. This gives a distinct operating cost advantage to the subsidiary form of organization by homogenizing the regulations and supervisory authorities overseeing the bank. The potential offsetting disadvantage, of course, is that subsidiaries have regulatory capital requirements that might have important cost implications.

The benefit of operating in Europe under a single regulatory authority depends on the degree to which regulation and supervision vary from one jurisdiction to another. The Second Banking Directive clearly indicates that countries will be under pressure to adopt a regulatory posture that is not much stiffer than that adopted by all.

To adopt a stiffer set of regulations imposes costs on local banks not faced by other banking units entering the European market. This principle does not extend to branches of foreign banks, however. Since they are regulated within the country of their location, market pressures are not present to force intracountry regulations of branches to a lowest, common level. Consequently, the potential exists for both different and more obstructive regulations on branches of foreign banking firms—especially, entry limitations on some services. This would directly raise the costs of U.S. and Japanese branch banking in Europe, both absolutely and relative to banking through a subsidiary structure. These costs are likely to be important and to vary considerably within countries and over time as individual countries attempt to sort out the optimal regulatory structure for dealing with foreign branches.

At the same time, subsidiary banking operations require devoted capital, which may increase costs in three ways. First, capital requirements for subsidiaries may be established by regulation at other than optimal levels. Second, capital requirements for subsidiaries may exceed the requirements for the firm on a consolidated basis. Third, the bank's operations may be proscribed by regulations that limit certain actions to a percentage of capital, for example, for loans to one borrower or for one class of loan. Given the marginal costs of capital faced by banks, only the third of these is likely to play an important role in creating a cost structure that substantially penalizes subsidiary forms of entry into European markets by foreign firms.

This cost is greater for some services than for others. Given the size of many transactions at the wholesale level, the cost will be greater here than in retail lines of business. If wholesale products and services are to be less fully regulated than retail activities by the individual countries, then the cost comparisons might very well favor the branch structure for wholesale markets, with subsidiary structures optimal for all other banking pursuits.

Finally, relating to the production and distribution of banking services, are investment banking activities. Under reciprocal national treatment, banks prevented from engaging in the securities business in the United States will be able to engage in such activities in Europe. Thus, although both foreign and domestic bank operations are limited by the Glass-Steagall Act in the United States and by similar restrictions in existence in Japan, banks operating in Europe are free to engage in all types of primary securities market transactions.[6] Given this environment, U.S. and Japanese bank operations in Europe will be asking three questions in particular: First, are economies of scope such that only banks that offer both standard bank services *and* underwriting services will be able to compete effectively in the market for wholesale business? Second, will U.S. banks be able to compete side by side with European banks for underwriting business when they cannot undertake those same activities within U.S. markets? Third, if offering both banking and investment services allows firms to achieve significant economies of scope, will other financial service firms, such as investment and merchant banking organizations, have a competitive advantage over commercial banks in supplying some or all of these services? The third issue asks if economies (or current presence) are such that it is easier for investment banking firms to enter the banking business than for banks to enter the securities business.

There are few solid answers to these questions. Economies of scope seem obvious in investment banking markets. Most large corporate clients use no more than one or two investment banking organizations, because familiarity with the corporate customer is a necessary prerequisite to providing most services. Recent casual evidence suggests that economies of scope extend at least from some investment banking activities into traditional banking services, and vice versa. Citibank, Bankers Trust, and other large U.S. banks currently are pressing the limits of Glass-Steagall by offering fee-based services that traditionally have been performed in the securities industry. Similarly, investment banking firms are offering corporate liability management services that are closely related to lending and leasing arrangements traditionally undertaken with banks. Moreover, economies of scale clearly are present in many investment banking activities. Securitization, merger and acquisition financing arrangements, and underwriting require enormous amounts of capital and, possibly, management teams with rather large fixed costs.

The apparent significance of both economies of scope and scale lead many to argue that large universal banks will dominate the European scene. But investment banking and wholesale commercial banking firms frequently form informal joint ventures and partnerships to enable them to effectively serve their clients. Not all of the individual participants in joint ventures have the capacity to offer the variety of services required by the client. As a consequence, firms that specialize in less than a full complement of services can survive. Significant economies of scope and scale are achieved by renting capacity from other commercial banks and investment banks. The system works rather well and seems to allow firms with a narrow range of services to exist side by side with firms that offer a broader range of services. In this manner, then, it seems likely that even if foreign banks cannot enter the investment banking market in Europe

338

on their own, because of their lack of an investment banking base in the United States, they still may be able to enter the market through partnership arrangements with U.S. or European investment banking organizations.

Even if economies of scale do not prevent U.S. banks from entering Europe, however, they may face a competitive disadvantage in the investment banking markets where U.S. firms already have a substantial presence. At a minimum, substantial price concessions are likely to be necessary to capture a significant portion of what will be a growing market. U.S. and British investment banking firms already have a clear advantage in providing securitization, merger and acquisition, and underwriting services to the European market-place (and, conversely, have little to offer in the way of traditional banking services). A few major European and Japanese banks and a number of Japanese securities firms will no doubt participate in the expansion of these markets—and some will offer a full range of banking services as well. As long as Glass-Steagall is in effect and the economies that go with larger levels of investment banking outputs remain, U.S. banks are not likely to enter the investment banking business in Europe in the same way that investment banking firms will (nor will investment banking firms enter the European banking business without their being able to offer those services in the United States as well). Nevertheless, there is no reason to expect them to be excluded from this market, either, as they provide specific services within partnership arrangements created to service the range of needs of European business firms. These services will involve banking activities, as well as such traditional activities as securitization and merger and acquisition financing.

Competitive structure in the United States. If the European Community adopts reciprocal national treatment as its standard, the competitive structure of financial services in the United States will not be greatly affected. Most of the large banks of the world are already operating in the United States (of the 100 largest banks in the world, 94 already have an office in the United States, as do 70 of the next hundred largest), and American rules on banking operation would not need to change. With the consolidation of EC banks, larger banks will be competing in the United States, but American banks are already exposed to that; it is also possible that the number of foreign banks in the United States will decline.

Foreign banks expanded rapidly in the United States during the 1970s. Although the pace of expansion has slowed somewhat, they have continued to increase their share of the U.S. market. Fears that the U.S. banking system might be taken over by foreign banks have proved groundless. And although some foreign banks have been highly successful, some have given up on a number of their U.S. ventures (for example, Midland Bank acquired Crocker, but then sold it to Wells Fargo after suffering significant losses; Marine Midland Bank, a subsidiary of Hong Kong and Shanghai Bank, recently abandoned plans to acquire First Pennsylvania).

Foreign-controlled U.S. banking assets now represent about 20 percent of total domestic banking assets. That figure has grown steadily, from about 5 percent in 1975, to 10 percent in 1979, and 15 percent in 1983. These figures probably overstate the penetration of foreign banks into the domestic market, since much of the activity of their U.S. offices is with other banks and with the home country. A majority of their assets are interbank, as are 70 percent of their liabilities. Nevertheless, foreign-controlled banks accounted for more than 25 percent of the commercial and industrial (C & I) loans of banks in the United States in 1987 (their share was 10.3 percent in 1977). A significant portion of that share represents loans originated by U.S. banks and sold to foreign banks. Many analysts argue that the real profit in business lending comes from the origination function, not portfolio investing.

Japanese banks are by far the largest foreign participants in the U.S. banking market. At the end of 1987, Japanese banks held $45.8 billion of C & I loans in the United States, out of a total of $86.2 billion held by all foreign-controlled banks. Canadian banks were a distant second, with $8.9 billion. The largest volume held by an EC country's banks was $6.4 by Italian-controlled banks.

Within the past few years, foreign entry has been more significant in investment banking. In 1986 Sumitomo Bank bought a substantial interest in Goldman, Sachs & Co. Earlier that year Union Bank of Switzerland became the first foreign bank to lead and manage a U.S. domestic bond offering. Several foreign firms are now primary dealers in U.S. government securities. If universal banking becomes prevalent in Europe, European banks are likely to play a larger role in this market as they gain experience at home.

There is some prospect that foreign banks will have less interest in operations in the United States after 1992. Some large banks will be under pressure to meet the new risk-based capital requirements that must be fully phased in by 1992. These capital requirements may put severe constraints on growth for some banks, although many may be able to raise sufficient additional capital. Since the announcement of the Basle agreement on capital standards, the Japanese banks have raised enormous amounts of new capital, and it appears that their growth will not be constrained (the high prices of Japanese bank stocks make this easier than for other banks). Banks under such constraint may decide to limit their expansion to Europe rather than the United States. For most EC banks, the logical path of expansion lies in other EC countries, rather than in third countries. After 1992 a French or German bank will be able to expand in Italy or Spain with virtually no additional regulatory burdens. Moreover, developments in Eastern Europe may open up that potentially large market, and financial firms in Western Europe may find a more attractive market there than in the United States.

A decline in the competition provided by foreign banks will not be welcomed by American consumers of financial services, although U.S. markets will remain competitive. A more serious result may be a lessening in the competitive position of the United States (and New York City in particular) as the major financial center of the world. After 1992 there may be advantages in centralizing international financial activities in London or Frankfurt rather than the United States. Direct cost considerations—labor, rents, communications, and so on—will play a role in such a decision, as will the availability of the necessary resources. But regulatory considerations may also play a large role. Differences in regulatory costs may well make New York a less attractive financial center than some European locations. Differences could exist in the cost of reserve requirements, deposit insurance, financial reporting, consumer protection, examination and supervision, and other regulatory burdens.

A forecast that the U.S. financial structure will not be significantly affected by the EC initiative would be a positive one if the U.S. financial structure was optimal. But this structure has significant shortcomings that the United States has been reluctant to face up to in the absence of a real crisis. Indeed, the long-smoldering problems with the federal deposit insurance system and with the savings and loan industry were ignored by the administration and Congress until the savings and loan situation erupted into a crisis. The U.S. financial services business needs to be overhauled, and the EC initiative could be the appropriate catalyst for change.

Strict Reciprocity. Early statements by European leaders indicated that proposed requirements for reciprocity would be interpreted strictly. All such statements, even when viewed as most threatening by American bankers, stressed the use of reciprocity as a means of forcing an opening of markets rather than as a protectionist device. Although most Americans (though not necessarily the Japanese) have breathed a sigh of relief as more recent statements have indicated a willingness to accept true national treatment, it is by no means clear how this issue will finally be resolved by the Europeans. If they do insist on a mirror-type reciprocity, U.S. interests will obviously be affected differently, depending on whether the United States adjusts to such a demand.

The United States does not provide reciprocity. This would be the worst of all possible outcomes, although some observers believe that it is impossible. They argue that if the United States makes it clear that U.S. laws will not provide such reciprocity, the European Community will either back down or accept a compromise that saves face on both sides, but does not significantly change U.S. banking law.

If EC demands for reciprocity are not met and American financial service firms are then excluded from Europe, the policy decision for the United States is whether to retaliate. The European Community has clearly indicated that firms already operating in Europe will be grandfathered, regardless of what is done about reciprocity. That is, the London-based subsidiary of an American firm will be treated like any other EC company, and its operating and expansion rights will not be affected by the dispute over reciprocity. U.S. retaliation, then, will probably be limited to a restriction on new entry by EC banks. There would be little support for a policy of massive retaliation in the form of ousting all EC banks from the United States (besides damaging U.S. financial markets, such an action could lead to an ouster of U.S. firms from Europe). But nearly all European banks that would be logical entrants into the U.S. market are already here, so such limited retaliation would have little effect.

Since most European banks are already operating in the United States, the effects of an impasse over reciprocity, even with U.S. retaliation, would be rather insignificant in domestic financial markets. U.S. financial services firms would suffer greater effects, however. A number of such firms do not have subsidiaries in the European Community. It is important to recognize that an existing *branch* in London is *not* an EC firm with automatic expansion rights. Furthermore, interstate consolidation among U.S. banks may increase the number of such firms with the interest and the capability of operating successfully in the European Community. Exclusion from the single market will be a significant barrier to their development into worldclass institutions.

Exclusion of these firms from Europe will also have adverse effects on the U.S. balance of payments—first, because they would expect to earn profits abroad; and, second, because if they did operate in Europe, a significant part of their activity would tend to be financing the export transactions of their American customers.

Although these effects are difficult to quantify, the direction is rather clear—the United States would be adversely affected by a dispute over reciprocity that leads to the exclusion of American firms from the European Community.

Accommodating EC demands: the issues. The negative effects described above would pose a serious dilemma for American policy if accommodating EC demands for reciprocity required undesirable changes in the U.S. financial system. Fortunately, that is not the case. The evidence suggests that the United States would benefit from changes in U.S. law that would represent full reciprocity for EC firms.

The principal restrictions in U.S. law that are relevent here are the barriers to interstate banking (specifically, the McFadden Act and the Douglas Amendment to the Bank Holding Company Act), restrictions on combinations of commercial banking and securities activities (Glass-Steagall Act), and perhaps the prohibitions in the Bank Holding Act of common corporate ownership of a commercial bank and a nonfinancial firm (although only those provisions that restrict bank involvement in insurance and real estate may pose any real problem).

The clearest example of the difference between U.S. financial regulation and that of the European Community is the current U.S. restriction on interstate banking. The heart of the post-1992 change in EC banking is that any bank in the European Community will be allowed to branch or establish subsidiaries anywhere within the EC (with no approval needed from the host government). In this regard the twelve-nation community will be much more a single market than the United States. U.S. law (the McFadden Act) does not allow national banks to branch across state lines. State-chartered banks may be allowed by their home state to branch across state lines, but they can do so only if the host state allows such branching, and none do. The Bank Holding Company Act allows bank holding companies to acquire or establish subsidiaries across state lines only if the host state explicitly authorizes such entry.

There have been no changes in federal law concerning interstate banking since the restrictions imposed by the Bank Holding Company Act of 1956 (except limited authorization for interstate acquisitions of failing banks). The recent liberalization of interstate banking restrictions has come entirely at the state level. Several states now do allow interstate holding company activity (but not branching), but much of the country is segmented by regional interstate compacts. These laws are more restrictive for foreign banks than might be apparent because of their bias against New York banks. That is, the laws of several states were enacted with the support of their local bankers, who wanted interstate opportunities and were willing to accept interstate competition from some quarters but not all. They were most concerned with keeping out the money center banks. Thus

343

Connecticut authorizes interstate operations by holding companies based elsewhere in New England, but excludes New York banks. Since most foreign banks find it essential to have a major part of their U.S. operations based in New York, they are excluded from entry into most states in the United States. Some states with regional reciprocal laws do have a future date at which interstate banking becomes national. Some of these require reciprocity, but New York already authorizes interstate banking. Nearly all such laws have trigger dates earlier than 1993.

The current situation is not likely to satisfy those EC banks interested in building a national operation in the United States. (But note that U.S. laws do not preclude interstate operations for securities firms or insurance companies.) Equity seems to be on the side of the Europeans: why should an American bank be granted the authority to operate in London, Frankfurt, Milan, and anywhere else in the European Community, while a French bank is allowed to operate in New York City and Buffalo?

It is not clear whether elimination of the Douglas Amendment would represent a satisfactory resolution from the European point of view, or whether modification of McFadden would also be necessary. Branching is clearly superior to maintaining a separate subsidiary as a means of providing services across state lines. The subsidiary must be separately capitalized, with a loan-to-one-borrower limit based on the subsidiary's capital. These are the same issues that bear on U.S. bank operations in Europe.

The problem of providing interstate banking powers for EC banks turns on the U.S. tradition of allowing individual states to control their own banking structure. This is not a matter of Constitutional requirements, but merely a decision by the Congress to defer to the wishes of the states. It is somewhat of an anomaly that the branching powers of national banks, an instrument of national policy, differ from state to state. Nevertheless, some recent decisions by the Congress and the Federal Reserve have broken with the long tradition of deferral to state preferences. Banks have not been allowed to make use of a liberal authorization of insurance powers by South Dakota, and the recent FIRREA legislation puts severe federal restrictions on the use by savings and loans of powers granted by the various states. The dual banking system has been an important component of the U.S. banking structure for more than a century, but it is certainly reasonable to consider anew whether its continuation is in the best interests of the United States.

The other point of controversy regarding reciprocity for EC firms is the mixing of commercial banking and securities services, as in the

German universal banking model. As noted earlier, universal banking is likely to become the rule within the European Community because of the mutual recognition concept. At present, the Glass-Steagall Act limits the securities powers of commercial banks. A number of actions by the regulatory agencies and decisions by the courts have broadened somewhat the securities powers of banks. There is substantial support in the United States for repeal or major modification of Glass-Steagall, but also a significant body of support for the separation of commercial and investment banking. Further chipping away at Glass-Steagall is likely, even without legislative action. Banks will be able to broaden their underwriting activities, but actions by the regulators cannot grant banks the power to underwrite corporate equities.

American banks have been interested in three types of securities business. Besides underwriting securities (investment banking) they are interested in brokerage services (American banks can provide discount brokerage services, and, in some cases, serve as full service brokers) and in marketing and managing mutual funds.

The controversy over Glass-Steagall in the United States is primarily a turf battle, with securities firms (other than those that would like to acquire commercial banks) trying to limit competition from the banks. The Glass-Steagall Act was a response to problems supposedly caused by the mixing of commercial banking and investment banking activities during the 1920s. Recent careful historical research has rather convincingly demonstrated that the reputed abuses never occurred, or could not reasonably be attributed to a combination of commercial and investment banking (Benston 1989). The fact that there was no historical basis for enactment of Glass-Steagall does not make the turf battle any less bitter, but it does mean that we should appraise the issues with a clean slate.

The Second Banking Directive will allow banks to sell insurance products and to provide real estate services throughout the European Community. American banks are now generally prohibited from providing these services in the United States. Real estate services are not likely to generate much controversy, but insurance is important. The creation of the single market in Europe will offer opportunities for consolidation and economies of scale that will lead some European firms to be interested in offering insurance products in the United States.

The separation of banking and commerce in the United States has by and large prevented banks from entering the insurance business, although there are some exceptions. National banks in small towns have been allowed to operate insurance agencies, and the Bank Holding Company Act has allowed bank affiliates to offer credit life insurance. In some states, bank officers have been able to operate as insurance agents, and some state laws have allowed somewhat broader powers to state-chartered banks. Savings and loan associations have had much broader powers to provide insurance services.

The implications of banks underwriting insurance and banks acting as insurance *agents* are quite different. Underwriting carries financial risks, although those risks differ significantly between life insurance underwriting and casualty insurance. Obviously, selling insurance entails no financial risks, and the restrictions on the bank sale of insurance products stem in part from a concern for consumer protection. Like the Glass-Steagall issue, debate over the bank provision of insurance services has been primarily a turf battle.

Banks offer some convenience advantages in the sale of insurance. The car buyer or home buyer usually needs a loan to finance the purchase. It may be convenient for the customer to be able to buy auto or homeowner's insurance at the same time. The insurance agents believe that this gives the bank an unfair advantage in selling insurance and argue that there are opportunities for forced tie-in sales. They fear that the bank will make approval of a loan application contingent on the purchase of insurance from the bank. Economic theory holds, however, that the ability to force a tie-in requires market power, and if the banks have market power they can exploit that directly in the lending market. Moreover, if forced tying is the issue, why are banks allowed to sell credit insurance, where the tie-in potential is most immediate? (The Bank Holding Company Act prohibits tying.)

Some other aspects of reciprocity may also have to be negotiated, but they are unlikely to pose unsolvable problems. For example, foreign banks (branches or subsidiaries) will no doubt continue to be subject to U.S. reserve requirements. A more important issue is the general concept of home-country supervisory responsibility. It is a virtual certainty that the United States will not leave supervision of EC banks operating in the United States to their home countries, even when there is full respect for the capabilities and motivation of the home-country supervisors. But the Europeans are not likely to expect such mutual recognition. This is not to suggest that all EC bankers will be happy with U.S. supervisory procedures and requirements. Disputes may arise over the applicability of certain American consumer protection rules to limited service foreign financial institutions, but even the EC rules accept the legitimacy of home-country concerns about the protection of its consumers. Specific legislation will probably be needed to deal with these issues. Although such negotiations may be difficult, particularly since the specific resolutions may have significant effects on particular institutions, disagreement over them is not likely to cause the collapse of an otherwise acceptable reciprocity agreement.

Accommodating EC demands: the evidence. As noted earlier, American antipathy toward interstate banking has its roots in concerns about the concentration of financial power and the rights of states to determine the structure of banking on their own territory. For much of U.S. history, the ability of banks to branch, even within their state has been a controversial matter. One important issue addressed with substantial empirical literature on branching (see, for example, Gilbert and Longrake 1974) is whether branching, by facilitating an increase in bank size, allows large banks to achieve economies of scale that lead to undesirable levels of concentration. In general, economies of scale are thought to be relatively modest, with significant economies exhausted at a relatively small asset size. Moreover some agree that branch structure does appear to produce diseconomies such that the operating costs of small unit banks do not put them at a disadvantage in competition with large branch banks (see Benston et al. 1982; King 1983). Others conclude that freer entry, or an increased number of competitors, results in better service and lower prices to bank customers.

Some legal means are already available for banks to operate on an interstate basis, however, and technological changes are allowing banks to offer interstate competition without a significant brick-and-mortar presence (see, for example, Bennet and Haywood 1983). Over the past several years, nearly all states have changed their laws to allow at least some sort of interstate banking (usually bank holding company acquisitions, frequently with a regional limitation on the location of the acquirer). Some of these changes have been motivated by perceived benefits from encouraging interstate activity; other states may have recognized the extent to which interstate activity was already taking place.

The evidence clearly shows that the public can benefit from the increased entry into banking markets that wider interstate banking would bring. If the European Community insisted on authorization for EC banks to operate on an interstate basis in the United States and the United States changed the McFadden Act or the Bank Holding Company Act to accommodate that demand, the evidence strongly suggests that American consumers of banking services would benefit.

The prohibition of bank participation in securities activities was based on the view that securities activities were risky and posed a threat to the survival of banks in the securities business. Evidence does not support that interpretation of U.S. banking history. Even

347

during the 1930s, when 26 percent of all national banks failed, only 7.2 percent were national banks with securities operations (White 1986).

Although the earnings of securities firms are greater than those of banks, risk, as measured by the variability of earnings, also appears to be greater for securities firms (see, for example, Wall and Eisenbeis 1984). Even if this is so, a combination of commercial banking and investment banking may reduce risk if the correlation of returns from the two activities is negative or low. Furthermore, if average returns from the securities business are higher, the combination may reduce the probability of failure, even if the variability of returns (risk) increased. Some studies find high correlations, indicating that the risk-reduction benefits from diversification would be small (Stover [1982] finds a correlation coefficient of .77). Litan (1985) concluded that securities activities would be included in an optimal portfolio for a bank holding company, but the optimal percentage of assets was only 1.6 to 3 percent. A careful study by Kwast (1989: 123) concluded that "Some evidence of diversification potential is evident. . . . However, the results of this study suggest that the burden of proof should be on those who would claim substantial diversification benefits."

Benston (1989: 298) has summarized the evidence as follows:

All of the studies reviewed indicate that there would be benefits in terms of higher returns from combining commercial and investment banking. They also report higher standard deviations of returns from investment banking than from commercial banking. Some find that total risk, measured by the total standard deviation of returns, from combining the two activities would not increase significantly or might be negative, while some find higher total standard deviations than were experienced by banks alone.

The evidence is certainly not sufficient to conclude that allowing banks to participate in the securities business will reduce the risk to commercial banking. Nor can we conclude that keeping commercial banking and investment banking separate is necessary to, or even contributes to, maintaining commercial banking safety. Since allowing commercial banks (and foreign commercial banks) to provide securities services in the United States will increase competition, and presumably improve service to American consumers of such services, some gains could ensue from the elimination of the Glass-Steagall barriers to combinations of commercial and investment banking.

As already mentioned, the possible insurance activities of commercial banks cannot be analyzed without distinguishing between insurance underwriting and insurance agency functions. Whereas insurance underwriting involves a degree of financial risk, operating an insurance agency is clearly a low-risk activity. Studies of potential combinations of banks and insurance companies generally find some risk reduction from such combinations. In this case, even high correlations can reduce risk at least to a modest degree since the insurance activities themselves do not carry greater risk than banking (see Heggestad 1975; Stover 1982; Wall and Eisenbeis 1984; Rose 1989).

Consumers are likely to benefit significantly from the provision of insurance services by commercial banks, both because of the increased competition and the increased convenience. Banks have been prevented from providing such services not because of concerns about risk (as might be the case with securities activities), but because of the efforts of insurance agents to fend off the threat of increased competition. Clearly, insurance agents will be worse off if the United States allows commercial banks to engage in a full range of insurance activities, but the U.S. national interest is not likely to be harmed by dropping the present restrictions.

Conclusions

A reduction of barriers to the provision of financial services on a transnational basis within the European Community will open up opportunities to a limited number of U.S. financial firms, but will also increase the strength of the competition in a number of European markets. American firms bring some advantages and some disadvantages to this competition. Although the outcome cannot be predicted, these disadvantages, nor the regulatory regime set by the Second Banking Directive and the forthcoming Investment and Insurance Directives, do not appear to be barriers to the expansion of American firms.

The effects in the United States will depend on how EC proposals for reciprocity are resolved. For their part, the Europeans are likely to follow policies that are in their own best interst. It is in the interests of European financial firms to seek a liberalization of U.S. financial regulation. The European Community may therefore use the reciprocity provision to encourage change in the United States. But if it threatened to limit access to the European market by American financial firms, this would not be sufficient to coerce the U.S. Congress or administration to take action that runs counter to the best interests of the United States. We believe, however, that it is in the interests of the United States to change the laws that now restrict interstate banking and the activities of banking firms. The changes in

Europe regarding the provision of financial services are certain to benefit European consumers and business. They could also serve as a catalyst for a long-needed reform of the market for financial services in the United States.

References

Baer, Herbert L., Jr., and Larry Mote. 1989. "Preparation for Globalization in the Americas: The Domestic Operations of U.S. Banks." Paper presented at Conference on Financial Globalization: Private and Public Strategies, Federal Reserve Bank of Chicago, November 2.

Bennet, Vironica M., and Charles R. Haywood. 1983. "Technology and Interstate Banking." *Economic Review* (May).

Benston, George J. 1989. *The Separation of Commercial and Investment Banking: The Glass Steagall Act Revisited and Reconsidered.* New York: St. Martin's Press.

Benston, George J., Gerald A. Hanweck, and David B. Humphrey. "Scale Economies in Banking: A Restructuring and Reassessment. *Journal of Money, Credit and Banking.* November.

Bierman, Leonard, and Donald R. Fraser. 1988. "The Canada-United States Free Trade Agreement and U.S. Banking: Implications for Policy Reform." *Virginia Journal of International Law.* Fall.

Cecchini, Paolo, with Michel Catinat, and Alexi Jacquemin. *The European Challenge: 1992: The Benefits of a Single Market.* Aldershot: Wildwood House.

Commission of the European Communities. 1988. "The Economics of 1992: An Assessment of the Potential Economic Effects of Completing the Internal Market of the European Community." *European Economy.* March.

Dewey, Davis R. 1910. *The Second Bank of the United States,* Washington, D.C.: U.S. Government Printing Office.

Gilbert, Gary, and William Longbrake. 1973. "The Effects of Branching by Financial Institutions on Competition, Productive Efficiency and Stability: An Examination of the Evidence." *Journal of Bank Research.*

Heggestad, Arnold A. 1975. "Riskiness of Investments in Nonbank Activities by Bank Holding Companies." *Journal of Economics and Business.*

Holdsworth, John T. 1910. *The First Bank of the United States,* Washington, D.C.: U.S. Government Printing Office.

Key, Sidney J. 1989. "Mutual Recognition: Integration of the Financial Sector in the European Community." *Federal Reserve Bulletin.* September.

King, B. Frank. 1983. "Interstate Expansion and Bank Costs." *Eco-*

nomic Review (May). Federal Reserve Bank of Atlanta.

Kraus, James R. 1990. "U.S. Banking Laws Called Unfair." *American Banker*. April 25.

Kwast, Myron L. 1989. "The Impact of Underwriting and Dealing on Bank Returns and Risks." *Journal of Banking and Finance*.

Litan, Robert E. 1985. "Evaluating and Controlling the Risks of Financial Product Deregulation." *Yale Journal on Regulation*.

Pavel, Christine, and John N. McElravey. 1990. "Globalization of the Financial Services Industry." *Economic Perspectives* (May/June). Federal Reserve Bank of Chicago.

Peter Merrill Associates. 1981. *Foreign Banking in the U.S.* Washington: American Bankers Association.

Rose, Peter S. 1989. "Diversification of the Banking Firm." *Financial Review*.

Stover, Roger D. 1982. "A Reexamination of Bank Holding Company Acquisitions." *Journal of Bank Research*.

U.S. International Trade Commission. 1989. *The Effects of Greater Economic Integration within the European Community on the United States*. Publication 2204. Washington, D.C., July.

U.S. Treasury Department. 1979. *Report to Congress on Foreign Government Treatment of U.S. Commercial Banks*, Washington, D.C.: U.S. Government Printing Office.

Wall, Larry D., and Robert A. Eisenbeis. 1984. "Risk Considerations in Deregulation Bank Activities." *Economic Review* (May). Federal Reserve Bank of Atlanta.

Wolf, Martin. 1989. "1992: Global Implications of the European Community's Programme for Completing the Internal Market." Paper prepared for the Lehrman Institute, New York, April.

16
Commentaries on Financial Services

A Commentary by Geza Feketekuty

Paul Horvitz and Richardson Pettit have raised three important issues: the competitive impact on U.S. firms relative to European firms; the competitive impact on the U.S. *market* compared with the European market; and the pressure on U.S. regulations.

With respect to the competitive impact on firms, and their analysis of economies of scope and scale, I would add that we have to look at the future and see where banking is going. Banking still faces enormous challenges in adapting the new computer technologies for the delivery and customization of the financial product. To the extent that American firms have been in the forefront of using computers and telecommunications to deliver banking services, they have an important competitive advantage.

As the individual national markets in Europe are merged into a single market, the electronic intracorporate networks that have been developed by the American banks will be an important competitive element because in managing a continental-size financial network, you need a highly integrated system for managing and delivering financial services. These electronic networks are vital for obtaining economies of scale and scope. Consideration of the U.S. strength in the use of computers and telecommunications is an important addition to the evaluation of the competitive impact of EC 92 on U.S. firms.

As for the competitive impact of EC 92 on the U.S. financial market, I would have liked to have seen, frankly, more analysis of the extent to which liberalization in Europe will be a disadvantage for the New York financial market and other U.S. financial centers. Horvitz and Pettit state that after 1992 there may be advantages in centralizing international financial activities in London and Frankfurt rather than the United States. They go on and say, "Differences in regulatory costs may lead to a decline of New York as a financial center relative to some European locations."

There could have been more analysis to back up this statement because the source and nature of the competitive pressure could have important implications for U.S. policy, including U.S. regulatory policy. I suspect that the pressure that could emanate from Wall Street for changes in the U.S. regulatory structure in order to compete with Europe is going to be more powerful than perhaps some of the pressures that the authors examine. We therefore need a clear idea of which aspects of liberalization in Europe will draw business away from New York and what pressure will that create to change specific American regulations in order to even the competitive balance.

Turning to the potential pressure of EC 92 on U.S. regulations, both Linda Powers and Geoffrey Fitchew have laid to rest the reciprocity issue. We oppose sectoral reciprocity, and we are in favor of reciprocal national treatment. According to Fitchew, that is also the European policy, and furthermore the debate now has shifted to negotiations that are focusing, among other things, on trade in services, especially in the Uruguay Round. This is where some of the details regarding the treatment of foreign banks will have to be ironed out, including the treatment of branches.

We also have to decide what national treatment means in the U.S. context. Does it apply to the states? If it doesn't apply to the states, will the federal government at least break the link between federal banks and state banks, which it has maintained up to now. Federal regulators have extended a courtesy to state regulators by not giving foreign banks federal charters in states that prohibit foreign banks. This becomes an important issue from the point of view of national treatment.

I was a little bothered by the shift in terminology—from "effective market access" to "effective market treatment." I am not sure those two terms mean exactly the same thing, yet the authors seem to use them interchangeably.

On the question of U.S. regulatory reform, the key issue is American economic interest. Many people who favor regulatory reform in the United States have argued that tying fundamental regulatory reform to trade negotiations is like trying to hitch a Sherman tank to a donkey. You know, it just won't pull. But if there is an economic interest in basic regulatory reform, trade negotiations could lead to some regulatory changes that are both in the U.S. interest and the European interest. In other words, it is not only the donkey pulling the tank, but several caterpillar tractors also pushing the tank.

The frustration of Canadian bankers was mentioned in the context of the U.S.-Canadian negotiations. But we did make some regulatory changes to accommodate the Canadians. That is, we allowed

Canadian banks to deal in Canadian treasuries. This is, at least, a precedent. It is an instance in which we were prepared to make some domestic regulatory changes in the context of a trade negotiation.

U.S. regulatory reform, I think, really depends on whether the wall that prevents banks from crossing state lines and prevents banks from engaging in investment banking is rapidly being eroded by the growth of the non-bank financial sector and by electronic networks in the United States. Ultimately, these economic forces will work some changes into the U.S. regulatory structure.

A Commentary by Geoffrey Fitchew

A striking change appears to be taking place in American attitudes toward what is going on in Europe. Two or three years ago, many were still fairly skeptical about the success of the single market venture, about the success of 1992. Today Paul Horvitz and Richardson Pettit convey an unspoken assumption that we are going to succeed in creating a single market in financial services. That is obviously an assumption that we in the commission share.

Another change, is that the reciprocity issue appears to be pretty well settled, despite the attempts to revive it. Actually, I am a little surprised to find people still questioning the good faith of both the commission and the community in this respect.

The fact is, we are making rapid progress in adopting all the financial services legislation needed to liberalize the market. The directive that obliges member states to liberalize capital movements came into effect on July 1, 1990. That completely liberalizes capital movements down to and including the right of citizens and corporations to open bank accounts anywhere within the Community. It means that the countries will liberalize their capital movements not just within Europe, but owners of the rest of the world too.

Moreover, the large majority of member states anticipated that requirement and liberalized their capital movements completely, or almost completely in advance of the July date. In addition, Belgium and Luxembourg have finally removed the two-tier foreign exchange market that had previously operated in those two countries.

All the necessary banking legislation needed to create the single license—the Second Banking Directive the own funds directive, the solvency ratio directive to implement the 8 percent capital ratio—have been agreed by the council of ministers and will come into effect on January 1, 1993.

As for the securities market sector, the work is well advanced.

The Investment Services Directive to create a single license for investment firms is under discussion in the council now, and before the end of April we will be publishing a proposal on the capital adequacy requirements to be applied to investment firms in respect of market risks—that is, position, foreign exchange, and counterparty and settlements risk.

On insurance, progress has been slower because it is a more complicated industry and because there is a greater history of protectionism. Even so, we reached an important agreement on the liberalization of large commercial risks in 1988, and the council is close to an agreement on own-initiative life insurance for both individuals and groups that was under discussion at the end of last year.

We are also bringing forward three further proposals to complete the liberalization of the insurance market; a directive to liberalize mass risks (the so-called personal lines), insurance for nonlife, and insurance for life; and a third proposal for pensions.

More generally, one of the conditions of success has been that the financial services industry in Europe believes the single market is going to be achieved. They have already demonstrated that by the rapid growth of mergers and acquisitions, joint ventures, joint marketing agreements, and so on.

Our goal is to have the largest and most liberal financial market in the world, and we think that that will become a reality. We also want to remain an open market. We welcome outside competition and inward investment. The entry into our markets of American and Japanese banking and securities firms not only adds competition but, particularly in the securities sector, adds desirable depth and liquidity to securities markets. So we will certainly not be a Fortress Europe. On the contrary, we are trying to set an example of a liberalized financial market that we hope other countries will follow.

We hope to pursue those objectives of liberalization internationally, both in the GATT, in the OECD and, where necessary, in bilateral negotiations. In the GATT, the community and the United States have been in close cooperation, and I believe that what we are hoping to achieve in the GATT negotiations, the goals that we are setting ourselves for opening up market access in third countries, are very close, indeed.

Turning to the prospects for U.S. businesses and U.S. banks, I agree that there will be substantial growth and demand for financial services in the Community. At the same time, competition will increase significantly. Perhaps the important question to consider here, whether universal banks are the model for the future. In our community legislation, we are certainly not requiring people to operate in the form of universal banks. In that sense, our legislation is permissive or, if you like, agnostic. We are certainly not seeking to restrict universal banks, but neither are we seeking to favor universal banks in comparison with other forms of organization.

Undoubtedly, there will be some movement in the direction of universal banking, but the scope for specialist operations will also be there. Indeed, the Deutsche Bank decided that in order to conduct securities operations in London, it wanted to have a specialist securities subsidiary and acquired Morgan Grenfell.

On the question of branches as against subsidiaries, Horvitz and Pettit suggested that subsidiaries might have one disadvantage as a vehicle for American banks: they would have to be specifically capitalized, whereas branches would not.

That suggestion overlooks one prominent feature of the treatment of foreign branches in Europe. A majority of member states—ten out of twelve, at present—require the branches of third country banks to have dedicated capital for those branches as if they were separately capitalized banks. Under the Second Banking Directive, with its single license, the requirement for endowment capital for branches of any banks that are incorporated in the community is entirely removed. So, that disadvantage of the subsidiaries seems is overstated.

Arguing in the opposite direction, Horvitz and Pettit suggested that foreign branches might be at a disadvantage because it would remain open to member states to impose different and more obstructive regulations on branches than on subsidiaries. Clearly, the endowment capital requirement is an example of that.

In the longer term, however, the European market and other markets are likely to move in the direction of a more liberalized treatment for branches as well. Indeed, that ought to be one of the objectives of the Geneva negotiations in the GATT.

The question of where new opportunities are most likely to arise is still debatable, but I see them in the provision of banking services to medium-size and then later to small companies, rather than to the retail sector, that is the man in the street. As I think was mentioned, Europe is heavily overbranched. Therefore, few foreign banks will be seeking to create a new network of branches. There will be acquisitions to acquire foreign presence, but few new branches.

Let me turn, finally, to the question of reciprocity and national treatment. In our view, there is no ambiguity in the Second Banking Directive. It is absolutely clear that we have decided on a reciprocal national treatment test and that we have drawn a sharp distinction between two different situations.

On one hand, we are denied reciprocity in the broad sense, that is to say, where community banks are not allowed to do in a third country what foreign banks can do in its community. Securities market operations are an obvious example. In this talk, we have said that we will negotiate, and we will do so with determination and persistence, to try to persuade our partners to remove what we regard as unnecessary barriers of that kind. But we will not deny access to the third country banks in those circumstances.

We will only refuse a license or limit the scope of a license in cases where we are denied national treatment and effective market access. Effective market access, in that context, means that we can actually get into the market, because a number of countries—not the United States but a number of other countries—ration banking licenses. There are quantitative limits on the number of new banks that can be opened, and that is a denial of effective market access. National treatment has to be de facto, not just de jure. That is the other reason why we use the phrase "effective market access."

We have also made it clear that the grandfathering provision does not stop at a particular date. It is not just banks in the community now that will benefit. The grandfathering is a continuing process and would apply to any new bank that comes into the community and is established there until we hit a problem and are denied national treatment and decide to invoke the sanctions. It is difficult to imagine a more liberal and generous approach to the problem than that.

One impression that needs to be corrected, by the way, concerns the single banking license. It is not valid for insurance and real estate operations in the community. It is valid for all traditional banking functions and for securities business, but not for insurance. On the contrary, community legislation specifically prohibits banks or, indeed, anyone other than insurance companies from underwriting insurance.

But there are no prohibitions at the community level and few prohibitions at the national level on banks operating as an insurance agent and selling insurance. A great deal of that is already going on. We would certainly encourage movement in that direction elsewhere, but it is not something that comes into the Second Banking Directive.

Another serious concern for some people is national treatment. My question is whether the United States itself is consistent in all cases with the principle of national treatment that the administration has endorsed. At least two states, Florida and Virginia, discriminate against foreign-owned banks in regard to interstate branching. Furthermore, the limits the FEDWIRE System imposes on daylight overdrafts, which do not take into account the worldwide capital of foreign banks, operate, in effect, to restrict the activities of foreign banks.

So all those countries that are committing themselves, as the United States has done, to the principle of national treatment and, indeed, that are trying to advance that principle further in the GATT negotiations and elsewhere, need to examine their own practices on this matter with great care. Needless to say, we in the Community will also do.

One other point that seems to require a comment is that the Community has been urged to use the reciprocity instrument to promote banking reform in the United States. The more important question is, Does the United States and its banking community perceive such reform as being in their own interest? We in the Community would say that we certainly think it should be in your own interest and that it would make your market more attractive for European banks, as well. The reasons have to do with competition. For various reasons, banks are going to find themselves under continuing and increasing competitive pressures. That strongly underlines the desirability of the kind of banking reforms that have been undertaken within the Community.

PART FOUR
Agriculture

17

Agricultural Trade Conflicts in the 1990s

Timothy Josling

Conflicts between the European Community and the United States over agricultural trade have enlivened the international scene for many years. From the chicken war of the 1960s to the disputes over pasta and beef hormones in the 1980s, disagreements over relatively small volumes of trade have bedeviled transatlantic commercial relations. Tensions have spread beyond agricultural markets, both through the use of retaliatory trade sanctions on other products and through the souring of bilateral trade relations. Commercial relations between the United States and the European Community have improved with the Bush administration, and cooperation rather than confrontation seems to be on the rise. But tensions over agriculture remain just beneath the surface and could erupt again at any time. These bilateral differences have often stalled progress in multilateral trade discussions. Such differences lie at the heart of the problems facing the GATT Uruguay Round discussions on agricultural trade.

There is little mystery as to why governments get into conflicts about agricultural trade. They take on, through their agricultural policies, the responsibility of finding markets for domestic farm products. By and large, governments do not control output decisions: that is left to the millions of small and medium-size family businesses that make up the farm sector. Sometimes governments attempt to bribe or coerce farmers to restrict output of various products, although often without notable success. On other occasions they allow the market to determine prices and they top up farm income with an extra payment. Occasionally, they give farmers payments related to income need or to environmental contribution rather than output. But the main thrust of farm support policies has been to provide sufficient "markets" to maintain chosen levels of price. These markets are often the creation of policies rather than of consumer choice. They are created through protection against imports, state purchas-

I would like to thank Wally Falcon, David Kelch, and Stefan Tangermann for helpful comments on an earlier draft.

ing and intervention schemes, export restitutions and enhancements (note the variety of pseudonyms for subsidies), and the taxing of substitute products.

If more than one government is trying to create such an artificial market, then each will come into (potential) conflict with the others. Such policies impose a financial and administrative cost on the policies of all other governments. Some of these costs go unnoticed, as a part of the trading environment; others are made apparent and cause friction. What causes a particular potential problem to emerge as a conflict is in part a result of world market forces, in part a reflection of the political influence of particular producer groups, and in part a consequence of the policy instruments used. Conflicts will diminish if world market conditions improve (that is, if prices increase, and therefore the cost of providing the artificial market declines); if the political influence of producer groups diminishes (which may happen if the public loses sympathy with farmers); or if governments shift to other types of policies (such as direct payments or supply control).

One question for the 1990s is whether this state of trade tension is likely to continue, or whether we can expect an easing of the situation. The answer depends in part on the changes that Stefan Tangermann has examined elsewhere in this volume. But other factors are also at work. Changes in U.S. agricultural policy and that of other industrialized countries will have a bearing on the climate for trade relations. Developments in the former Soviet bloc countries and in the developing world will also have an important influence on the state of world markets. Technology has a habit of posing new challenges for policy makers, as well as new opportunities for humankind, and how these challenges will be met will undoubtedly influence trade relations. And don't forget the weather. It often takes a decisive hand in agricultural matters and will no doubt help determine the trend in commercial temperatures over the decade.

The factors that will influence the climate of trade relations are deceptively easy to identify—easy because so many factors come into play and deceptive because they tend to hide an important facet of agricultural (and other) policies. These policies are largely reactive to events outside their control. Developments in domestic farm policy follow closely changes in the market situation for agricultural commodities. To describe likely trends in such policies without reference to these world market conditions is clearly inadequate. But world market trends are at least partly a function of domestic policies in the larger countries. As a consequence, EC and U.S. policies toward agricultural can materially alter the assumptions on which those same policies are based. (These might be called "large" policies, in contrast to "small" policies, where there is no discernible feedback between policy actions and the situation that the policy is trying to correct.) One might well ask, "Which came first: the common agricultural policy (CAP) or unstable world markets?"

U.S.-EC Agricultural Trade Conflicts in the 1980s

U.S.-EC trade conflicts reflect a clash of domestic farm policies. More often than not, the conflict pits U.S. export interests against the CAP of Europe. The United States strongly believes in the capacity of its own agriculture to compete on level terms with other countries. It has consistently objected to subsidized competition from other countries that seek to use world markets to avoid domestic resource adjustments and hence prevent true competitiveness from emerging. The European Community is singled out as a major player in the game of subsidized exports and high domestic market prices. As a result, the CAP has achieved a particular status in U.S. agricultural policy circles as public enemy number one.

This continued attack on the Community is not without cause. The EC's CAP has been almost a caricature of a trade-distorting policy. The principal instruments developed in the late 1960s are the variable import levies applied at the border in such a way as to keep domestic markets stable, the intervention purchases that put a floor in the domestic market, and the variable export subsidies that keep domestic intervention stocks at a reasonable level. Only for sugar was a quota system chosen, on a "temporary" basis, although for some products protection came through fixed tariffs (as in beef, sheep, fruits, and vegetables), and in some cases the intervention system was weak or absent (as in pigmeat, poultry and eggs, and fruits and vegetables). More recently, quotas have been introduced for milk, and the intervention system for cereals and meat has been weakened (see Tangermann, this volume; Moyer and Josling 1990). Despite these changes, the emphasis on border protection has contributed greatly to trade tensions. In contrast, the U.S. policy for cereals and oilseeds operates mainly at the farm and internal market level, in spite of the growth in export subsidies in recent years. As a result, trade tensions are not so marked or so clearly focused.

Trade Balances and Trade Conflicts. The conflicts in agricultural trade go back twenty-five years to the founding of the CAP in the early 1960s. Until recently, these conflicts looked as if they were under control, but they have intensified since 1980—that is, ever since EC

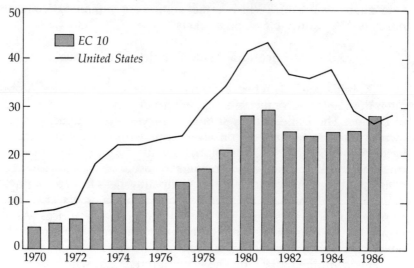

FIGURE 17–1
AGRICULTURAL EXPORTS FROM THE UNITED STATES
AND THE EUROPEAN COMMUNITY, 1970–1987
(billions of U.S. dollars)

NOTE: EC exports exclude intra-EC trade.
SOURCE: Newman, Fulton, and Glaser (1987).

agriculture emerged as a major exporter in temperate-zone markets.
The United States has seen its exports to the European Community
diminish over the past decade and has faced increasing competition
in third-country markets. EC exports have also penetrated the U.S.
domestic market to an increasing extent. During the 1970s, U.S.
exports rose rapidly (figure 17-1). The United States had in place the
capacity to meet the surge in demand from the USSR and from the
developing world. European exports lagged until 1977 but accelerated
with the generally favorable trade conditions until 1981. That year
represented a peak for U.S. agricultural exports, at $43 billion. Over
the next five years, U.S. exports declined sharply to a low of $26.1
billion in 1986. EC exports stalled a little, then recovered, and in 1986
were actually higher than those of the United States. The European
Community, always thought of as the "largest import market" for
U.S. agricultural products was now the world's largest exporter. A
recovery in U.S. exports since 1987 has helped restore the earlier
balance somewhat.

The trend in total exports sets the tone for U.S. farm policy. The

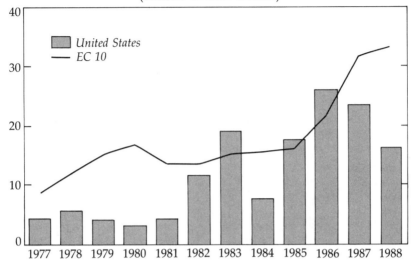

FIGURE 17–2
FARM SUPPORT EXPENDITURES IN THE UNITED STATES
AND THE EUROPEAN COMMUNITY, 1977–1988
(billions of U.S. dollars)

NOTE: 1988 is estimated.
SOURCE: Newman, Fulton, and Glaser (1987).

budget cost largely reflects the balance between domestic production and export demand. The escalation of budget costs over the 1980s was a serious policy concern in the United States, as it was in the European Community. In the 1970s, farm support costs stayed low—with buoyant export markets and firm prices (figure 17-2). Support costs in the United States took off when exports dropped in 1982 and generous policy prices were set under the 1981 farm bill. A drought-induced drop in production in 1983, coupled with the cost-shifting effect of the payment-in-kind (PIK) scheme, gave a temporary respite, but by 1986 expenditure had reached a peak of as $25 billion. Indeed, as EC representatives in Brussels and Washington were quick to point out, U.S. support costs exceeded those in Europe at that time. More recent developments have returned this relationship to its more normal state.

Bilateral trade figures point to the same story (table 17-1). Over the last half of the 1970s, trade was increasing steadily in both directions. The situation changed abruptly after 1980. U.S. exports of agricultural products to the EC-10 fell from a high of $9.6 billion in 1980 to $5.2 billion in 1985, recovering the next year to $6.6 billion in

TABLE 17-1

U.S.-EC BILATERAL AGRICULTURAL TRADE, 1975–1986

(billions of U.S. dollars)

Year[a]	United States to European Community	European Community to United States
1975	6.0	1.1
1976	6.8	1.3
1977	6.9	1.4
1978	7.5	1.9
1979	8.1	1.9
1980	9.6	2.1
1981	9.1	2.3
1982	8.4	2.5
1983	7.4	2.8
1984	6.5	3.2
1985	5.2	3.6
1986[b]	6.6	4.1

a. Calendar year.
b. EC-12 figures are given for 1986. EC-10 trade flows are 5.6 and 3.8 billion, respectively, for that year. Portuguese accession, and the United States has lost some of its rather small share in the EC wine market in recent years.
SOURCE: Newman et al. (1987).

part because of the enlargement of the Community in 1986. In contrast, EC agricultural exports to the United States continued to rise, reaching $4.1 billion in 1986 ($3.8 billion for the EC-10). That same year, the EC-12 sold $71 billion of nonagricultural goods to the United States and purchased $44 billion of those goods. The agricultural trade surplus of $2.5 billion went only a small way toward offsetting the U.S. merchandise trade deficit with the Community.[1]

The fall of U.S. exports to the Community in the 1980s was primarily in the big-ticket items of grains, nongrain feed ingredients, and oilseeds and products (see table 17-2). Corn sales were hard hit by emerging surpluses of barley in the European Community and by the continued attractiveness of nongrain feed ingredients in livestock rations. Soybean sales were hit by increased oilseed production in the European Community, which grew from 3.2 million tons in 1980–1981 to 11.6 million tons in 1987–1988. Domestic oilseed production now accounts for nearly one-half of the total EC oilseed use (U.S. Department of Agriculture 1989). More recently, other markets have been affected. Beef and variety meat sales to the European Community from the United States had surpassed $100 million in 1988, when the ban on imported meat produced with hormones was introduced.

TABLE 17-2

U.S. AGRICULTURAL EXPORTS TO THE EUROPEAN COMMUNITY,
SELECTED PRODUCTS, 1982–1986
(millions of U.S. dollars)

Commodity	1982	1983	1984	1985	1986
Oilseeds and products	5,173	4,403	3,378	2,318	2,506
Grains and feeds	3,403	2,488	2,621	1,800	1,507
Animals and products	987	788	793	649	765
Tobacco, manufacturing	616	636	669	663	549
Nuts and preparations	301	250	263	330	357
Fruits and preparations	229	183	156	136	161
Cotton	215	209	369	375	123
Vegetables and preparations	178	152	147	128	137

NOTE: Fiscal year, exports to EC-12.
SOURCE: Newman et al. (1987).

Cotton sales fell away after 1985, in part as a result of Spanish and Portuguese accession, and the United States has lost some of its rather small share in the EC wine market in recent years.

Added to the concerns about import access has been the intensified competition in third countries, particularly in the case of wheat. EC wheat production has more than doubled since 1962, largely as a result of yield increases (U.S. Department of Agriculture 1989). In the face of stagnant consumption, self-sufficiency was reached in the mid-1970s, and the European Community emerged as a leading exporter of wheat, capturing 15 percent of the world market by 1987. The U.S. share declined sharply in the 1980s, from 48 percent in 1981 to below 30 percent in 1985 (ABARE 1989b). Whatever the true cause of this decline, the Community's generous export subsidies were held in part to blame. This experience led to a small subsidy war, with the United States using the Export Enhancement Program (EEP) to target export subsidies at markets lost to the European Community. These EEP sales accounted for about 50 percent of U.S. wheat exports from 1985 to 1988 (1989). The struggle for markets was particularly intense in the North African countries of Morocco, Algeria, Tunisia, and Egypt, which import large quantities of wheat and wheat flour. With the aid of considerable subsidies, the United States was able to regain market shares in this region. The incident, however, left a mark on U.S.-EC relations that perhaps exceeded its real significance.

Oilseeds and Animal Feed. Certain agricultural markets have provided the lion's share of trade conflicts. The longest-running battle has been over soybean exports to the European Community. The United States received a concession from the Community in the Dillon Round (it was actually negotiated in the Article XXIV (6) negotiations that preceded) that the tariff on soybeans and meal would be bound at zero. This action, more than any other, dominated the next twenty-five years of trade and trade relations. To the European Community, it was a concession easily made, since trade was fairly small in those commodities and domestic production almost nonexistent. Low tariffs on imports of oilseeds in any case favored the domestic crushing and refining sectors. To the United States, it seemed like a useful concession, but the United States was generally unhappy with the outcome on other products. It carried out of the Dillon Round "unsatisfied negotiating rights" to be used in later trade talks.

What followed is well known. High wheat prices set for the new CAP (a political compromise made to satisfy German rural interests) drove feed demand to corn—much of it imported from the United States. When grain prices were harmonized in the European Community under the so-called silo system (moving corn prices up to meet the higher wheat prices), feed compounders switched to non-grain feeds. The pressure was particularly strong in Germany and the Netherlands, where "green" exchange rates ensured higher cereal prices than in other parts of the European Community. Compounders found that a mix of soybean meal and cassava chips (from Thailand) made an excellent substitute for corn, barley, and wheat (see Schmidt and Gardiner 1988).

Soybean sales to the European Community boomed over the 1970s and continued high when EC corn market imports slowed down. The hole in the dike was letting in a flood of imports. Later, when the European Community entered into a bilateral agreement with Thailand on a limit to cassava imports, other starchy feed ingredients such as citrus pulp, maize germ meal, and distillers dried grains began to be used to replace cereals in feed rations—many imported from the United States. Corn gluten feed, a by-product of the corn wet-milling process in the United States, became the ingredient of choice in the 1980s. (The wet-milling of corn is used to produce high fructose corn syrup, isoglucose, a substitute for cane and beet sugar, and ethanol, used as a an additive to gasoline.) The European Community classifies all these starchy products as "cereal substitutes": the high-protein meals are, of course, better considered "cereal complements." But the distinction is not always so clear. At times feed ingredients high in protein have been used for their carbohydrate content.

The conflict simmers on three fronts. The EC proposal to institute a fats-and-oils tax, often rejected by the Council of Ministers but never quite abandoned by the EC Commission, is seen in the United States as a scarcely disguised tax on soybean imports. The fact that the tax would apply to domestic as well as imported oils cuts little ice. To be effective, the fats-and-oils tax would undoubtedly have to reduce the consumption of soybean oil, benefiting the market for butter and perhaps olive oil. U.S. opposition to the tax has been made abundantly clear, and this has perhaps influenced the member states (the United Kingdom and Germany) that have consistently opposed it with the European Community.

The attempt in 1985 to limit imports of corn gluten feed from the United States—following the "success" of the voluntary export restraint agreement with Thailand—also received a rebuff from the United States. Why enter voluntarily into an agreement to limit a booming export market when the open market was due to a firm commitment in GATT? (The duty on corn gluten feed had also been bound at zero in the Dillon Round.) At least, if the negotiations were undertaken in the GATT, the United States could have expected to be offered compensation. Unilateral action of this kind was ruled out of the question in Washington.

The third "front" of this conflict has been the growth of oilseed production in the European Community, promoted in part by subsidies to crushers who use domestic oilseeds (and pay at least a minimum price). Production of soybeans has increased in Italy, rapeseed has become a popular crop in the north, and sunflower production has expanded in the south. The threat to U.S. soybean exports has not gone unnoticed. The U.S. Soybean Association has lodged a complaint against the EC oilseed program, and the U.S. administration has successfully pushed for a GATT investigation of the case. The U.S. view is that the European Community is trying to promote the production of one of the few products that it has actually allowed in from abroad. The GATT binding is being avoided by the back-door method of subsidizing production, and hence U.S. rights under the GATT are being impaired. The GATT panel has ruled on this complaint, although its findings have yet to be accepted. Its members found that the way in which the European Community operated its oilseed policy did indeed interfere with trade, over and above the bound tariff agreed in the GATT. But the resolution of this dispute will have to be a part of the Uruguay Round agreement later this year.

Beef Imports and the Hormone Issue. A recent trade conflict that illustrates well the tenuous state of trade relations in agricultural markets is that over beef imports. The European Community is not a major market for U.S. beef. Most exported beef goes to Japan, a market that seems to appreciate the grain-fed beef with the marbled texture produced on U.S. feedlots. The United States in turn imports considerable quantities of grass-fed manufacturing beef from Australia and Central America, together with some cooked meat from South America. The European Community has moved from being a steady importer of South American and Australian beef to one of the world's largest beef exporters. Beef imports are controlled by both a tariff (of 20 percent) and by variable levies, to protect the domestic market price. Beef is still imported under a number of schemes for preferential access, however, such as levy-free quotas and tariff-free quotas. The United States has a levy-free quota for high-quality (Hilton) beef, accounting for some $10 million annual sales. But much more important has been the growth in the market for variety meats, comprising beef offals used in making pies and sausages in Europe. This market had reached $100 million and has provided a valuable outlet for beef by-products not commonly used in the United States. It is this trade that was threatened by the import ban.

In December 1985, the European Community decided to ban the use of anabolic hormones in livestock production. The ban followed rising consumer concern over the health effects of such hormones, spurred by the well-publicized incidents in Italy involving the use of a synthetic estrogen, diethylstilbestrol (DES). DES had been banned in the European Community (and the United States), but consumer confidence in the safety of cattle feeding and in the ability of the regulatory authorities to control such practices was shaken. The hormone ban, applicable at first to domestic production and then extended to exporting countries in January 1989, was ostensibly a reaction to this consumer pressure. The United States reacted to the loss of the trade in beef and offals by imposing a 100 percent tariff on an equivalent value of EC exports to the United States. An EC counterretaliation was announced, but has so far not come into force, pending the outcome of bilateral negotiations.

U.S.-EC Negotiations on Agricultural Trade

This sampling of agricultural problems might suggest that there is little pattern to these skirmishes and little that can be done to help prevent them from recurring. In fact, these conflicts do have a pattern and it may help in their resolution. The agricultural trade conflicts between the United States and the European Community can be

TABLE 17-3

CATEGORIZATION OF U.S.-EC AGRICULTURAL TRADE CONFLICTS

Categories	Examples
1. Conflicts among exporting countries over declining market share	Wheat sales to China Wheat flour to Egypt
2. Exporter-importer conflicts over decline in market access	Corn sales to the European Community Fats and oils tax Spanish accession to European Community EC beef hormone ban
3. Domestic policy conflict with rising imports	Corn gluten feed to European Community Soybean meal imports Section 22 quotas in United States

SOURCE: Author.

grouped under three broad headings corresponding to different market situations (table 17-3). These categories distinguish between the conflict in markets where both the European Community and the United States are exporters; the trade problems that involve declining market access in each other's markets; and the problems surrounding the increasing penetration of imports into each other's markets.

The first category includes those problems that came about as a result of conflict among exporters, typified by the situation in the wheat and wheat flour market. Problems exist when the overall market stagnates or when market shares change rapidly. The U.S. market share for wheat seems to trigger such conflicts: when this share rises, the transatlantic climate is peaceful, but when it drops, the situation becomes more acrimonious. Since the European Community had an export subsidy for wheat (and wheat flour) in all except two years of the past twenty, and the United States had added export subsidies to its own arsenal, these conflicts have largely centered on the role of these subsidies and their legality in the GATT.

The second category of conflicts are those involving issues of falling market access into EC and U.S. markets for each other's goods. Examples of such conflicts include declining corn sales to the European Community. When a traditional market declines, many factors may be responsible—including macroeconomic forces, world market

371

developments, demand shifts, and technology changes. To those concerned with export policy, such nice distinctions are less appealing. If a lucrative market is shrinking, then someone must be responsible. Governments set policies, and policies influence trade. When imports drop, the first place to look is government policy. In the case of trends in U.S.-EC trade, the culprit is obvious: the CAP is clearly to blame.[2] The exporter takes the initiative in such cases, and the importer is put on the defensive.

Trade problems in the third category arise when imports rise. In this case the importing country government will be the initiator of action, usually in an effort to support domestic policy instruments. The clearest case of such a conflict (between the European Community and the United States) is that of imports of corn gluten feed and of soybean products into the European Community. The European Community has tried for some years to get the United States to restrain exports of these products, on the grounds that the growing level of imports makes domestic policy more expensive.

Although most trade conflicts of these three types are generated by market trends or sudden shifts in world price, some are exacerbated by the use of a particular type of trade instrument. An example of this is the use by the United States of sugar and dairy import quotas under the GATT waiver of 1955, necessitated by section 22 of the Agricultural Adjustment Act. Domestic policy dictates to trade policy and reduces the scope for change. On the EC side, the existence of the variable levy and the variable export subsidy determine the type of trade policy the Community can maintain. This has a significant bearing on EC trade policy options and can lead to demands from the United States for more radical changes in EC domestic policy than can be accommodated.

Other trade problems arise from the spillover effects of a nonagricultural policy change on agricultural trade. Two examples of this type of conflict are the changes in the import regime for Spanish corn (and Portuguese oilseeds), after their accession to the Community in 1986, and the recent change in the beef import regulations as a result of the domestic hormone ban in the European Community. Neither issue was really the result of an agricultural policy change, nor did it reflect market share developments. Both problems were precipitated by events outside the normal scope of policy decisions.

The three alternative market situations point up the different actions taken by the European Community and the United States to try to resolve these conflicts. The actions were unilateral, bilateral, or multilateral in scope. Matching this choice with the source of the trade conflict yields some useful lessons concerning the control of trade relations in the future.

Unilateral Action. The first reaction to many agricultural trade problems is to take unilateral measures to alleviate the situation. In a conflict involving declining exporter market shares, that action will tend to be a form of export subsidy. The subsidies can either be general or targeted at certain markets. The fall in the U.S. share of the wheat market in the early 1980s elicited a sharp unilateral action, the implementation of the Export Enhancement Program. This program represented an abandonment of the policy initiated in the mid-1970s (when grain prices were high) to shun the use of export subsidies. The targeted nature of these new subsidies made them particularly attractive (if not always effective) for waging the battle of market shares, and countering the regionally differentiated EC export subsidies. Although the United States still considered export subsidies an undesirable element in farm policy, in 1985 they seemed a necessary adjunct to the more diplomatic approaches to conflict resolution.

Unilateral action is also possible but much more difficult in other areas of trade conflict. Export subsidies could in principle be used to keep up sales to declining markets, but in the case of EC-U.S. trade, specific export subsidies have not been widely used to counter the effects of declining import markets. Such subsidies would probably be offset by policies in the importing country, either automatically (as with the EC variable levy) or by deliberate retaliating action (as was threatened when it was alleged that the EC granted a premium on exports of wine to the United States). If rising, rather than falling, imports cause the trade conflict, then unilateral action is again an option for the importing country, but with considerable circumspection. The proposed EC tax on vegetable oil and fat consumption was action of the unilateral type, although great care was taken to ensure that the fats and oils tax was not a "trade" measure as such. Even so, such unilateral action caused a sufficiently noisy reaction in the United States as to dissuade the European Community from introducing the policy.

Bilateral Action. The essence of bilateral action is that both countries feel that a particular issue in agricultural trade must be resolved for the greater good of trade relations as a whole. The exporter conflict in the wheat and flour market also yielded an example of a bilateral approach to trade conflict. The European Community, through a mixture of guilt and expediency, offered in the early 1980s to keep their share of the world wheat market to 14 percent.[3] This informal pact held for about three years, but was abandoned by the European Community on the pretext that the United States has taken advantage of the agreement to expand production. It is unlikely that the EC could in the event have maintained that share in the face of rising domestic production. The commission has only limited control over exports, through its role in setting the level of export subsidy. If the export subsidy is inadequate to move all of the excess from the market, intervention stocks tend to rise. As stocks become unduly high, the level of exports will catch up again. Such a temporary benefit could confer some short-run advantage, but it illustrates the weakness of bilateral agreements. Market share agreements of this nature can only work if all participants have effective control over domestic supply. If this is not the case, then the pact is essentially worthless. Moreover, market share arrangements that only cover two exporters are ineffective in a world market where other exporters are free to follow their own interests.

Bilateral discussions on market access appear to have been more promising: they have in recent years become more popular in U.S. agricultural trade policy as a result of some apparent success in the opening of the Japanese market.[4] This success has not been reflected in the area of U.S.-EC trade. The United States has not been able to persuade the European Community to take action to stop the reduction in corn imports except in the specific case of EC enlargement. Neither has the European Community been able to persuade the United States to limit sales of corn gluten feed through a voluntary export restraint. Just as the European Community would claim that corn imports are declining as a "natural" consequence of a perfectly legal domestic policy, so the United States would claim that corn gluten imports into the European Community reflect the genuine demand from feed compounders seeking to mix low-cost feed rations in the face of high cereal prices. But even if few lasting bilateral agreements have been reached, biannual high-level discussions continue between the United States and the European Community on agricultural trade. The beef hormone issue is one that has been recently discussed in these meetings, and a joint EC-U.S. task force has been given the challenge of proposing a solution. The bilateral talks also create a possibility for the United States and the European Community to discuss issues relating to multilateral negotiations in the GATT.

Multilateral Action. In light of the limited success of bilateral action to solve agricultural trade conflicts, the focus of action has switched to the multilateral level. The exporter conflict is a clear example of the advantage of multilateral discussions of trading problems. The role of the GATT in such matters is unequivocal: a set of regulations governing the use of export subsidies would certainly seem an effective approach to the problem. Recognizing this fact, a great deal of effort has gone into the negotiation of rules on export subsidies for agricultural products. Similarly, issues of declining market access arising from policy changes are more satisfactorily dealt with in a multilateral setting. Problems posed for domestic policy by rising imports also fit into the normal multilateral trade framework that has provisions for safeguards and rules governing the reaction to dumping and to subsidies in the exporting country.

Multilateral action seems to be the dominant focus of conflict resolution in agricultural trade at present. The flurry of activity in the multilateral arena in the 1980s has been unusual. Governments have been engaged in an almost continuous dialogue, leading up to the current discussions of agricultural policy in the GATT Uruguay Round. Background work was undertaken in the Organization for Economic Cooperation and Development (OECD) to investigate the trade impact of domestic agricultural policies and to suggest ways in which negotiations could come to grips with the issue (the 1982 Ministerial Trade Mandate). The OECD work proved important both for convincing governments that domestic policies were at the root of the trade problems (a fact that many had sought to ignore) and for illustrating the magnitude of support in a way that could be compared across countries (Organization for Economic Cooperation and Development 1987). The GATT also set up a committee to look at the same set of issues. This committee studied ways in which "all measures affecting trade in agriculture would be brought under more operationally effective GATT rules and disciplines" (GATT 1986). As was to be expected, the OECD focused on domestic policies and the GATT on trade rules. An added high-level political boost was given to both GATT and OECD initiatives by the Tokyo summit of the heads of government of the largest seven industrial countries in May 1986. This was followed by the launching of the Uruguay Round in September 1986 and by a ministerial declaration from the OECD in May 1987. Multilateral solutions are at present "on trial." The GATT Round is a focus of attention, but it is by no means clear that a constructive agreement will emerge.

World Trade Developments and Pressure on World Markets

The pattern of U.S.-EC agricultural trade problems of the 1980s suggests that such problems are more severe when budget costs of domestic policies are high. Such periods correspond to times of low world prices—in part caused by the policies themselves. A vicious cycle of high protection, dumping of exports, and depressed world markets was evident in the early 1970s, the late 1970s, and the mid-1980s. But in addition to policy-induced world price developments, other factors determine price levels on world markets. These include the production of agricultural goods in developing and centrally planned economies, as well as in other industrial countries; the levels of demand in world markets, influenced by population trends and income changes; and the availability of foreign exchange in those countries that need to import agricultural products. A full analysis of each factor is far beyond the scope of this discussion, but a few comments are needed to put the prospects for better trade relationships into perspective.

Production Trends. In contrast to the lavish protection often granted to agricultural producers in industrial countries, farmers in the developing world have often faced less favorable conditions. In part this has been a consequence of the notion current in the 1960s that agriculture was an undynamic, unresponsive sector that provided a poor basis for development. It also reflected the political strength of the urban worker and the attention many governments were giving to large-scale industrial projects. The overtly low prices for agricultural products were reinforced by the effect of an overvalued currency (see Kreuger et al. 1988). This bias against agriculture has been reversed somewhat in recent years. Institutions such as the World Bank and the International Monetary Fund have taken the lead in encouraging nations to restore reasonable market incentives to agricultural producers. In addition, the removal of major exchange rate distortions has in many cases led to higher prices for tradable goods. As a result of these better price incentives, production has risen steadily in recent years.

Higher prices bring forth more output, but removing a price disincentive may not change the rate of growth measured from the higher level. This is the role of technology, the development and dissemination of yield-increasing varieties, and the provision of information on improved husbandry practices. The rapid adoption of improved varieties of wheat and rice in developing countries in the past twenty years (the green revolution) has played a large role in realizing the potential of agriculture, through the application of scientific knowledge to farming practices. The question therefore arises as to whether such technology is likely to continue to appear and be adopted at the same rate as in the past. Falcon, reviewing the present state of agronomic research in the international agricultural research centers has concluded that "the development and adoption of cereal technologies between 1965 and 1985 were quite unprecedented and are unlikely to be repeated" (Falcon 1989). The annual growth in Asian wheat production over that decade was 4.3 percent, whereas that for corn and rice was 2.5 percent and 2.4 percent, respectively (Falcon 1989). Only in Africa were the cereal production growth rates below the rate of population growth. There would seem to be considerable scope for increases in corn production over the next decade, where a significant gap exists between the yields of experimental stations and farms: for wheat and rice, this gap of "known but unused technology" is much smaller (Falcon 1989: 9). New technologies, particularly biotechnology, could, however, lead to sufficient applications in plant breeding to keep up the historical rate of growth.

Production trends in the developed world seem more difficult to call. Falling prices have imposed constraints on expansion for some years in the industrial countries. Yield increases in the major cereals are likely to be further kept in check by the emerging issues of ecological stability and environmental safety.[5] Sensitivity over the way in which animals are reared and doubts about the use of biochemical stimulants to growth have changed public attitudes toward livestock farming. These issues threaten to overturn, or at least modify, conventional views of agricultural progress. Modern farming systems involve the massive use of inorganic fertilizers, weedkillers, pesticides, and other farm chemicals. Dangers to workers and to the environment were always considered a small price to pay for higher yields and more acceptable crops. Now it seems that the environmental costs are much higher than had been previously thought. The notion is spreading that high-input (or high-nonlabor-input) agriculture is not sustainable. The search for a sustainable agriculture could dominate policy issues over the next decade. Low-input agriculture will imply lower output, as agriculture adjusts to the policies of environmental protection. Farming practices will involve less purchased inputs in the form of fertilizer and alternative methods of controlling plant disease. Animal production could also be affected by the same trends.

Environmental pressures may help to hold down the level of prices for farm products. High price supports have kept agriculture viable in many marginal areas. In several countries this has satisfied objectives in terms of population density in rural areas and in others has provided support for weekend and retirement farming for urban residents. But serious conflicts have arisen that make it difficult to equate modern intensive farming with the provision of other environmental amenities. Medical knowledge concerning the long-term hazards of exposure to chemicals has changed public perceptions about the "healthy" nature of farm work. Residues from such chemicals are seen as a threat to consumer health. The public in many countries distrusts modern farming methods and identifies intensive farming with environmental degradation. High prices are in turn held to encourage such farming. If there have been any environmental benefits from present farm support programs, they are not immediately visible. Population pressure and the accompanying urbanization have redefined attitudes toward the countryside. It is now seen as a resource for the public good. Conflicting ideas on the appropriate use of this resource are likely to become a more common feature of farm policy debates.

Demand Trends. The prospect of some slowdown in the growth in production need not lead to markedly higher prices if demand is also weak. Food demand is driven by population pressures, income growth, and taste changes. Of these, population is the easiest to predict, at least on a global level. World population expands at just less than 2 percent per year. This presents a formidable challenge to agricultural production even in the absence of any income growth. This challenge has been met for the past decade, but such a situation cannot be taken for granted. Global economic growth (per capita) averages about 3 percent when things are going well, although the period from the 1980s on has seen a considerable slowdown in this growth rate. Many developing countries have experienced negative growth for much of the decade: at the same time, India and China have achieved historically high growth rates over the same period. Three percent per capita growth adds just less than one percentage point to the increase in the demand for food. As a result, supply needs to increase at about 2.5 percent to prevent price increases.

Demand has to be reflected in the marketplace to be effective in attracting supply. Much of the demand in the past decade has not been effective. Countries without foreign exchange do not buy much on world markets. Developing country debt rose from $151 billion in 1975 to $454 billion in 1981; by 1987 it had reached $881 billion, with the debt service averaging about 16 percent of exports (U.S. Agency for International Development 1989: 131). Many of the African countries have accumulated debt equal to one-half their GNP. Under such circumstances, continued growth in imports will be difficult. Just as in the 1980s, some significant part of the potential growth in market demand will fail to materialize.

Until recently, one could have placed consumer tastes in the category of variables that change so slowly as to be easy to ignore.

Such an approach looks short-sighted today. The demand for particular foods can shift markedly as a result of a change in preferences. The meat sector offers a case in point. Much of the dynamic of the world food system in the past twenty years has come from the upgrading of consumer diets, from starchy to protein-rich foods. In the process, considerable demand for animal feeds is generated— exceeding by far the grains not needed for direct consumption. Many of the predictions of food shortages common in the early 1970s (and again at the beginning of the 1980s) were based on this phenomenon. But the process has begun to go in reverse. High-income consumers, buying some supposed health benefits, are switching away from meat and using more cereals. As a result, the consumption of red meats has stagnated in recent years. Whether the middle-income countries skip over the high-meat phase will be interesting to observe. If they do, then demand pressures from that source could be alleviated in the 1990s.

A key determinant of the climate of U.S.-EC agricultural trade relations is whether world market prices for the main commodities rise or fall over the next decade. The arguments in this section tend to point to some continued decline, unless the global economy strengthens considerably. But a period of high prices is clearly on the cards, as happened in 1974–1975 and 1980–1981. On those occasions, shortfalls in harvests followed periods of surplus production. Stocks were unable to prevent price rises. Stocks of grain are low at present, as a result of the U.S. drought in 1988 and modest harvests in the United States and Europe in 1989. Wheat stocks are forecast by the International Wheat Council to be about 95 million tons, the lowest level since the 80-million-ton carryover in 1975. Any further drop in grain production could spark the panic in the market that characterized the world food crisis in the mid-1970s. Should prices rise as a result of such a development, trade conflicts will ease. U.S. market shares tend to do well in expanding export markets, and U.S. farmers gain the full benefit of higher world prices. But the subsequent fall in world prices after a temporary boom seems to redouble the trade conflicts.

Technology, Food Safety, and Emerging Trade Problems

It is in the nature of new technology that it brings problems as well as benefits to humankind. Agricultural technology is no exception. The chemical industry has provided agriculture with an impressive array of products to enhance yields and to control pests and diseases. At times of surplus, such yield-enhancing technologies add to the strain of adjustment and make harder the task of running farm policies. Several types of agricultural chemicals carry with them negative externalities in the form of groundwater contamination and other environmental hazards. It is natural that governments should exhibit some ambivalence toward such chemically based technologies. But an equally tricky problem is posed by a new set of technologies related more to biology than chemistry.

For several decades, agricultural progress has centered around improvements in crop yield. There are signs that many of the most interesting technologies of the 1990s will be in the area of animal production. Conventional research in animal production focused largely on breeding by selection and on improved feeding practices. Biotechnology has opened up several other possible lines of advance. Some of the most immediate possibilities have to do with the genetic engineering of microorganisms to increase the production of naturally occurring substances. These substances include growth hormones and other valuable products. Commercial production and the sale of such products pose a particular challenge to policy (for a concise review of the agricultural uses of biotechnology, see Longworth 1987).

Food Safety. As if the increased output from biotechnology were not enough, policy makers face an additional problem associated with the acceptability of food products from biotechnology. In part reflecting the general shift toward a healthier diet, consumers seem to be questioning the safety of several new techniques of agricultural production and food marketing. Governments are reacting to this concern by revising food legislation and standards. As laboratory instruments become more sophisticated, technicians can detect even smaller amounts of harmful substances. This adds to the fears of consumers, whether founded or not, and leads to an even longer list of suspect food items. The products of biotechnology generally fall in this category of foods that are "guilty until proved innocent."

The food industry is not always to blame for these heightened concerns. Many food-related illnesses have been linked to poor food handling by retailers and by the consumers. Anxious to consume only "natural" foods, many consumers have avoided products with "preservatives," without at the same time improving their own methods of inventory control in the food closet or refrigerator.

This leaves the government with an uncomfortable dilemma when it comes to food standards. Pressure from consumer groups (and environmental lobbies) tends to lead toward more regulation and the banning of substances with even minimal health risks. But such tighter regulation goes against the trend toward less government intervention in business and consumer affairs. Moreover, exporters will see such regulation as a form of protectionism.

The beef trade conflict mentioned above is a good example of this dilemma. The EC Commission claims to have been reacting to consumer concerns about the health hazards of hormone-treated beef. The U.S. view of the beef hormone ban is that the commission's actions are of a protectionist nature, bowing to pressure from cattle producers and being concerned with the buildup of intervention stocks of beef. Not that anyone doubts that there have been consumer concerns over the health effects of hormone use in cattle, but as yet there is no credible scientific evidence that the hormone treatment of beef cattle, under proper conditions, leaves any harmful residue in the meat sold to consumers. The U.S. Food and Drug Administration (USDA) tests artificial growth hormones before approving their use in livestock production, and it has a test program to check for chemical residues in meat. Therefore, in the absence of protectionist motives, the role of public authorities in the European Community could have been to educate consumers on the matter, and to make sure that (both domestic and foreign) producers followed accepted practices.[6]

The whole issue of the role of government in shielding consumers from small or imagined risks is under review in both the European Community and the United States (see Archibald and Winter 1989). A "liberal" approach to standards would be to legislate for full disclosure on labels along with regular inspection of food production and handling facilities. Authorities would regulate food content only in clear cases of consumer safety, rather than impose a strict risk-averse consumption strategy on consumers. Indeed, this is the intention of the EC Commission in its directives to complete the internal market by the end of 1992 (Gray 1990). But this approach has come under pressure from those who favor greater intervention and suggest that such action might be taken at a national level. Nor is this centrifugal threat confined to the European Community: the United States has also recently introduced legislation to improve food labeling in part to forestall the proliferation of diverse state regulations. There is the possibility that this legislation will prove to be even more restrictive to trade than that of the European Community.

Two issues that seem destined to precipitate such problems in the future are the use of bovine somatotropin (BST) as a growth stimulant in cattle (and the related product porcine somatoprin, PST, in pigs) and the use of irradiation of food. BST is a naturally occurring hormone in cattle. Experimentation has revealed that milk yields can be increased by 15–25 percent by feeding dairy cattle additional BST. Biotechnology has made it possible to produce the hormone in large quantities at a cost that makes it use profitable. There are no obvious side effects, either to the cow or to persons drinking the milk. But the side effects on farm policy are all too clear. The EC Commission, concerned about the prospect of different regulations springing up in each member state, has been considering whether to allow the use of BST in the Community. The licensing of such a product would normally require the commission to consider its safety and efficacy, along with its reliability. In this case, however, the commission has considered introducing a "fourth criterion," that of economic and social need. Since the social value of additional milk in the European Community is rather low at present, such a criterion would presumably have militated against licensing BST. One could also argue that, as a cost-reducing technology, it is precisely in those areas where costs exceed value that such a technology is needed. In the event, the commission has postponed a decision on the use of BST for three years, until the results of further studies are available.

The U.S. Food and Drug Administration also has yet to pronounce on the acceptability of BST, although the decision is expected in early 1991. In the United States there is somewhat less concern about the impact of higher milk yields on budget costs. But some fear that the technology might benefit large dairy farmers rather than those with fewer cows. Largely for this reason, the dairy-producing states of Minnesota and Wisconsin have recently banned the sale of milk from BST-treated cows. The fourth criterion is clearly not the exclusive preserve of the European Community.

Although the repression of known cost-reducing techniques presumably creates a loss for the economy, it is not easy to see consumer pressure for its use. The story of PST is somewhat different. The addition of extra PST has led to impressive gains in the live weight of pigs, thereby improving feed efficiency. But it has also been shown that the fat content of the meat is reduced. This leads to the interesting possibility that the product, a leaner cut of pork or slice of bacon, may have considerable consumer appeal and be difficult to dismiss on health grounds. PST has not yet been developed on a commercial scale, and its use is a few years away.

Food irradiation is another example of a technical advance that brings with it problems of acceptance. This technique has been used for many years in certain instances, but is now becoming more widespread. A low dose of radiation kills bacteria (though not viruses) in the food without causing the cell structure of the food to break down. The result is "purer" food, with a longer shelf life: there is no residual radiation. Many scientists have welcomed the technology as having considerable benefit in the control of storage losses in developing countries, and others have argued that it can prevent many of the health hazards arising from the swing away from the use of preservatives.

Such a desirable development is apparently not welcomed by those who would benefit. The prospect of irradiation arouses negative reactions in many circles. In the past this was due to the links with the emotional issues of both military and peaceable uses of nuclear reactions. The irradiation of food is seen by some as a potential legitimization of nuclear reactors and hence is to be discouraged. Even consumers who do not make these connections are wary about the notion of irradiated food. At present, food irradiation is allowed only in specific cases, such as spices in the United States and imported shrimp in some members of the European Community. The use of irradiation will be slow to expand as long as consumers are reluctant to accept the scientific evidence, or those with other agendas succeed in confusing food safety with nuclear energy.

Standards and Trade Barriers. The issue of biotechnology, together with "new" food technologies such as irradiation, promises to be a continuing source of trade tension between the United States and the European Community. Whether such conflicts can be avoided depends on the way in which standards are administered. The link between trade and technical standards can be better understood by examining two types of concerns that may motivate governments to inspect and regulate foodstuffs. One is consumer health and safety. A health hazard is a negative externality associated with the consumption of tainted food. The other is the safety or health of those in the production or processing sectors (or those affected by the process). Such a hazard is a negative externality associated with the production of the good in question. There are also two main ways of testing for such hazards—and hence controlling them. Product standards, enforced by the testing of samples, lay down the content (recipe) of foodstuffs. In contrast, production and processing methods can be regulated with on-site inspection of the process rather than the testing of the product.

The link between the type of externality and the method of testing and regulating is shown in table 17-4. Consumption externalities could conceivably be avoided by testing the product either at (or near) the point of consumption or by regulating the method of production (or processing). Similarly, production externalities can be controlled either by testing the product or by regulating the method

383

TABLE 17-4
OPTIONS IN APPLYING HEALTH STANDARDS

	Externality in Consumption	Externality in Production
Product standards (recipes)	Test near point of consumption	Test domestic production Test production for export
Production and processing methods	Regulate domestic production or processing Test imports at border for equivalent standards	Regulate domestic production or processing

SOURCE: Author.

of production. In a closed economy, these procedures are likely to be the same.[7] If there is no trade it may not much matter whether one tests the process or the product as long as the results are the same. For some commodities, it may be more convenient to regulate at the wholesale level; for others, regulation at the production level may be easier. Both production and consumption externalities can be guarded against by the most convenient method.

Once the economy is opened up to trade, the picture changes considerably. If testing for consumption externalities is done by monitoring the production method, one also has to test imports—or regulate the production method in other countries. This is the most common reason for imposing standards checks on imports. Domestic production has already "passed the test" and imports have to be checked for consistency with local regulations.[8] Whenever border checks are needed, the mechanism is at hand for protection. And even if protection is not intended, the suspicion of it is always present.

Is it inevitable that countries must rely on border controls to maintain their own standards (that is, to intervene optimally to offset the negative externalities in consumption and production)? Or is this source of trade friction a relic from the days when trade was a small part of economic activity? Another glance at table 17-4 suggests that trade controls need not be used even if countries have different standards. Suppose one tests for consumption externalities close to the point of consumption, say, at the wholesale or retail level. If testing is done at a point in the marketing chain *after* imports have entered, then no border testing is required. Similarly, one can regulate for production externalities exclusively at the production (or processing) stage. In this way, no monitoring of trade would be needed. Such a shift in the location of testing and regulation may make sense even in a closed economy. Testing for food quality near the point of consumption (or retailing) will catch any postprocessing deterioration or adulteration. Controlling production methods directly also seems to be an intrinsically better way of checking for production externalities. In an environment of expanding international trade—either in the context of completing the EC internal market or of liberalizing trade in the GATT Uruguay Round—the advantages become striking. Trade controls would no longer be needed to maintain domestic standards if the testing were to be moved to the appropriate point in the marketing chain.

The notion that different standards can coexist with free trade needs to be qualified, however. If the externality that is the reason for the policy arises from the *act* of trading itself, then controls at the border are still necessary. The spread of animal and plant diseases often falls into this category. In this case, different standards reflect the geographical incidence of the diseases. But it should be clear that this does not in itself justify testing at each national border: there will be disease-related boundaries that can be used to define inspection points. This is the approach that the Community has taken with respect to its internal borders, and international trade rules could move in that direction. Once the link between national borders and national standards is weakened, optimal systems of control of plant and animal disease can be implemented free of the temptation to use such control for the protection of domestic profits.

If domestic regulatory policy were to move in this direction, several implications would follow for agricultural trade relations. The GATT assurance of equal treatment of domestic and imported products would become the crucial organizing principle. The origin of most goods, even if labeled for purposes of consumer information, would become irrelevant in terms of the standards to be met and the testing to be performed. Even if some of the actual testing were to be performed at or near the ports, the *importation* of the product would not be conditional on any separate tests. Equivalency (of product testing and production and processing method regulation) would no longer be an issue: countries would use product testing to protect their own consumers, regardless of whether some other government had regulated the method of production. Mutual recognition of the standards of other countries would still be an option, but would not be a condition for free trade. A European Community without internal barriers could still have different consumer standards in different countries as long as regulations were imposed at the wholesale or retail level and did not discriminate among sources. Countries could still regulate worker health or pollution from domestic industries without trade barriers. International harmonization of consumer and worker health standards would not be necessary.

It would be unduly optimistic to expect such a development to resolve all international conflicts over standards. As long as national standards differ, there will be unexploited scale ceremonies. This may be the price to pay for autonomy in consumer health policies. Moreover, domestic producers will always call for trade controls to shield them from any cost-increasing effect of domestic production restrictions. But having to resist such demands is the political price for autonomy in environmental policies. Mutual recognition of the standards of other countries will expand market size, and harmonization of production standards will reduce the calls for protection. But both will proceed only as far as allowed by real national differences in perceptions about externalities arising from the production and consumption of foods. Neither are needed for trade liberalization once testing is moved from the border.

Farm Policy Instrument Choice and Trade Problems

At the same time that agricultural trade relations have been under stress, domestic policies have come under scrutiny at home. It has been recognized for some time that the standard form of income supports, consisting of government action to raise domestic market prices, gave most benefits to those farmers with the most to sell. It was equally clear, though less often stated, that raising incomes through price support put a disproportionate burden on middle- and low-income households, through their spending on food. In recent years other criticisms have come to the fore.

Support for Agricultural Commodities. The basis for farm-income support rests on the suppositions that farm incomes are both low and unstable and that farm and rural incomes significantly affect the health of the rest of the economy. If farm incomes are low, then government support for farm incomes can be justified on grounds of equity or income distribution. Pockets of rural poverty exist in both the United States and the European Community, and returns on farmland tend to be rather low. But average household incomes of farm families (from farm and nonfarm sources) do not appear to be significantly below the average of nonfarm families. That farm incomes are inherently unstable is clear from the nature of the industry. Providing a more stable economic environment for agriculture is clearly a reasonable objective for policy. Similarly, putting in place a safety net under rural family income is, on social grounds, likely to find widespread support. Farm programs can be seen as part of social and regional policy. The gain in economic stability is a form of public good. Such income support is also likely to have beneficial macroeconomic effects, although the national impact of stable farm incomes is now much less than earlier in the century, when it was said that recessions were farm-led and farm-fed.

Also implicit in the case for income support is the assumption that farm incomes would be lower without government assistance. This contention is more problematic: to be true, it requires labor and capital markets to be segmented within the economy. The growing realization is that price supports may not in fact work to raise farm incomes. The agricultural sector in most industrial countries is now small relative to the rest of the economy and well integrated into the capital and labor markets. As a result, labor and capital tend to earn roughly what they would in the nonfarm sector (taking into account skills and regional labor market conditions), irrespective of the amount of price support given. Price support does many things: it generates an economic rent on the specific factors (that is, land suited to farming); it bids up prices on specialized equipment; it encourages factors to enter or stay in the industry; and it generates costly surpluses. But it does not have much effect on the return to new capital investment or to mobile labor. The increase in land prices benefits those already in the sector: the new entrant into farming gets almost no benefit from the billions of dollars spent by consumers and taxpayers on price support. Thus, after a generation or two, when many have taken the rents and left the industry, the program is all costs and no benefits.

This effect of price supports, to generate surpluses without raising returns to labor, has implications for the rest of the economy. Agriculture competes with other sectors for capital and labor. Even if price supports do not raise wages significantly, they can still have an effect on nonfarm factor markets. Since much of agriculture is capital-intensive, agricultural expansion can crowd out capital from more socially profitable investments. Beyond that, spending on agricultural support will raise taxes or decrease funds available for other government projects. Food costs will tend to show up in wage contracts. Import taxes and export subsidies on farm products will tend to appreciate the exchange rate through the foreign exchange market. This, too, acts as a tax on nonfarm businesses operating in the

TABLE 17-5
EXTERNAL EFFECTS OF PRICE SUPPORT TRANSFERS FOR SELECTED
COUNTRIES, 1984
(percent transfers to producers)

	Offset by Policies in Other Countries[a]	Loss of Income by Farmers Abroad[b]
United States	57.6	33.2
Canada	54.5	41.0
European Community	48.7	62.5
Other Western Europe	45.5	68.7
Australia, New Zealand	479.4	72.1
Japan	6.9	31.8

a. Percentage of transfer to producers in home country that is necessary to offset the policies in the other countries listed.
b. Percentage of transfer to producer in home country that represents a loss to producers (or consumers and governments) in other countries listed.
SOURCE: Author's calculations based on Roningen and Dixit (1987).

international market. These negative effects on the nonfarm sector, coupled with the doubts about the effectiveness of the policies to raise income levels and returns on capital, have weakened the support for agricultural policy among nonfarm groups in the economy.[9]

In addition, there is a growing realization that price-support policies are being undermined by their own international effects. Quite apart from any question of peace and tranquility in international relations (and conformity with the GATT), the policies themselves are having to work harder just to offset the impact of other similar policies in other countries. Studies that have incorporated the effect of developed country prices support policies on world markets come up with surprisingly large values for this external impact. Table 17-5 shows one set of results. The proportion of transfers under U.S. farm-support policies that simply go to offset the negative impact of the policies of others was 58 percent in 1984. For the European Community, 49 percent of the transfers under the CAP in that year went merely to offset the effect of other policies. Australia and New Zealand would have had to make almost five times their 1984 transfers to offset the impact of the policies of other countries. Looked at in a different way, the negative impact of EC and U.S. policies on other countries could be as high as 63 and 33 percent, respectively, of the amount of domestic income transfer (see table 17-5).

Whether or not such numbers impinge upon the policy process, the perception that distortion of the world market puts up policy costs is causing a recalculation of policy instruments. Those policies that give an open-ended stimulus to production and choke off domestic demand (such as import levies and export subsidies) have the most serious impact on world prices. Those that vary the level of levy and subsidy inversely to world prices have an exaggerated impact, keeping up domestic production and restricting consumption when world market prices are falling. In contrast, fixed tariffs have the advantage of allowing domestic prices to respond to international events; deficiency payments allow consumption to be at market prices; supply control limits the burden put on world markets of domestic price supports; and direct income payments are the least trade-disruptive instrument of all.

Decoupling Payments to Farmers. All these arguments point to one conclusion. If the objective of government agricultural policy is to maintain incomes, then supporting prices is a poor way to proceed. The problem is that all of the sensible alternatives are politically difficult. Farmers like to feel that they get their income through the marketplace rather than as a welfare payment. Devising an efficient way of transferring income is not too difficult; making it look like a market transaction is more tricky. An exploration of some of the new agricultural policies that are under discussion will illustrate this dilemma.

In recent years, the concept of decoupling has been introduced to cover the notion of separating income transfers from output decisions. A decoupled policy supports farm income but does not encourage production. Decoupled policies make domestic objectives easier to attain and avoid the impacts on world markets. The move toward decoupled policies has a logic that should be able to make headway against the status quo. Unfortunately, policies are not easy to classify as decoupled or coupled—indeed, there may not be any purely decoupled policies. Imagine the case of a payment to a farmer based on his income level in the previous year. The farmer would well use the payment to invest in the business and hence increased output. An decoupled policy before the fact becomes coupled after the fact, although the output effect would presumably be less than if the payment had been made per unit of output.

Correcting Price Incentives. This issue of the definition of a decoupled policy should not unduly hold up the process of policy change. The most important aspect of the concept of decoupled payments is the improvement of price signals at the margin. As long as farmers are faced with a price for extra output that roughly corresponds to the value of that output to the country, then the most serious economic costs of the policy are mitigated. At present, the prices that farmers face exceed the value of the product by perhaps 40 percent.[10] The most important task facing agricultural policy makers is to reduce this premium to a level that is more in keeping with the incentives to produce other goods and services within the economy. It is generally assumed that a direct price cut, leaving current programs in place, is politically impossible. The search is on for ways to correct incentives without causing such a massive change in farm incomes as to create economic or political instability.

Seen in this light, decoupling is only one way of correcting price signals. The search for a perfectly decoupled program is neither necessary nor even desirable. If the farmer chooses to invest in a particular product in the face of correct incentives (that is, undistorted market prices), then it is difficult to see why such investment should be discouraged. The important element of decoupling is the price correction. Others have suggested alternative ways to the same end. Hathaway has proposed that countries allocate to farmers a share of domestic use (Hathaway 1988: 151) on which a support payment is made; any production for export would receive no subsidy. The term *producer entitlement guarantee* (PEG) has been coined for a similar concept (Blandford et al. 1988). Governments would set PEG quantities at a level no higher than the free-trade production level. Payments on the PEG quantity would support income, but decisions to produce above that level would be based on world market (unsupported) prices. In the absence of any policies that distort consumer prices, such a scheme would give a close approximation to free-trade patterns.

Governments are likely to move toward such instruments in the next decade as they provide a way of limiting the budget exposure under support policies. To the extent that this happens, trade frictions will decrease. But such policies have a serious problem: any country that reversed its policies would get a free ride from those that were limiting support payments. This suggests that some international restraints may be needed to back up this policy change. The international discussions that are under way in the GATT are aimed at this objective. Without such discussions and any agreements that emerge, domestic policy reform will be slow and erratic.

Changes in the CAP and Improved Trade Relations

The discussion in the previous section suggests that farm policies have to change in certain respects if problems of trade are not to get worse over the coming decade. How do these principles apply to the CAP? Are there signs that the CAP is moving toward such a trade-neutral state? Or are domestic interests so firmly in charge that the trade considerations will be once again ignored? And have the changes recently made in the CAP improved the transatlantic trade climate?

Reform of Dairy Policies. The European Community has been going through an extended period of reform, particularly with the introduction of milk quotas in 1984 (and the further reduction in the size of these quotas in 1986) and the agreement on budget stabilizers in February 1988 (see Moyer and Josling 1990). The changes in milk policy were not of great importance to U.S. trade interests. The United States is roughly self-sufficient in dairy products. It imports specialty cheeses from the European Community, while disposing of American cheese under domestic and foreign concessional programs. The United States disposes of limited amounts of skimmed milk powder (nonfat dried milk) abroad, mainly through overseas aid programs. There is little U.S. trade in butter, although there are occasional domestic surpluses. CAP reform in the dairy sector has clearly reduced EC dairy capacity and firmed up world dairy product prices, but it is largely domestic reform, aimed at cutting budget costs.[11] The introduction of quotas, as an alternative to the politically more difficult price cuts, is not a great contribution to removing trade tensions. Although the United States and many other countries use variations of quotas in controlling the dairy industry, it is seen as moving in a direction counter to that of deregulation. Since quotas, once introduced, are hard to remove, the net result may be to reduce the chances for true liberalization in the future.

Stabilizers. The relative lack of impact of EC dairy quotas on U.S. trade explains why that aspect of reform did little to ease trade tensions. Could more be expected from the stabilizers program, and the introduction of set-asides and direct income payments that together make up the CAP reform package of February 1988? How the EC tackles its grain surplus and the growing expenditure on oilseeds payments is clearly of direct importance in trade relations.

That stabilizers program itself is a fairly modest quasi-automatic device for linking price levels to output at the Community level. Guarantee thresholds have been around for much of the 1980s, but were generally regarded as ineffective. The 1988 program extended their use to most major products, including cereals, and made more certain the penalties for overproduction. Large-scale cereal producers now face an additional coresponsibility levy of 3 percent (in addition to the 3 percent levy already in place), which will only be reimbursed if output falls short of the maximum guaranteed quantity (MGQ). The levy is translated into a fall in the intervention price the following year. Assuming that the commission does not negate these automatic price reductions at the annual price review, the price restraint could have an effect on output. But set against productivity changes in the cereals sector, the fact that small farmers are exempt from the coresponsibility levies (as is grain used for feed on farm) and the generally upward movement of prices due to the green currency system, the restraint is modest. And since the cereals stabilizer lasts only for three years, there is no guarantee that any permanent change has been achieved.

Oilseed and protein crops are included in the stabilizers program in part because of the steady rise in support costs for these products and in part to anticipate any possible shift out of cereals toward these commodities.[12] The net effect on the price of rapeseed and protein crops (field peas and beans) is expected to be minimal, although the program may help to inhibit the growth of soybean production in Spain (ABARE 1989a). It could be argued that the United States has not shown enough appreciation for this attempt to control the growth of oilseed production, but from the outside the policies look less than dramatic.

Set-Asides. The introduction of set-asides in the European Community should have triggered a sympathetic response. The United States has been using set-asides since the 1930s, and in recent years has made participation in the major price-support programs conditional upon compliance with mandatory acreage adjustment. The reaction to EC set-asides has hardly been enthusiastic. The national schemes on the books at present will not be sufficiently attractive to entice many acres out of production. The commission's estimate of 1 million hectares (and 3.5 million tons of grain) is considered optimistic. Individual countries have varying degrees of commitment to the scheme, which was pushed by the German government as an alternative to the stabilizer price cuts. Since national governments will have to pay up to 65 percent of the cost, their incentives to encourage participation are relatively weak. Add to this the fact that even the most extensive set-aside programs in the United States seem to have a relatively modest impact on production, as farmers find ways of idling acres without losing output, and the attitude is cautious at best and scornful at worst.

Direct Income Assistance. One aspect of the European Community's reform package that might seem to be high on the popularity charts is the element in the recent sociostructural measures that allows for direct income assistance to farmers. Farmers earning significantly below the national average farm income level could receive up to ECU 1,500 per year, with the member states covering up to 70 percent of the cost. At present this seems to be a relatively minor add-on to the range of structural programs that are available. Much depends on how the member states decide to administer the scheme. Funding for regional and structural programs as a whole, both agricultural and more general schemes, has been increased sharply. But there is little indication that the commission is considering moving any significant part of the present price support transfers to direct income payments of a decoupled nature. From the Community's perspective, the introduction of a scheme of this type is significant. It establishes the principle and allows the political process to get used to the idea; it may also provide useful experience in administration. In terms of U.S. trade, the scheme cannot be too significant if it is so small and underfunded.

The muted U.S. response to what is often regarded in Europe as a large change in policy may seem churlish. In part, this response is conditioned by the experience of years of well-meaning efforts by the commission to make significant changes in the CAP, only to be rejected by the Council of Ministers. In part, it reflects the different viewpoint, where results count and the amount of political contortions needed to achieve the decision is not of interest. In part, it is a function of the present stage of multilateral negotiations, where to recognize that the European Community has made major changes may itself squander negotiating capital. That the CAP is less trade-disruptive than it might have been is undeniable. These changes to date do not, however, remove the prospect of continued frictions with the United States in years to come.

Changes in U.S. and Other Farm Policies to Improve Trade Relations

The changes in domestic farm policy under way in the European Community have a parallel in other developed countries. The pace of change varies from country to country, and the particular form of reform is also country specific. But the direction is similar. Before changes in domestic policy can reduce trade frictions, they have to continue in several countries for a sustained period of time.

U.S. Policy Reform. U.S. policy has been changing in significant ways

393

since 1985, largely as a result of budget pressures. The 1981 farm bill left agriculture with high price supports for the leading products—in anticipation of a firm world market that did not materialize.[13] In 1982 U.S. farm exports slumped (as described above) and the surplus was absorbed by the government. By the time the 1985 farm bill was under consideration, both the administration and Congress were willing to countenance fairly dramatic shifts in policy. The administration proposed a policy that would have phased out much of the price-support programs over a period of years. This was to be achieved by reducing both the target prices and the loan rates, thus regaining competitiveness and reducing program cost. Senators Rudi Boschwitz and David Boren added their own radical solution, for paying temporary compensation to farmers for the removal of price supports.[14]

In the event, the 1985 farm bill was not a radical departure from its predecessors. The loan rates were reduced to improve the competitiveness of U.S. agricultural exports, but target prices were to come down only marginally. As a result, the cost escalated rapidly in the face of weak world markets. One change that did become effective was the treatment of the base acreage and yield for farmers participating in the cereals program. Payments had previously been on a base that had been regularly updated, giving producers the incentive to raise output to expand the base. The new regulations tied the base to a historical period, and thus potentially decoupled the program payments.

In the United States, as in Europe, much of the political steam has recently gone out of the movement to reform agriculture policies. Farm program costs are sharply down, and stocks are at a relatively low level. Discussions are well under way on the 1990 farm bill, but so far no radical options have been proposed. Decoupling is still on the agenda, but in a more subtle form than the Boschwitz-Boren proposal discussed in 1985. The element of decoupling introduced in the 1985 farm bill, basing deficiency payments on a historical farm base acreage, could be extended. Other provisions allowed payments to be made even if the base acreage were not fully planted. There has been discussion of introducing a further element of decoupling the deficiency payments by allowing a portion of the base to be considered as entitlement, not varying with market conditions (the triple-base option).

Reform in Other Countries. The movement for reform of farm policies has not been confined to the United States and the EC (for details, see Sanderson 1990). Even Japan has not escaped the movement to reform farm policies. Some aspects of this reform are linked with direct pressures from trading partners—notably, the U.S. citrus and beef markets have been opened up in a series of bilaterally negotiated agreements. Also significant have been changes in the marketing system for rice and other grains. As in other areas of trade, the real protection in Japanese markets lies not in tariffs or other transparent barriers but in the network of firms in the distribution chain that determine the fate of imports. As regulations are relaxed in the distributive trades, imports will continue to penetrate the Japanese market further. Apart from some shifting out of rice, and possibly citrus production, the scope for substantial change in farm production is limited in Japan. Notions of decoupling support nevertheless have relevance, even in an economy without subsidized exports. Finding ways to pay rice farmers without encouraging production is a farm policy challenge for Japan.

Canada has gone further than most countries in the direction of replacing an emphasis on open-ended price support with such policies as income insurance schemes. Although the transfers to producers under Canadian policies are substantial (particularly if one includes provincial policies), many aspects of these policies are illuminating for other countries. Canada has refined the idea of stabilizing farm incomes—as opposed to price levels. A fund, financed both by the government and by producers, makes payments to Western Canadian farmers if their income from a group of commodities falls below a predetermined level. There have been suggestions to extend this scheme to supplant the price-support policies. But Canada also employs policies that have proved irritants to trading partners. Marketing boards abound, on exported and imported commodities, and these tend to dictate trade policy decisions. Quantitative controls over imports often provide the basis for the market power of these boards. Transportation subsidies give indirect benefit to grain farmers in the west and livestock producers in the east. It may take a substantial change in thinking in Canadian farm policy to introduce a truly market-oriented system.

Among the few countries that have made considerable steps down the road toward reform of farm programs are the two southern exporting countries, Australia and New Zealand. In the case of New Zealand, the structure of price supports erected in the late 1970s was almost completely removed in the period after 1985. Although this can hardly be taken as an indication of the ease with which the U.S, EC, Canadian, and Japanese programs could be removed, it does indicate that farmers and farm groups can live without subsidies if obliged to by wider economic considerations. Agriculture was swept

395

into a market-orientation by liberalization in the rest of the economy. The process has started in Australia, although the structure of state marketing institutions makes full reform difficult to achieve.

Taken as a whole, the experience of the 1980s reflects a remarkable shift in both attitudes and policies toward developed country agriculture. Much of this was prompted by depressed world markets from 1982 and encouraged by a broader trend toward economic deregulation. But the trend may be difficult to reverse. The agenda shows signs of moving toward issues other than farm income— particularly those concerned with the environmental impacts of agriculture and of the safety of foodstuffs. If farm lobbies and rural politicians have to fight on these fronts, they will be less able to resist calls for the removal of excessive price supports. This will have a positive effect on trade relations, inasmuch it will be easier to modify domestic policy to offset trade conflicts.

Defining a Successful Uruguay Round Outcome for Agriculture

The start of the Uruguay Round of GATT negotiations, in September 1986, has provided a new setting for U.S.-EC discussions on agricultural policy. It provides the opportunity to resolve old problems. But embedded in the context of a formal trade negotiation, U.S.-EC conflicts begin to take on an added significance. Agreement or disagreement could have wide-ranging implications for the trading system as a whole. This is particularly true of the current round. Failure of the negotiations could lead the large countries to lose confidence in multilateral trade arrangements. The agricultural stakes are also high, since by mutual agreement domestic agricultural policies are on the table.

Countries have traditionally taken the view that domestic agricultural policies, supported as they are by strong political interests at home, take precedence over the rules on international trade. The operation of these policies has given rise to persistent problems in international markets, with harmful effects on both developed and developing countries. The development that makes the Uruguay Round different from earlier efforts to discuss agricultural trade is that these domestic policies are, at least in principle, subject to negotiation. Countries have expressed their willingness to discuss constraints on these policies that would make them more compatible with stable world markets.

The Negotiations So Far. Progress achieved in the Uruguay Round on agriculture has been considerable, at least in comparison with previous GATT negotiations. This has been due to solid groundwork before the negotiations began, a relatively unambiguous statement of objectives, and some imaginative national proposals on negotiating modalities. The Punta del Este agreement in September 1986 came after a period of intense negotiation on the content and procedures for the round. The declaration itself defined the negotiating objectives. These included "greater liberalization of trade in agriculture" and the bringing of "all measures affecting import access and export competition under strengthened and more operationally effective GATT rules and disciplines." The declaration defined the structure of the negotiating groups and established a time limit of four years. It called for countries to present their ideas on the method for negotiating on agricultural trade by the end of the following year, 1987.

Several proposals emerged during 1987 that took the objectives laid down at Punta del Este and elaborated on them. First to be announced was the U.S. proposal of July 1987; the Cairns Group and the European Community followed in October of that year. (A separate proposal by Canada was also tabled at that time, although Canada is also a member of the Cairns Group.) By early 1988, two more proposals had been introduced, by Japan and by the Nordic countries (Sweden, Finland, Norway, and Iceland). Papers by Korea and by a group of developing countries (Egypt, Jamaica, Mexico, Morocco, and Peru) together with declarations from India, Nigeria, and Switzerland, were also tabled.

The U.S. proposal called for the elimination of "all policies which distort [agricultural] trade" over a ten-year period. Certain domestic policies would be exempt, as only having a small impact on production and trade. These would include domestic food assistance programs, international food aid, and any safety net farm-income programs not linked to the level of production. The Cairns Group shared the U.S. view of a liberalized agricultural market, but added a preliminary stage of a freeze in present subsidy levels. The EC paper appeared more concerned with short-term market imbalances but agreed that a reduction in support prices was necessary over the long run. At the other extreme, the Japanese position implied that trade problems were the fault of the exporting countries, and that domestic policies were not subject to international negotiation. Negotiations on domestic policies pose a tricky problem for the comparison of trade effects. All the major proposals, except for that of Japan, supported the use of an aggregate measure of support (AMS) based on the OECD's PSE. Most countries suggested that this be modified to take into account supply control and exchange rate changes.

These proposals were discussed during 1988, in the GATT in

Geneva. Seven meetings of the Agricultural Negotiating Group were held between February and November. In addition, the group set up technical working parties to consider the issues of the use of an AMS and of sanitary and phytosanitary regulations. In addition, participants spelled out their own proposals over the year. The Cairns Group introduced the notion that countries, in addition to the freeze in support levels, should agree to a two-year down payment on longer-term reform. This would ensure that policy changes were started during the negotiations, rather than awaiting their conclusion. The European Community elaborated on its own short-term proposals, but declined to spell out what they had in mind for the longer-term reform. The United States stuck to its position for much of the year that no short-term action was required, other than an immediate start on the long-term program. By the end of the year, the United States indicated its willingness to talk about short-term measures as long as the goal of long-term elimination of support had been agreed. The European Community found this position unacceptable, claiming that it went far beyond the mandate of Punta del Este.

The lack of agreement on the longer-term program for agriculture threatened the timetable for the Uruguay Round as a whole. The midterm review, held in December 1988 in Montreal, was intended to endorse at the ministerial level the progress so far and set the agenda for the remaining two years of negotiations. In the event, the Montreal meeting broke up with no agreement on agriculture, and several agreements that had been reached on other issues were put on hold. The GATT director-general was asked to try to find a compromise on this (and some other outstanding issues) to allow the round to continue. Such a compromise framework for negotiations was finally agreed on April 7, 1989, in Geneva, to complete the midterm review.

The Midterm Agreement. The April agreement did not resolve the many issues that had separated the negotiating positions of the major participants, but it did provide a framework for their eventual resolution. It also mandated a timetable for the work plan that instills some urgency and discipline into the negotiations. The main provisions of the agreement are a short-term commitment to freeze policy prices, a decision substantially to reduce support levels over a period of years, and an obligation to discuss revision of GATT rules governing agriculture—including those dealing with plant and animal health regulations and food safety. Countries also agreed to specify to what extent developing countries would be expected to accept all the obligations of the GATT rules.

The short-run program calls for a two-year freeze in support levels, import access, and national prices in nominal terms. It adds an agreed "intent" to reduce protection in 1990 by an unspecified amount. Policy prices have been edging downward over the past four years, in the European Community, the United States, and Japan, as a reaction to high budget costs and low world prices. It is not clear that the freeze has had a major impact on policy decisions. But it does appear to have helped guard against an upsurge in domestic prices in the light of firmer world prices.

The second element of the April agreement was long-term reform in agricultural policies. Countries agreed to negotiate a "substantial, progressive reduction in agricultural support sustained over an agreed period of time." The time period remains to be decided, and the level of reductions was not specified. The United States appeared to accept that its goal of zero trade-distorting support within ten years is not going to be agreed by others. Also still to be agreed is the mechanism for achieving this reduction. The two main candidates are negotiations on specific policies and negotiations of commitments of an aggregate measure of support (AMS). Both are likely to be used in various ways during the negotiations.

The United States originally pushed for the use of an AMS, as a way of capturing the totality of agricultural policy instruments in one comparative figure. When it became clear that a zero target for the protection level was not feasible, concern grew that countries might try to evade the trade implications of support reductions by shifting policies. Reductions in the AMS might not be translated into trade gains. Although many of the these concerns can be met by an appropriate definition of the AMS, the feeling grew that it would be desirable to deal with specific policies to enable exporters to target priority importer practices. The Cairns Group also broadly took this line, thinking of the AMS as a scorecard to keep track of progress obtained by specific policy bargaining. Meanwhile, the European Community had warmed to the notion of using an AMS as the main form of negotiated commitment. To the European Community, negotiations on specific policies meant attacking the CAP. AMS negotiations would move some of the focus back onto the United States and Canada, who emerged with surprisingly high PSEs in 1986 and 1987. And an AMS negotiation might allow the European Community to spare some sectors and even to achieve an element of rebalancing in its policy. The European Community is now the main enthusiast for an AMS approach and has spelled out its ideas in more detail.[15]

The third element in the April agreement was for changes in GATT rules. Two rules in particular have been particularly significant in agricultural trade. Article XI specifies conditions under which quantitative trade barriers are allowed. Among these exceptions is one for situations in which domestic supply is also controlled by quantitative means. Some countries would like to remove this exception. The United States was granted a waiver from even this condition in 1955, and operates import quotas for dairy products without effective supply control. To compound matters, the variable levy, used extensively by the European Community to maintain stable domestic prices, is not even included specifically by the GATT. As a result, large parts of EC and U.S. farm policies are de facto excluded from GATT scrutiny. Participants in the negotiations seem to agree that it is time to get rid of the exceptions and waivers (although the negotiating value of relinquishing a waiver has yet to be tested) and to clarify the status of grey area import measures.

The issue of export subsidies is among the most urgent in the negotiations. Article XVI allows export subsidies on primary products, although saying that countries should "seek to avoid their use." Countries have not taken this advice, and even with the negotiation of a subsidies code in the Tokyo Round, the problem has proved intractable. Moreover, many domestic policies act as subsidies to exports, including U.S. deficiency payments for grains. No consensus has emerged as to how to deal with export and domestic subsidies by changing rules. An outright ban on such subsidies has been suggested, but the European Community views this as both impracticable and inequitable. Constraints on the level of export subsidies may be possible, and the quantities exported with the aid of such subsidies could be limited. With firm world prices, such agreements could be workable. Whether they would be sustainable at a time when world prices were depressed, as happened in 1986, is much less certain.

Less dramatic than support reduction and export subsidies, but still important for agricultural trade, is the area of sanitary and phytosanitary regulations (SPR). The Punta del Este declaration made special mention of the need to "minimize the adverse effects that sanitary and phytosanitary regulations and barriers can have on trade in agriculture." Behind this apparent agreement, the different approaches to the problem are still to be reconciled. The U.S. view emphasizes the need to base domestic regulations on internationally agreed standards, not to recognize the equivalence of different regulations (that is, those that provide substantially the same protection to the consumer). The European Community has been less explicit on such matters and has argued for the negotiation of a "framework of rules" governing harmonization of standards. The need of equivalence is not fully accepted, and the European Community also places less emphasis on the scientific basis for international regulation. The Cairns Group also favors a negotiation on a long-term framework based on strict justification for protecting human and animal health, and argue for equivalence where harmonization is not possible.

The Comprehensive Proposals. Under the timetable of the midterm agreement, countries were to present their ideas for a package of reforms, including the reduction in support and the changes in GATT rules, by the end of 1989. In October, the United States presented the first of these comprehensive proposals. The U.S. proposal builds upon earlier papers but contains considerably more detail on the implementation of reforms. The proposal itself is organized by category of policy instrument—import access, export subsidies, domestic subsidies, sanitary and phytosanitary barriers, and distinctive treatment for developing countries. As discussed above, the three negotiating methods under consideration are changes in GATT rules, reducing support by an AMS, and negotiating on specific policies and commodities. Table 17-6 attempts to place the U.S. proposals into this framework, as a way of highlighting its approach and facilitating comparison with other proposals.

The U.S. proposal places a heavy burden on negotiating changes in GATT rules. Import access is to be tackled by getting rid of all nontariff import barriers. Tariff quotas protect the exporter interests over a ten-year transition period, and other safeguards are designed to prevent too rapid an increase in imports. Quantitative restrictions would be removed by the end of the transition, thus eliminating the need for the current waivers and exceptions. Export subsidies would also be removed (over a five-year period) and the GATT rules changed accordingly. (The U.S. proposal also calls for the removal of the clause that allows export restrictions in time of domestic shortage.) For domestic subsidies, a set of regulations would define those that are prohibited (that is, those that reward farmers on the basis of current output) and those that are permitted (that is, those that are effectively decoupled or indirectly linked to output). New procedures would be developed to strengthen notification, consultation, and dispute settlement obligations for sanitary and phytosanitary trade barriers.

Policy-specific negotiations would also be crucial to the success of the U.S. plan. Specific levels of tariffs, along with the amount of the tariff-rate quota, would be negotiated. Countries would need to present and agree on sweeping changes in domestic price-support programs. Each country would have some flexibility on the transition

TABLE 17-6

Categorization of U.S. Comprehensive Proposal by Negotiating
Methods and Policy Area

	GATT Rules	AMS Reduction	Policy Specific
Market access	Tariffs only after transition Eliminate Art. XI (2) c		Negotiate levels of tariffs and interim tariff quotas
Export subsidies	No export subsidies after transition		
Domestic subsidies	Specify acceptable subsidies	Bind and reduce	Negotiate removal of unacceptable subsidies
Sanitary and phytosanitary barriers	Revise procedures Amend article XX(b)		

Source: Author.

mechanism but be locked in to a ten-year program of domestic policy reinstrumentation. The AMS find only a minor role in the U.S. proposal, as a way of measuring policies that fall neither into the prohibited nor the permitted list. These discipline policies—largely input and investment subsidies that are not tied to particular commodities—would be subject to a phase-down over a period of years.

The Cairns Group tabled its own comprehensive proposals for the agricultural negotiations in December 1989. Like the U.S. plan, the Cairns Group proposal emphasized import access and the control of export subsidies. It also advocated the conversion of nontariff measures to tariffs and stressed the need for bringing all import measures under GATT coverage. For export subsidies, the Cairns Group proposal argued for a freeze and a progressive phase-out of these programs. It also argued that the option of converting export subsidies to food aid should be made less attractive by limiting such aid to outright grants of food. The Cairns Group sees a somewhat larger role for the AMS than does the United States, but treats it as a scorecard to keep track of progress obtained by specific bargaining. The Cairns Group proposal on the reform of domestic policies is somewhat more flexible than that of the United States as it allows somewhat more choice of domestic policy instrument.

The EC global proposal showed perhaps the most willingness to bend from its previous position.[16] The Europeans reluctantly concede that tariffs, in a modified form, could replace the present levy system on EC imports, and a careful reading between the lines suggests that a similar modification could be applied to EC export subsidies. As long as equivalent concessions were available on the main policy instruments of other trading partners, one could envisage a significant modification to EC policy following from such an agreement. But the main thrust of the EC proposal falls not on changes in instruments. To the European Community, negotiations on specific policies means attacking the CAP; in contrast, AMS negotiations would move some of the focus back onto the United States and Canada, which proved to have surprisingly high PSEs in 1986 and 1987. And an AMS negotiation might allow the European Community to spare some sectors and even to achieve an element of rebalancing in its policy. The European Community is now the main enthusiast for an AMS approach. Whether other countries will shift their own positions to accommodate the EC on this issue remains to be seen (for an explanation of the common points in the proposals, see Josling et al. 1990).

Prospects for a Peaceful Decade in Farm Trade

The changes that are needed to improve both the domestic performance and the international acceptability of farm programs will not be easy. They will require significant skill in international negotiations and considerable political will at home. Success requires that traditional forces that opposed these changes, and that have been able to block them in the past, be persuaded to remove their opposition, or else be countered by others. The Uruguay Round cannot dictate domestic farm policy change. To attempt to undertake such a task would condemn it to failure. But the round cannot ignore domestic policy and concentrate on trade rules or the exchange of trade concessions. Such tinkering with the symptoms would have little lasting impact. What is needed is a trade reform outcome that promotes the process of domestic reform; just as the domestic reform is needed to improve the trading system.

This suggests three criteria for success in the Uruguay Round negotiations on agriculture: (1) the agreement should specify a substantial reduction in the levels of support given by farm programs; (2) the agreement should encourage the reinstrumentation of policies toward more decoupling income subsidies from output decisions and some recoupling of domestic prices with world market conditions;

and (3) the agreement should modify GATT rules to encourage and underpin these developments and to ease the resolution of any conflicts that may arise in the future.

Observers of the process tend to fall into two camps. One group, the realists, consider the Uruguay Round an exercise in illusion, a game played by trade officials at the periphery of agricultural policy. Whatever comes out of the round will amount to minor changes in the trade rules and some collective but empty encouragement to domestic policy reforms. The chances of major farm policy changes being adopted in Geneva are remote. To pretend otherwise is fanciful at best and possibly even dangerous since the focus on multilateral processes for farm policy reform could in some situations slow down the domestic reform process (Paarlberg 1987). It flies against all the experience of recent history and ignores political realities. Under such an interpretation, the United States and the European Community should not look to the GATT to reduce trade tensions. Some hard bargaining on a bilateral basis could yield results, but the solutions lie in domestic politics and initiatives.

History and logic are so firmly on the side of this realistic interpretation that it seems foolhardy to argue otherwise. But there is another more optimistic interpretation of current events that is worth passing consideration. Suppose that special-interest politics and middle-class entitlement programs have now become less attractive to politicians. Imagine agricultural price policy becoming identified with transfers to wealthy families and with the degradation of the environment. Add a sense of frustration over agricultural trade squabbles from those in charge of commerce and commercial policy. It is not inconceivable that the GATT Round under these circumstances could play a nontraditional role. The tail of trade policy could for once wag the domestic policy dog. A bold agreement in the GATT could essentially dictate the framework for domestic policies for the next decade.

If the realist interpretation is proved correct, then trade relations between the United States and the European Community will be determined largely by the level of demand for temperate-zone products in nonindustrial countries. Firm demand, from general economic growth and a resolution to the debt crisis, unmatched by any dramatic change in supply trends, would ease the burden on domestic policies. Although program costs would decline and the political visibility of farm programs would be reduced, the underlying problems will remain as long as the instrumentation of farm policies was unchanged. Domestic pressures would continue slowly to move support away from surplus-generating measures, but without external disciplines the temptation to resort to passing the burden to other countries would be irresistible. But if demand were to turn weak, then all of the problems of the early 1980s would quickly return. A scramble for markets would push up program costs and set in train another cycle of reform.

The current GATT Round offers a short cut to this process. By constraining domestic policies within effective GATT rules, countries will incur much greater risks when running policies that offer excessive protection to agriculture. Domestic policies will run up against the constraints and adapt more quickly. U.S.-EC agricultural conflicts will not disappear overnight, but they will take place within a clearer framework of rules and obligations. This attractive scenario could be enough to persuade negotiators to come to an agreement in the Uruguay Round. But few would put the probability of a strong agreement high. More likely is a continued period of tension, with both the European Community and the United States trying to interpret the terms of a weak agreement in their favor, at the same time accusing the other of bad faith. The prospects for a peaceful decade in farm trade do not look bright.

References

ABARE. 1989a. *The 1988 EC Budget and Production Stabilisers*. Discussion Paper 89, no. 3. Canberra.

———. 1989b. *U.S. Grain Policies and the World Market*. Policy Monograph 4. Canberra.

Archibald, Sandra O., and Carl K. Winter. 1989. "Pesticides in Food: Assessing the Risks. In *Chemicals in the Human Food Chain*, edited by Carl K. Winter, James N. Sieber, and Carole F. Nuckton. Agricultural Issues Center, University of California.

Batie, Sandra S. 1989. "Sustainable Development." *American Journal of Agricultural Economics* (December).

Blandford, David, Harry de Gorter, and David Harvey. 1988. "Production Entitlement Guarantees (PEGS): A Minimally Distorting Method of Farm Income Support." Background paper for Annapolis Symposium, International Agricultural Trade Research Consortium.

Falcon, Walter P. 1989. "Future Linkages between U.S. Agriculture and the World Food Economy." Photocopy.

GATT. 1986. *Recommendations: Draft Elaboration*. Committee on Trade in Agriculture, AG/W/9.

Gray, Paul. 1990. "Food Law and the Internal Market: Taking Stock." *Food Policy* 15, no. 2 (April).

Hartwig, Bettina, Tim Josling, and Stefan Tangermann. 1989. "Design of New Rules for Agriculture in the GATT." Photocopy.

Hathaway, Dale E. 1988. *Agriculture and the GATT: Rewriting the Rules.* Report 20. Washington, D.C.: Institute for International Economics.

Josling, Tim, et al. 1990. "Report of the Task Force on the Comprehensive Proposals for Negotiation in Agriculture." International Agricultural Trade Research Consortium.

Krueger, Anne, Maurice Schiff, and Alberto Valdes. 1988. "Agricultural Incentives in Developing Countries: Measuring the Effect of Sectoral and Economy-wide Policies." *World Economic Review* 2 (3).

Longworth, John W. 1987. "Biotechnology: Scientific Potential and Socioeconomic Implications for Agriculture." *Review of Marketing and Agricultural Economics* 55, no. 3 (December).

Moyer, H. Wayne, and Timothy E. Josling. 1990. *Agricultural Policy Reform: Politics and Process in the EC and USA.* Hemel Hempstead: Harvester-Wheatsheaf.

Newman, Mark, Tom Fulton, and Lawrence Glaser. 1987 *A Comparison of Agriculture in the United States and the European Community.* FAER 233, USDA/ERS. Washington, D.C.

Organization for Economic Cooperation and Development. 1987. *National Policies and Agricultural Trade.* Paris.

———. 1989. *Agricultural Policies, Markets and Trade: Monitoring and Outlook 1989.* Paris.

Paarlberg, Robert L. 1988. *Fixing Farm Trade: Policy Options for the United States.* Cambridge, Mass: Ballinger.

Roningen, Vernon, and Praveen Dixit. 1989. "Impact of Removal of Support to Agriculture in Developed Countries." *Food Policy.*

Rosenberg, Norman J. et al. 1989. *Greenhouse Warming: Abatement and Adaption.* Washington, D.C.: Resources for the Future.

Sanderson, Fred H., ed. 1990. *Agricultural Protectionism in the Industrialized World.* Washington, D.C.: Resources for the Future.

Schmidt, Stephen C., and Walter H. Gardiner. 1988. *Non-Grain Feeds: EC Trade and Policy Issues.* FAER 234, USDA/ERS. Washington, D.C.

U.S. Agency for International Development. 1989. *Development and the National Interest.* Washington, D.C.

U.S. Department of Agriculture. 1988. *Estimates of Producer and Consumer Subsidy Equivalents.* USDA/ERS. Washington, D.C.

———. 1989. *Western Europe: Agriculture and Trade Report.* USDA/ERS. Washington, D.C.

18
European Integration and the Common Agricultural Policy

Stefan Tangermann

Unfortunately, trade relations between the United States and Europe are time and again strained by problems in agriculture. U.S. policy makers complain that Europe is taking natural markets away from American farmers by what looks like a set of particularly unfair agricultural and trade policies. For their part, policy makers in the European Community consider the common agricultural policy (CAP) to be a matter of essentially domestic concern, and they cannot understand why the United States should interfere. Moreover, they feel that U.S. agricultural policies are not that much different from those in Europe, so why should the United States constantly attack the CAP.

The common agricultural policy is indeed a central factor determining agricultural developments in the Community and in its agricultural trade. A number of factors will shape the CAP in the years to come, beginning with the current EC program of reform. But external factors are also bound to change the course of the Community's agricultural policies, the most notable being the Uruguay Round of GATT negotiations. If anything, these negotiations should help liberalize the agricultural trading regime in the Community. Also important is the internal market to be completed by the end of 1992, but it is not quite clear how this development may affect European agriculture. Will it create a Fortress Europe in agriculture, or will it support the reform of the CAP?

These issues are at the heart of this discussion. I do not, however, describe the institutional design and the instrumentation of the CAP, nor the economic consequences of the Community's agricultural policies, since such information is readily available in the literature (see, for example, Harris et al. 1983; Bureau of Agricultural Economics 1985; Koester and Tangermann 1989).

Helpful comments by Ann Hillberg-Seitzinger on an earlier draft are gratefully acknowledged.

The Role of Agriculture in European Integration

There are only a few economic sectors of Western countries where government interference is as pervasive as it is in agriculture. Moreover, given the politically sensitive nature of issues related to food and agriculture, agricultural policies in all countries are considered a matter of particular national concern—agriculture is special everywhere, but domestic agriculture is even more special. In addition, an unbelievably wide variety of policy measures have been invented by agricultural policy makers. Hence, not only do the objectives of agricultural policies differ among countries, but the nature of the instruments used varies considerably from country to country. As a result, the opening up of borders for agricultural trade and the harmonization of agricultural policies across nattons, even if these nations have much in common, is a truly Herculean task. The failure of the GATT to come to grips with even modest steps toward agricultural trade liberalization bears witness to the difficulties involved in agricultural matters.

Against this background, one can only admire the enthusiasm and optimism with which the fathers of a united Europe approached the matter of agricultural integration. There was never any serious doubt that agriculture should be included in the common market to be created in Europe. Indeed, the negotiations on the establishment of a European Economic Community (EEC) had been preceded by attempts to set up a purely agricultural scheme of integration. In parallel with the creation, in 1951, of a "black pool" in the form of the European Coal and Steel Community (which involved the six countries that later were to become the first members of the EEC), and in spite of the abortive debate about the possible establishment of a European Defense Community, various efforts were made to integrate European agriculture into a "green pool." In 1950 the Consultative Assembly of the Council of Europe launched a study on the organization of a common agricultural market in Europe (which led to the Charpentier Plan). In 1951 the French government proposed negotiations with the objective of setting up a European Agricultural Community (the Pflimlin Plan). At the same time, the Dutch government issued even more ambitious proposals for agricultural integration in Europe (the Mansholt Plan). On the basis of these proposals and plans, fifteen Western European countries launched a series of conferences entitled the Organization of European Agricultural Markets in Paris between 1952 and 1954. In the end, the green pool in Europe did not materialize, but important precedents had been set for the way in which agriculture would be treated when it came to the formation of the European Economic Community (for details, see Tracy 1982: 261ff.).

The 1956 report by the intergovernmental committee set up to prepare the Treaty for a European Economic Community (the Spaak report) did not contain concrete suggestions regarding the way agricultural policies should be treated in the Community. But it left no doubt concerning the fundamental importance of including agriculture in the process of European economic integration. Agricultural specialization in the emerging Community, it was suggested, could result in significant economic benefits. Above all, the inclusion of agriculture was needed to balance trade advantages among the member countries. In particular, the agricultural exporters—France, the Netherlands, and Italy—saw free access to the German food market as a quid pro quo for opening up their borders to industrial exports from Germany.

Although Germany had a strong foreign policy interest in European integration, particularly in having close links with France, its interest in agricultural integration was lukewarm at best. After all, German agriculture was at a disadvantage because of its fragmented farm-size structure and low competitiveness. What agricultural integration would mean became abundantly clear when the 1955 bilateral trade agreement with France led to a doubling of German cereals imports from France (Kluge 1989: 1: 226). But the fundamental German interest in harmonious political relations and economic integration in Europe was so strong that agricultural concerns were not allowed to inhibit progress toward a European Community.

The Treaty of Rome, which was largely based on the Spaak report, clearly provided for the inclusion of agriculture in the European Community. As in the case of other goods, tariffs and quantitative restrictions on trade between the six member countries had to be removed for agricultural commodities, too. Moreover, a common agricultural policy had to be established, with the rather general and vague objectives laid down in the famous Article 39 of the Treaty of Rome, but the treaty left considerable scope regarding the nature of the CAP.

Among the three possible options for agricultural market integration envisaged in Article 40 of the Treaty of Rome—that is, common rules for competition, coordination of national market organizations, and establishment of common market regimes—the Community later chose the most ambitious approach when it decided to replace the existing national market policies by European market regimes for nearly all agricultural products. This decision meant that responsibility for all elements of agricultural market policy, in particular the setting of support prices and the instrumentation of agricultural trade policies in relation to third countries, was removed from national governments and handed over to the Community's Council of Ministers. Hence, after long and intense debates about the exact form of the instruments to be used in the common market regimes, particularly about the level of price support in the Community (between the low French and the high German level of price support), the individual market regimes for the various commodities were designed and introduced in the course of the 1960s. At the same time, and again not without intense debate, the decision was taken to finance the CAP at the Community level.

The fundamental decision to pursue and finance agricultural policies at the level of the European Community has never been challenged. During the preparation of the first enlargement of the Community (to include the United Kingdom, Ireland, and Denmark in 1973), there was some debate about possible modifications of the CAP. The six original member countries successfully maintained, however, that the newcomers had to agree to full acceptance of the *acquis communautaire*. In the preparation of the later rounds of enlargement (Greece 1981; Spain and Portugal 1986), there was not even a discussion about changing the CAP, and the negotiations concentrated on the modalities of adjusting the agricultural policies in the acceding countries to the existing CAP.

Agriculture has thus become an integral element of European integration in two respects. On the one hand, agricultural trade among the member countries of the European Community is seen as an important balancing factor in the overall exchange of goods and services among EC nations. On the other hand, the need for and the possibilities of pursuing and financing common agricultural policies at the level of the European Community has led to a functional integration of policy making and administration in Europe.

A few figures can illustrate the significance of agriculture in European integration. In 1968, one-third of all agricultural imports of the six member countries came from within the Community (Commission of the European Communities 1987: 41, 44). In 1987, the corresponding figure for the twelve member countries stood at 59 percent (Commission of the European Communities 1989b: T/153–54). Thus, the significance of intra-EC agricultural trade as opposed to trade with third countries has nearly doubled over the past twenty years.

Of all the merchandise traded within the Community of twelve member countries in 1987, 13.4 percent was food trade; in total world trade the share of food trade was only 10.1 percent (GATT 1988:

tables AB3, AB5). Thus, food is about one-third more important for intra-EC trade than for world trade on aggregate.

Among all operations of the Community, activities related to the CAP have a high share. In 1987 (as in earlier years), two-thirds of all expenditure from the Community budget was spent on the common agricultural policy (Commission of the European Communities 1989b: T/83). A large part of all council meetings are held by agricultural councils. And the many other committees dealing with the CAP—above all, the Special Committee on Agriculture (preparing agricultural council meetings) and the various management committees (involved with the day-to-day administration of the CAP)—add to the number of occasions on which member country representatives deal with agricultural issues in the Community. In the second half of the 1970s, more than four-fifths of the total of legislative acts in the Community were concerned with agricultural matters, of the total administrative staff of the EC Commission, close to one-tenth is in the Directorate General for Agriculture (DG VI) (Harris et al. 1983: 33, 16).

Quite apart from the sheer quantitative significance of agricultural issues in the European Community, there is no doubt that the early and undisputed decision to include agriculture in the process of creating a European Community has had a major impact on the way in which European integration has developed. The self-imposed need to agree among member countries on such difficult matters as those involved in agricultural policy decisions has certainly influenced the thinking and behavior of politicians and government officials, and hence attitudes toward European integration in general. Moreover, agricultural difficulties and successes have often had wider implications for the process of integration in the Community. Two striking examples of political turning points in the history of the Community may suffice to illustrate the extent to which agricultural issues have influenced European integration in general.

In 1965, a decision had to be made regarding the establishment of a permanent system for financing the CAP. The commission proposed, in line with the philosophy of the Treaty of Rome and with earlier tentative decisions, that all income from levies and duties on agricultural imports should accrue, as "own resources," to the Community budget and that the European Parliament should be given more significant influence over the Community budget. President Charles de Gaulle was in opposition to these proposals, and in spite of earlier French pressure for making progress with all aspects of the CAP, including the financial regime, he blocked the acceptance of these commission proposals. For more than half a year France did not participate in council meetings. This empty-chair crisis did not end before the Luxembourg compromise was reached in January 1966. The substance of this compromise was that the treaty provisions for majority voting, which should have become effective on January 1, 1966, were overruled by an agreement that in cases where "very important interests" were at stake the council would try to find solutions that could be accepted by all member countries. Hence the Luxembourg compromise effectively allowed retreat to the principle of unanimous council decisions wherever a member country claimed that vital national interests were concerned. For a long time this voting principle was to have a significant impact on the way in which decisions were taken in the Community—until the Single Act became effective in 1987.[1]

One of the many other occasions on which agricultural issues affected the overall process of integration in the Community was the Brussels summit in February 1988. This summit dealt extensively with what was called the reform of the CAP, which included a program for the set-aside of agricultural land, stabilizers for agricultural markets, and a budget guideline for agricultural expenditure. But the Brussels summit was primarily concerned with overcoming the depressed mood that had spread in the Community. It did so by laying the political and financial foundations of further progress toward the internal market. In particular, in addition to announcing the agricultural provisions, the 1988 Brussels summit decided on a new scheme for a substantial increase of own resources for the Community budget, on a doubling of structural funds to provide aid for disadvantaged regions in the Community, and on acceptance of January 1, 1993, as the deadline for the completion of the internal market. In the debate among EC heads of state (and in the earlier council meetings), these more general decisions were closely linked with the resolve to reform the CAP, and, in the absence of agreement on agriculture, the other elements of the package would in all likelihood not have been adopted. When the whole package was finally agreed, it was regarded and celebrated as a breakthrough that would pave the way toward a successful completion of the internal market and, more generally, a brighter future for the Community.

Thus, although the share of agriculture in total GDP of the Community is down to 3.5 percent, the significance of its role in European integration is by far higher than proportional (this figure is for 1986; see the Commission of the European Communities 1989b: T/20). Inclusion of agriculture in the common market is essential for at least some of the member countries. Community activities are largely devoted to the pursuit of the common agricultural policy, and agricultural issues have often been pivotal points in decisions regarding the future development of the Community at large. It is important to keep this in mind in debates about the prospects for the CAP and, for that matter, about future developments in the Community at large.

Agriculture and the Completion of the Internal Market

The Community's move toward the internal market is an interesting exercise in political psychology. By establishing the work program for the completion of the internal market and by setting the deadline of January 1, 1993, Community politicians have managed to affect people's expectations, both inside and outside the Community. In the end, these changes in expectations may turn out to be more important than the actual modifications in the legal framework and the policies of the Community. It is true that the 279 Community directives that are supposed to create the internal market will establish new factual conditions in a number of fields. In many cases, however, the resulting adjustments in legal conditions will be marginal compared with the mental changes that have already taken place and that will continue to occur and remain effective.

Teachers at village schools in the Community, for example, are reconsidering their programs in foreign languages—in what they feel is a necessary preparation of their students for competing for jobs in the internal market. Companies in branches where intra-EC trade is already as free as it can possibly be are setting up new subsidiaries in other EC countries—in order to benefit fully from the internal market. Business consultants are organizing seminars on 1992 affairs—and making money out of educating managers who wish to be better informed than their competitors. Governments are reorganizing ministries—and creating branches that exclusively deal with matters relating to intra-European competition. All of these activities could have taken place long ago. But it required the inspiring idea of a new age in the Community and of a given date (not too near and not too far in the future) for all this to happen. The 1992 program has thus turned out to be a masterly designed approach toward effectively overcoming the phenomenon of Eurosclerosis. Whatever the legislative situation concerning the internal market will be in the years to come, the mental changes triggered by the Europe 1992 campaign will shape reality, and possibly more so than any of the changes actually taking place at the Community's internal borders.

Agriculture, though, may be a specific variation of this theme. Except for the internal border taxes and subsidies related to the Green

Money system of the Community, agricultural trade among member countries has been free of restrictions since the establishment of common market regimes in the late 1960s and early 1970s. Some trade barriers concerning plant and animal health regulations remain, and a number of the directives in the 1993 work program relate to such sanitary and phytosanitary regulations. Most of the roughly 100 (out of a total of 279) directives that deal with agriculture and food, however, are of immediate concern only for the food-processing and trading industry, and they will probably have only marginal effects on the farming industry and on trade in raw agricultural commodities.

Moreover, in contrast to the food industry, which is very much on the alert in view of the internal market, Community farmers appear to be relatively relaxed about 1992. There is the occasional conference about agriculture in the internal market, studies are being pursued on the relative competitiveness of farming in different member states, and functionaries of cooperatives are considering modifications to their operations. Yet, on the whole it appears that there is less excitement about 1992 in agriculture than there is in other industries (including the food industry).

Contrary to expectations, it may well be that some things in agriculture will change significantly with the creation of the internal market. Such changes, though, may come about through the way in which the internal market affects the pursuit of the CAP, rather than through changes in product standards and similar modifications that are typical of what will happen in the area of industrial products (including processed foods). Outstanding CAP issues in this context are the green money system and the national agricultural policies of member countries.

Green Money after 1992. In agriculture, the Community has rather peculiar currency regulations, the infamous Green Money system. There are specific agricultural exchange rates (the Green Rates), and related monetary compensatory amounts (MCAs). MCAs are specific agricultural taxes and subsidies that are implemented at the internal borders of the Community. (Equivalent MCAs are also implemented in trade with third countries.) Agricultural imports into strong-currency countries that have not adjusted their Green Rates to the market exchange rate are taxed, and exports from these countries are subsidized. Equally, imports into weak-currency countries are subsidized and exports from these countries are taxed. These taxes and subsidies at the border are used in order to maintain the divergent levels of support prices among member countries which result from the common institutional prices being converted into national currencies through Green Rates rather than through market exchange rates. In the absence of border MCAs, agricultural produce from weak-currency countries would flow into intervention in strong-currency countries since it attracts higher prices (in "real" money) there. With such arbitrage, prices in all member countries would move up to the level of support prices prevailing in the member country with the highest prices (in real money terms). Hence border MCAs are a technically necessary concomitant of price differentiation among member countries that results from the lack of adjusting agricultural support prices to exchange rate changes.

If the Community abandoned internal border controls after 1992 and maintained the Green Money system of the CAP in its current form, this would obviously be inconsistent, because without border controls it would be technically impossible to implement MCAs. Hence, the natural solution would be to eliminate the Green Money system, and this is exactly what the EC Commission would like to happen. Not all member countries would be happy about the disappearance of Green Money, however. The German minister of agriculture, in particular, would like to maintain the possibility of protecting support prices in Germany against the effects of deutsche mark revaluations. In this situation, a number of options can be considered. Some of these options would allow the Community to continue price differentiation among member countries.

First, border controls could be maintained for agricultural trade in order to collect and pay MCAs. This option would appear somewhat ridiculous since the abandonment of border controls is the single most visible indication of the creation of a truly internal market; maintaining border controls and actually checking all trade across borders, only because of relatively minor taxes and subsidies on some agricultural goods, would appear to be far too high a price to pay for agricultural policy purposes. Hence, even the most determined proponents of the continuation of some form of a Green Money system do not appear to consider this option seriously.

Second, the implementation of MCAs at borders could be shifted to domestic points of sale (as is being actively considered at least by the German government). This solution would be analogous to one option that is currently being considered for dealing with the general value-added tax (VAT) system in the Community in case it should not prove possible to harmonize VAT rates sufficiently among member countries. In this case, the compensation of different rates of the VAT, which currently is also implemented at the border, could be done, it is suggested, at the level of the individual firms, based on documents to be provided and books to be kept by the firms. MCAs could then also be implemented at the level of firms rather than at the border. Such a solution, if it were technically possible at all, would involve enormous administrative efforts and costs. Moreover, it would open up many opportunities for manipulation and fraud. Even the current system of border MCAs, which is much easier to implement and control, has permitted much manipulation and fraud (Court of Auditors 1989). Hence, it seems unlikely that this option is really feasible.

A third option would be to give up on the application of special agricultural exchange rates, but to allow member countries to compensate farmers and consumers for exchange rate changes by manipulating the VAT system for agricultural and food products. For example, if agricultural support prices in a given country were to be reduced by 3 percent following a revaluation of that country's currency by 3 percent, the government of that country could be allowed to increase VAT rates on agricultural and food products by three percentage points, and to let farmers retain the additional revenue. This system would generalize a provision that was used, with reluctant agreement by the Community, by the German government when positive German MCAs had to be reduced in 1985.[2]

Although such a system would probably be easier to implement than true MCAs collected and paid at the level of firms, a number of considerations speak against it. Technically, the maximum level of negative MCAs that could be implemented in this option would be limited by existing VAT rates (because a VAT rate can be reduced to zero, but probably cannot become negative). The system would run counter to the existing attempts at harmonizing VAT rates among member countries. To the extent that it increases differences of VAT rates among member countries, it would add to the need for tax compensation at the level of firms, and would expand related possibilities of manipulation and fraud. Politically it would require a complete turn around in the position of the commission and some member countries that have successfully urged Germany to gradually reduce its VAT compensation to farmers.

Given all the difficulties with these various options for maintaining agricultural price differentiation among member countries, a strong point can be made for giving up on the Green Money system after 1992. Indeed, even more important than the technical difficulties with implementing price differentiation in the absence of borders is the simple economic argument that a common market is only common if the same price prevails everywhere (except for transportation costs, for example). MCAs have always been a violation of the spirit

416

of market integration in the Community. In the internal market they would be an outrageous anachronism, even if they could be technically implemented without border controls. Government-induced price differentiation distorts competition among countries, and it is diametrically opposed to what the creation of a truly internal market is supposed to achieve. It is therefore no wonder that the EC Commission strongly argues for eliminating MCAs completely and irrevocably by the end of 1992.

Yet some member countries, in particular Germany, argue that the need for compensating the effects of exchange rate adjustments on farmers will exist until a monetary union with fixed exchange rates (or a single European currency) has been established. The reverse of this argument is undoubtedly true: in a monetary union there is no need for MCAs, simply because there are no longer any exchange rate changes that could call for compensation. This does not mean, however, that MCAs *are* necessary as long as there is not yet a full monetary union.

The arguments for and against the Green Money system are well-known (see, for example, Ritson and Tangermann 1979). In spite of all the debates and fights about MCAs, no really convincing economic argument has yet been advanced to indicate why MCAs should be generally necessary (although they may, under particular circumstances, have welfare benefits). The only slightly rational argument why agriculture may need some protection against exchange rate changes, while all the rest of the economy is exposed to them, is that the prices of homogeneous bulk commodities, like agricultural products, react more strongly to exchange rate variations, particularly if these prices are controlled by the government. If some compensation for abrupt price changes appears necessary in agriculture, the more economic approach would be to grant or levy that compensation in the form of direct payments or taxes, rather than in the form of price interventions. In other words, the Community would be well advised to use the occasion of 1992 to abandon the Green Money system, even if a monetary union were still far in the future.

One slight technical difficulty, though, could arise for those member countries that still allow their exchange rates to float in relation to the ECU. Theoretically, these member countries would have to adjust market regime prices (in particular intervention prices) continually to variations in their exchange rates. But now that the importance of intervention buying is declining as a result of the reform measures adopted in various market regimes in recent years, actual market prices are becoming increasingly independent of short-term changes in intervention prices. At the same time, this says that

417

even with some variations in exchange rates, intervention prices in national currencies can probably be kept constant for some time without inducing massive arbitrage flows. Hence, a possible approach in countries with floating currencies would be to keep intervention (and other market regime) prices constant as long as the exchange rate variation does not exceed a given margin.

If the Community should manage to abandon its Green Money system by 1993, this could have significant consequences for the pursuit of the CAP and for market developments. Indeed, the consequences could well go far beyond any other changes in agriculture that may occur as a result of the completion of the internal market. In particular, divergencies of support price levels among member countries would disappear, and the trend of support prices in the Community could change.

Even under the existing Green Money system, divergencies of support price levels among member countries have decreased recently, as a result of adjustments in Green Rates and of more exchange rate stability in the Community. They are still in some cases, however. For example, because of the Green Money system, support prices in Greece for a number of products were 36.3 percent below the theoretical Community price level toward the end of the 1988–1989 crop year (April 1989). At the same time, support prices for a number of products in Spain were 7.4 percent above the Community level. For some products, in other words, Spanish prices were more than 68 percent higher than those in Greece. It is clear that the elimination of such price gaps would have a significant impact on the allocation of production and consumption in the Community. After all, not only do institutional prices differ among member countries, but so do market prices. As Koester (1989) has shown for a number of agricultural products, coefficients of variation of market prices among member states are as large as 10 to 20 percent, and throughout the 1970s and 1980s there has not been any clear indication that these price divergencies are beginning to disappear (Koester 1989). Green Money has been an important factor behind such price differences, and the elimination of this peculiar element of the CAP would therefore be a large step in the direction of really creating a homogeneous market for agricultural products in the Community.

Moreover, in a number of member countries price relativities between different products would change. This is because there are currently different Green Rates, and hence different MCAs, for various products in a number of member countries. For example, in both Spain and Greece, Green Rates are set separately for ten different product groups (although some of these Green Rates may actually be the same). In April 1989, the product group with the highest negative MCAs in Greece had MCAs of minus 34.8 percent, whereas MCAs for other products in Greece were zero. (The MCA applied is less than the price divergence referred to above because MCAs are set somewhat below the actual currency gap.)

It would be surprising if any other changes brought about by the completion of the internal market, such as elimination of border controls and technical barriers to trade, could have price effects in agriculture that came close to the price distortions, among both countries and commodities, that currently result from the Community's Green Money system. In this sense, the abandonment of Green Money, if it should be achieved, would likely be the most important effect of the 1992 program on agricultural market integration in the Community. In addition, and possibly even more important, the elimination of the Green Money system can also have consequences for the level at which support prices are set in the Community, and hence for the level of protection in EC agriculture.

The immediate short-run effect of removing MCAs on the level of support prices in the Community would be that the average price level would increase, because there are now more and higher negative MCAs around than positive MCAs. More important than this one-time effect would be the longer-run consequences that the elimination of Green Money might have on the development of support prices in the Community. The most obvious consequence here would be that the elimination of Green Money would also do away with the switchover provision that currently exerts an automatic upward pressure on agricultural support prices in the Community.

The switchover provision was introduced in 1984 to alleviate political problems plaguing the German minister of agriculture, who was under constant pressure from other member countries and the EC Commission to reduce positive German MCAs—contrary to what German farmers wished him to do. The trick introduced by the switchover provision was that positive (German) MCAs were converted into negative MCAs (in other member countries) by lifting the theoretical Community price level (to which all countries would have to align if MCAs were eliminated). In order to avoid, also, the creation of new positive MCAs in cases of revaluations (of the deutsche mark), it was agreed that the Community price level would in the future move up with the strongest EC currency (in practice, the deutsche mark) in cases of currency realignments. Technically, this is done through a correction factor that is applied to central rates before MCAs are calculated. In effect, the Community has in this way

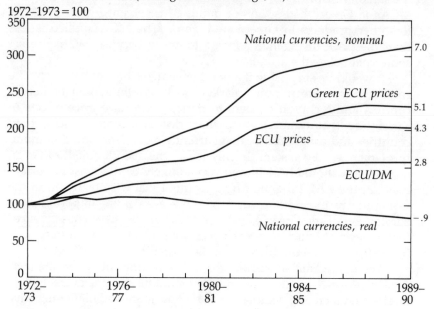

FIGURE 18–1
CAP PRICE DECISIONS, 1972–1990
(average annual change, %)

1972–1973 = 100

National currencies, nominal — 7.0

Green ECU prices — 5.1

ECU prices — 4.3

ECU/DM — 2.8

National currencies, real — −.9

1972–73   1976–77   1980–81   1984–85   1989–90

SOURCE: EC Commission (1987, 1989a).

created a new type of currency unit, the Green European currency unit (ECU), the value of which is equal to the value of the (normal) ECU times the correction factor. As long as the deutsche mark remains the strongest currency in the Community, the Green ECU is essentially pegged against the deutsche mark. In effect the Green ECU has been revalued by more than the deutsche mark, because the correction factor has on two occasions been raised by "by hand." MCAs are now calculated from the difference between the Green Rate of a country's currency and its rate against the Green ECU.

As a result, new additional negative MCAs for all but the strongest currency are created whenever there is a currency realignment in the Community. Since MCAs can be (and according to a council decision have to be) reduced and eliminated within a given period, a revaluation of the deutsche mark now automatically leads to an increase in the level of CAP support prices. In other words, since 1984 the Community's agricultural support prices are no longer fixed in ECU, but effectively they are set in deutsche marks. In 1987, this system was modified slightly.

The implications of this scheme are pictured in figure 18-1, which represents the effects of CAP price decisions taken by the EC Council

420

of farm ministers since 1972–1973.[3] Support prices in ECUs as set by the council have increased in every single year until 1983–1984. Since 1984–1985, the council has embarked on what has sometimes been described as a rigorous price policy. The indication of this change in direction, it is said, is the fact that support prices have now been cut. Indeed, ECU prices have been slightly reduced, and in 1989–1990 they were 1.3 percent below their 1983–1984 level. The seeming reform of price policy, however, has been accompanied by the switch-over provision and the related correction factor. As a consequence the relevant prices to look at now are the ECU prices including the correction factor, that is, CAP prices in Green ECUs (in figure 18-1, this is the line above the ECU price line, beginning in 1984–1985).

The correction factor now stands at 1.137182. In practical terms, this means that actual support prices in the Community are 13.7 percent above the level indicated by the (now meaningless) ECU prices. Hence, rather than having been cut by 1.3 percent, CAP support prices are now 12.4 percent above their 1983–1984 level. Indeed, until 1978–1988 one could not really speak of a reform of CAP pricing, because there was hardly any change in the trend of CAP support prices if one takes the correction factor into account, and it is only due to the exchange rate stability and to the absence of deutsche mark revaluations since 1987 that the support price level has not further increased since 1987.

The same basic conclusions can be drawn by looking at the development of support prices in national currencies (averaged over all member countries, as shown, on the basis of EC Commission calculations, in figure 18-1). After all, it is these prices in actual money received by farmers that determines market developments. The increase of average prices in national currencies has usually been higher than the increase in ECU prices. On average, over the period 1972–1973 to 1989–1990, support prices in national currencies have increased by an annual rate of 7.0 percent (in nominal terms), although ECU prices (exclusive of the correction factor) have increased by only 4.3 percent a year over this period (see figure 18-1).

The fact that support prices in national currencies have increased more than those in ECUs is not only due to the switchover system. As figure 18-1 shows, this happened continuously even before 1984–1985. Some critics have argued that this gap between price developments in national currencies and those in ECUs reflects a disguised (though possibly deliberate) form of raising agricultural price support in the Community. Such criticism is not fully justified. The gap between national currency prices and ECU prices reflects two main factors. On the one hand, the gap results from a tendency to reduce negative MCAs more rapidly than positive MCAs for farm income reasons. This is clearly an agricultural policy issue, and it does reflect a propensity to raise the level of price support. On the other hand, the gap between national currency prices and ECU prices is also due to the fact that the (statistical) weight of agricultural production in weak-currency countries, relative to aggregate agricultural production in the EC, is higher than the weight of these countries' currencies in the formula for calculating the value of the ECU.[4] Of course, this is a purely statistical effect that has nothing to do with the pursuit of agricultural policies.

What is important in the end is the development of real (that is, deflated) prices in national currencies. These support prices in real terms have gone down in most of the years since 1977–1978, on average by an annual rate of 0.9 percent over the period 1972–1973 to 1989–1990 (see figure 18-1).[5]

What does all this have to do with the completion of the internal market? If the Community should really manage to abandon its Green Money system by 1993, the switchover device and the related correction factor would disappear. The quantitative effect that this could have on the future development of agricultural support prices in the Community can be significant.

As described above, the correction factor largely traces the development of the deutsche mark in relation to the ECU.[6] In the past, the deutsche mark has time and again been revalued against the ECU. Over the period from 1972 to 1989, the average annual rate of appreciation of the deutsche mark against the ECU was 2.8 percent (see figure 18-1). If one assumes that this development of the deutsche mark rate against the ECU continues in the future, then the correction factor would tend to increase by an annual rate of 2.8 percent. The abandonment of Green Money would then result in the elimination of an equivalent annual rate of upward pressure on CAP prices. This would mean a doubling of the rate of decline in real support prices in national currencies against what it has been since 1984–1985 (from 2.8 to 5.6 percent). If such a development should continue over a ten-year period (say, from 1993 to 2003), CAP support prices would be roughly one-quarter below what they might have been in the absence of the internal market and, hence, without the elimination of the Green Money system.

Of course, this would have profound implications for market developments in the Community and for EC agricultural trade with third countries. There is probably no other single factor related to the internal market in agriculture that would ever come close to such a significant impact, and even the totality of all other changes that may take place with the creation of the internal market is unlikely to have a similarly pronounced effect.

It is unlikely, however, that the elimination of Green Money would have quite as dramatic an effect on future pricing policy in the CAP, for a number of reasons. First, the mechanics of the switchover system have already been slightly changed, such that its impact should now be somewhat more moderate. In 1987 the provision was introduced that, in the case of a revaluation of the deutsche mark (or another stronger currency), the common level of support prices in ECUs will be reduced by one-quarter of the rate of that revaluation. Hence, the switchover system is now only three-quarters as inflationary as it was originally. Instead of its possible trend effect of 2.8 percent a year, the switchover system might, therefore, result in only a 2.1 percent a year upward drift of CAP support prices over and above what is decided in ECU terms. This new provision has not yet been tested, however, for there was no currency realignment in the European Community since it was introduced. It may well be that in practice this new provision will be overruled by other decisions if and when it comes to a new currency realignment in the Community. After all, this new provision would automatically lead to a reduction of support prices in the country with a revaluing currency. Germany, which is the country most likely to suffer from this provision, may well oppose the actual enforcement of such price reductions, given the strong opposition of German agricultural policy makers to price cuts.

Second, CAP price-support setting may not work quite as mechanically as suggested above. In particular, the setting of support prices in ECUs may not be completely independent of the development of the value of the Green ECU. Indeed, if there were no money illusion at all among ministers of agriculture, the EC Council would realize that it is in effect setting support prices in deutsche marks rather than in ECUs, and it would increase institutional prices by less (or reduce them by more) than it would do if prices were actually determined in ECUs. Hence, on the assumption that the trend of a 2.8 percent annual revaluation of the deutsche mark against the ECU would continue to prevail, the EC Council would, in its annual price review, raise prices in Green ECU by 2.8 percentage points less than what it would have done had prices been effectively set in (normal) ECU terms. If this were the case, then the elimination of Green Money along with the creation of the internal market would not change the trend of support prices in the Community.

It is not clear to what extent the Council of Ministers and the EC Commission in its price proposals actually suffer from money illusion. One could argue that developments after 1984 demonstrate that there is only very little money illusion involved in setting CAP support prices. In particular, the development of CAP prices in Green ECUs (that is, ECU prices plus the correction factor in the years after 1984 has essentially continued along the trend earlier exhibited by CAP prices in the old ECU, as is obvious from figure 18-1. Hence it could appear that the Council of Ministers has immediately and effectively reacted to the change in the definition of the currency unit in which CAP prices are determined.

The problem with such an argument is that CAP support price decisions since 1984 were explicitly meant to be on a firm reform track, with much lower increases than earlier—indeed, with price cuts. When CAP support prices were, for the first time in the history of the CAP, cut in 1984 (by 0.4 percent in ECU terms), this was celebrated as a turning point in the CAP, and the courageous decision of the EC Council was accordingly advertised. The media believed it, and the general public got the impression that the CAP now was on a new track. The fact that at the same time the switchover system had been introduced and that the new correction factor immediately raised the value of the Green ECU by about 3.4 percent—which meant the CAP prices had in effect been increased by 3 percent rather than having been cut by 0.4 percent—completely escaped the attention of the general public. The conclusion is that either the Council of Ministers *did* suffer from money illusion and believed that it was cutting prices while it did not, or that it has deliberately misled the general public. It is difficult to say which of these two cases is the sadder one.

Two other arguments can be advanced in support of the assumption that the council is at least not completely free of money illusion. The new provision introduced in 1987, on the insistence of the commission, that one-quarter of any new revaluation of the deutsche mark is to be compensated by a reduction of ECU support prices, can only make sense if one assumes that there *is* some money illusion, for otherwise there would not be any need for such a provision. More important, the automatic price cuts at the core of the stabilizer provisions established in 1988 are determined as nominal price cuts in ECUs—independently of how the correction factor develops. In other words, cereal prices are supposed to be cut by 3 percent (when cereal production exceeds 160 million tons) regardless of whether the correction factor remains constant (in which case the price cut would actually occur in national currencies) or whether it increases as a result of a deutsche mark revaluation. Thus it could happen that in a given year in which the deutsche mark is revalued the 3 percent price cut is partly or wholly, or even more than wholly, compensated by a deutsche mark revaluation. In such a situation, the elimination of Green Money could have a significant impact on actual price developments.

A final reason why it is not really appropriate to project CAP price developments as mechanically as was done above, is that it is far from certain that the deutsche mark will continue to appreciate against the ECU to the same extent that it has appreciated in the past. Indeed, it is likely that the deutsche mark–ECU rate will be much more sticky in the future, for two interrelated reasons. First, differences in rates of inflation among EC member states have come down considerably, and there is therefore less need for currency realignments. Second, in view of the preparations for a later monetary union in the Community, some member countries are now resisting exchange rate changes. In particular, the French government strongly opposes any change in the franc–deutsche mark rate, although the high balance of payments surplus that Germany is again experiencing (and the resulting excessive growth of aggregate demand in Germany) would speak in favor of a revaluation of the deutsche mark. Of course, these two reasons are closely interrelated, because the fixing of exchange rates in the end leads to a convergence of rates of inflation among the countries concerned. The strong inflationary pressure that the German economy currently is experiencing (largely as a result of strong demand for German exports) is a case in point.

Should the deutsche mark really appreciate less against the ECU in the future, then the correction factor would rise less, and the effects of removing the Green Money system would be less pronounced than suggested above. Indeed, if EC governments should actually manage to live with essentially fixed exchange rates in the Community (with or without a true monetary union), then the whole Green Money business dissipates, and the formal elimination of the Green Money system would not make any practical difference.

In this case, the average rate of inflation across member states of the Community may well be higher than it could be in the absence of essentially fixed exchange rates among European currencies. In particular, countries that have traditionally had relatively low rates of inflation, such as Germany and the Netherlands, will be forced into higher inflation, and the consequent reduction of inflation in the other countries may not be sufficient to balance the average. Should this happen, then CAP prices in real terms would come under pressure from the side of overall inflation. Thus, higher inflation as a result of sticky exchange rates may in the end have an effect similar to the elimination of the Green Money system as a concomitant of the creation of an internal market.

What is the bottom line below this lengthy story about Green Money in relation to the internal market? The elimination of Green Money on the way toward the internal market could have significant effects on agricultural markets and trade of the Community, effects much more pronounced than any other agricultural consequences of the internal market. It would certainly lead to a reshuffling of agricultural production incentives among strong- and weak-currency countries in the Community. But it could also accelerate a fall in the level of real support prices in the Community. But there are a number of uncertainties. First, it is not impossible that Green Money will continue to exist after 1992, even if in some other technical form. Second, even if the Green Money system should be abandoned, it is not clear whether this would fully eliminate the inflationary tendency that is an indigenous feature of that system in its current form. Whatever the institutional arrangements, monetary developments after 1992 are likely to push down CAP prices (in real terms) somewhat faster than would otherwise happen. But it is impossible to indicate, with any degree of precision, the extent to which this will happen.

National Agricultural Policies of Member States. Although agricultural policy has become such a large part of the overall set of common policies in the European Community, it not all agricultural policies in the EC are pursued at the Community level. National agricultural policies of the member states still play an important role, and they differ widely among member states.

It is difficult to measure the significance of national agricultural policies, as opposed to the common agricultural policy, in any quantitative way. If public expenditure on agricultural policies is taken as an indicator, then national agricultural policies of member states have actually been more important than Community policies for a long time, and it appears that this is still the case, although this statistic has (deliberately?) not been published recently.[7] As an example, the development of Germany is depicted in figure 18-2. National expenditure on agricultural policy measures (including tax benefits for farmers) at the federal, state, and local levels has grown significantly over the past thirty years, and it has continued to do so even under the CAP. Indeed, in recent years (between 1985 and 1988) the growth of German national expenditure has actually accelerated.[8] Of course, Community expenditure in Germany has grown more rapidly from its zero base in 1955. In 1988, however, national German expenditure still accounted for two-thirds of total public expenditure on agricultural policy in Germany.[9] Incidentally, as is also shown in figure 18-2, total public expenditure on agricultural policy in Germany has

FIGURE 18–2

PUBLIC EXPENDITURE ON AGRICULTURAL POLICY IN WEST GERMANY,
1955–1988
(billions of deutsche marks)

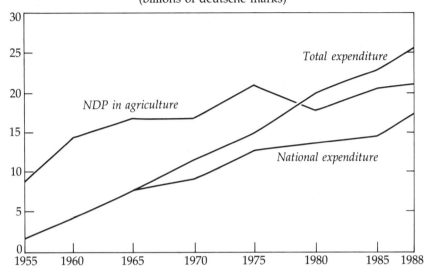

SOURCE: Schmitt and Tangermann (1988).

been higher than total net domestic product for some time (that is,
sectoral income) originating in German agriculture.[10]

One has to remember that a considerable part of the agricultural
policy measures pursued by member countries, and hence a significant part of the national expenditures involved, is related to the
implementation of Community policies at the member state level.
This is particularly true for those policy measures in which the legal
implementation of the CAP takes the form of directives (which set a
framework for national legislation and policy) rather than regulations
(which are directly applicable and binding in the member states). For
example, so-called structural policies (directed toward improving the
farm-size structure, regional development, and so on) are implemented in the form of directives. In these cases, national member
states have to implement their own legislation, within the constraints
defined by the Community directive, and the budget expenditure
involved in these policies is usually shared among the Community
and the member states. This cofinancing by the Community has a
double purpose. It is supposed to result in a fairer sharing of the
financial burden of these policies, but it is also expected to provide
incentives for member states to stick to the Community rules for

427

designing and implementing the respective policy measures. In contrast, CAP market and price support policies are pursued on the basis of regulations—that is, at the Community level—with all budget expenditure borne by the Community.

It is not easy to say whether policy measures implemented in these areas are national policies or Community policies. On the one hand, the Community directive defines the objectives of the policy concerned and the nature of the instruments to be used, and there is a financial contribution by the Community. In that sense, one can speak of Community policies. On the other hand, the member countries have a fairly wide say in the design of the actual measures. Member state governments are often quite vocal in this regard, and hence the policies and their results can differ widely among the member countries. For example, the CAP program for set-aside, introduced in 1988, was not greeted equally by all member countries, and some member countries implemented in a way that was not attractive for their farmers, who accordingly seldom used by them.

Surprisingly, however, there is scope for national differentiation even within some CAP measures that are in principle pursued by the Community. For example, the details of the rules for intervention buying can differ among member countries,[11] although price support—and intervention buying as its main instrument—is the central element of supranational Community policies for agriculture. The price equivalents of such differences in intervention rules for cereals, for instance, have in some cases been as large as 5 percent of the intervention price.[12] There is no doubt that differences as large as that can have an influence on the allocation of production and on trade among member countries.[13]

In addition, many agricultural policy measures are still pursued, and financed, by member states in their own right. Examples of such policies are social policies for farmers (old age pension schemes, health and accident insurance), tax concessions for agriculture, measures to improve the structure of marketing, financial support for research and extension in agriculture, disaster payments, measures to improve infrastructure in rural areas, and environmental policies (such as restrictions on the intensity of fertilizer use). In these policy areas there is still relatively wide room for maneuvering through the use of national policies, although member countries are supposed to consider the constraints on the nature and extent of national measures defined by the general Community rules on national aids, as set out in Articles 92 to 94 of the Treaty of Rome.

Some policies are also set at the Community level, but with a deliberate differentiation among member countries. The outstanding measures in this category are production quotas, as they exist for sugar and milk. These production quotas are allocated to individual member countries (and within member countries to processing plants and farmers), and they cannot be transferred among member countries. It is a matter of definition whether these measures should be called national policies. After all, they are determined at the level of the Community, and in that sense they are common rather than national policies. Undoubtedly these measures affect competition among member countries significantly, and in that sense they have much in common with national policies.

The point to be made about all these policies, in the context of assessing the implications of the internal market for Community agriculture, is that, for the time being, no initiative has been taken to change anything in this area before 1993 (or, for that matter, even after the creation of the internal market). None of the 279 directives included in the work program for 1992 would affect the national agricultural policies, and the EC Council of agriculture ministers does not appear to have the intention to do anything significant in this area. For example, there is no plan to reduce the flexibility that national governments have when it comes to designing structural policy measures within the framework set by Community directives; there is no talk about shifting responsibility for social policies in agriculture to the Community level; there is no sign of harmonizing the systems of income taxation in agriculture among member countries (or, at least, to harmonize the extent to which member countries grant tax benefits to their farmers); and there is no plan to make sugar and milk quotas freely transferable among farmers in different member countries.

This is certainly a potentially serious shortcoming of the Community's efforts to create a truly internal market in agriculture. National agricultural policies of the member countries can have significant effects on the allocation of resources in agriculture, and they can strongly affect competition among farmers in the different member countries. If the process of creating an internal market is supposed to result in more intensive and less restricted competition between producers in different parts of the Community, in order to make better use of productive resources in Europe, then all government measures that interfere with the free allocation of production (and consumption) among member countries should be reconsidered in this process.

Even from the point of view of a better allocation of resources in the Community, it is not necessarily true that all of the national policies mentioned here are really candidates for harmonization or elimination in the process of creating a truly internal market. On closer inspection, it turns out that the broad set of these national policies includes rather different categories of measures.

A first category of national measures deals with external effects, for example, in relation to the environment. Farmers in individual member countries tend to feel that such measures, if they make life more difficult in their home country, distort competition and that they should, therefore, be harmonized. For example, German farmers complain about German legislation that requires odorous emissions from farm buildings (such as hog barns) to remain below a given limit, or about German legislation that imposes limits on the amount of fertilizer that can be applied to farmland in certain sensitive areas (water basins)—on the grounds that legislation in other member countries is less restrictive and that therefore their competitors in the other member countries have an unfair advantage. Farmers in other member countries have similar concerns regarding other measures that are more restrictive in their home countries. Consequently, there are calls for harmonizing such measures, in order to allow for fair competition. Alternatively, it is argued, farmers in countries with more restrictive regulations should be compensated financially by their governments. In public debates, farmers' representatives often argue that they are not afraid of more intensive competition in the internal market—if only the playing field is level in the sense of conditions at home being no more restrictive than those in other member countries (although it is never argued that farmers in other member countries should also receive the same national subsidies that the government pays the farmers at home).

That farmers should argue in this way is not surprising, but there is no reason to harmonize legislation that deals with the external effects of the production process as long as these external effects do not cross borders. If German society is more concerned about ground-water quality than, say, French society, then it is fully acceptable that Germany imposes more rigid restrictions on fertilizer use than is the case in France. Either German farmers are sufficiently competitive to honor these restrictions and still produce profitably, or else production shifts to France. In both cases, groundwater pollution in Germany is reduced, which is exactly what German society wants. The fact that groundwater pollution in France possibly increases, because of agricultural production being reallocated from Germany to France, is no reason to provide protection for German farmers. It may be a reason for the French government to consider the establishment of more restrictive environmental rules in France as well. If this is not done in France, however, it probably reflects the fact that the French are less concerned about groundwater quality (or that for technical reasons groundwater pollution is less of a problem in France).

In other words, national legislation that specifies requirements for production processes is part of the overall economic and social environment of the country concerned. Cost differences that result from such national legislation cannot be said to distort competition. On the contrary, such cost differences reflect comparative advantages, and they should affect the allocation of production among countries, rather than being compensated through forced harmonization or national government subsidies. The need to harmonize such policies internationally arises only where external effects cross borders.[14] For example, if fertilizer applied by French farmers pollutes groundwater being used in Germany, then there is reason to develop consistent rules in France *and* Germany. Such cases of intercountry external effects are not common in agriculture.

A second category of national agricultural policies contains measures that transfer income from national budgets to farmers but that may have only limited effects on the allocation of agricultural production among member countries. Thus, one could argue that these policies do not noticeably distort competition and that therefore there is no need to harmonize these measures. For example, disaster payments that are unpredictably made in only rare cases of extreme hardship can be assumed to be such production-neutral measures. The real problem is that this category of national policies is difficult to define and there is no clearcut borderline between these policies and other measures that clearly affect the allocation of production and that distort competition.

The issues that the Community would have to deal with, if it were to do something about national agricultural policies in the preparation of the internal market, are the same issues that the contracting parties of the GATT have to consider in the agricultural negotiations of the Uruguay Round when it comes to defining decoupled policies in the context of deciding on policy coverage for an aggregate measurement of support. Few, if any, forms of government support to agriculture are 100 percent production-neutral. Hence, a subjective distinction has to be made between policies with negligible production effects and other policies that have a more pronounced effect on agricultural production. The dividing line will be drawn where it appears convenient for the purpose at hand, and political convenience will be at least as important as economic considerations.

One could argue that the Community has already decided on where a convenient dividing line should be drawn between production-neutral measures and policies that have the potential of distorting competition in agriculture. After all, the European Community has decided to pursue some agricultural policies at the Community level (and these are assumed to be the policies that could otherwise have distorted competition among member countries), whereas other policies have been left in the hands of member countries (because their production effects are presumably negligible). For example, agricultural price support is a Community policy (because national price policies could heavily interfere with the free allocation of agricultural production across member countries), whereas social policy for farmers is left to national governments (because its effects on agricultural trade among member countries are so small that there is no reason to bother about harmonization or even internationalization of this type of policy). In view of the given sharing of responsibilities for agricultural policies among the Community and the member states, one could argue that the European Community has solved the question of which policies are production-neutral and which are not, and hence there is no need to reconsider this complex set of issues in relation to the internal market.

This argument is not fully convincing. The Community itself is not really sure about the appropriateness of the current allocation of agricultural policy responsibilities. Under current conditions, social policy for farmers is clearly a matter of national responsibility. But no one seems to know how far member countries can go in this policy domain. The EC Commission has recently begun to reconsider the scope that should be given to member countries for pursuing social policies in agriculture. As a first practical step, the commission has warned the German government that a further increase in its financial contributions to the social security schemes for German farmers might violate Germany's obligations in the Community (Breuer 1986). The commission may well be right in assuming that these contributions provide German farmers with a noticeable competitive advantage over farmers in other member countries. It is not clear, however, why this would not already have been the case in the past. After all, the German federal government has made massive financial contributions to agricultural social security for a long time. For example, in 1988 government subsidies for the social security scheme for farmers in Germany were DM 4.8 billion, which is equivalent to 28 percent of total net value added in German agriculture (Bundesregierung 1989). German farmers pay only about one-quarter of the contributions that industrial workers in Germany have to pay to receive equivalent social security benefits (Wissenschaftlicher Beirat 1979). It would be surprising if such massive national government subsidies to agriculture did not distort competition among member countries.

Moreover, the argument that the Community has already solved the question as to which agricultural policies need to be harmonized or integrated is not convincing, because the same argument could have been advanced in relation to all other sectors—so that there would have been no need at all to change anything in order to create free trade in the Community. The free movement of people, goods, services, and capital among member countries has already been stipulated in the Treaty of Rome, and one could have argued that what the Community had reached by the mid-1980s was what an internal market should look like. But still the Community has decided to go much further than that. Hence, there is no reason to argue that in agricultural policy matters the Community has already done everything to allow a free play of the forces of competition among member countries. It may well be necessary to reconsider the allocation of agricultural policy responsibilities between member states and the Community, and the occasion of the internal market process may provide a good opportunity for doing this.

This opportunity should also certainly be used to reform the category of measures wherein Community agricultural policies deliberately restrict competition among member countries. In particular, production quotas that are not transferable among member countries (as in the cases of sugar and milk) are difficult to reconcile with the concept of more intensive competition in the internal market. Technical progress and changes in the economic and social environment constantly comparative advantages, and agricultural production should be allowed to respond to such shifts.

In the absence of production quotas, this can happen. As figure 18-3 shows, before the introduction of milk quotas (in 1984) the growth of milk production differed considerably among the individual member countries. Between 1973 and 1983, milk production in the Netherlands grew by more than 40 percent, whereas French milk production went down slightly. Hence, the allocation of milk production in the Community changed continually before the introduction of quotas. With the establishment of quotas, however, which are not transferable across the borders of member countries,[15] the Community's structure of milk production is now frozen, and productivity gains that could be made by moving milk production to areas where competitive advantages have improved will be forgone. Such frozen structures of production across member countries are certainly not in line with the basic philosophy of the internal market.

Why, in any case, should policy makers establish regulations that prevent farmers who would like to do so from selling their quotas to other farmers? Some people seem to think that the original regional

FIGURE 18–3

GROWTH OF MILK PRODUCTION IN EC MEMBER COUNTRIES, 1973–1983

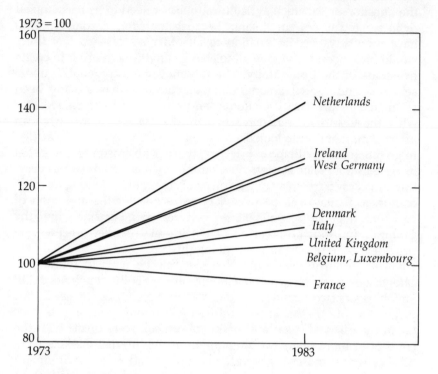

SOURCE: Author.

distribution of production, particularly of milk, is something worth protecting. "Farmers in certain regions have no alternative to milk production, and therefore they need to maintain their production rights" would be a typical argument advanced by policy makers who are not willing to make quotas transferable. Why these policy makers should be able to make better judgments than the farmer who is willing to sell his quota rights (because he obviously has a more attractive alternative to milk production) is one of the many mysteries of agricultural policy. In any case, there is so far no plan to make quotas transferable across borders among member countries in the process of creating the internal market.

The Community is not only far from eliminating all national agricultural policies, but there are actually proposals for introducing additional national measures. In particular, the EC Commission has proposed that when MCAs are eliminated, member countries that find it necessary should be allowed to grant national compensation to their farmers if their currencies should be revalued. Of course, these national aids should be production-neutral. As argued above, however, there is probably nothing like a 100 percent production-neutral subsidy, and hence the Commission proposal amounts to suggesting that member countries should have the right, under certain conditions, to interfere with the free competition of farmers across borders. From a slightly different perspective, such proposals amount to substituting domestic policies in individual countries for measures that are effective at the borders among the member states.

Consequently, the Community's concept of an internal market appears to be rather a superficial one, at least in agriculture. Efforts are made to eliminate visible border measures and to open restrictions to trade among member countries. For example, enormous energies are invested in making sure that countries do not use food standards in a way that would interfere with the free marketing of products across borders. Similarly, other regulations that impose publicly noticeable constraints on the free exchange of food and agricultural products across borders are being revised in the work program for 1992. Even so, the less visible, but at least as distorting, policy measures that are pursued domestically by member states, either in national responsibility or on behalf of the Community, are not being reconsidered in the process of completing the internal market. In some cases, the national measures used domestically may be substituted for border measures. In other words, it does not appear that free and unrestricted international competition in agriculture is really the objective of the internal market. Rather, it is to eliminate border controls—the most visible indication of a still divided Europe. As far as agriculture is concerned, the current plans for 1992 are a far cry from removing all distortions among member states. A truly free internal EC market in agriculture, without government influence on competition among the farmers of Europe, is not at all in sight.

The Future of CAP Reform

In several respects, the creation of the internal market is closely tied to CAP reform. The most direct link is through the possible elimination of the Green Money system when border controls are removed. As argued above, the related change in the monetary basis of CAP price fixing could have a significant impact on the future development of agricultural prices in the Community. Significant changes could also take place if the internal market were taken seriously enough and more rigid limits are imposed on national agricultural policies of the member states. This is not yet being considered, however.

A less direct link between the internal market and CAP reform can be seen in the competition between agricultural policy and other Community policies for budget expenditure. This link was explicitly established at the 1988 Brussels summmit when the decision was made to expand the spending power of the Community budget, primarily to buffer the regional and social consequences of increased competition in the internal market.

This decision was part of a larger package of agreements among heads of state that contained, in particular, a number of provisions for CAP reform. The summit decisions on CAP reform were thought to be appropriate not only in their own right (because the CAP was in need of an overhaul anyhow), but also in order to make sure that the CAP did not use up all the additional money made available to the Community for structural policies outside agriculture.

Another, less direct, relationship exists by virtue of the overall political climate in the Community. The process of creating the internal market has significantly affected the political dynamics in the Community, and this has both diverted attention from CAP matters and supported the feeling that agricultural issues must not be allowed to get in the way of more important developments in the Community.

In other words, one could get the impression that the process of creating the internal market has influenced the CAP positively in the sense of making its reform more likely. That the CAP is on a new track or that it remain there is by no means certain. What is clear, however is that developments external to both the CAP and the Community are likely to have a hand in the future of CAP reform.

Agricultural Developments in the Community

The reform of the CAP, as initiated in 1984 and more firmly established in 1988, is a mixed bag of old and new elements, of more and less promising approaches (for details, see Tangermann 1989a). The central element in the 1984 CAP reform package (apart from the rather unconvincing changes to the green money system) was the introduction of production quotas for milk. Such quotas may appear to be a drastic reform measure since they obviously depart from earlier policies of unlimited price support. But quotas are not actually a policy reform. They constitute a method of reducing some undesirable consequences of earlier policies without having to reform the policies as such.

The immediate purpose of production quotas is to allow the continuation, if not intensification, of high price support through the suppression of (a part of) the market surplus and, hence, through the reduction of budget spending on surplus disposal. Production quotas are a method of substituting transfers from consumers to farmers through higher support prices for transfers from taxpayers to farmers through public budget expenditures. In this sense, production quotas simply disguise the underlying problem. Production quotas do nothing to make domestic agriculture more internationally competitive and therefore less dependent on government support. On the contrary, quotas limit the adjustment of production to changing economic and technical conditions and thereby reduce the efficiency of resource use. Typically, farmers demand higher support prices under a quota system, and such higher prices are often granted by policy makers, because there is no longer the danger of increasing surpluses and budget exposure. This is exactly what has happened in the Community's milk market policy since 1984.

Most EC agricultural policy makers and farmers are happy with higher milk prices, and they consider the quota system to be a marked success. Minor technical problems (such as the need, resulting from a decision of the European Court, to allocate additional quotas to certain farmers) have caused a few concerns. By and large, however, the milk quota system is regarded as a successful element of CAP reform, and it will remain a permanent feature of the CAP, along with production quotas for sugar.

The 1988 reform package contains another element that points in a similar direction. The set-aside—introduced in 1988 as a voluntary and paid idling of land—is another means of reducing the surpluses (particularly of cereals) without additional price cuts. The set-aside also reduces the efficiency and international competitiveness of the EC farming industry, by increasing land prices and preventing the movement of land from less to more efficient farmers.[16] Hence, it leads to more rather than less government intervention in agriculture. The only reason that it may be a less durable policy than production quotas is that the paid set-aside requires budgetary expenditures (possibly even more than what is saved on surplus disposal), and so any attempt to expand this measure may eventually meet with some resistance. The real danger, however, is that set-asides as currently implemented in the CAP will lead to the adoption of production quotas for crops (see Tangermann 1989a). In other words, both the milk quotas established in 1984 and the set-aside introduced in 1988 cannot be considered measures of CAP reform. They relieve some of the symptoms, but they do not cure the underlying problems.

The 1988 reform package also contained so-called stabilizer mechanisms that are supposed to cut support prices automatically whenever production in the Community exceeds a predetermined quantity. This is quite the opposite approach of that reflected in production quotas and set-asides. It can increase to market orientation in European agriculture by establishing a link between market developments and prices and by bringing CAP prices closer to those on world markets. It has the potential of gradually reducing the degree of government interference in agricultural markets in the Community and thus of making EC agriculture more internationally competitive.

This is not to say that the new CAP stabilizers are an ideal policy. Their actual design (in terms of the volume of production at which prices are cut and the magnitude of the price cuts envisaged) lacks any economic justification. It is not clear why their design should differ so much among commodities (particularly among cereals and oilseeds); and they seem to create too many unnecessary technical complications (for example, in the extra coresponsibility levy applicable to cereals if the threshold quantity is exceeded). Nonetheless, the stabilizers are a step in the right direction since they have the potential to reduce the level of price support in the CAP.

The important issue is whether this potential will actually be used by the Council of Ministers. Apart from the fact that stabilizer price cuts are determined in nominal ECUs and that they are therefore subject to monetary developments, including manipulations of the green money system, their principal shortcoming is that the Council of Ministers will still be able to interfere with price developments. The reason is that the prices from which cuts have to be made, in accordance with the stabilizer provisions, are those valid for the current year. Hence, in principle, the council could increase prices before they are cut according to the stabilizers and thereby counteract the intended effects of the stabilizers on future price developments.

The fear that this could happen is justified by history. The stabilizers are in reality not a new provision of the CAP. As early as 1981 the council established what at that time was called guarantee thresholds. These thresholds were, like the more recent stabilizers, supposed to lead to price cuts if EC production exceeded given quantities. Experience with these precursors of the stabilizers was rather depressing. The guarantee threshold for milk finally was instrumental in establishing production quotas (on the pretext that the price cuts otherwise required under the guarantee threshold mechanism were politically not feasible). The guarantee threshold for cereals was overruled when the German minister of agriculture in 1985 blocked a council decision on the EC Commission proposal to cut cereal support prices by 1.8 percent, in the first and only case in which a German government has dared, in spite of the determined pro-European attitude of the Federal Republic, to revert to the Luxembourg compromise (see Tangermann 1989b). There is basically no guarantee that the Council of Ministers will in the future stick to the self-imposed price discipline of the stabilizers than it did to that of the guarantee thresholds.

How the stabilizers will fare will depend on the general mood concerning CAP reform. The stabilizers have so far passed only their first test in the CAP price decisions for the 1989–1990 crop year (adopted in April 1989). This test was indeed successful in the sense that there was no debate whatsoever in the council as to whether the stabilizer provisions should be overruled. Prices were actually cut in accordance with the stabilizer mechanisms, and in some cases the council even adopted additional implicit reductions of price support through the weakening of provisions for intervention buying. At that time, the council was still reform-minded, under the influence of earlier difficulties with financing the CAP and confirming the new schemes being applied.

The situation already appears to have changed, however. The budget savings (relative to appropriations) in 1989, mainly the result of high world market prices for agricultural products, have created a demand for more generous agricultural policies. Some farmers' groups and national agricultural policy makers are furious that in this situation the commission has "dared" to estimate the 1989 cereals crop at 160.5 million tons, which is just enough above the 160 million tons maximum to trigger price cuts in the coming year.

Whether the stabilizer mechanisms will work will depend on budget developments in the Community. The willingness to reform the CAP in the past has greatly depended on the budget situation in the Community, and there is no reason to believe this situation will change—although one other element in the 1988 reform package may turn out to be the decisive factor in this regard.

The 1988 Brussels summit has adopted a budget guideline for Community spending on agricultural market and price support (that is, for what is called the Guarantee section of the Fonds Européen d'Orientation et de Garantie Agricole, FEOGA). According to this guideline, FEOGA Guarantee expenditure should not grow from a given basis in 1988 by more than 74 percent of the growth rate of the Community's GNP. This guideline would require agricultural expenditure to deviate significantly from past developments. From 1976 to 1985, for example, the growth of FEOGA Guarantee spending was 151 percent of the growth of GNP in the Community.[17] Thus, the CAP will have to cope with a completely different financial future.

Here, too, the lessons from the past are not encouraging. The idea of imposing financial constraints on the CAP is not new. In 1984, the principle of budget discipline was established to ensure that CAP expenditure would not grow by more than the own resources (that is, potential budget income) of the Community. This principle was supposedly strengthened by a provision requiring ministers of finance to be involved when agriculture ministers were about to take decisions that threatened to violate budget discipline. Despite all these provisions, the Community still came close to a financial collapse in the following years.

The new 1988 budget guideline for CAP spending may be more effective than the old budget discipline, because it is now coupled (according to a new interinstitutional agreement) with the provision that not only the Council of Finance Ministers, but also the European Parliament has to be involved, in a rather complex process, if there is a threat of excess spending. Furthermore, the commission now has more responsibilities and powers in the budget process. But these more rigid provisions are not entirely reassuring, given that the Community has in the past violated even more fundamental budget principles. Between 1984 and 1987, the Community continuously spend more than its income, and only through a number of rather questionable trick solutions was it possible to conform, on the face of it, to the legal requirement that the Community must not overspend.

The most important threat to the new agricultural budget guideline probably is the fact that the 1988 Brussels summit also decided on a significant increase in the Community's own resources and thereby lifted the ceiling for the EC budget. This increase in the amount of money available to the Community went largely unnoticed by the general public, because of the technical complexities involved in determining the overall budget ceiling and individual member countries' financial contributions, and because the overall increase in the own resources was (deliberately?) coupled with a new mechanism for fixing the budget ceiling and member countries' contributions.[18] This new mechanism was advertised to be fairer than the old system, but the fact that it also provides much more money to the Community was not explained. Taken together with the 1986 lifting of the budget ceiling, the Community can now command roughly 40 percent more money than would have been the case had the financial system applied up to 1985 not been changed.[19]

The budget guideline for the CAP is supposed to ensure that this additional money is not spent on agriculture, and for some member countries (above all the United Kingdom) the adoption of the agricultural budget guideline and of the other elements of CAP reform was a condition for accepting the rise in the Community budget. These member countries may well try to make sure that the constraints on CAP spending are more effective than in the past. The new financial provisions have not yet been tested and so it remains to be seen how they will work if they are challenged.

Developments External to the CAP. The most important external factor for the development of the CAP—external to the CAP and to the Community—is the ongoing Uruguay Round of GATT negotiations. Agriculture plays an important role in these negotiations, and the CAP is obviously one of the main targets being eyed by agricultural exporters such as the United States and the countries of the Cairns Group.

Opinions on how the Community has behaved and is behaving in the agricultural negotiations of the Uruguay Round differ widely. In the eyes of free traders, the Community has been an obstacle to progress, because EC negotiators have time and again emphasized that the Community is not prepared to sacrifice the CAP on the altar of the GATT negotiations. Even worse, the Community wants to use the occasion of the Uruguay Round negotiations to increase the protection for its currently low- or zero-taxed imports of cereal substitutes, oilseeds, and protein feeds (the infamous EC proposal for rebalancing).

Others point at the difference between the Community's negotiating position in the Uruguay Round and its behavior in earlier GATT rounds. This time, EC negotiators have been much more forthcoming than usual. In its initial proposal for the agricultural negotiations of the Uruguay Round, the EC has suggested negotiations on "a significant, concerted reduction in support" and on "GATT bindings . . . of the maximum levels of support, protection and export compensation" (GATT document MTN,GNG/NG5/W/20, October 26, 1987). EC negotiators have actively and constructively participated in the negotiations and have made practical proposals for limiting and reducing support for agriculture. Furthermore, in the agreement adopted at the midterm review (in April 1989) the Community has, for the first time in the history of the CAP, accepted internationally agreed constraints on the level of its domestic agricultural support prices.

Whichever view one wants to adopt, there is no doubt that the Uruguay Round will be a decisive factor for the future of the CAP. Even if the Community should avert requests for major changes in GATT rules for agriculture and significant concessions regarding domestic and trade policies in agriculture, such as those put forward by the United States, the GATT negotiations will still have an impact on the way in which the CAP is pursued for the remainder of this century. The reason is that the Community itself has already advanced proposals that, if they were to form part of the eventual package of GATT agreements, would alter the nature of the CAP.

One of the central elements of the Community's approach to the agricultural negotiations of the Uruguay Round is its willingness to bind the level of support granted to agriculture. Indeed, the possibility of such bindings is extensively discussed in the Uruguay Round negotiations, under the title of "aggregate measurement of support." The Community was not the first party to suggest this approach for the Uruguay Round. The plurilateral interest in the measurement of aggregate levels of support in agriculture essentially originated in the OECD (1987a) and its work on national agricultural policies and agricultural trade. In the Uruguay Round negotiations, the United States was the first to suggest the use of an AMS. Early in the negotiations, the Community accepted the possibility of AMS commitments, and it presented its own suggestions as to how this approach could be put into practice.

The Community's view is that the AMS approach should be used to bind agricultural support as measured against a fixed external reference price. Thus, changes in world market prices and exchange rates would not require adjustments of domestic support prices (or other support policies). Hence, what would be bound, according to the Community's proposal, is the level of domestic support prices. The Community's negotiators have named this concept the "support measurement unit" (SMU). To some extent, the SMU is similar to the *montant de soutien* approach suggested by the Community during the Kennedy Round, but not accepted by the United States at the time. In that sense, one could argue that in the Uruguay Round the United States and the Community are about to meet somewhere in the middle. More important is the fact that something like binding levels of support along such lines are obviously not strange to the philosophy of the Community, since the European Community made similar proposals twenty years ago.

Most other parties in the Uruguay Round negotiations on agriculture do not appear to be happy with the Community's approach of binding support against fixed external reference prices, on the grounds that the resulting domestic agricultural markets would not be sufficiently responsive to developments in international trade. Actually, the world's agricultural system would function much better if domestic markets in all countries were more closely linked to international markets. Hence, much can be said for the U.S. proposal of not only binding domestic support for agriculture against actual world market prices, but also converting all existing nontariff border measures into bound tariffs. Domestic prices everywhere would then move up and down with world market prices, and this would greatly improve the stability and transparency of the international market system in agriculture.

Moreover, the point is made by the Community's negotiating partners that by suggesting the SMU concept and, probably, relatively low rates of reducing the level of support over time, the Community is merely trying to sell internationally its domestic decisions concerning price cuts under the stabilizer mechanisms introduced into the CAP in 1988.[20] According to this view, the Community is offering something to which it is already committed, while it expects other countries to make new concessions.

It is probably true that EC negotiators hope to get away with a GATT agreement that does not require the Community to do much more, in terms of reducing support to EC agriculture, than what is already envisaged internally. This does not mean that it is pointless to consider an agreement along such lines. Even if the only commitment to which the Community could be pushed was that the price cuts envisaged in the CAP stabilizer mechanisms would be bound in a multilateral agreement, this would constitute valuable progress on two fronts.

First, the legal character of the CAP would change in terms of international commitments. For the time being, the Community is free to set its domestic support prices where it wants, since the variable levies it uses escape any effective GATT discipline (because they belong to the grey area measures that are not explicitly regulated in the GATT). Hence, the variable levies allow the Community to defend any level of price support under the CAP. The only GATT discipline that could constrain the level of price support in the Community (as in any other contracting party of the GATT) is the rule that subsidized exports connected with high domestic price support must not exceed the famous equitable share of the world market. Since this GATT rule has proven basically ineffective, however, it does not really constrain the CAP.

If the Community should accept the binding of its domestic level of price support (and other domestic support policies), this would lend a completely new legal quality, in international terms, to the CAP. One of the principal benefits for other countries would be that from then on the CAP would be internationally negotiable. Therefore, the Community's trading partners could later sit down with EC negotiators and talk about further reductions of CAP support. Even if the commitments accepted by the Community did not bring the level of CAP price support down very much in the first round, the chances of exerting an effective permanent pressure on the CAP in later negotiations would be greatly enhanced.

At the same time, bindings of the level of agricultural price support in the European Community would change the domestic nature of the CAP. After all, such bindings would seriously interfere with one of the primary privileges and functions of the Council of Ministers of Agriculture—namely, the setting of support prices in the annual price reviews.

Second, even if the Community bound only the prospective effects of its existing stabilizer mechanisms, this would not necessarily produce immediate benefits for the Community's trading partners. After all, as argued in the preceding section, it is not certain that the stabilizers will really stick. Farmers in the European Community, who have originally been rather impressed by the overall momentum for CAP reform, are becoming angry about the stabilizers, and they may try to oppose the continuation of this policy. If EC agricultural policy makers could then point to the fact that the stabilizers are bound internationally and that, therefore, they cannot be weakened, this might help them to avert political pressure to soften the CAP reform.

Finally, as in all negotiations, it is always worthwhile to try pushing the negotiating partner a little beyond the initial negotiating position. Thus it may not be impossible to convince the Community to consider somewhat deeper cuts in support rates, somewhat more flexibility with regard to external reference prices for measuring the level of support, a gradual shift from its current variable levies toward tariffs, more effective limitations on its export subsidization, and more operationally effective GATT rules for agriculture. Even with modest steps in these directions, the CAP could not continue as it stands now, and some of these changes might affect the future of the CAP far more than any of the recent reforms. Such benefits may even be worth considering in negotiations about the Community's despised proposal for rebalancing.

For the Community's trading partners, the trick is to find out how far the EC Commission can be pressed before it completely loses the confidence of the member countries. For the time being, it appears to be deliberately trying to use the GATT negotiations as a lever to push the member countries in the direction of a more rational CAP. In order to do so, the commission occasionally has to speak and balance in two different ways. This is a delicate task, and it has to be careful not to raise too much opposition too soon among the member countries. Any support that the commission can receive in this process would be in the interest of a successful round of negotiations.

Among the other external factors that may influence the future of the CAP is the possible enlargement(s) of the Community before the end of the century. Some of the countries that are, or might be, candidates for accession—for example, Austria, Norway(?), Sweden(?), and Turkey(?)—have more protectionist agricultural policies than the CAP. Hence, such countries, if they were to become members of the Community, might try to influence the CAP according to their agricultural policy tastes and thereby exert an upward pressure on the level of agricultural protection in the Community.

At the same time, any further enlargement of the Community would almost automatically strengthen the role of the commission in relation to the member countries. Decision procedures in the council and the Parliament become more and more difficult as the number of member countries grows, and this adds to the (relative) weight of the central institution, namely, the EC Commission. Moreover, the technical complexity of Community matters appears to increase exponentially with the size of the Community. This, too, strengthens the role of the central administrative unit, which in many cases is the only institution with access to all the relevant bits of information. A growing weight of the Community in CAP decision making could mean that more rationality and consistency will be brought to bear on the Community's agricultural policies. It could also mean that EC representatives in international negotiations will have more flexibility and be better able to commit to the Community to agreements reached in the negotiations.

If all these external factors are taken together, they point in the direction of a continuation, if not modest acceleration of CAP reform. It will be interesting to see how the balance between internal and external factors finally affect the future of the CAP.

Possible Impact of Reforms in Eastern Europe

EC agricultural policy is also bound to be affected by the developments in Eastern Europe. Although structure and organization of agriculture differs widely among the Eastern Europeans countries, ranging from small family farms in Poland to socialized state enterprises in East Germany, one common feature is widespread inefficiency. This prevents Eastern European agriculture from producing at its technical yield potential. The reasons behind this inefficiency differ from country to country, but the political and economic reforms now being pursued in Eastern Europe have the potential of releasing a significant production capacity. If agriculture in Eastern Europe were to become as productive as agriculture now is in Western

445

Europe, output would increase significantly. Such reform would require many ingredients—and much time.

Furthermore, a switch from central planning to decision making on individual farms is going to cause much turmoil and upset existing delivery relations, although it will soon correct the inadequate allocation of production to individual regions and farms. A return to financial responsibility of individual farms and to free wage and income formation will improve the incentive structure. Both changes can, if the political will is there, be made relatively rapidly, and they will certainly improve efficiency.

Without sufficient supplies of inputs and investment goods, however, such improvements will remain limited. As long as the foreign exchange situation of some Eastern European countries remains precarious, they will find it difficult to make more inputs and investment goods available. As long as their efficiency is not high enough, capital formation on farms will remain limited and scarce savings from the rest of the economy would have to be made available for agriculture (either through financial markets or in the form of government subsidies). The process of reducing excessive labor input in agriculture will have to be kept slow in order to prevent massive unemployment. Most difficult, the process of returning from socialized farms to private holdings will be slow, not least because people have become used to secure wage incomes and the social safety nets which their farms provided.

Taken together this means that productivity in Eastern European agriculture is likely to improve and that the growth of production will accelerate in the years to come, but not in big jumps. After some time, however, Eastern Europe may again be willing and able to play the role of a strong agricultural producer, which it played so successfully before socialism and a totalitarian political system put a brake on its development.

Food consumption, on the other hand, is relatively high in most Eastern European countries, compared with their level of economic development. As far as economic factors are concerned, this has mainly two causes. First, food prices are heavily subsidized. Second, the nonavailability of other consumer goods has distorted consumption patterns toward higher consumption of food. Both factors will change significantly in the years to come. Governments will have to reduce their budget deficits, and they will have to cut subsidies. The opening up of markets will make a wider choice of consumer goods available, and consumption may turn away from overemphasis on food.

As far as agricultural trade is concerned, such changes in production and consumption of agricultural products in Eastern European countries would mean that their imports of many basic agricultural products would tend to go down and their exports of these products to expand. Such changes in the agricultural trade balance of the Eastern European countries will not happen rapidly. But they may accelerate significantly during the 1990s. If this scenario is correct, many farmers in Western Europe and in other temperate-zone countries may find that their market prospects will deteriorate as a consequence of reforms in Eastern Europe. Farmers in tropical countries and farmers producing specialty products, on the other hand, as well as food-processing companies, may face improving market prospects.

Western countries will and should feel obliged to support the reform process in Eastern Europe in whatever way they possibly can. As far as economic support is concerned, an important contribution is to improve access to western markets for exports from Eastern European countries. Such improved market access should include agricultural products. For the time being, the international comparative advantage of agriculture in Eastern European countries is still limited to a small set of products. But this is no reason not to open market access in Western Europe and elsewhere. In the future, there is likely to be a wider array of products and a larger export potential for which Western countries could and should offer attractive markets.

In addition to such changes in the agricultural market situation, the ongoing reforms in Eastern Europe may have more general consequences for agriculture and agricultural policy in Western Europe, particularly in the European Community. For one thing, Eastern Europe will, to some extent, divert attention from traditional day-to-day business. Support for and reaction to developments in Eastern Europe will bind all sorts of resources in Western countries—political, economic, financial, and intellectual resources. These resources will not be available for other activities.

For example, the European Community will be faced with applications for accession. Hungary has already announced its wish to become, at some stage, a member of the European Community. For the time being, the European Community is not considering more than the possibility of an association with Eastern European countries. But such an association would require much political and economic attention and may open a whole array of completely new problems for the European Community. The process of finding solutions to these problems will compete with other activities of the Community. Moreover, support for Eastern Europe could strain the budget of the European Community rather significantly.

447

These developments could further displace the Common Agricultural Policy from the center stage of Community policies. This process has already begun as a consequence of the efforts to complete the internal market. The CAP is now less important than it used to be in the early days of the Community. With increasing attention being attributed to developments in Eastern Europe, the Community may begin to treat agriculture as no more than one among many of its activities. But that may not be a bad development.

Conclusions

In purely statistical terms, agriculture makes up no more than 3.5 percent of economic activity in the European Community. In political terms, however, the weight of agriculture is much larger in the Community. A far more than proportional share of political attention and administrative efforts is spent on agriculture, and the CAP is still by far the largest single expenditure item in the Community budget. On many occasions it is difficult to avoid the impression that the agricultural tail is waging the Community dog.

Apart from the typical overemphasis on agricultural policy in many industrialized countries, the CAP has been in a special situation for a long time, because agriculture has historically been one of the primary candidates for policy integration in the Community. This situation is changing now. One of the more positive side effects of the creation of an internal market and of other steps in the direction of a full economic and monetary union will be that the Community will take over responsibility for an increasing number of other policies. This will dilute the weight of the CAP in EC policy making. The political status of the CAP will therefore become increasingly normal in the sense of being less prominent in the overall set of Community affairs.

Whether this will lead to a more economically rational pursuit of the CAP is an open question. Less visibility of the CAP can mean that more technocratic rationality is brought to bear on it, but it can also mean that political extravagance can blossom more safely in the agricultural policy niche. As far as the more immediate consequences of the creation of the internal market are concerned, there is some hope that the process of CAP reform will be strengthened. One of the main factors working in this direction could be the elimination of the Green Money system of the CAP. Abandonment of Green Money would, among other things, remove of the automatic inflationary pressure on CAP support prices that is a built-in feature of the current system. This change alone could reduce the level of support prices by one-quarter over a ten-year period, although in practice the effect will likely be smaller.

The most effective consequences of the internal market for agriculture are not likely to come about through the harmonization of standards and other typical elements of the 1992 work program, but through the effects that the internal market may have on the way in which the CAP is pursued. It is also obvious that the Community's current concept of an internal market is a rather superficial one, at least in agriculture. National agricultural policies of the member countries still play an important role, much more important than the celebrated and reviled CAP of more than twenty-five years would suggest. These national agricultural policies probably distort competition among farmers in the member countries of the Community much more than all the measures that are supposed to be eliminated or harmonized as a result of the existing work program for 1992. But no attempt has so far made to change these national policies in the process of creating an internal market.

The Community is determined to eliminate visible border controls and similarly noticeable barriers to trade, but it has—not yet—embarked on the much more difficult and politically less remunerative process of creating the appropriate environment for undistorted competition among farmers in different member countries. It may be that the endogenous dynamics of the internal market process will one day push the Community to do something about national agricultural policies of the member countries. If this should happen, it could become by far the most important and quantitatively significant consequence of the internal market for agriculture.

The internal market, however, is only one of the many factors affecting the future of CAP reform. Other factors are the more indigenous developments of agriculture and agricultural policy. The Community has taken a number of steps to reform the CAP, but they are not really solving the underlying problems of agriculture and agricultural policy in the Community. As a result, other reform elements may turn out to be less durable than they look at the first glance.

The process of reforming the CAP must coincide with the Uruguay Round of GATT negotiations. The Community's negotiating partners are often critical of the conservative attitude of the European Community in the agricultural talks, but the Community's behavior should be assessed in historical perspective. Nor should people overlook the fact that the Community is now making substantive offers, from an internal EC point of view. It may be true that the Community is trying to get away from the Uruguay Round with selling internationally the CAP reforms on which it has already embarked domestically. But even this would not be a minor achievement, because the Community would therefore have to put its plans for CAP reform into practice and the international legal status of the CAP would change significantly.

The 1990s will be an interesting time for the Community. Some of the developments that are taking place there are as important as the original common policies were in the late 1950s and early 1960s. Agriculture will be affected by these developments, and the common agricultural policy may change noticeably in the years to come. If all goes well, agriculture in the European Community will become more market oriented, and in the agricultural sense Europe will be less of a fortress by the end of the century.

References

Breuer, J., 1986. "Das Sozialversicherungs-Beitragsentlastungsgesetz (SVBEG)." *Soziale Sicherheit in der Landwirtschaft* 4: 229–57.

Bundesregierung, Agrarbericht. 1989. Bonn.

Bureau of Agricultural Economics. 1985. *Agricultural Policies in the European Community: Their Origins, Nature and Effects on Production and Trade.* Policy Monograph 2. Canberra.

Court of Auditors. 1989. "Special Report on the Agrimonetary System, accompanied by the Replies of the Commission." *Official Journal of the European Communities* C 128.

European Economic Community. 1984. *Public Expenditure on Agriculture.* Study P. 229. Brussels. November.

Commission of the European Communities. 1980. *The Agricultural Situation in the Community—1980 Report.* Brussels, Luxembourg.

———. 1987. *The Agricultural Situation in the Community—1986 Report.* Brussels, Luxembourg.

———. 1989a. "Green Europe." *Agricultural Prices 1989/1990.* Decisions from the Council, 1. Brussels.

———. 1989b. *The Agricultural Situation in the Community—1988 Report.* Brussels, Luxembourg.

Harris, S., A. Swinbank, and G. Wilkinson. 1983. *The Food and Farm Policies of the European Community.* Chichester.

Kluge, U. 1989. Vierzig Jahre Agrarpolitik in der Bundesrepublik Deutschland. *Berichte über Landwirtschaft* 202. Sonderheft. Hamburg, Berlin.

Koester, U. 1989. "Implications for the Reform of the CAP." Paper presented at the International Conference on the Completion of the Internal Market, Kiel Institute of World Economics, June 21–23.

Koester, U., and H. Terwitte. 1988. "Durchbruch in der Agrarpolitik oder weiteres Politikversagen?" *Wirtschaftsdienst* 68(3): 130–35.

Koester, U., and S. Tangermann. 1990. "Agricultural Protectionism in the European Community." In *Agricultural Protectionism in the Industrialized World*, edited by F. Sanderson. Forthcoming.

Organization for Economic Cooperation and Development. 1987a. *National Policies and Agricultural Trade*. Paris.

———. 1987b. *National Policies and Agricultural Trade. Study on the European Economic Community*. Paris.

Ritson, C., and S. Tangermann. 1979. "The Economics and Politics of Monetary Compensatory Amounts." *European Review of Agricultural Economics* 6: 119–64.

Schinke, M. 1989. "Der Handel mit Getreide innerhalb der Europäischen Gemeinschaft." *Struktur, Entwicklung und "administrative Verzerrungen"*. Kiel.

Schmitt, G., and S. Tangermann. 1988. "Regulierte Märkte mit extremer Fehlentwicklung: Die Agrarmarktordnungen in der Bundesrepublik Deutschland und der EG." Paper presented at the 1988 annual conference of the German Economics Association (Gesellschaft für Wirtschafts- und Sozialwissenschaften—Verein für Sozialpolitik), Freiburg, October 5–7.

Tangermann, S. 1989a. "Evaluation of the Current CAP Reform Package." *World Economy* 12: 175–88.

———. 1989b. *Agricultural Policy Reform in Germany: Domestic Concerns and International Trade Negotiations*. Göttingen: Resources for the Future.

Tracy, M. 1982. *Agriculture in Western Europe. Challenge and Response 1880–1980*. 2d ed. London.

Wissenschaftlicher Beirat beim BMI. 1979. Agrarsozialpolitik—Situation und Reformvorschläge. Landwirtschaft—Angewandte Wissenschaft, Heft 233. Münster-Hiltrup.

19
Commentaries on Agriculture

A Commentary by Ralph Ichter

Fundamental philosophical differences between the United States and the European Community lie at the heart of the problems facing the GATT Uruguay Round of negotiations on agriculture. Furthermore, U.S. policy makers are under the impression that, for the European Community the Uruguay Round has taken a political back seat to the 1992 integration process and, more recently, to the formidable changes that have been taking place in Eastern Europe. Before addressing the possible outcome of the Uruguay Round of negotiations, I would like to comment on the different nature of our respective agricultural policies, which in my view are rooted in deep philosophical differences about the role of governments in supporting agriculture and regulating commodity markets.

When the common agriculture policy (CAP) was being worked out in the early 1960s, farming in the six founding member states, handicapped by antiquated structures, was, on the whole, inefficient. The European Economic Community, as it was then, depended heavily on imports for most basic food products. This formed the background against which the CAP was devised, its goals began to make the European Community self-sufficient in basic commodities, support farmers' income through high market prices, and bring stability and predictability to agriculture. The CAP worked all too well—it generated huge surpluses and unbearable budget expenditures in the early and mid-1980s, a problem we shared in common with the United States.

Something remains to be said about stability and predictability in markets and prices. The issue of the impact of wild price fluctuations on the farming industry has not been properly addressed by the proponents of the so-called zero option in the GATT negotiations. More than the level of protection, price stability and predictability are of great concern to farmers in Europe, and in the United States, too. This is the most important reason why the liberal option was politically dead on arrival, at least in the European Community.

Whereas the European Community relies heavily on double-pricing mechanisms to support market prices at a level higher than the world market, the United States has put the emphasis since the 1985 farm bill on direct payment to producers, which allows domestic U.S. prices to clear at the world market level for most commodities. One quickly realizes that these differences in our domestic agricultural policies are by no means trade-neutral.

One might ask why the European Community cannot, or will not, change its policies into a deficiency-payment kind of system, which would probably solve most of our trade conflicts and consequently bring about a happy conclusion to the agricultural negotiations in the GATT. There are several reasons for this. Some good, some not as good.

The first good reason is of a budgetary nature: when you have 10 or 12 million farmers, it is still cheaper to support market prices, rather than income, whether decoupled or not. Well, things will change. Even at today's level of support, the number of farmers is decreasing rapidly. Ten years from now, an income-support policy might make sense. There are already signs that the EC Commission and certain member states want to move into that direction.

The second reason is political: farmers in general are opposed to direct payments because they do not want to rely on governmental entitlements that might be axed in the budget process. From an economical standpoint, however, it does not make much difference whether the farmer gets a check in the mail or gets the same amount of money from the taxpayer through price supports.

The third reason is philosophical and relates to the role of governments in managing the economy. Although liberalization has been the trend for the 1992 integration process, most governments in the European Community still believe that agricultural markets ought to be regulated by government intervention. They also believe that production should be brought in line with demand through mandatory government intervention, such as production controls, rather than relying solely on price policies to bring about long-term supply and demand adjustments. When the European Community takes credit—and rightly so—for adjusting its surplus production to world demand since 1986 in dairy, oilseeds, and grain, this has been achieved through a combination of price cuts, producers' assessments, and production quotas, such as those in the dairy industry.

These are among the most important reasons why EC officials have repeatedly stated that the CAP, and, to be more specific, the dual-price mechanisms, are not negotiable. But that is no reason to say that the European Community is not engaged in significant deregulation of its agricultural policies. What we are about to see in agriculture is the start of a coordination process among the big players, much along the same lines that we are seeing in macroeconomic and monetary policies with the G-5 and G-7 processes.

The main issues at stake here are, first, price supports: both the United States and the European Community have significantly lowered supports in real terms for leading commodities in the past five years. This trend should continue, although at a slower pace. Germany, for instance, has repeatedly said that reductions of supports has reached a limit and that a pause is needed. If an agreement is reached, it will have to address the question of coordination of inventory management policies, such as set-aside and stockpiling.

Second is the question of export subsidies. The United States and the Cairns Group (comprising Canada, Australia, Argentina, and others) want to eliminate all export subsidies. The European Community has said that these subsidies will be brought down at the same pace as domestic supports, clearly linking the Community's external mechanisms to the fate of the U.S. deficiency payment.

The EC proposal also foresees a partial tariffication of the variable levy, splitting it into a fixed tariff and a fluctuating component. The fluctuating part of the levy would take into account exchange rate fluctuations and, beyond a certain limit, straight decreases in world market prices. To what extent the variable part of the levy would absorb world market price decreases is subject to negotiations. The fixed part of the levy would come down at the same pace that domestic price supports. The European Community has also linked tariffication to its "infamous" proposal for rebalancing external protections. In exchange for some degree of liberalization in grain imports through tarrification, the European Community would raise its protection through tariffs on soybean and grain substitutes.

Health and sanitary measures are an often overlooked, but important, factor of trade, especially in animal products. It seems that an agreement is possible in this area, based on internationally recognized standards and more effective dispute settlement procedures that rely on sound scientific evidence.

The positions of the United States and the Cairns Group, on one hand, and the European Community, on the other hand, are still far apart. But if you look at the broader picture, there is some cause for optimism: (1) the growth of environmental concerns related to agricultural practices will probably reduce political support for agriculture both in the European Community and the United States; (2) although agriculture is the most important subject on the table, the Uruguay Round remains a global negotiation with other important issues at stake, such as services and intellectual property. Therefore, special-interest groups that stand to gain from the negotiation tend to counterbalance interest groups that stand to lose; and (3) in both the United States and the European Community there is a strong political will at the highest level to conclude the round successfully. Also, a failure of the GATT negotiations would probably be perceived by our leaders as the wrong signal to send to Eastern European countries, at a time when these emerging market economies look toward the West as an example to follow.

Two other events will affect agricultural policies and agricultural trade. First, agriculture is not really an important part of the 92 process, since the CAP is already an integrated policy in itself. Therefore, Europe 1992 is not directed at agriculture, although the food industry and, indirectly, agricultural trade will be affected.

From an economist's point of view, the CAP is still an overregulated dinosaur in an increasingly unregulated environment. Although it has not been left untouched, its political sensitivity make changes painful and slow to bring about. I simply cannot imagine that deregulation in other sectors will not affect agriculture, at least inside the European Community. The Uruguay Round of negotiations will undoubtedly bring about a cautious and slow liberalization of external mechanisms, which will make EC agriculture more responsive to world market signals. For the foreseeable future, however, agriculture will remain a highly regulated industry, certainly in the European Community, and most likely in the United States.

Second, the combination of gradual external trade liberalization and less regulated internal mechanisms (such as the elimination of monetary compensatory amounts, MCAs, which should be a natural outcome of monetary union) will lead to a certain degree of specialization in European agriculture.

The recent evolution in Eastern Europe, too, will greatly affect the CAP and agricultural trade in general. The financial resources of the Community will probably have to be stretched to provide assistance to East European countries, which in addition to other resources devoted to new EC policies will constrain agricultural spending. Also, Germany will become a more efficient and larger agricultural producer of grains and livestock products, with a competitive impact on other EC exporting countries such as France, as well as a budget impact on the CAP.

Many challenges also await agriculture on the global level. Although global demand—especially for soybean and cheap proteins for human consumption—will probably increase, the key to exporting to the USSR in the near future will probably be financing. The Soviet economy is in chaos, and the country seems to be running out of hard currencies to pay for its huge grain and food needs. Government-guaranteed export credits will soon be an issue. So, watch out for competition on credit terms between the United States and the European Community on sales of wheat and other commodities to the USSR. Cuba may be another wild card in all this. In order to supply the growing markets for feedgrains, soybeans, and some value-added products, producers will have to compete not only on prices, but also on financing arrangements provided by commercial banks or, when needed, by governments.

A Commentary by Michel Petit

I have a few comments on the chapters by Stefan Tangermann and Timothy Josling. I agree with Stefan Tangermann that the common agricultural policy (CAP) will change noticeably in the years to come. If all goes well, a more market-oriented EC agriculture policy will emerge. The EC should be less a fortress by the end of this century.

Timothy Josling concluded his chapter by predicting that U.S.-EC conflicts would not disappear overnight but would take place in a framework of rules and obligations. Although Mr. Josling might not believe the optimistic scenario, he holds it as a definite possibility. I think that the possibility is indeed there, and perhaps I am a little more optimistic than he is.

I do differ with Mr. Josling's view that this attractive scenario might be enough to persuade negotiators to defy history and challenge political reality. That is where I find a sticking point: I do not believe that negotiators will challenge political reality. I believe that political reality, particularly in Europe, has changed. As we shift the focus of the main questions to why policies are what they are and what the dynamics of those policies are, we can begin to make predictions about the future and worry less about whether the policies are the right ones or whether they are moving in the right directions.

I offer a few examples of what I call the "explicit political economy" perspective to explain why domestic agricultural policies will not be touched in the 1992 work program.

In the 1970s the monetary compensatory amounts (MCAs) were necessary for the pursuit of national objectives within a framework of a common policy. That policy needed to be somewhat flexible for the national politics and interests involved. That is the thrust of the argument that Mr. Tangermann used ten or fifteen years ago. As a result, we do not need the concept of a superficial internal market for agriculture in 1992 to explain the process. I, like everyone else, believe

1992 is a very important process: it is not superficial in general, and it is not superficial in agriculture in particular.

I believe, too, that the budget process is more binding than Mr. Tangermann suggests. The budget plan discusses a ceiling on the common agricultural policy spending, stabilizers, and budget disciplines. Of course, while these are not as constricting as budget constraints, they are nevertheless important. I would argue that, agricultural policy making in Europe, like that in the United States, may be driven by budget considerations.

In addition, a contribution of what I call political economy leads me to slightly different interpretations of quotas and set-aside programs. It is true that quotas and set-asides do not solve the problem, because the problem is prices that are too high.

From a political-economic perspective, given the dynamics of the policies, those changes are extremely important. They mark a turning point. Therefore, from the political-economic perspective, they are very significant. And we must take this significance into account if we want to say anything about the future.

I disagree with Mr. Tangermann's claim that "the reform of the CAP since 1984 is not quite as convincing as it is sometimes advertised, and much will depend on the willingness of ministers of agriculture to let the summit decision of 1988 work to full vigor." It is not the willingness of ministers involved here but the political and economic forces that shape the policies. For that reason I believe that reform is more serious and is independent of the willingness of the ministers.

Finally, I think a political economy perspective can explain why agricultural negotiations in the Uruguay Round are very different from what they have been before. This difference comes not only, as Mr. Josling says, because of solid groundwork or clarity or imagination of the negotiators but also because of the changed political reality of policy making, particularly in the European Community.

Having nitpicked with the authors of these chapters, I have a few other matters to raise. The first one is the obvious neglect of the problems that emanate from the United States. The only problem affecting U.S.-EC agricultural relations is *not* the common agricultural policy. Some speculate whether anything will be done to reform agricultural policy, and some tell us what the international consequences will be of possible reforms, as if there were new obstacles on the U.S. side and as if we could take at face value as current U.S. agricultural policy the positions defended by previous administrations.

The reality of agricultural policies in the United States is, in fact, very similar to the reality elsewhere. Indeed, we can draw a parallel between the actions of the U.S. administration in its efforts to apply external pressures and the actions of the GATT to pressure domestic interests and domestic agricultural policy. Rumor has it that Rep. Kika de la Garza told Clayton Yeutter some time ago that the U.S. farm bill will not be written in Geneva but in Washington.

These are the political realities in the United States, which, I think, cannot be ignored. My own conviction is that the real stumbling block for an agreement in GATT will come from the United States.

The other stumbling block I see comes from the World Bank, that is, from the developing countries. We should not dwell on U.S.-EC relations in agriculture at the expense of agricultural trade relations in the broader world context. I believe that the greatest consequence of the U.S.-EC squabbles, problems, and trade confrontations has been a major increase in the instability of agricultural prices in the international market. In a historical sense, volatility in international prices surely existed before the CAP. But instability has doubtlessly increased, and the principal consequence of all squabbles between the United States and the Europeans is a sharp increase in instability on the world market, with dramatic impact on developing countries. Argentina and its problems of wheat exports, for instance, come to mind. But this instability brings on many of the problems we have in investing in agriculture in a developing country through the World Bank or in financing investment in agriculture in the World Bank. Unless agriculture can develop in these countries, they will not experience general economic development. Without general economic development, they cannot provide a market for foreign products. Therefore, we must put the U.S.-EC trade relation in a broader context. Moreover, the issues go beyond trade to issues of political insecurity. Focusing on U.S.-EC trade without considering what impact that has on developing countries for the present and the future is seriously shortsighted.

A Commentary by John Sault

Australia covers approximately the same area as the contiguous United States, but in terms of soil quality and water availability, it is far from being as well endowed for agricultural production as this country is, or the European Community. Conditions are such that, in general, Australian farming is characterized by extensive dryland, low-input, and low-cost production of livestock and crops. The domestic market is relatively small. The population of Australia is some 17 million, compared with about 250 million in the United States.

Our main agricultural industries are therefore heavily export oriented. Some 80 percent of the food and fiber Australia produces is exported. Also the size of the Australian economy is relatively modest in international terms. Our GDP is only about 5 percent that of the United States.

Australian broadacre agriculture is therefore largely unsubsidized. The relatively small domestic market and modestly sized economy do not provide a basis for significant transfers to producers, either from consumers or taxpayers. In fact calculations of the Organization for Economic Cooperation and Development and U.S. Department of Agriculture indicate that Australian subsidy rates are about the lowest of the leading agricultural exporters.

The incomes of Australian farmers therefore depend on world market prices and access. And most Australian farmers have come to adopt a free-trade stance. Any developments or policies that have an impact on the level and variability of world commodity prices are of direct interest to us. The trade disputes and competitive subsidization programs across the Atlantic are not only costly to the economies concerned—those of the European Community and the United States—but also have significant implications for countries that do not subsidize and are heavily reliant on the world market.

Our speakers have correctly identified that these trade frictions have their origins in domestic agricultural policies; also that high support levels for agriculture in ways that distort markets do not achieve their objectives or, if they do, only in a highly inefficient way.

In Australia, we have placed particular emphasis on endeavoring to make more transparent the costs and inefficiencies of protectionist agricultural policies, especially for the countries carrying them out. I refer in particular to the work of the Australian Bureau of Agricultural and Resource Economics. Our two main speakers have pointed out that there have been some adjustments to the agricultural policies of both the United States and the European Community. They have demonstrated that these changes have not been as significant as sometimes proclaimed, especially, for example, when factors such as variations in EC Green Rates are taken into account. Also, it cannot be guaranteed that the trend will continue. Nevertheless, to the extent that the adjustments represent some reduction in the total levels of government support, they are steps in the right direction.

Both Professor Josling and Professor Tangermann highlight the opportunity that the Uruguay Round of multilateral trade negotiations provides to sustain and accelerate these changes and to resolve trade frictions. They also refer to the real dangers for the international trading system and the world economy should the round fail.

Australia sees the Uruguay Round as providing a unique opportunity to curb the excesses of national agricultural policies and bring about a more liberalized and less distorted international trading environment for agricultural products. It was apparent to us that given the dominant role of the major trading countries, particularly the United States and the European Community, in previous negotiations, there was a need for a new force in the negotiations, representative of smaller to medium economies that were dependent on agricultural trade. Accordingly, Australia played a leading role in the formation of the Cairns Group. We believe that the Cairns Group has been a key factor in moving comprehensive reform of agriculture to the center stage of the negotiations—the first time this has occurred in an MTN Round—and keeping it there.

Cairns Group pressure also played an important part in achieving the breakthrough in the agricultural negotiations, which emerged last April, following the deadlock that occurred in the review held in Montreal in December 1988. Although the April agreement provided a solid framework for the remainder of the round, much remained and still remains to be done in negotiating the details. All the main players—including the United States, European Community, and the Cairns Group, tabled comprehensive proposals toward the end of last year.

There is a consensus about the need for greater market orientation in farm policies, which is a positive factor, but there is wide divergence on the manner, degree, and time frame in which this should occur. In this respect, the U.S. and EC proposals set the main boundaries in which the negotiations will occur.

The United States has tabled a comprehensive, integrated, and market-oriented proposal on agriculture. It addresses the four policy areas that can lead to distortions in international trade: market access, domestic support, export subsidies, and sanitary and phytosanitary measures. The Cairns Group has also tabled a comprehensive proposal addressing these four areas. Although it differs in points of detail and adopts a somewhat more flexible approach on some issues than the U.S. proposal, the closest affinity exists between the objectives of the two proposals.

I must, in passing, take issue with Professor Josling's comment that the Cairns Group has given less than full support to the United States on SPS issues. The Cairns Group, along with the United States, has been an active progressor of SPS issues in the round, and there is a large measure of commonality in U.S.-Cairns Group positions.

The European Community has tabled a proposal that shows greater flexibility than hitherto. It contains a number of elements on which the community has not previously indicated a willingness to negotiate. But these are heavily circumscribed and tied to undesirable features, such as rebalancing. Moreover, the proposal is vague and open to varying interpretations.

I note Professor Tangermann's view that even if the European Community was prepared to do no more than be committed internationally to the CAP reforms that it has already embarked on internally, this would be a positive achievement. I can only say that such a minimalist result is most unlikely to be acceptable to other players. And if an acceptable outcome is not achieved in agriculture, the round as a whole will fail. Montreal demonstrated that.

There can be no satisfactory outcome to the GATT Round without assurances that agricultural trade in the future will be conducted according to a common set of rules and will become progressively freer and fairer. Although certain elements of agricultural policies are being adjusted in the right direction, others are not, and the favorable adjustments cannot be guaranteed to continue. The process of reform needs to be intensified and locked in by international commitments.

Let me add another dimension to this point. The events in Eastern Europe are moving rapidly. The outcome of the Uruguay Round will determine the agricultural policy structures toward which East European countries might evolve. Likewise, unless we see a substantial change in the world trading system, we can expect many Asia Pacific developing countries to block off growth in their agricultural markets by following the Japan-Korea mould of high agricultural protectionism. Thus, the massive trade potential offered by this rapidly developing area of the world would be seriously curtailed. For the sake of world economic prosperity and all our individual economies, the Uruguay Round cannot be allowed to fail.

A Commentary by Daniel Sumner

In response to Professor Tangermann's chapter, I think agriculture plays a fairly small role in the 1992 European integration. The major issue is Green Money. Perhaps there is cause for some liberalization on that front. But on the list of reasons for optimism, the one I would choose is this: that 1992 seems to be encouraging Europe to move toward liberalization. To the extent that liberalization helps EC-U.S. relations, that is welcome.

With respect to Eastern Europe, we have heard that not just East

Germany but perhaps many East European countries want to participate in the European Community. Czechoslovakia indicated its interest. The question is, Can one imagine the CAP (common agricultural policy) throughout Eastern Europe? I think the answer is no. It would be too expensive and unmanageable—although, of course, they brought in Spain and Portugal. That leads me to think that reform is likely to continue.

Let me come back to the 1990 U.S. farm bill debate and consider how it fits into this discussion. Radical reform was not on the table in 1990, either from the Congress or from the administration. There was general satisfaction with the 1985 farm bill. There was a prevailing conservatism because 1990 was an important election year for Congress. And there was a sense that the more appropriate vehicle for fundamental reform was the Uruguay Round.

A second point is that the mood is one of consultation and consideration rather than confrontation. We in the administration feel that the reception to our proposals has been quite good.

I will mention three of those proposals. One is flexibility; with respect to program crops, growers would be allowed more movement to react to market forces, rather than simply to target prices.

A second concerns stocks policy. This program is a market-oriented move to eliminate complicated release rules and acquisition rules, leaving release and acquisition up to the individual growers for the farmer-owned reserve. There will still be subsidized storage, but we in Washington will not determine when and under what conditions the stocks move in and out. The third proposal concerns the administration's commitment to budget restraint for farm programs. We are committed to saving $1½ billion, and that is an important underlying factor in the discussion of future policies.

Perhaps even more important, we plan essentially to stay the course with respect to international policies, at least until the end of the Uruguay Round. The Export Enhancement program indicates that no one is proposing to eliminate or substantially modify the EEP immediately. The strategy for the farm bill in 1990 was thus to move in an appropriate direction.

Notes

Chapter 1: Structural Change and Market Integration, *Fabrizio Onida*

1. Since reinvested earnings play a large role in these figures on direct foreign investment, one should take into account the arithmetic impact of strong movements in the dollar exchange rate. Reinvested earnings in European currencies are downplayed in dollar terms when the dollar becomes stronger, and vice versa. For recent geographical trends in stocks of direct foreign investments by major country of origin and destination (see tables 1-1 and 1-2; see also the *Economist*, May 13, 1989, pp. 80–84).

2. The sentence handed down by the EC Court of Justice (in Luxembourg) prevented the German government from forbidding the importation of Cassis de Dijon from France by the German importer Rewe Zentral AG ("an unsung European hero," according to the *Economist*, 1988).

3. Medieval cities typically supported local producers' cartels (guilds) and put up several barriers to free trade among cities. Only the jurisdictional integration linked to the rise of central (national) governments brought about freer trade and lower transport costs. This applied to the Dutch United Provinces at the beginning of the seventeenth century when they gained their independence from Spain and took advantage of their particularly favorable external environment (with its canals, rivers, and plains) for low-cost trade. Germany's and Italy's accelerated growth in the early period of industrialization took place at the same time the central government authority was being established (Olson 1982: chap. 3, 5).

4. Public procurement may see some of the greatest gains from the single market (although their actual implementation is still uncertain). Of an overall market of ECU 530 billion (about 15 percent of total European GDP), ECU 240–340 billion (6.8–9.8 percent of European GDP) is likely to be affected by liberalization (Commission of the European Communities 1988a: table 3.4.1). The remaining ECU 190–290 billion will arise from current public expenditure (such as rents, materials, and electricity consumption), which is not traditionally subject to formal public procurement procedures and therefore is less likely to feel the cost-cutting benefits of liberalization.

5. Legal, fiscal, and straightforward political constraints are generally considered to be the significant obstacles to mergers with and acquisitions by foreign firms in countries such as Germany, France, and the Netherlands. Political and psychological barriers, however, are likely to weaken under the pressure of increasing competition in large-scale and intensive operations such as motor vehicles and components, semiconductors, computers, domes-

tic appliances, consumer electronics, and food and tobacco. During 1982–1985 new intra-EC joint ventures among the leading 1,000 European firms rose from about forty-five to eighty per year over all sectors in industry and services (De Jong 1988; see also table 1-4).

6. The EC absorbed $21 billion (15.1 percent of the total $139 billion) of the cumulative 1951–1987 stock of Japanese direct foreign investment, but only $3.3 billion of the $36.0 billion (less than 10 percent) manufacturing stock of direct foreign investment. Within Europe, the United Kingdom, Luxembourg, and the Netherlands accounted for $13.7 billion, or 65 percent of the total European stock. Foreign production in 1986 was only 3.2 percent of total Japanese industrial production, compared with 18.1 percent for the United States (in 1985) and 19.3 percent for the Federal Republic of Germany (in 1984) (data from Japan's Ministry of International Trade and Industry, quoted by Fukuda 1988). In the automotive sector, the big three (Honda, Toyota, Nissan) have already channeled almost $4 billion into direct European investments, thereby creating more than 8,000 jobs. Their cumulative production in Europe has reached 230,000 units (cars, special trucks, etc.), the official target being around 600,000 units by 1992, 200,000 of which are Nissan-Bluebirds in the United Kingdom. Local content is subject to debatable evaluation. Honda officially is aiming at 80 percent local European content by 1992 (see also Jones 1988).

7. Strategic alliances, whose business relevance goes well beyond traditional licensing agreements, imply

> commitments of two or more firms to reach a common goal, entailing the pooling of their resources and activities. Thus a strategic alliance might include one or more of the following: (i) an exclusive purchase agreement; (ii) exclusionary or manufacturing rights; (iii) technology swaps; (iv) joint R & D or codevelopment. Thus a strategic alliance denotes some form of mutual control. By this nature, it is not a passive instrument. (Teece 1989: 26)

The importance of a time horizon for strategic decisions, and of vertical (user-producer) cooperation for enhancing productivity, is stressed by Ferguson (1989). Aoki (1989) dwells on the importance of various internal coordination in work organization. The need for a pragmatic approach to competition and antitrust policy is emphasized by Jacquemin (1987), particularly in reference to R & D cooperation. Geroski (1988) carefully explains and tries to test the coexistence of the direct and indirect effects of industrial concentration on the incentive to innovate (the former showing an expected negative sign, the second and more powerful one showing a positive sign).

8. It should be kept in mind that R & D statistics seriously underestimate the volume of incremental innovation, which plays a crucial role in many mechanical and electrical engineering activities, and in general at the level of small and medium firms (see, among others, Pavitt 1980; Ergas 1984, 1987; Patel and Pavitt 1988).

9. The share of European subsidiaries' production and U.S. exports over total sale in Europe is remarkably high: more than 60 percent in overall information technologies (*Economist* 1989: 82), 35 percent in personal comput-

ers, 23 percent in motor vehicles, and 23 percent in pharmaceutical products. Motorola and Texas Instruments are among the top five sellers of integrated circuits in the European market. The geographical distribution of recent flows of U.S. direct investment in Europe is rather uneven: about one-third goes to the United Kingdom, 16 percent to the Federal Republic of Germany, 13 percent to Switzerland, 10 percent to the Netherlands, and only 6 percent to Italy.

10. European producers of computers, such as Nixdorf-Bull-Olivetti, are heavy users of imported DRAMs, whose share of the value of final products is close to 40 percent. Therefore they tend to oppose the antidumping actions demanded by the few European producers of electronic components and semiconductors (such as Philips and Siemens). The EC Commission has to mediate among domestic producers before negotiating restrictions or voluntary export restrictions with Japanese producers of semiconductors (see, for example, *Wall Street Journal*, 27 July 1989; *Financial Times*, 23–24 June 1983). Since June 1, 1989, Japan has negotiated to end its VERs on the export of semiconductors to the European Community.

11. In sensitive sectors such as passenger cars and consumer electronics, there is a consensus among member governments (of course among the leading European producers!) that Japanese imports (including parts and components for final assembly in Europe) need to be kept under some sort of surveillance to force greater reciprocity and to avoid the settlement of purely screw-driver operations. Opinions differ, however, as to the instruments that should be used and what constitutes a tolerable rate of increase of import penetration. German and British officials are among the least enthusiastic about the nontariff barriers to be erected against the disruptive penetration of Japanese products, both imported and assembled (see, for example, Healey 1988).

CHAPTER 3: THE AUTOMOBILE INDUSTRY, *Frank D. Weiss*

1. The reasons for these agreements need not be of concern here. Keohane's hegemon theory of policy making in international trade may be of relevance. Some sectors, notably agriculture and textiles, were indeed taken out of normal international trade diplomacy at the behest of the United States in the early postwar years. See Yoffie (1983) on textiles and clothing and Winham (1986: 152ff.) on agriculture.

2. Heinrich von Moltke argues that the motive for imposing quotas was the legally required preservation of free trade in steel within the European Community. Precisely: had there not been quotas, no one would have acquiesced in the free movement of goods (steel) across Community members' borders because of the mechanisms outlined.

3. Sources vary. Bronckers (1983) states that 1981 imports were to be limited to 110 percent of the 1980 level. De Malo and Messerlin (1988) take the VER to mean that Japan's market share was to be limited to an annual expansion of 10 percent, but they find it to have been redundant.

465

CHAPTER 7: TELECOMMUNICATIONS EQUIPMENT, *Claude G. B. Fontheim*

1. Within five months after the 1988 trade act was enacted, the U.S. trade representative was required to designate "priority" foreign countries that deny "mutually advantageous market opportunities" to telecommunications products and services of U.S. firms. The president is required to enter into negotiations with these "priority countries." The president is then required to impose trade sanctions against these priority countries if no market opening agreement is reached by the end of a one-year negotiating period. The negotiating period may be extended twice for not more than one year in each case.

2. The trade data in this section are taken from the U.S. Department of Commerce market summaries for the European Community, United Kingdom, and Germany.

3. CPE is taken to be synonymous with the term "terminal equipment," as used in the directive.

4. The proposed directive on type approval sets out the detailed rules by which the member states "will put into force the mutual recognition of type approval to common type approval specifications" and repeals an earlier directive on the initial stage of mutual recognition of CPE. Under this directive, common approval specifications will be limited to "essential requirements," including user safety; safety of telecommunications authority employees; protection of the public network from damage; protection of network users from network degradation, denial of service, and incorrect charging; interworking of equipment, that is, establishing, modifying, charging, and clearing connections; and interworking to the extent justified by the nature of the service.

5. A public hearing was held on March 23, 1989; the International Trade Commission invited written submissions from interested parties. Its report is classified and thus not available to the public.

6. The larger and more sophisticated U.S. telecommunications firms are already implementing such strategies, many of which include investments in European manufacturing facilities, acquisitions of European firms, and the formation of alliances with European firms. A thorough treatment of such strategies, however, is beyond the scope of this discussion.

CHAPTER 9: TELECOMMUNICATIONS AND INFORMATION SERVICES, *Jonathan D. Aronson*

1. Even before the sweeping changes in Eastern Europe, it was evident that the establishment of a single European market would create new challenges for U.S. export control policies. An integrated European market will make it impossible to maintain controls on reexports within the community, particularly through a newly reunited Germany. In mid-June 1990, the United States announced that it would relax restraints covering about $300 billion in exports (*Los Angeles Times* 1990). It also is unlikely that changes in Eastern

Europe will distract top-level economic and political decision makers away from Brussels and force them to concentrate more time on Eastern Europe. Just as European leaders worked hard a decade ago to pull Spain, Portugal, and Greece in the European Community to reinforce their democratic tendencies, so there will be a strong pull in Germany and elsewhere to build on present breakthroughs and start to reintegrate East European economies into Europe. The big question is, Can rapid progress toward 1992 and the revitalization and integration of Eastern Europe be accomplished simultaneously? Some slippage in implementing measures for 1992 is likely.

2. At the beginning of the June 5–9, 1989, meeting of the Group of Negotiations on Services of the Uruguay Round, the representative of the European Communities noted that the telecommunications services sector was particularly important because of its relationship to other service sectors, but he asked whether trade in services could even be envisaged without liberalization of trade in equipment (Group of Negotiations on Services of the Uruguay Round 1989b).

3. Definitions and distinctions in the telecommunications and information realm are the subject of continuing dispute and debate. This is compounded by the now legendary, but somewhat overblown, merging of communications and computer technologies and the less well understood merging of communications and broadcast technologies. One systematic, legalistic approach to these distinctions is Bruce, Cunard, and Director (1986).

4. The critical document in the European context is Commission of the European Communities (1984). On trade in such services see Wildman and Siwek (1988).

5. An intriguing possibility is that Eastern Europe, in its effort to rapidly upgrade its communications infrastructure without paying for a full-scale backbone network, may permit broad use of VSAT (Very Small Aperture Terminals). European Community Telecommunications Authorities have opposed the introduction of VSAT, because they feared they would encourage bypass and push competition too far, too fast. The European Community may prod individual countries to license VSAT so that East European nations do not leapfrog them.

6. For example, Japan prefers to distinguish between Type I and Type II carriers. Their service offerings do not correspond to basic and enhanced services.

7. Although the conceptual boundaries are eroding rapidly, companies that grew up in one segment of the information business have not easily entered other segments. Thus, the much ballyhooed competition that was expected when AT&T moved into computers and IBM into telecommunications has fizzled in both directions. AT&T's attempt to acquire NCR is just its most recent attempt to strengthen its position in computers.

8. An often noted but relevant fact is that two decades ago, 80 percent of the investment to develop a new computer or telecom switch was spent on the hardware and 20 percent on the software. Today these percentages are reversed.

9. AT&T persuaded the U.S. government that in the negotiations to

establish a U.S.-Canadian free trade agreement and in GATT negotiations basic services (and network facilities) should not be considered explicitly in the negotiations. They note that Telecommunications Authorities strongly oppose the inclusion of these gigantic revenue-generating services and suggest that if basic services are put on the table, telecom-service negotiations are likely to collapse under their weight. Users, system integrators, and other newcomers, by contrast, fear that if basic services are excluded from the bargaining arena, the TAs could choose to undercut their interests in other service segments. For example, TAs could choose to undercut their interests in other service segments. For example, TAs could make it difficult for EDS or GEIS to operate private leased networks that provide basic services.

10. Several years ago Ann Reid put forward the then controversial view that before the 1970s technology changed relatively slowly: services were homogeneous, easily distinguished from each other, and vertically integrated; the same basic range of services was found in all countries; and services were offered under more or less the same regulatory conditions in each country. Since then, she argued, none of these givens remain valid (Reid 1985: 16–18). On the evolution of the international telecommunications regime, see Cowhey (1990b).

11. The most far-reaching reform was undertaken by New Zealand, which on April 1, 1989, privatized and segmented its telecommunications monopoly and invited all comers to compete in all segments of the market. Bell Atlantic and Amerited bought what was once the publicly owned New Zealand Telephone Company. Eli Noam is probably the leader in tracking the comparative changes under way in Europe and Asia (Noam 1988: 257–97).

12. The USSR and East European countries can be expected to lay as much fiber as they can afford, try to develop their own versions of ISDN, and allow foreign firms and consortiums to participate in building and operating new overlay networks. Poland has accepted cellular bids from abroad, and Czechoslovakia has agreed to let Bell Atlantic and US West help modernize its network. For a background review of the current state of telecommunications in Eastern Europe, see U.S. Department of State (1990).

13. Detailed discussions of national regulatory changes in key industrial nations and some smaller European countries can be found in Temin and Galambos (1987); Bruce, Cunard, and Director (1986); Foreman-Peck, Haid, and Muller (1988); Snow (1986); and Noam (1991).

14. In addition to the perpetual worry about the technical standards that might be foisted upon their private networks and might prevent them from using their own technical protocols, U.S. firms were particularly concerned about leased circuits. Would they be available promptly when they were requested? Would they continue to be leased for a flat monthly rate? Would rates be closely tied to costs? Would users be allowed to share leased circuits or resell their capacity for use by third parties? Would they be allowed to interconnect their leased circuit networks to the public network?

15. The French, for example, wanted to hold on to their monopoly over packet-switching, and Italy tried to keep its videoconferencing monopoly.

16. Belgium seems intent on turning Brussels into the "Singapore of

Europe." To do so, RTT, the Belgian TA, would need to provide a wider variety of services more efficiently and at lower prices. Competition in basic services need not be introduced. Indeed, Belgium generally has less interest in competition than other EC members.

17. Witte Commission for Telecommunications (1988). For analysis of the early acceptance of the Witte Commmission report, see Haid et al., *Alternate Market Configurations*, in Foreman-Peck (1988: 155–180) and European Telecommunications Research (1988).

18. France carefully planned the renovation of its network. Favored innovations such as packet switching thrived, but as of 1990 Britain enjoyed a penetration rate for cellular and other overlay services five times higher than France's.

19. PanAmSat complains vigorously that even though France licensed their operations, it has thus far blocked them from offering their services because of a series of technicalities.

20. During the 1970s users were generally passive. Even the large banks did not want to risk possible retaliation by the Bundespost or other powerful PTTs. This situation began to change when European users organized at the middle-management level through the International Telecommunications Users Group (INTUG). Pressure for change accelerated when top management in large firms such as the Deutsche Bank and Volvo organized the Roundtable of European Industrialists and began to lobby national and EC leaders on behalf of large users.

21. Directive 77/62/EEC, OJ L 13, 15. January 1, 1977; Ungerer and Costello (1988: 129).

22. This task force was so successful in shaping an active policy approach for Europe that it was combined with other commission departments, given a broader scope and increased power, and reconstituted as the Directorate-General for Telecommunications, Information Industries, and Innovation—DG-XIII.

23. The most cited national example was the 1978 Nora-Minc report commissioned by French President Giscard d'Estaing, which coined the term "telematics" and led to a major rethinking of French policy regarding information (Nora and Minc 1980).

24. One reason for U.S. business concern is that SOG-T inevitably must rely mostly on the TAs for technical expertise. The main advisory panel for SOG-T and ultimately for DG-XIII is the Groupe d'Analyse et de Prévision (GAP).

25. Interviews with EC Commission officials, Brussels, June 1984.

26. Ungerer and Costello (1988: 137) provides the complete list.

27. Ungerer also describes several subsequent cases, involving the right to establish terminal equipment to the network, the disclosure of interface standards by IBM, international air courier cases, and so forth that established telecommunications as commercial undertakings subject to rules of competition. Also see Bruce (1988: 302–20).

28. France led Italy, Belgium, and Spain in opposition to the use of Article 90(3). Apparently the French wanted to make certain that voice traffic would

not migrate to private networks. In February 1990 the European Community's Advocate General backed the French challenge with regard to the terminal directive that Article 90(3) did not constitute an appropriate legal base for the commission's directive liberalizing terminal equipment. This opinion, if backed by the European Court of Justice, could undercut the commission's authority to liberalize the market for telecommunications services, which is also dependent on Article 90(3) (Telecommunications Reports 1990, February).

29. After an initial round of feedback the commission issued another document to clarify the proposed mechanism for implementing the Green Paper (Commission of the European Communities 1988c).

30. The Green Paper suggested that restrictions might be continued on the first telephone set, but this exception was later dropped.

31. Critics believed, however, that the language left open the possibility of discrimination against new competitors and cross-subsidization of competitive services provided by the TAs.

32. The commission seems poised to require the elimination of exclusive or special rights granted to telecommunications entities for the provision of nonreserved telecom services.

33. Traditionally, European telecommunications standards were in the hands of the European Conference of Postal and Telecommunications Administrations (CEPT), a body made up of the telecommunications authorities of Europe plus British Telecom. Frequently CEPT participants were more interested in establishing local than regional standards. Over time this created three major problems for Europe. First, telecommunications equipment manufacturers could not capture necessary economies of scales that would have been possible with a large, homogeneous market. Second, new services carried over the telephone lines were discouraged. Third, business users that exchanged large amounts of data were frustrated because their communications were more time-consuming and less efficient than desirable (Dodsworth 1988).

34. For example, Meyers and Harper (1989: 403) list a total of sixteen EC directives, regulations, decisions, recommendations and proposal taken between 1984 and 1989. The directives and proposed directives cover the following areas: (1) Directive 85/372/EEC: definition phase for a research and development program in advanced communications technologies for Europe (RACE); (2) Directive 86/361/EEC: initial stage of the mutual recognition of type approval for telecommunications terminal equipment; (3) Directive 86/529/EEC: adoption of common technical specifications of the MAC/packet family of standards for direct satellite television broadcasting; (4) Directive 87/371/EEC: availability of frequency bands for the coordinated introduction of public pan-European digital mobile communications in the European Community; (5) Directive 88/28/EEC: community program in the field of telecommunications technologies (RACE); (6) Commission Directive 88/301/eec: competition in the markets in telecommunications terminal people; (7) COM(88)378: *proposal* for a directive on procurement procedures of entities operating in telecommunications sector; (8) COM(89)289: *proposal* for a direc-

tive on approximating laws of the member states concerning telecommunications terminal equipment; (9) COM(89)325 *revised proposal* for a directive on establishing the internal market for telecommunications services through the open network provision.

35. So far the European Community has not focused on the provision of international basic services except to say that the TAs may maintain their monopoly.

36. "The directive does not apply to telex, radio-telephony, paging, satellite services, cable television, and mass communications radio or broadcast television" (U.S. Department of Commerce 1990: 63).

37. For example, in April 1989 CEPT agreed on a framework for common standards for commercial, public ISDN by 1992. The agreement covered "a common range of services which all signatories will provide, and a list of further optional services which will be provided to common standards as the market demand develops." The pact also defines arrangements for interconnection of national ISDN systems for international services (Telecommunications Reports 1989, April, 11).

38. "Member states may require private service operators to submit a declaration indicating they will not engage in simple resale of leased line capacity for data communications until 1993. States may also request an extension of the transition period until 1996, provided they show the Commission that their national network for packet-switched data services is undeveloped" (U.S. Department of Commerce 1990).

39. The ministers did agree to allow member countries to request an extension until December 31, 1995, of the time during which the restriction on simple resale of capacity can remain in effect, but only on the grounds that their PTT otherwise would not be able to meet its public service obligations. The provision for such extensions was adopted in the expectation that countries might qualify whose telecom infrastructures were relatively underdeveloped (Telecommunications Reports 1989, December, 12–13).

40. If that presumption for compliance did not guarantee interoperability for transborder services within the community, the standard in question could then be made mandatory to the extent "strictly necessary to assure such interoperability." For example, each member state might be requested to make certain that a service that complied with the standard was offered by at least one service provider in its territory (Telecommunications Reports 1989, December, 13; Telephony 1989, December 16).

41. Major fears about "Fortress Europe" have diminished somewhat. Still it is clear that EC1992 could be quite unfavorable to Japanese concerns that try to export to the European Community, as long as Japan buys relatively little from Europe. U.S. firms are taking pains to separate themselves from the Japanese so that the same rules do not apply to them.

42. Companies move in and out of groups, depending on their interest in specific issues, but companies involved with this group usually include GEIS, EDS, Citicorp, Manufacturers Hanover, and American Express. IBM's interventions are somewhat less predictable, but they often join this group as well.

43. AT&T cautions against including basic services in current negotiations. MCI generally follows AT&T on these issues and does not usually get involved. In the mid-1980s, as a negotiating ploy, US Sprint was somewhat more vocal in support of including basic services on the negotiating agenda, but since it received most of the concessions it sought, it now seems to be more supportive of the AT&T position. Except for Nynex, which intervenes from time to time, the RBOCs have not been active either.

44. See Cowhey (1990a) on the possibility that Europeans may coopt the competition through such groups as Infonet, Eucom, and the Managed Data Network Services (MDNS).

45. The treatment of satellite services is especially unclear. Does the exclusion of satellite services include value-added services that use satellite links or use satellites as a backup for users and providers of value-added services? Presumably, these issues will be at least partially clarified by the forthcoming satellite directive.

46. Michael Calingaert argues that the success of U.S. firms in Europe after 1992 will depend on (1) the level of transparency in general and on the extent of U.S. participation in the standard-setting process in particular; (2) whether testing and certification at U.S. facilities will be recognized in the European Community; and (3) the "extent to which European, as opposed to international standards are adopted" (Calingaert 1988: 117).

47. Although agreement was reached on services at Montreal, a full and final agreement on the round proved elusive. The final text and agreement was finally hammered out in Geneva by deputy trade ministers in April 1989. This section draws heavily on Bruce, Cunard, and Director (1989).

48. A detailed discussion of the concept access as applied to services and telecom services is beyond the scope of this chapter. Bruce, Cunard, and Director (1989: 50–58) detail some of the fine points and discuss two sets of issues: whether obligations should be imposed only on "network" or "transport" services or on all services, and whether services provided pursuant to a government regulated, limited competition—but not a monopoly—as in the United Kingdom, bear access obligations.

49. Another issue that has not yet been classified as a trade issue but is garnering considerable attention in Washington is international settlements policy. U.S. regulators have begun to argue that the settlement rates and methods for determining them have resulted in a gigantic balance-payments-deficit for the United States on simple telephone calls. Americans place more international calls and send more data abroad than they receive. For handling their ends of the calls, foreign firms and TAs are compensated. They also keep a larger portion of the revenue from calls to the United States. U.S. officials suggest that reform in this area would boost calls to the United States, would provide lower tariffs for users, and would lower the U.S. deficit in telecommunications services.

50. The greatest consternation over the reciprocity standard was raised by U.S. bankers who argued that U.S. banking law made it impossible to grant foreign banks the same rights in the United States that they enjoyed in Europe. Partly in response to repeated discussions in the financial realm the

472

European Community backed away from reciprocity in the financial realm in mid-1989.

51. At the time that selection of priority and candidate countries was under way in late 1988 and early 1989, it was still not clear whether German liberalization was real or a mirage. Believing that progress was real, however, Alfred Sikes, then head of NTIA, was determined that Germany should not be named. Another round of reorganization of Italian telecom was underway. Standard-setting and procurement remained relatively closed in Spain despite a recent law that introduced reforms in telecommunications.

52. The failure to reach closure in December 1990 was not unexpected. Four years was not enough time. Indeed, before negotiations began Michael Aho and I predicted that the Uruguay Round would take at least as long as the seven-year Tokyo Round (1973–1979) (Aho and Aronson 1985).

53. This allowed a group of developing countries led by India and Brazil that had opposed putting services onto the GATT agenda to exact promises that any agreement would be concerned with development issues, and to put off a final decision about the future role of services within the GATT. At the final ministerial meeting of the round the ministers may decide to roll services into the general agreement.

54. It was first suggested that separate sectoral agreements might be negotiated. That would have meant that in order to participate at the sectoral level, countries would be obligated to become signatories of the framework agreement. Countries that signed the framework agreement, however, chose whether or not they were prepared to sign each sectoral agreement. By moving to an annex instead, countries will have to accept or reject the framework and all the annexes as a group. This limits the ambitiousness of telecommunications and any other proposed services annexes.

55. The best summary of the development of negotiations for trade in services is Geza Feketekuty (Feketekuty 1988). On telecom services specifically, also see Feketekuty 1989.

56. The SPAC sought to ensure fair competition between private firms and public monopolies and to guarantee access to and use of public telecommunications systems (Services Policy Advisory Committee to U.S. Trade Rep. 1987; Aronson and Cowhey 1988).

57. At meetings of the GNS held June 5–9, 1989, those represented reviewed two documents, "Trade in Telecommunications Services," MTN.GNS/W/52 and a list of questions that might be addressed in the examination of concepts, MTN.GNS/W/51. The brief discussion that follows is drawn from GNS (Group of Negotiations on Services of the Uruguay Round 1989b).

58. The Mexican delegate emphasized "that applying national treatment in the communications sector was difficult, especially for developing countries. He noted that it was most difficult to grant national treatment when many countries did not even have domestic provision capabilities for certain services. Likewise, assuming that domestic providers did exist, they would probably be in early operating stages and might need infant industry support, although in the long run national treatment might need to be applied

to foreign providers. He felt that one way of strengthening competition would be by allowing infant national industries to use networks set up by foreign operators. This he likened to a technology transfer" Ibid., p. 32.

59. Predictably, the proposal includes a plan for progressive liberalization of services trade through application of trade principles such as national treatment, right of establishment, and transparency. Procedures for resolving disputes and enforcing any agreement are suggested. The United States proposed that signatories would be allowed to take limited "reservations" for measures that do not conform to the agreement as long as these measures were understood to be subject to removal in future negotiations (Group of Negotiations on Services of the Uruguay Round 1989a; New York Times 1989, October 24, C9; CSI Reports 1989, December 3).

60. In addition, the U.S. council paper advocated that services individual countries agreed to liberalize should be specified in a "negative list." AT&T participated in the drafting of the U.S. council statement, but after it was issued changed course and opposed the document.

61. AT&T did not block the U.S. council statement; indeed, AT&T participated in its drafting. After further reflection at higher levels, however, in the words of one official, "AT&T went ballistic" in opposition to it.

62. Specifically, the U.S. council asked authorities to provide a menu of terrestrial and satellite telecommunications services and leased lines and other transport services. They seek reasonable, nondiscriminatory cost-based rates. They want the ability to interconnect leased lines to the public switched network for the purpose of dial-up access and the freedom to choose and attach equipment to the network on the basis of "no technical harm to the network" consistent with national standards and policies. Users should be free to use proprietary protocols and to interconnect in accordance with commercial considerations. Information should be free to move consistent with the protection of personal privacy, intellectual property, public safety and national security. Finally, there should be minimal and reasonable licensing requirements, if any (U.S. Council for International Business 1989).

63. The proposed annex is reproduced in *Transnational Data and Comunications Report* (1990, April 27–29). The other sectoral annex likely to be appended to the framework agreement would cover financial services. There is a more remote chance that an annex covering professional services might be added at the end of negotiations as well. The difficulty with an annex is that signatories to the framework agreement are automatically signatories to any annexes as well. Each signatory, however, has the option of not "binding" certain parts of the agreement, thus providing a loophole.

64. AT&T wanted to exclude basic services entirely from the U.S. proposal. It feared that the price the United States would have to pay for taking an exception to protect AT&T might be too high. It worried that other countries' TAs and firms could enter AT&T's market without earning reciprocal access for AT&T. On the other side, companies that ran their own private networks such as EDS and GEISCO were concerned that private basic networks of the type they ran would be excluded from the agreement unless the U.S. position were more ambitious.

65. An exclusive provider of service is one of a limited number of government-designated providers of a service. Thus, British Telecom and Mercury are exclusive providers of some services in the United Kingdom, not monopoly providers of services.

66. With regard to leased lines they seek broad scope for resale and shared use; flat-rate pricing of leased circuits at cost-based prices; the right to attach CPE equipment to the network subject only to a no-technical-harm-to-the-network requirement; the right to perform proprietary CPE switching and signalling functions in connection with their leased lines; the ability to interconnect leased lines with the public switched network on fair or reasonable terms and the right to refuse to interconnect to the public switched network; and the ability to interconnect leased lines with other leased lines.

67. Peter Cowhey and I argued in *When Countries Talk* (Aronson and Cowhey 1988) that it was probably a mistake to overload a telecommunications services agreement by including basic services at this time. We also suggested that it was a mistake to seek an obligation to permit the free flow of information. We suggested that by achieving guarantees over the operation of the conduit. free flow of information, with some restrictions, was bound to follow. In addition, the focus of attention on transborder data flows would raise problems for many industrial countries and could further persuade developing countries not to become parties to the agreement.

68. A more controversial question is whether TAs might under some circumstances be able to reclaim some of the rights they gave to their competitors. In other words, if the trend in telecommunications services shifts from deregulation toward reregulation, what consequences would that have for the TAs and the annex?

69. This might be done for a specific service sector such as telecommunications by representatives with technical skills, or it might be done in conjunction with continuing meetings of higher level trade officials to review the progress on implementing the entire Uruguay Round agreement.

70. Traditionally, the GATT secretariat served as a fair broker, trying to craft compromises. This time it evidently threw all the competing concepts together in an inevitably contradictory heavily bracketed document. By contrast at the 1988 World Administrative Telecommunications Conference (WATTC) of the ITU, then Secretary General Richard Butler threw out competing national proposals and submitted his own compromise proposal which was ultimately the basis for agreement.

71. Peter Cowhey (Cowhey 1990a) makes a strong case that it will be difficult for U.S. firms to make much headway in the fiercely competitive, relatively slowly growing telecom equipment market. There may, however, be significant opportunities for U.S. firms to sell advanced transmission and terminal equipment.

72. One telephone company that has done well in the VAN business is US Sprint's Telenet. By comparison, Pacific Telesis, US West, and Motorola have each been granted licenses to participate in PCN ventures in the United Kingdom, and Pacific Telesis is part of the winning coalition that received the second cellular license in West Germany (*New York Times*, December 10, 1989)

RBOCs, other phone companies, and equipment suppliers also should experience a robust jump in sales in Eastern Europe and the Soviet Union now that COCOM rules are being relaxed. For example, US West has signed a cellular deal with Hungary (*Telephony*, December 11, 1989); US West is also at the head of a seven-company consortium that won the contract to lay a 12,000-mile fiber-optic cable across the Soviet Union. (The U.S. government, however, is trying to block US West participation in the project on security grounds.) Poland agreed to buy a standard 5ESS digital switching system from AT&T (*Telephony*, January 22, 1990); and foreign firms have won licenses to provide overlay services in Poland.

73. In addition, the RBOCs cannot try to integrate service and equipment because they are banned from the U.S. equipment market.

CHAPTER 15: FINANCIAL SERVICES, *Paul M. Horvitz and R. Richardson Pettit*

1. The Cecchini report predicted substantial declines in the price of financial services in some countries (16–26 percent in Spain, and 9–19 percent in Italy) and significant declines even in countries that are now believed to have efficient, competitive banking systems (5–15 percent in Germany and 2–12 percent in England) (see Cecchini 1988).

2. The EC Commission is to prepare a periodic report on the treatment of EC banks in outside countries that appears similar to the U.S. Treasury study mandated by IBA.

3. In a study prepared for the American Bankers Association in 1981, foreign bankers operating in the United States commented on the willingness of American businessmen to do business with foreign banks. A British banker noted that on the Continent, French and German businessmen would prefer to deal with domestic banks. His only edge was that the French would rather deal with a British bank than a German bank, and the Italians would prefer a British bank to a French bank. This suggests that such attitudes are not exclusively Japanese, although they are (much to the regret of American bankers) not common in the United States (Peter Merrill Associates 1981).

4. This statement holds for all but the largest of European business firms. Large European producers have access to debt and equity markets that rivals the access held by large U.S. and Japanese firms. Nevertheless, although medium-sized American firms have almost the same access to U.S. debt and equity markets as their large counterparts, the same is not now the case in Europe.

5. In fact, the distinct lack of success of some otherwise successful financial institutions in lending to developing countries, real estate development lending and equity participations, oil and gas lending, and credit cards suggests that management talent is more product unique than many have thought.

6. The lowering of walls between investment banking and commercial banking is a relatively new phenomenon in some countries. For example,

explicit relationships between the two types of firms were permitted only as recently as the "big bang" in Paris for French financial institutions. Thus, in many markets it does not seem that a "long tradition" of operating in the securities business will place U.S. banks that are new to these services at a competitive disadvantage—at least in some European markets.

Moreover, the level of investment banking activities is likely to expand sharply in the 1990s. U.S. and Japanese investment in European stock and bond markets expanded manyfold in the 1980s. The growth and integration of these markets, the expected activity in mergers and acquisitions, and the need for capital by European business firms will create a substantial new demand for corporate financial underwriting and securities trading activity.

CHAPTER 17: AGRICULTURAL TRADE CONFLICTS, Timothy Josling

1. Economists may point out the irrelevance of bilateral deficits in a multilateral trade system. Such balances do, however, play a significant role in shaping trade policy attitudes.

2. This tendency to hold governments accountable for trends in bilateral trade balances is not confined to agriculture, nor is the European Community the only state to be under pressure to change policies for these reasons. But the way that this view comes to dominate commercial relations is perhaps reflected as clearly as anywhere in the U.S. attitude toward the CAP.

3. It is not clear what action the United States undertook as its side of the bargain. This might better be described as a unilateral action, bilaterally negotiated.

4. The Japanese market for farm products has been growing, but has been subject to quantitative controls. These have proved a lightning rod to attract the attention of exporting countries. Trade liberalization seems simpler to negotiate bilaterally when the importer has quantitative restrictions operated through parastatal enterprises. The agreements are, however, not restricted to U.S.-Japan trade.

5. In addition to the impact of environmental policy changes on agricultural yields, there is the issue of the changes in the environment itself. The greenhouse effect of global warming has potentially significant implications for agriculture (Rosenberg et al. 1989). But the time scale and uncertain direction of these changes make it unlikely that they will have much influence on world markets over the next decade.

6. A recent example of such a response is the case of the outbreak of bovine spongiform encepalopathy (BSE) in the United Kingdom. First Germany and then France tried to ban U.K. beef exports. The EC commission has taken a scientific approach to the problem and sought to reassure consumers that there is no health risk involved in beef consumption.

7. The equivalence of product standards and production method regulation is a principle championed by the United States in discussions of revision of the GATT sanitary and phytosanitary rules.

8. A similar, though less common, problem arises with the enforcement of product standards to regulate the production process; exports have to be

monitored (or other countries must enforce similar product standards on their imports) before these regulations can become effective.

9. The nonfarm effects of farm policy have been made apparent by the use of general equilibrium models in recent years. Some of these models even show that total employment is reduced by agricultural support policies, as a result of the impact on the nonfarm sector. If accepted, this finding would undermine much of the macroeconomic premise of farm policy.

10. The average level of producer subsidy equivalent as calculated by the OECD (1989) was 34 percent for 1988. Translating to a world price base suggests a level of protection of 40 percent.

11. The United States has had its own dairy scheme in recent years, the Dairy Herd Replacement Program, which significantly (if temporarily) increased dairy cow numbers.

12. One might have expected the Community to have welcomed any shift out of cereals, since that presumably was the rationale for price restraints in that sector.

13. Domestic prices were fixed in the farm bill in nominal dollars and based on the assumption of continued inflation. A sharp reduction in the rate of inflation thus contributed to the high prices levels mandated by the act.

14. This proposal would have granted decoupled cash payments to farmers as compensation for a removal of all price support over time. The payments would have been based on historical farm output and would have declined over time. See Paarlberg (1988: 119).

15. The European Community has labeled its measure a support measurement unit (SMU). It is the OECDE PSE corrected for supply control and measured using reference prices and exchange rates rather than current world prices.

16. Tangermann (this volume) makes the point that the United States has considerably hardened its line on the reinstrumentation of domestic policies, while abandoning its goal of a zero level of trade-distorting support. The EC position has moved some way to meeting U.S. requests on changes in domestic policy, perhaps more than the rhetoric of the proposal would suggest. The Europeans also appear to have made such policy changes contingent upon agreement to rebalancing protection among sectors.

CHAPTER 18: AGRICULTURAL POLICY, *Stefan Tangermann*

1. The Single Act has not formally done away with the Luxembourg compromise, since it has introduced majority voting for issues on which the Treaty of Rome (rather than the Luxembourg compromise) required unanimity. In the practice of council procedures, however, the changed atmosphere after the Single Act has meant that an increasing share of decisions are taken by majority voting.

2. The German compensation through the VAT system provided only for higher retained VAT revenue of farmers, but not for higher taxes on food consumption.

3. Price developments shown in figure 18-1 represent the effects of council decisions on changes in *support* prices (as opposed to actual *market* prices), averaged over all CAP commodities and countries (until 1981–1982 EC-9, from 1982–1983 EC-10).

4. If there were no MCAs and if the share of each member country's agricultural production in the EC aggregate were equal to the share of its currency in the basket that determines the ECU, then there would be no difference between average price developments in national currencies and price developments in ECUs.

5. Closer inspection reveals that the decline in real prices has increased considerably since 1984–1985. Because of significant increases in real prices between 1972–1973 and 1976–1977, the subsequent reductions in real support prices until 1983–1984 were no more than just sufficient to bring them back to their 1972–1973 level. Yet since 1984–1985, real support prices have declined by an average annual rate of 2.8 percent.

6. Part of the existing level of the correction factor has, however, been set by hand: When the correction factor was created in 1984, it was immediately set at 1.033651, in order to implement reduction in German positive MCAs by around 3.4 percentage points. Moreover, in 1987 it was, through a discretionary decision, raised by another 1 percent, in order to allow for another reduction in German MCAs without reducing German deutsche mark prices. Thus, of the existing level of 13.7 percent extra price support due to the correction factor, 4.4 percentage points are artificial, and only the remainder is due to deutsche mark appreciations since 1984.

7. In 1980 (which appears to be the latest year for which the Community has published such statistics), 55 percent of total budget support for agriculture in the Community was expenditure by member states (see the Commission of the European Communities 1980). For a more detailed survey of national expenditure by member states in 1979 and 1980, see the summary of EEC (1984) in OECD (1987b).

8. The more rapid growth of national expenditure in Germany recently is largely related to national compensation for reductions in positive German MCAs and to significant increases in government contributions to the social security system for farmers.

9. The difference between total expenditure and national expenditure in figure 18-2 is CAP expenditure in the area of the Federal Republic.

10. In other words, if all public expenditure were directly paid, in the form of completely decoupled payments, to farmers rather than being spent on market support and other measures, German farmers would be better off in terms of income.

11. Such differences relate, for example, to the required technical characteristics of produce eligible for intervention (for instance, maximal humidity in the case of cereals) and to the time lag between delivery to the intervention agency and payment of the intervention price. Intervention buying is done, on behalf of the Community, by agencies that are part of the member countries' administrative setup. Member countries have some legal scope (and also use, to some extent, the lack of Community control) for setting the intervention parameters as they see fit.

12. This means that farmers in one member country receive an intervention price that is 5 percent above the equivalent intervention price in one other member country. See Schinke (1989), who also examines other administrative distortions of intra-Community trade in cereals. From this analysis, it is obvious, that even a relatively smoothly functioning Community market such as the one for cereals is quite removed from the situation of a truly internal market, as it would exist in one nation.

13. Profit margins in cereals trade are usually assumed to be about 1 percent of revenues. Differences in intervention rules that are equivalent to 5 percent of the intervention price and therefore result in significant trade flows across borders of member countries. See Schinke (1989).

14. Note that the effects of national regulations that shape the product (rather than the production process) tend to cross borders as long as the product concerned is tradable. Hence, product standards are a legitimate object of harmonization activities, and it is appropriate that they play an important role in the Community's 1992 work program.

15. In some member countries, milk quotas are still not transferable among individual farmers (except in conjunction with transfers of land).

16. Participation in voluntary set-asides with given premiums per hectare of land is more attractive for a farmer with low profits per hectare. Hence, it tends to take less efficiently farmed land out of production, instead of making it available to more efficient farmers. In the existing design of the EC program, however, it is not certain that a positive contribution is made to ecological objectives.

17. Expenditure under the new budget guideline cannot really be compared with past spending since some expenditure items will remain outside the budget guideline. Although the agricultural guideline will grow by 1.9 percent a year according to the Community's financial forecasts for 1992, actual expenditure from the FEOGA guarantee can grow by 5.5 percent a year, according to an estimate by Koester and Terwitte (1988).

18. The basis for determining the budget ceiling was switched from the value added tax base to the (much larger) GNP of the Community, and the new financial source are contributions by member countries based on their GNP. This twofold usage of GNP has further added to the confusion in the mind of the general public and has helped to mask the overall increase in the budget ceiling.

19. The 1986 lifting of the budget ceiling was achieved through an increase of member countries' contributions from 1 to 1.4 percent of their value added tax base.

20. The Community has not yet proposed any particular rate of reducing support after 1990, but the general assumption is that EC negotiators would not envisage large cuts.

A Note on the Book

*This book was edited by Venka V. Macintyre
and the figures were drawn by Hördur Karlsson.
The text was set in Palatino, a typeface designed by
the twentieth-century Swiss designer Hermann Zapf.
Coghill Composition Company, of Richmond, Virginia,
set the type, and Edwards Brothers Incorporated,
of Ann Arbor, Michigan, printed and bound the book,
using permanent acid-free paper.*

The AEI Press is the publisher for the American Enterprise Institute for
Public Policy Research, 1150 17th Street, N.W., Washington, D.C. 20036:
Christopher C. DeMuth, publisher; *Edward Styles,* director; *Dana Lane,* assistant
director; *Ann Petty,* editor; *Cheryl Weissman,* editor; *Susan Moran,* editorial
assistant (rights and permissions). Books published by the AEI Press are
distributed by arrangement with the University Press of America, 4720 Boston
Way, Lanham, Md. 20706.